The World's Great Philosophers

The World's Great Philosophers

Edited by

ROBERT L. ARRINGTON

Blackwell
Publishing

© 2003 by Blackwell Publishing Ltd

350 Main Street, Malden, MA 02148-5018, USA
108 Cowley Road, Oxford OX4 1JF, UK
550 Swanston Street, Carlton South, Melbourne,
Victoria 3053, Australia
Kurfürstendamm 57, 10707 Berlin, Germany

The right of Robert L. Arrington to be identified as the Author of the
Editorial Material in this Work has been asserted in accordance with the UK
Copyright, Designs and Patents Act 1988.

First published 2003 by Blackwell Publishing Ltd

Library of Congress Cataloging-in-Publication Data

The world's great philosophers / edited by Robert L. Arrington.
p.   cm.
Includes bibliographical references and index. ISBN 0-631-23145-5
(hardcover : alk. paper)—ISBN 0-631-23146-3 (pbk. : alk. paper)
1. Philosophers.   2. Philosophy.   I. Arrington, Robert L., 1938–
B29 .W69 2003 109′.2—dc21
2002004264

A catalogue record for this title is available from the British Library.

Set in 10/12.5 pt Baskerville
by SNP Best-set Typesetter Ltd., Hong Kong
Printed and bound in Great Britain
by T J International Ltd, Padstow, Cornwall

For further information on
Blackwell Publishing, visit our website:
http://www.blackwellpublishing.com

Contents

Contents

Contributors

Robert L. Arrington is Professor Emeritus of Philosophy at Georgia State University, Atlanta, Georgia, USA.

John Beversluis is Professor of Philosophy at Butler University, Indianapolis, Indiana, USA.

Vernon J. Bourke, an Honorary Member of the Order of St Augustine, is Professor Emeritus at St Louis University in Missouri, USA.

Brian Carr is Senior Lecturer in Philosophy at the University of Nottingham, UK.

Indira Carr is Reader in International Law at the University of Kent and Senior Visiting Fellow at the Institute for Advanced Legal Studies, London, UK.

John C. Coker is Associate Professor of Philosophy at the University of South Alabama, Mobile, Alabama, USA.

Russell Dancy is Professor of Philosophy at Florida State University, Tallahassee, Florida, USA.

Michael H. DeArmey is Associate Professor of Philosophy at the University of Southern Mississippi, Hattiesburg, Mississippi, USA.

Georges Dicker is Professor of Philosophy at the State University of New York at Brockport, USA.

Lisa J. Downing is Associate Professor of Philosophy at the University of Illinois at Chicago, USA.

David Gauthier is Distinguished Service Professor in the Department of Philosophy at the University of Pittsburgh, USA.

Roger F. Gibson is Professor of Philosophy at Washington University, St Louis, Missouri, USA.

Hans-Johann Glock is Reader in Philosophy at the University of Reading, UK.

James Gouinlock is Professor of Philosophy at Emory University, Atlanta, Georgia, USA.

Bina Gupta is Professor of Philosophy at the University of Missouri, Columbia, Missouri, USA.

P. M. S. Hacker is a Fellow of St John's College at the University of Oxford, UK.

David L. Hall is Professor of Philosophy at the University of Texas at El Paso, USA.

Chad Hansen holds the Chair of Chinese Philosophy at the University of Hong Kong.

Peter Harvey is Professor of Buddhist Studies in the School of Social and International Studies, University of Sunderland, UK.

Jonathan R. Herman is Associate Professor of Religious Studies at Georgia State University, Atlanta, Georgia, USA.

James M. Humber is Professor of Philosophy at Georgia State University, Atlanta, Georgia, USA.

Peter Hylton is Professor of Philosophy at the University of Illinois at Chicago, USA.

Nicholas Jolley is Professor of Philosophy at the University of California, Irvine, USA.

John Knoblock is late of the Department of Philosophy at the University of Miami, Coral Gables, Florida, USA.

Genevieve Lloyd is Emeritus Professor in Philosophy at the University of New South Wales, Sydney, Australia.

E. J. Lowe is Professor of Philosophy at the University of Durham, UK.

Ladelle McWhorter is Associate Professor of Philosophy and Women Studies at the University of Richmond, Richmond, Virginia, USA.

J. N. Mohanty is Professor of Philosophy at Emory University, Atlanta, Georgia, USA.

G. Felicitas Munzel is Associate Professor in the College of Arts and Letters at the University of Notre Dame, Notre Dame, Indiana, USA.

Kai Nielsen is Adjunct Professor of Philosophy in the Department of Philosophy, Concordia University, Montreal, Canada.

C. D. C. Reeve is Professor of Philosophy at the University of North Carolina, Chapel Hill, North Carolina, USA.

Timothy Renick is Associate Professor of Philosophy at Georgia State University, Atlanta, Georgia, USA.

Tom Rockmore is Professor of Philosophy at Duquesne University, Pittsburgh, Pennsylvania, USA.

Richard Schacht is Professor of Philosophy and Jubilee Professor of Liberal Arts and Sciences at the University of Illinois at Urbana-Champaign, USA.

William R. Schroeder is Associate Professor of Philosophy at the University of Illinois at Urbana-Champaign, USA.

Thomas Sheehan is Professor of Religious Studies at Stanford University, California, USA, and Emeritus Professor at Loyola University, Chicago, USA.

Kwong-loi Shun is Professor of Philosophy at the University of California, Berkeley, USA.

George J. Stack is Professor Emeritus of Philosophy at the State University of New York at Brockport, USA.

Allen W. Wood is Professor of Philosophy at Stanford University, California, USA.

Preface

Most of the essays contained in this book were originally published in *A Companion to the Philosophers* (Oxford: Blackwell, 1999). Several have been revised, and three (on Aquinas, Zhu Xi (Chu Hsi), and Kant) are new.

The practice of reflective thought called philosophy has few geographical or temporal boundaries. Almost from the beginning of recorded history, and in almost all cultures and nations, individuals have engaged in thinking about the nature of ultimate reality, the human condition, and basic human values. Such philosophical reflections have a degree of abstraction that sets them apart from more practical, everyday concerns as well as from the enterprise we now call science. Philosophical issues are more fundamental, dealing not with individual or generalized facts but with core concepts, essential categories of being and knowledge, basic presuppositions, and ultimate moral and social principles. The line separating philosophy and religion is more difficult to draw, since philosophers and religious thinkers often address similar concerns, and the relationship between the two disciplines is seen differently in divergent philosophical traditions. Indeed, the nature of philosophy itself is a philosophical issue and a matter of dispute, and conceptions of philosophy vary with the schools of thought that embody them.

The goal of this book is to present the thoughts and theories of the truly major philosophers of the world throughout human history. Most of the essays are on "Western" thinkers, which label encompasses European, American, and other English-speaking philosophers. But the rich history of "Eastern" philosophical thought in India and China is also well represented. Inevitably such an project as this can only proceed selectively, and an editorial task that must be faced at the beginning is to choose figures that loom large in the editor's view of philosophy. Obviously, not everyone will agree with this selection. Disagreement may be particularly evident with respect to recent and contemporary thinkers. It is difficult to assess the long-term stature of philosophers who are currently active or were only recently so, but the criterion of selection operating here has been the level of interest shown in their work and the originality of their thought.

I hope these essays will provide stimulating reading for those who sample them. They are written at a level that is appropriate for a reader who is approaching these figures for the first time. But some philosophy is difficult, and although an effort has been made to keep technical terminology and mind-boggling argumentation to a minimum, some of the essays will stretch the minds of many readers. Stretching the mind, however, is a major part of what philosophy is supposed to do – the results, one hopes, are deeper insights into the human condition.

The authors of the essays are authorities on the thinkers about whom they write. In most instances, they have written other essays or books about the philosophers in question.

A bibliography is appended at the end of each essay. It gives a list of the major works of the philosopher under discussion in the essay, and it also indicates works written about the philosopher that will provide additional information and a deeper understanding of the figure.

To assist the reader in tracing the lines of connection (historical and intellectual) among the various philosophers, the names of other thinkers whose works bears some significant relationship to the thought of the philosopher being discussed are given in small capitals.

A few remarks may be appropriate here about the peculiarities of style in the essays on Chinese and Indian thinkers. Commentators on Chinese philosophy use two different systems of romanization in rendering Chinese names and words, the pinyin and Wade-Giles systems. In this book the pinyin system is employed, but because both formulations are common, the Wade-Giles equivalent is also provided within brackets (on the first occurrence of the term). The essays on Confucius and Mencius latinize the proper names of these philosophers but give other terms in pinyin. In some instance, several different proper names are associated with the same philosopher, and these names are also indicated in parentheses. The essays on the Indian thinkers contain many diacritical marks that are used in the original Sanskrit or Pāli languages.

The essays in this book portray the rich fabric of philosophical thought that has been woven over the centuries and throughout the world by some of humankind's greatest thinkers. Together the essays provide a chart to humanity's "philosophical condition." And they invite the reader to participate in a search that continues today. Philosophy is decidedly not simply a product of our past; it is an ongoing venture, but one frequently shaped by the issues found in its history while always on the lookout for new insights into reality and humanity. To read these essays, and to share in the intellectual excitement they convey, is to undertake, truly, an adventure of ideas.

1

Aquinas

Timothy Renick

Thomas Aquinas (1225–1274 CE) ranks among the most important thinkers of the medieval time period and among the greatest minds produced by Christianity. His systematic approach to theology helped to define the Scholastic movement, and his appropriations of the arguments of ARISTOTLE were instrumental in restoring classical Greek philosophy to the European intellectual mainstream. Furthermore, Aquinas's applications of natural law theory proved foundational to Enlightenment conceptions of the state and to the emergence of international law. Fitting neatly into neither the category of traditional theologian of the Middle Ages nor that of modern philosopher, Aquinas came to represent a new breed of Christian thinker: a defender of orthodoxy who turned to pagan, Muslim, and Jewish sources for support, and a Christian who used philosophical tools – including reason, induction, and empirical evidence – to understand and advance his faith.

Born near Naples, Italy in 1225 CE, Aquinas was sent at the age of five to study at the Benedictine monastery of Monte Cassino, where he remained for ten years. At fifteen, he enrolled at the University of Naples and first was exposed to the works of Aristotle (whose writings only recently had been reintroduced to European scholars after centuries of suppression). While at Naples, Aquinas joined the Dominican order, much to the displeasure of his family; Aquinas's family kept him under house arrest for almost two years in an unsuccessful attempt to force him to reverse his decision. When his family relented, Aquinas traveled to Cologne and Paris to study under the Dominican scholar Albertus Magnus (Albert the Great). In 1256, he became a professor of theology at the University of Paris, where he taught from 1252 to 1259 and from 1269 to 1272 (holding the Dominican chair). He also taught at Anagni, Orvieto, Rome and Viterbo. He died on March 7, 1274 on his way to the second Council of Lyons. Aquinas was canonized in 1323 and, in the late nineteenth century, his thought and ideas, collectively referred to as Thomism, were designated the official theology of the Roman Catholic Church – a designation that stands to this day.

During his relatively brief lifetime, Aquinas was the author of over sixty works, including extensive writings on scripture and commentaries on the works of such thinkers as Aristotle, Boethius, Pseudo-Dionysius, and Peter Lombard. He is best known, though, for two long theological treatises, the *Summa contra Gentiles* (in which he defends Christian beliefs against non-Christians) and the *Summa Theologica* (his "summation" of theology). Over two million words in length, the *Summa Theologica* has become the work which defines Thomism and which may well represent the pinnacle of Western systematic thought.

While Aquinas would define himself as a theologian and not as a philosopher, central to his importance historically is his claim that philosophy and reason are essential to theology. Challenging a prevailing view of his day which held that philosophy is a threat to faith and must be suppressed, Aquinas argues that philosophy in fact serves as a "preamble to faith." It rationally establishes the truth of claims such as "God exists" and "God is one" and thus provides a firm foundation for belief. Moreover, through "similitudes" – the use of conceptual analogies – philosophy supplies insights into the nature of religious claims that otherwise defy human understanding; for instance, while God's infinite "goodness" cannot be fully grasped by the finite human, reason applied properly allows one to construct an analogy between that which is knowable (the goodness seen in human experience) and that which is not (the perfect goodness of God), thus enabling one to discern aspects of the divine. Perhaps most significantly, philosophy provides the basis for defending the truth of Christian claims against Jews, Muslims, and other non-Christians by developing an independent and universal language of argumentation; for example, while pagans might not surrender their polytheism upon being told the Bible asserts that God is one, they surely will have to yield their belief, Aquinas thought, when confronted with a rational argument that establishes the truth of monotheism. (See the discussion of his *via eminentiae*, below.) Thus, philosophy becomes a useful tool for the church, particularly at a time when the insulation of Christendom was being pierced by events ranging from the Crusades to the founding of "modern" universities at Oxford, Cambridge, and Bologna.

While ostensibly giving Christian belief a privileged position over philosophy – "If any point among the statements of the philosophers is found to be contrary to faith, this is not philosophy but rather an abuse of philosophy" – Aquinas also holds that true theological claims cannot be patently false, "so it is possible, from the principles of philosophy, to refute an error of this kind" (*Exposition of Boethius on the Trinity*, II.3, c). Reason thus can serve as an instrument not only to understand but to perfect theology. For Europe as it emerged from the so-called Dark Ages, this new-found respect for the human person and for human reason would prove revolutionary.

For Aquinas, human beings possess two rational faculties. First, there is "reason" itself, the faculty which processes sensory data to draw general conclusions such as "fire is hot." Second, there is the "intellect" – a faculty which intuits non-empirical, *a priori* truths (which Aquinas labels "first principles") such as "good is to be done and evil avoided." While the ability to learn from sensory experience is common to all higher animals, the faculty of intellect is possessed by humans and angels alone. Aquinas argues that angels, in fact, are "pure intellect." As non-corporeal beings, angels lack the physical senses to see, smell, and hear; they can only "know" in the direct, intuitive sense afforded by the intellect. Alone among all creatures, humans combine reasonable and intellectual faculties – though, especially since the Fall, both faculties emerge as fallible and incomplete.

Many of Aquinas's most important philosophical arguments must be read in terms of these dual rational faculties. For instance, in his proofs of God's existence – historically referred to as the "Five Ways" – Aquinas borrows and builds upon concepts introduced by Aristotle (and, to a lesser extent, Maimonides and Avicenna) to offer five parallel "demonstrations" of the existence of God: the arguments from motion, cause/effect, contingency, gradation, and governance. Each demonstration starts with an empirical observation. In his first Way, the argument from motion, Aquinas simply observes that things move. Reason then recognizes a correlation in its examination of observable experience: "whatever is moved is moved by another." Each instance of motion is caused by some prior motion. But, Aquinas concludes, this sequence "cannot go on for infinity. . . . It is necessary to arrive at a first mover, moved by no other; and this everyone understands to be God" (*Summa Theologica*, Part I, question 2, article 3). If motion exists, and motion is caused, there must be some first mover that initiates the motion, lest everything would be at rest. Thus, Aquinas holds, we rationally arrive at God.

For modern critics like Immanuel KANT, this argument is fatally flawed. Although Aquinas starts with a correct empirical observation about the causal nature of motion, they contend that he contradicts himself by positing a first mover, God, who himself is able to cause motion but whose motion is not caused by anything prior. No empirical data support the concept of an unmoved mover, so it is irrational to posit such an entity.

If Aquinas believed that human rational capabilities were purely empirical in nature, he would have to agree with this conclusion. But Aquinas holds that intellectually each human is a *composite* of reason and intellect, and each faculty contributes in its own way to the proof. It is reason which surmises that all motion is caused; and it is intellect which at that point steps in and asserts that if all of the links in the chain of motion were contingent links, dependent on something prior, we would have no complete explanation of motion. The intellect, intuiting a first principle roughly equivalent to "there must be an explanation," is rationally compelled to posit, Aquinas thinks, an unmoved mover to account for the observable phenomenon.

Aquinas argues that reason and intellect not only give humans the ability to know that God exists, but also provide us with glimpses into the nature of God. An advocate of the *via negativa*, Aquinas holds that we can know about God through rationally examining what God is not; while we cannot grasp God's infinite nature, for instance, we can comprehend our own finitude and understand, by means of our rational faculties, ways in which God is *not* like us. Additionally, philosophy can play a more positive role in allowing us to understand aspects of God, the *via eminentiae*. For example, if one starts with the premise that God is a first mover, one can rationally prove (to the pagan, for example) that God is a unity, i.e. one and not many. That which is compound must be brought together by something prior; a first mover by definition has nothing prior to it (lest it would not be first); therefore God must not be compound. Of course, for Aquinas, what we can know of God by means of even the *via eminentiae* is limited: "The knowledge that is natural to us has its source in the senses and extends just so far as it can be led by sensible things; from these, however, our understanding cannot reach the divine essence" (*ST*, I, q.12, a.12). Complete knowledge of the divine comes only to those blessed with a supernatural gift from God.

Aquinas's response to the problem of evil echoes the positions of Plotinus and AUGUSTINE before him. Evil is not a substance created by God; rather, evil is a "privation" of the good and, as such, has no metaphysical status: "Hence it is true that evil in no way has any but an accidental cause" (*ST*, I, q.49, a.1–2). Since what we call evil is simply the removal of some of the good from a wholly good substance, evil is uncreated and, as such, unattributable to God.

Aquinas's response to the theological dilemma of free will – the question of how human beings can possess free choice in the face of a sovereign, all-powerful, and all-knowing God – is historically more novel. Aquinas describes each human act as being constituted by two components, an end and the means to that end. It is the intellect which intuits the end, which for humanity is ultimately the happiness found in the "knowledge of God." This end is supplied to humans by God, it is part of their created nature, and it is not subject to human choice. The empirical faculty of reason, through experience and the observation of precedent, then chooses the means to this end for which the human has been created. This choice in unencumbered by God: "People are in charge of their acts, including those of willing and not willing, because of the deliberative activity of reason, which can be turned on one side or the other" (*ST*, I–II, q.109, a.3). Are people, then, free? Yes and no. Just as human beings have no freedom to change the fact that they need a certain amount of vitamin C to survive, they have no choice over their created end. This fact is established by God. But just as a given human being can choose to refuse to select the proper means to satisfy his or her vitamin requirements – one could elect to eat nothing but proteins or nothing at all – humans have the unencumbered ability to choose whatever means they would like, even means that serve to take them away from their created end of happiness. Thus, both God and the individual contribute to every human act: God establishes the end and the human selects the means.

How, then, is God's sovereignty preserved within Aquinas's system? If (as he claims) the good and loving God wills that all humans reach happiness/perfection and if (as he also claims) humans have the ability to freely choose evil means, cannot humans thwart God's will? Aquinas thinks not. He introduces a distinction between two ways in which God wills events to occur. God wills some events to occur necessarily, and other events contingently. It was in the first manner that God willed "Let there be light" at the beginning of time; the mere fact that God willed the event in this manner brought it into reality. It is in the second, contingent sense, however, that God wills that all humans reach perfection. Much like a person might wish for double sixes in rolling dice, recognizing that the outcome rests contingently on natural probabilities, God wills that all humans attain perfection, knowing the ultimate result is contingent upon the vagaries of personal free choice. God's will is fulfilled and God's sovereignty is preserved, even when an individual person chooses evil, because God wills precisely that the individual's attainment of perfection come only if chosen freely by him or her. Thus, Aquinas argues, humans can be free, God can be good (willing perfection for all), and God's *contingent* will can be fulfilled even in cases in which individuals follow the path of sin (*ST*, I, q.19, a.8).

Since the end of humanity is created by God and pursued naturally by all humans, Aquinas believes that sin results not from an act of will or a failure of intellect but from ignorance in choosing means. People are literally good willed; they will the good as their end at all times. Immoral acts are caused by a failure of reason – a failure to choose means appropriate to attaining this created end. Aquinas's depiction of the nature of immorality is in sharp contrast to Augustine, who believes that humans often seek evil for evil's sake. For Aquinas, humans seek only good, but they end up doing evil when, through an ignorance which is often culpable, they choose inappropriate means.

Aquinas's concept of law focuses on the issue of what constitutes the appropriate means to the god-given end. A law properly understood is "nothing else than an ordinance of reason for the common good, promulgated by him who has care of the community" (*ST*, I–II, q.94, a.4). For Aquinas, there are four primary types of law: the *eternal law*, which is the plan of God that directs every entity in the universe – animate and inanimate alike – to its appointed end; the *natural law*, which is that aspect of the eternal law which is accessible to human reason; the *human law*, which is the equivalent of the positive law and must never conflict with the natural law; and the *divine law*, which supplements the other types of law through sacred text and direct revelation from God.

Of these, the natural law receives the greatest amount of attention in Aquinas's writings. In pursuing the natural law, humans must apply their reason to the task of determining which means will direct them to their god-given end. The more nearly an act approaches this end, the more just it is; the further it deviates, the more unjust. For example, Aquinas argues that the created ends of human sexuality include procreating the species and unifying a husband and wife in the bond of matrimony. Thus, reason tells us, fornication and adultery both emerge as immoral since neither act serves to unite husband and wife to each other, but adultery becomes the greater sin since it entails a more pronounced abuse of unity (through violating the existing marriage bond of at least one of the parties) (*ST*, I–II, q.153, a.2). Aquinas's natural law arguments on sexual matters still ground contemporary Roman Catholic opposition to such issues as birth control, *in vitro* fertilization, and masturbation. Each act is seen as a violation of the procreating and/or unifying end of sex. His natural law arguments also contribute significantly to the just war tradition. In the *Summa Theologica*, Aquinas expands upon pre-existing understandings of the rules for when one may initiate war (the *jus ad bellum*) and advances concepts such as double effect – the idea that if a single act has two results, one good and one evil, the act is only necessarily condemnable if the evil effect is intended – which are now integral to moral prescriptions for the fighting of war (the *jus in bello*).

Since a law, by definition, pursues the good, human laws which fail to do so – unjust laws – are "not laws at all" according to Aquinas. They have no moral claim on individuals (though they may be adhered to under certain, practical circumstances).

Aquinas's concept of the state reflects this insight. A supporter of a mixed form of government in which the monarch derives his power from an aristocracy and the aristocracy gains its power from the polity, Aquinas holds that government is only legitimate when it pursues the good (*ST*, I–II, q.105, a.1). A monarchy which turns from the good to evil in its policies and actions becomes, by definition, a "tyranny" and is undeserving of the citizen's allegiance. While Aquinas cautions against a citizenry pursuing rebellion cavalierly – the anarchy caused by the ensuing unrest is often worse than the tyranny itself, he warns – his views represent a significant break from the arguments of previous Christian thinkers. Unlike the hierarchical vision of the state offered by Augustine, in which God appoints rulers and rulers reign by God's authority (making rebellion against rulers equivalent to rebellion against God), Aquinas portrays the citizenry as equipped with the potent faculties of reason and intellect and possessing the resulting ability to determine for itself whether just policies – means appropriate to the common good – are being pursued. By its collective authority, the citizenry has the moral right to rebel against unjust rule: "Nor should the community be accused of disloyalty for thus deposing a tyrant, even after a promise of constant fealty; for the tyrant lays himself open to such treatment by his failure to discharge the duties of his office, and in consequence his subjects are no longer bound by their oath to him" (*On Princely Government*, chapter VI). Each citizen's moral obligation remains to the good; it is the tyrant who has turned from his appropriate path. By popularizing such concepts, Aquinas emerges as a seminal figure in the development of modern philosophical notions of political authority and obligation; historical figures including Thomas Jefferson and Martin Luther King cite his thought in justifying disobedience to unjust rule.

Thomas Aquinas's works in general and his *Summa Theologica* in particular remain among the most important and impressive examples of philosophical system building in the history of the West. While contemporary philosophy has come to reject many of the explicitly theological components of Aquinas's thought, especially with respect to his metaphysics, Aquinas still is widely and rightfully regarded to be the finest philosopher of the medieval time period and a pivotal transitional figure in the move to modernity.

Bibliography

Writings

"Exposition of Boethius on the Trinity," excerpted and ed. Vernon Bourke, *The Pocket Aquinas* (New York: Washington Square Books, 1960).

"On Princely Government," in *Aquinas: Selected Political Writings*, ed. A. P. D'Entreves (Oxford: Blackwell, 1984).

Summa contra Gentiles, trans. Anton C. Pegis (Notre Dame, IN: University of Notre Dame Press, 1997).

Summa Theologica, five volumes, trans. Fathers of the English Dominican Province (Allen, TX: Thomas Moore Publishing, 1981).

Further reading

Copleston, Frederick: *Aquinas* (New York: Penguin Books, 1991).

Finnis, John: *Aquinas: Moral, Political, and Legal Theory* (Oxford: Oxford University Press, 1998).

Gilson, Etienne: *The Christian Philosophy of St Thomas Aquinas* (Notre Dame, IN: University of Notre Dame Press, 1994).

2

Aristotle

Russell Dancy

Aristotle (384–322 BCE) was born in Stagira. His father, Nicomachus, was a doctor at the court of Macedonia. The profession of medicine may well have influenced Aristotle's interests, and his association with Macedon was lifelong: in 343 he became tutor to Alexander the Great. After Alexander's death in 323, the political climate in Athens turned anti-Macedonian, and Aristotle went into voluntary exile. He died shortly thereafter, in 322.

At the age of 17, Aristotle went to Athens and studied at Plato's Academy for twenty years, until the death of PLATO in 348/7. Plato was succeeded as head of the Academy by his nephew Speusippus (c.407–339). Aristotle left Athens, traveling with another Academic, Xenocrates (c.396–314), who later succeeded Speusippus. There is no solid reason for supposing that Aristotle was disaffected with the Academy, or ever expected to become its head; both Speusippus and Xenocrates were senior to him. It was during this period that Aristotle acted as tutor to Alexander; he also married Pythias, adopted daughter of one of Aristotle's fellow students at the Academy, Hermeias of Atarneus. Aristotle returned to Athens in 335 and founded his own "school," the Lyceum or the "peripatetic school" (either because Aristotle and others lectured while walking or because the grounds had noted walkways).

Writings

Aristotle, like Plato, wrote dialogues. None has survived, nor have other works he wrote "for publication"; there are quotations or paraphrases from these lost works in later authors, and such material constitutes collections of Aristotle's "fragments." Among the more important of the lost works are: *Eudemus, or On Soul, Protrepticus, Statesman, On Poets, On*

Philosophy, On Justice, On Contraries, On Ideas (or *On Forms*), *On the Pythagoreans, On the Philosophy of Archytas,* and *On Democritus.* Some of these works are datable, and most appear to have been published early in Aristotle's career, while he was still in the Academy.

Cicero (*Academica* 2.38.119) speaks of Aristotle's "golden river of eloquence," and it is the lost works to which he is referring; what survives cannot be so described. What survives, rather, appears to be lecture notes, in which the style is compressed sometimes to the point of unintelligibility. This leads to a false contrast with Plato: Plato seems lively, where Aristotle is dry as dust. Their surviving works do present that contrast, but there is no reason to extend that to a comment on the men themselves.

What we have of these lecture notes is divided into separate areas of philosophy: logic (broadly conceived), natural philosophy or "physics," "psychology" or the soul, biology, metaphysics, ethics, political philosophy, rhetoric, and poetics. This division into disciplines presumably does not go back to Aristotle, but is an artifact of the early editions of these writings: there are intricate interconnections among the views presented in these works that are to some extent masked by this compartmentalization, and some of the treatises (particularly the *Physics* and the *Metaphysics*) do not appear to have been composed by Aristotle as units.

Development

Some think that a developmental pattern can be discerned in the material we have: for example, the early dialogue *Eudemus* appears to have presented a radical body–soul dualism of a sort the later treatise *On the Soul* could not have countenanced. But the question of Aristotle's development is a highly controversial matter, and proponents of the developmental point of view do not agree.

The most famous developmentalist is Werner Jaeger, who believed that Aristotle started as a follower of Plato and gradually drifted in a more empirical direction. This has been challenged on the ground that the fragmentary material from the early lost works already shows Aristotle objecting to Plato's views; on more than one point, one might see Aristotle as later approaching rather than receding from Platonism. But many continue to find this approach unpromising.

Logic

The first several books of the Aristotelian *corpus* – *Categories, De interpretatione, Prior Analytics, Posterior Analytics, Topics* (with *On Sophistical*

Refutations) – are commonly referred to as the *"Organon"* or "instrument" of philosophizing.

Aristotle's categories are variously types of predication and kinds of being: the predicate term in "S is P" may indicate what S is, its "substance" (the traditional translation for *ousia*) – it's a man, a horse – or how much of it there is in one or another dimension, or one way or another in which it is qualified, or something to which it is related, where it is, when it is, and so on. Alternatively, these terms give us different types of being: substances, quantities, qualities, relatives, places, times, and so on. So construed, substances form the bottom level, and so-called primary substances the rock-bottom of that level. In the *Categories*, the primary substances are individuals: men, horses, etc. Aristotle's fullest list of these categories (*Categories* 4, *Topics* I 9) enumerates ten; elsewhere fewer are listed: the enumeration is not fixed.

If we conceive "logic" more narrowly, as the analysis of the structure of argument or the study of validity, only the *Prior Analytics* and the *Topics* qualify for the label. The former gives us Aristotle's formal analysis of argument, in which all arguments are said to reduce to "syllogisms": arguments having three terms in two premises employing one of the four quantified predicational patterns "every B is an A," "some B is an A," "no B is an A," and "some B is not an A." Aristotle's treatment of these arguments is awesome, as is his formulation of a completeness theorem for his logic: the claim that all arguments can be so analyzed. His attempt to prove it (in I 23) is less fortunate, since the claim is false.

Aristotle attempts to extend his syllogistic to include modal syllogisms (premises such as those above modified by "necessarily" and "possibly"). This is some of the most difficult material in Aristotle, and there appears to be some confusion in his treatment of it.

In the *Topics* Aristotle gives rules of thumb for "dialectical" argument: argument that takes place between two individuals in dialogue. This work goes back to the Academy, where such "dialectical" arguments were used as training techniques. It antedates the *Prior Analytics*, and, although it is concerned with validity, it does not have as systematic a method of analysis as does the latter.

The *Posterior Analytics* goes back into the area of logic more broadly conceived: it concerns the analysis of knowledge. According to the analysis, exemplary knowledge is systematic, laid out in premise-and-proof form, almost always in syllogisms. That layout gives to each of the domains of knowledge, or each of the "sciences" (not a separate word in Greek), a particular structure: each "science" considers a single domain of objects, a "genus" or "kind," by starting from unproven assumptions about that kind and deducing ever more specific conclusions about it. Two sorts of examples dominate the treatise: biological ones and mathematical ones. Aristotle's picture of mathematics was based on a pre-Euclidean axiomatization of "elements" about which we have no independent information: this is most unfortunate, since there is no plausible way of applying syllogistic to actual mathematical argument as we know it from Euclid on. If biology is construed as simply taxonomic, syllogistic might more plausibly apply.

There is a characteristic tension in this treatise between two tendencies: on the one hand, only eternal, non-fortuitous, and universal connections can be the objects of knowledge or science (I 8, 30, 31), and on the other, *contra* Plato, science or knowledge arises from sense-perception (II 19). This looks like a tension between vestiges of Platonism and a nascent empiricism. Arguably, Aristotle never fully resolved the conflict.

Natural philosophy

Aristotle's "physics" in fact comprises all of what takes place in nature: his views on the soul and on biology as well as what is more conventionally regarded as "physics."

Physics I is devoted to problems pertaining to change, and it is here that Aristotle introduces the tripartite analysis of change – involving form, matter (subject), and privation – that stays with him throughout the rest of his work. To illustrate: when Socrates goes to the beach and gets a tan, he starts out pale and ends up dark, and he is there all along. He constitutes the subject for the change, and his initial pallor might be the privation and final tan the form he acquires in the change. This analysis is extended to cover the case in which he is born or dies: he can no longer be the subject that undergoes the change, since, in the latter case, he does not survive it; what does survive it is referred to as matter: the term "matter" is used for any continuing subject that survives a change, but comes into its own in cases such as the death of Socrates. The notion of matter did not appear in the *Organon*, and some think this significant, especially as it is prominent, and raises prominent difficulties, in later work (see below on Metaphysics).

In II we encounter the famous "four causes," known now by their scholastic titles: the "material," "formal," "efficient," and "final" causes. "Cause" translates a word (*aition*) that meant, used in a law court, the "guilty" or "responsible" party. Aristotle is listing four sorts of thing that might be held responsible for something's being the way that it is. As an example (Aristotle's), consider a bronze statue. Taking the causes in the above order, you might ask what it is made of (bronze), or what sort of thing it is (a statue), or what initiated whatever changes brought it into being (its sculptor), or what it is for (decoration).

As the example illustrates, Aristotle does not in the first instance focus on cases in which one event causes another (the situation taken as typical for the analysis of causality at least since HUME), and the extension of his analysis of efficient causality to such cases is somewhat difficult. But to the extent that Aristotle does take account of cases in which events cause events, one important difference between him and us is that Aristotle employs nothing like a principle of inertia, to the effect that once something is set in motion it will continue to move until something stops it. Rather, for Aristotle, the motion that causes another motion is exactly contemporaneous with it: the hand that pushes the book along the table is acting causally for precisely as long as the book is moving, and when the hand stops, the book stops. This model of causality (which we think of as motion modified by the effect of friction) gives Aristotle and his successors trouble over projectile motion, which Aristotle tried to explain, to his own dissatisfaction, by an aerodynamic theory in which the projectile causes eddies in the air that push the projectile along as it moves.

Books III and IV give analyses of motion, the unlimited (infinite), place, void, and time. Aristotle's procedure in each case is the same: he raises problems, discusses the views of others, and finally presents an analysis that solves the problems and explains the views he takes to be erroneous. It is plain that this is not a presentation of the "science" of "physics" such as the *Posterior Analytics* might have led us to expect; it is more like the philosophical groundwork that might have preceded such a presentation. Since part of Aristotle's aim is to preserve what he can of the views handed down to him, his results are generally conservative, but not altogether: he denies that there can be an actual infinite or a void.

Later books of the *Physics* deal with temporal and spatial continuity and with theology. The last book, in particular, gives the most detailed treatment to be found in Aristotle of the familiar proof (adapted by Thomas AQUINAS) for the existence of an "unmoved mover": something that causes motion without itself moving. The proof is based on a causal principle: motion requires an efficient cause. This sets up a regress of efficient causes that must, Aristotle thinks, be stopped by at least one first efficient cause or unmoved mover (there could be many, but Aristotle prefers one as the simpler hypothesis). The contemporaneity Aristotle demands of efficient causal action with its effect has an important corollary here: the first cause of the motion in the universe does not precede that motion but goes along with it. This makes it possible for Aristotle to argue for the existence of a first mover although part of his proof requires that the universe has always and will always exist. Aristotle's first mover is not a creator.

There are further elaborations of Aristotle's views on these matters in *Metaphysics* XII: see below.

The treatise *On Coming-to-Be and Passing-Away* deals with the nature of such changes and ultimately with the four "so-called 'elements'" earth, water, air, and fire, which are not really elements since they undergo transformation into each other, but are still as simple as any material can get. It remains a disputed question whether this drives Aristotle to the notion of a characterless "prime matter" that provides the material continuant for such changes.

The treatise *On the Heavens* adds a fifth element, unnamed there but "aither" in the later tradition, which is different from the previous four in that its motion is naturally in a circle whereas their motions are rectilinear. This is the element that composes the heavens. The treatise appears to be relatively early, and comes as close as anything in Aristotle to adhering to the syllogistic model that dominated the *Posterior Analytics*. Despite its title, its last two books deal with sublunary bodies and with the four elements – here Aristotle unhesitatingly so refers to them – once again.

The four books of the badly titled *Meteorology* (the Greek is much vaguer, and has no proper English translation) cover such things as comets, the nature of the sea, and chemistry, as well as winds, rain, and lightning.

Aristotle's treatment of the soul (*psuchē*), at least in the surviving treatises that deal with it, is that of a biologist: the soul is that aspect of an organism (including plants under this head) that constitutes its capacity for performing the activities characteristic of the sort of life it leads. A plant has a soul that enables it to grow and reproduce; an animal one that enables it to do that much and also to move around and perceive; a human being has one that enables it to do all that as well as think. In one of the most vexed chapters in any philosophical work in all of history (*De anima* III 5), Aristotle seems to be suggesting that there is a sort of immortality accorded to this last aspect of soul, but it is not an immortality that gives much comfort, since it does not carry any memory with it: even if Aristotle is allowing that you can think of your soul surviving your death (and it isn't entirely clear whether he is allowing this), he isn't allowing that your soul remembers anything of your life.

Book II contains an analysis of perception. Each sense has a domain of properties, which Aristotle refers to as "forms" (see above on the use of the matter–form distinction in *Physics* I), proper to it – colors for sight, etc. – and the sense organ is composed of a matter capable of taking on those forms: the eye is composed of something transparent, and so it can take on colors.

Aristotle's biological works make up between a fifth and a quarter of the entire Aristotelian *corpus*. His interest in biology was plainly fostered by the twenty years he spent in Plato's Academy, in which a fair amount of activity was devoted to biology. What we hear of it virtually all has to do with taxonomy, and this plays a large role in Aristotle as well.

The biological works, especially the enormous *Historia Animalium* (*Investigation of Animals*), incorporate some material that comes from other researchers in the Lyceum (such as Aristotle's student Theophrastus), but for brevity the following is phrased in terms of Aristotle.

In a letter to William Ogle (translator of and commentator on *On the Parts of Animals*) Darwin spoke of his "two gods" Linnaeus and Cuvier as "mere schoolboys to old Aristotle"; he also found "curious" Aristotle's "ignorance on some points." The combination of insight and ignorance runs all through Aristotle's biological work. There is a description of the development of the chick embryo in *Historia Animalium* VI 3 of remarkable accuracy that must have involved a great number of dissections and observations. But in the same work, in II 3.501^{b}19–21, Aristotle tells us that women have fewer teeth than men. No doubt a research group embarking on the task of codifying the enormous amount of information to be found in the Aristotelian biological works is going to include a certain amount of misinformation as well.

One of the most interesting and controversial aspects of Aristotle's biology is his use of final causes: his explanations of the parts of animals in particular are "teleological": "each of the parts of the body is for the sake of something . . . also the body they compose exists for the sake of a full activity" (*Parts of Animals* I 5.645^{b}14–17). The eye is composed of transparent material *so that* it can take on colors. Aristotle's explanation opposes the final cause (the function to be served by an organ) to the material cause or matter (the nature of the materials available to constitute that organ). The final cause is at the same time the essence of the organ, its formal cause: *what* it is, is an eye, and what an eye is, is an organ *for seeing*. For the organ to fulfil its function certain demands are made on the material (the eye-material must be transparent), but the matter makes demands back: transparent liquid, which is better for the purpose than air, which is very difficult to contain, still requires a certain sort of container. And the matter may, independently of all this, be responsible for such accidents as eye color. This picture gives the essence–accident distinction a respectable scientific role: it is the distinction between features that play a functional role in the life of the organism, e.g. the transparency of the cornea, and those that do not, e.g. eye color.

The biggest difficulty is seeing how Aristotle might account for natural teleology. He cannot appeal to a cosmic designer, and he nowhere tries: one of his favorite sayings, "nature does nothing in vain," should presumably be read as saying "an organism's nature does nothing in vain." Aristotle's teleology is sometimes called "immanent" for that reason: it is somehow "in" the organism that it has organs that are advantageous for its lifestyle. But Aristotle firmly rejects (*Physics* II 8) evolutionary explanations in the only form in which they were known to him, that employed by Empedocles, who had described a history of the world in the course of which organisms came into existence but were "unfit" to survive, and hence died out. To Aristotle, there could not have been any such history: the universe not only has always existed and will always exist, it has been and will be just the way it is, with all its species of organisms. So explanations of the purpose of organs that turn on survival value are ruled out.

Still, Aristotle's teleology leads him to an immense amount of detailed work devoted to teasing out the purposes of various organs, and some of his descriptions (e.g. some of the minutiae concerning crabs and crayfish in *Historia Animalium* IV 3–4) have only recently been matched for accuracy.

Unfortunately, some of his errors in biology were more influential than these accurate observations; the most famous of them is his endorsement of the idea that some animals are spontaneously generated, e.g. certain shellfish and insects.

Metaphysics

The term "metaphysics" does not go back to Aristotle; it seems merely to be a title in early editions of his works meaning "Appendix to the *Physics*." Aristotle himself describes what we count under this head as "first philosophy" or "wisdom." There are two tasks he allots to this discipline: the investigation of beings in general, and the investigation of a particular being or set of beings, namely god or the gods. These look to be different tasks, and it is not clear how Aristotle himself meant to connect them. In fact, he mostly pursues them separately.

Metaphysics XII contains an account of theology, sketchier in most respects but fuller in others than that in the *Physics*: in particular, it connects theology with astronomy by coming down on the side of a plurality of unmoved movers each associated with one of the spheres that carry the heavenly bodies in their rotations. Aristotle accepts from the mathematician and astronomer Eudoxus (who was present in Plato's Academy) and Eudoxus' student Callippus a scheme for explaining the observed motions of the sun, moon, and planets, according to which each of those heavenly bodies is fixed to the innermost sphere of a set of nested spheres rotating on orbits inclined with respect to each other: the motion of the body then becomes a composite motion, one of whose features was that it could perform something like a figure eight from the point of view of an observer at the center of the set, thus account-ing for retrograde motion. Aristotle, in order to turn what seems to have been a purely geometrical model into a physical one, added spheres to the Eudoxan total, and each of these was to have its motion explained by appeal to an unmoved mover. The result was a total of 47 or 55 unmoved movers (there is some confusion over the arithmetic).

The consideration of beings in general, or of "beings *qua* being," is prominent in *Metaphysics* IV and VII–IX. The question under consider-ation here is: what is imported by the notion of *being*, all by itself? What follows from the claim that something *is*? There are not separate words in Aristotle's vocabulary for "to be" and "to exist"; the question could as well be put by asking: what does a thing's *existence* consist in?

In IV, Aristotle argues that a thing's existence carries with it obedi-ence to the laws of non-contradiction and excluded middle; the argu-ment is mostly negative, opposing those who would reject the laws of logic.

Books VII–IX are hard, particularly VII and VIII, which contain some of the most difficult chapters in all of Aristotle. It has been plausibly claimed that they are not continuous expositions of doctrine but expo-sitions of argument, sometimes on opposite sides of the same question, without resolution.

The general position, essentially stated in book IV, is that anything whatever that can *be* can only do so on the basis of its enjoying some relation or other to a privileged set of beings, the substances: a quality such as a color can only exist by being a quality of a *substance*, so that the substances turn out to be the existence-makers. This much Aristotle might have said back in the *Categories*. But in *Metaphysics* VII he turns to the question: what, after all, *is* a substance? To settle the question whether Platonic Forms or Aristotelian individuals are rock-bottom beings or substances, to what can we appeal? This, on Aristotle's account, is not an all-or-nothing affair. Lots of different things will count as substances, so the question becomes: which of them has the best credentials?

Aristotle, somewhat confusingly, speaks of the substance *of* a thing in this connection: a thing's substance is what you point to by way of justifying the claim that it *is* a substance. There are three main candidates for the title of a thing's substance: its matter, its form, or its being a composite of matter and form. The first of these three is the weakest candidate, although it is not excluded altogether. The third, the fact that a thing is a composite of matter and form, is seen as derivative. So the form of a thing is left as its primary substance, what primarily makes it count as a substance.

But the individuals referred to as primary substances back in the *Categories* are now composites of matter and form, and once we make this fact about them derivative, we weaken or even destroy their claim to be primary substances. On the face of it, if there were any such thing as a pure form that had no admixture of matter, this would have the strongest claim to being a substance, a rock-bottom being. And this sounds a good deal more like Plato than like the Aristotle of the *Categories*.

But this is where the metaphysics of these books seems to fail to come to a stable position: Aristotle seems to be going in different directions at different junctures. There are many possibilities: perhaps Aristotle is here pointing toward his own unmoved movers as the primary substances, supposing that they are matterless forms. Then the individuals of the *Categories* are demoted. Or perhaps Aristotle thinks he has a way of making the fact that an individual is a form–matter composite less damaging to its claim to be a substance. Some (including the present author) see in the very lack of resolution, the open-endedness, of these books something very exciting: a great philosopher at work, without dogmatic answers.

Ethics

There are four books in the Aristotelian corpus devoted to ethics; the authorship of one, the *Magna Moralia*, is in great dispute, and the treatise *On Virtues and Vices* is universally declared spurious, but the remaining two, the *Eudemian Ethics* and the *Nicomachean Ethics*, are generally thought to be genuine, and a smaller consensus would make the *Eudemian* the earlier of the two. Books IV–VI of the *Eudemian* are the same as V–VII of the *Nicomachean*, and, although they are always printed with the latter, they probably belonged to the former. Comments here are confined to the *Nicomachean Ethics* as standardly printed.

Aristotle's ethical views (like Plato's and most of the other ancients') are of a type known as "eudaimonistic": their primary focus is on happiness (*eudaimonia*), or the good for man, and how to obtain it. Happiness is not here to be construed as a subjective feeling of well-being, but as human well-being itself. Aristotle explains the "human good" in *NE* I 7 as "activity of the soul in accordance with excellence" (or "virtue," *aretē*): the realization of the capacities distinctive of human life, particularly contemplation and political activity. The role of these latter activities in happiness overall is a matter of some dispute: sometimes Aristotle seems to paint a comprehensive picture in which both figure, while at other times he seems to place exclusive emphasis on contemplation (compare *NE* I with X).

Aristotle differs from Plato in the *Republic* in insisting that a minimum of external goods is a prerequisite for human well-being. But he rejects hedonism, one of whose advocates was Eudoxus and one of whose strongest enemies was Speusippus. But he devotes more time to refuting the arguments against hedonism than he does to refuting hedonism itself, and the two discussions of pleasure (*EN* VII 11–14, X 1–5) reflect differing attitudes toward hedonism: in the latter, Aristotle seems to reject hedonism on the ground that pursuit of pleasure as a goal, rather than the activities in which one takes pleasure, is bound to be frustrated.

We are responsible for our actions, even when they emerge from our characters, which are settled relatively early in our lives: Aristotle appears to recognize no problem about the "freedom of the will," unlike the Stoics and the Epicureans in the next generation of philosophers. The purpose of studying ethics is, he thinks, to make ourselves good, but Aristotle supposes that we already want to become good: he is lecturing to male Greeks who have been well brought up and have come of age.

The account of excellence or virtue he offers locates each virtue in between two opposed vices: the simplest example is courage, which is a mean between the two opposed vices of cowardice and rashness. His notion of virtue as a mean is not an ethics of moderation, as is sometimes supposed; he certainly recommends moderation, but as one virtue among others: a mean state between being self-indulgent and being "insensible" (a term Aristotle coins for this otherwise nameless vice: *EN* II 7).

He takes up (VII 1–10) Socrates' denial of moral weakness, and rejects it, but not without sympathy: when we do something we know to be wrong, this involves a momentary suppression of that knowledge. *EN* VIII–IX is a detailed discussion of friendship, an essential component of human well-being. Friendship may be based on utility, on pleasure in each other's company, or on mutual respect for each other's goodness. The last is the best and stablest.

Politics

The closing chapter of *NE* is an introduction to politics, not exactly to the *Politics*, which is a collection of treatments originally separate, but plainly Aristotle thought of ethics and politics as continuous disciplines.

Politics I argues that various institutions, including the *polis* (conventionally translated "city-state"; plural *poleis*) itself, are natural. The *polis* is natural because man is by nature "political": suited for a life in a *polis*. Slavery is natural because some humans are naturally suited to be living tools, which is what slaves are. The subjection of women is natural, because men are naturally more fit to rule than women.

II discusses proposed and actual *poleis*, including Plato's *Republic*; the discussion of this does not always correspond to the *Republic* as we have it.

III attempts to say what a *polis* is via explaining what a citizen (*politēs*) is: the *polis* will be a community of citizens. And a citizen is defined as a participant in government, someone entitled to hold office. (Aristotle does not envisage representative democracy; he is talking about those who may actually rule in the *polis*.) But then it turns out that different types of *poleis* differ in who counts as a citizen, and each type has a "correct" form and a "deviant" form, depending on whether the rule is for the common good: government may be by a single man (kingship is the correct and tyranny the deviant form), a few men (aristocracy and oligarchy), or many men ("polity" and democracy). Books IV–VI go into some detail about these (V is a historically rich discussion of revolutions, their causes and prevention, very Machiavellian in tone).

VII and VIII take up Aristotle's own ideal *polis*, including lengthy consideration of education in it.

Rhetoric

Rhetoric is a speaker's manual. It is not the first, but none earlier has survived. Aristotle's own emphasis is on the importance of argument for persuasion, and has a good deal in common with the *Topics*, but also includes (in II) a discussion of the emotions notably missing from the psychological works. And III, on style, is very detailed: there is even a discussion of prose-rhythms (the alternation of long and short syllables that is regimented in Greek poetry but not in prose, where it requires special attention).

Poetics

Looking at all the Aristotelian treatises, the ratio of influence to size in the case of the *Poetics* is the greatest: it is tiny (and fragmentary) but of enormous historical importance. It was at some point organized into two books; the second, on comedy, is now lost (although a sketch of it may survive in the so-called *Tractatus Coislianus*). The first considers the general nature of poetry, which Aristotle takes to be *mimesis*, "imitation" or "representation," and then takes up tragedy and epic.

Tragedy is defined (chapter 6) in terms of the representation or imitation by actors in poetic speech of a serious action in its entirety that by means of pity and fear achieves the catharsis of such emotions. The most controversial aspect of this definition is the catharsis or "purification" claimed for tragedy; there are two main lines of interpretation, one adopting a sort of medical model (tragedy purges one of excesses of pity and fear) and the other an educative model (one learns the appropriate degree of pity and fear to have). Epic (chapter 23) represents the same sort of thing but in narration, at greater length, and in a fixed verse-structure. Aristotle's elaboration of both these forms of poetry represents a considerable advance: Aristotle initiates the idea that they have their own rules of construction and are not simply to be criticized on a moralizing basis.

Influence

Aristotle has been one of the most influential philosophers of all time, sometimes beneficially and sometimes harmfully. But had his successors been as critical of his views as he was of his predecessors', the balance of benefit to harm would have been greater. Those who acquiesced in Aristotle's wisdom without questioning it have only themselves to blame.

Bibliography

Writings

Aristotelis Opera, five volumes, ed. I. Bekker (Berlin: W. de Gruyter, 1960 and later, first published in 1831–70).

The Complete Works of Aristotle, two volumes, ed. Jonathan Barnes (Princeton, NJ: Princeton University Press, 1984). [For description of individual works see above.]

Further reading

Barnes, Jonathan (ed.): *The Cambridge Companion to Aristotle* (Cambridge: Cambridge University Press, 1995). [Articles on all aspects of Aristotle's thought and extensive bibliography.]
Ross, W. D.: *Aristotle*, 5th edn (London: Methuen, 1949, often reprinted). [Remains among the very best introductions.]
Wians, William (ed.): *Aristotle's Philosophical Development: Problems and Prospects* (Lanham, MD: Rowman & Littlefield, 1996).

3

Augustine

Vernon J. Bourke

Born in Thagaste, sixty miles south of the Mediterranean coast, Augustine of Hippo (354–430 CE) was the first important Christian philosopher. Since his writings are very extensive, he is also the most prolific African author. Augustinian philosophy has been influential in every century of Western civilization (see Rist, 1994). Son of a pagan father (Patricius) and a Christian mother (Monica), he was not baptized as a child. Four years of classical education were followed by advanced studies in 370 at Carthage, where he eventually taught rhetoric. He fathered a son (Adeodatus) by an unnamed mistress in 373 and read the *Hortensius* written by Cicero, which stimulated his first interest in philosophy (*Confessions* III, 4, 7; cf. Bourke, 1992). In 383 he sailed from Carthage to Rome in search of a career in the heart of the Roman Empire.

Not yet a Christian, Augustine was an auditor in the religion of Mani (third century CE), which taught that two great cosmic forces, good and evil, competed for power in the universe as well as within each person (see Brown, 1967, chapter 5). Plagued by doubts about this cosmic metaphysical dualism but still nominally a Manichean, he was appointed to teach rhetoric in Milan, where he encountered a group of Christian scholars headed by Bishop Ambrose and Simplicianus, who sparked his interest in the relation between Platonic philosophy and Christian theology. Owing largely to his study of PLATO and Plotinus, he was converted to Christianity and baptized by Ambrose in 386. In 388, after the death of his mother, he returned to Africa, where he set up a monastic center for meditation, teaching and dictating to students and scribes many dialogues and treatises. While visiting Hippo (now Annaba in Algeria) in 391, he was ordained priest by Valerius, who needed a preacher who spoke Latin. After the death of Valerius in 396, Augustine himself became bishop of Hippo. His major works were composed during the following thirty-five years. He died in 430 during the siege of Hippo by invading Goths (for details on his life, see Brown, 1967; Bourke, 1973; Rist, 1994).

Augustine's philosophic thought takes its preliminary form (Markus, 1972) in a dozen short treatises dictated between 386 and 391. Typical of these are the dialogues *On Order, Immortality of the Soul, On Music, The Teacher, On the Good,* and *Free Choice.* These works represent a rethinking by Augustine of Platonic philosophy, influenced by his reading of the Old and New Testaments in the Bible (Battenhouse, 1955; Gilson, 1960). These early works already sketch Augustine's psychological interiorism, his introspective meditation on his own mental experiences (see O'Meara, 1954; Bourke, 1992; Clark, 1994). More profound rethinking starts around 400, with the *Confessions* (O'Donnell, 1992) onward to the *Retractations,* a review of nearly all his writings preceding the year 427. The great works – the *Commentary on the Psalms, The Trinity, Literal Meaning of Genesis,* and the *City of God* – are primarily theological in content, but they also include many philosophical sections.

Since Augustine does not present his philosophy as a methodical or organized system but rather as discrete insights into the meaning of wisdom as the highest grasp of both speculative and practical truth, the following seven key views are chosen to represent the essence of Augustinian philosophy. There is as yet nothing approaching a standard English edition of Augustine's works; references in the following are to two collections: BW is *Basic Writings of St Augustine;* and EA is *The Essential Augustine* (selections from 32 works).

Three levels of reality

The simplest version of this idea is found in a *Letter to Coelistinus* (18, 2; EA 45–6), written in 390, where Augustine explains: "There is a nature that is susceptible of change with respect to both place and time, namely the corporeal. Another nature is in no way changed with respect to place but only in regard to time, namely the soul. And there is a third Nature that can be changed neither in respect to place nor time: that is God. These natures of which I have said that they are mutable in some way are called creatures. The Nature that is immutable is called Creator." In this quotation "nature" (*natura*) means any sort of being, because the late Latin word "being" (*ens*) was not in use in Augustine's time (see Bourke, 1992, pp. 32–3).

The three-level theme appears throughout the writings of Augustine. In the *Nature of the Good* (1, 25; BW I, 431; EA 48–57; written in 405) the three levels are explained in terms of goodness: God is the highest good, the human soul is next, and bodies are the lowest, but they *are* goods. Reacting from Manichean dualism, Augustine decided that evil is a lack or failure in being or action, not a positive entity. Two different applications of this triadic ontology are found in the *City of God*. Book V, 9 describes a descending order of causality. God is the ultimate cause of all change but is Himself unmoved. Created spirits (angels and souls) are real causes but are divinely moved from above. Bodies cannot move spirits, "they do what the wills of spirits do by them." Later Platonic philosophers are praised because they see that God alone is immutable being, while souls change in time, not in space, and bodies change in both time and space (*City of God* VII; EA 58–61). Augustine finds some support for his Christian belief in a supreme God in earlier philosophies: Plato's World Maker (in *Timaeus*); ARISTOTLE's Prime Mover (in *Physics*); and Plotinus' One from which emanate the Many (*Ennead I*). Augustine does not offer a discursive rational proof for the existence of God that starts from some aspect of the physical world. Bodies do not provide a sufficient base for such reasoning. It is by turning from itself to look upward that the human soul discovers God.

Rationes: eternal and seminal

The Latin word *ratio* has several meanings for Augustine and it is not easy to find the proper English equivalents. In Augustinian psychology *ratio* (reason) means the gaze of the soul (*aspectus animae ratio est, Soliloquies* I, 13; BW I, 266) looking for understanding. In another meaning the term *ratio* (usually in the plural) is used more objectively to name the eternal exemplars (*rationes aeternae*) of all things and truths (like Platonic Ideas) which Augustine finds in the creative Mind of God (see *83 Questions*, p. 46; EA 62). Still another sort of *rationes* (formal reasons) exist in all creatures, giving them their specific character as individuals. Such seminal reasons are all created at the beginning of time, but they may develop into existing realities at any point in time (*Trinity* III, 8, 13–19, 16; EA 102–3). Throughout the *Literal Meaning of Genesis* all explanations of creation involve this distinction. Augustine bluntly says: "a bean does not grow from a grain of wheat . . . or a man from a beast" (17, 32; EA 103). This sort of statement has been used to make Augustine a foe of scientific evolution. Actually he would not have been surprised to learn that new species appear to arise by change from earlier ones. All he requires is the recognition that all species are eternally known to God, whatever their time of arrival in the universe.

Man's soul and its functions

The soul is a created spirit, with a beginning in time (hence not eternal) but no temporal ending (i.e. immortal), because the soul has no parts into which it might disintegrate. Several early works argue that the human soul is the container of eternal truths, and so immortal (*Soliloquies* II, 13, 23; BW I, 289). The *Immortality of Soul*, written in 387, has several arguments for such immortality, but Augustine was not enthusiastic about this work when he reviewed it in *Retractationes* (chapter 5).

The dialogue *On Free Choice* (II, 3, 7–10; EA 69–74) describes four psychic functions: vitalizing, sensing, understanding, and willing. Most distinctive is the treatment of sensing. Here and in Book VI (*On Music*), sense perception is called activity, not of bodies affecting the soul (since the lower cannot move the higher) but of the soul actively recording the changes that it observes in its body. Augustine is not skeptical about the veracity of most sense observations. Memory is viewed as a very distinctive function of the soul. Along with understanding and willing, memory becomes part of a triad of psychic functions in the later writings, notably in *Confessions* (Book X) and *Trinity* (X, 17–18). Awareness of self is a key feature of memory in its experience of past, present, and future. The present (*praesentia*) is not merely the past eating into the future (as in some present-day thinking, such as Bergsonism); Augustine sees the mind as being "present" to a "now" that ranges over broad expanses of remembering experiences extending over long periods of time (see Bourke, 1992). Freedom of choice or decision (*arbitrium*) is a special feature of the soul as willing. How such freedom is possible under the supervision of divine providence is a problem treated in the *City of God* (V, 10; BW II, 68 ff. and EA 181–5). More recent disputes about divine predestination have been much influenced by Augustine; but these theological discussions go beyond the scope of philosophy.

Divine illumination of the mind

The most debated topic among interpreters of Augustine is the theory of divine illumination. Augustine contends that, just as the eyes need physical light so that the soul can see visible objects, so the human intellect requires an immaterial light of the mind to make thought objects and truths intelligible. The *Literal Meaning of Genesis* (XII, 6–11; EA 93–7) distinguishes three kinds of vision: corporeal through the eyes of the body; imaginative as when one sees images of things never witnessed through the eyes (such as the great city of Alexandria where Augustine had never been); and intellectual as when one grasps the meaning of eternal reasons, such as charity and all the virtues. It is in this highest vision that divine illumination shines. Its objects include the meanings of numbers and mathematical concepts such as unity and equality (*Free Choice* II, 8, 22–4). Other examples of such objects are justice, faith, and goodness.

The intellectual light is available to all persons, not simply a few favored ones such as the mystics (*Confessions* XIII, 3, 4; 31, 46). However, interpretations of the working of this illumination differ widely. The Thomistic view that the light is really the agent intellect is most unlikely. A second interpretation, that the light of the mind is God's impression of certain truths directly on the intellect when needed, is more plausible. Most plausible of all is the interpretation holding that God guides the mind in its primitive acts of judgment.

Time as measured in the mind

The opening sentence of Book XI of the *Confessions* stresses the contrast between time and eternity. Augustine admits great difficulty in understanding both of these concepts, but he is sure that "time does not exist without some movement and transition, while in eternity there is no change." Repeatedly he insists that "I measure periods of time." He rejects Aristotle's notion that time is the number of movement from before to after in bodies (*Confessions* XI, 24, 31).

Some interpreters (see Sorabji, 1983) minimize the importance of the subjective view of time in the *Confessions*. Certainly Augustine recognized the objectivity of historical times. In any event, he has influenced many modern approaches to the nature of time.

Morality, happiness and the virtues

Much of Augustine's ethics depends on his conviction that all persons naturally desire to be happy. Ancient philosophers usually were eudaimonists, stressing happiness as the ultimate end of a good life. In the early work, *The Happy Life* (5, 33), happiness is equated with the attainment of wisdom. Here wisdom means "a measured quality of mind whereby the mind balances itself so that it never goes to excess and is never reduced below its proper fulfillment" (cf. *On the Psalms*, Ps 32, Sermon 3, 15–16; EA 151–3). The usual objects of desire – wealth, worldly magnificence, honors, physical beauty – are not guarantors of happiness or moral goodness. Only God, the supreme Wisdom, brings ultimate satisfaction. A philosophical discussion of this claim appears in *The Trinity* (XIII, 3–9).

While Augustine recognizes the value of moral laws (*Confessions* X, 29, 40), his ethics is not legalistic. It is virtue that leads men to the good life (*Morals of the Catholic Church* 6; EA 153–8). The four great virtues of ancient philosophy – prudence, temperance, fortitude and justice – are adopted by Augustine as affective parts of charity, the love of God. To these he adds the Christian virtues faith, hope, and charity (*City of God* XIX, 25; BW II, 504). Augustine speaks very openly about the iniquities of his early life in the first books of the *Confessions* (see also *Enchiridion* 18–22; EA 166–9). His view that every lie is a sin is also very strict, but he admits that there may be circumstances justifying concealment of the truth (*On the Psalms* 5, 7; EA 169–71). Some of this ethical severity is owed to his effort to show how much he is indebted to divine forgiveness (see Bourke, 1979).

Two cities: terrestrial and celestial

Although the societal and political philosophy of Augustine is most fully developed in the *City of God* (see Burleigh, 1944), the theme of two different societies of men is already evident in *The True Religion* (26, 49), where those who love God are the pious and those who love inferior goods are impious. In the Psalms the holy city is called Jerusalem, the unholy Babylon (see *On the Psalms* 64, 1–2). Augustine takes Jerusalem to mean the vision of peace. A long passage in the *City of God* (XIX, 13; BW II, 488–9) sums up much of his thinking on peace with the conclusion that the essence of peace is "the tranquility of order."

Bibliography

Writings

The Works of Aurelius Augustinus, 15 volumes (English), ed. M. Dods (Edinburgh, 1871–6).
Oeuvres de Saint Augustin, 85 volumes (Paris: Desclée de Brouwer, 1949–). [The best editions of the Latin works.]
Partial critical editions: *Corpus Scriptorum Ecclesiasticorum* (Vienna: Tempsky, 1866–); and *Corpus Christianorum. Series Latina* (Turnholti: Brepols, 1953–).
Augustine's Works, ed. P. Schaff (New York: Scribners, 1892–1902). [Some new English versions in *Ancient Christian Writers* (Westminster, MD: Newman Press,

1946); and *Fathers of the Church* (New York and Washington, DC: Catholic University of America Press, 1947–).]

Basic Writings of St Augustine, two volumes, ed. W. Oates (New York: Random House, 1946). [Cited as BW.]

The Essential Augustine, ed. V. Bourke (Indianapolis: Hackett, 1974). [Cited as EA.]

Further reading

Armstrong, A. H.: *Saint Augustine and Christian Platonism* (Villanova, PA: Villanova University Press, 1967).

Battenhouse, R.: *A Companion to the Study of St Augustine* (London and New York: Oxford University Press, 1955).

Bourke, V. J.: *Augustine's Quest of Wisdom* (Albany, NY: Magi Books, 1973).

——: *Joy in Augustine's Ethics* (Villanova, PA: Villanova University Press, 1979).

——: *Augustine's Love of Wisdom: An Introspective Philosophy* (W. Lafayette, IN: Purdue University Press, 1992).

Brown, P.: *Augustine of Hippo: A Biography* (Berkeley: University of California Press, 1967).

Burleigh, J. H. S: *The City of God: A Study of Saint Augustine's Philosophy* (London: Macmillan, 1944).

Clark, Mary T.: *Augustine* (Washington, DC: Georgetown University Press, 1994).

Gilson, E.: *The Christian Philosophy of St Augustine*, trans. L. Lynch (New York: Random House, 1960).

Markus, R. A. (ed.): *Augustine: Critical Essays* (Garden City, NY: Doubleday, 1972).

O'Donnell, J. J.: *Augustine: Confessions*, three volumes (London: Oxford University Press, 1992). [Introduction, critical edition, commentary.]

O'Meara, J. J.: *The Young Augustine. The Growth of St Augustine's Mind up to His Conversion* (London: Longmans, Green, 1954).

——: *Charter of Christendom: The Significance of the City of God* (New York: Macmillan, 1961).

Rist, J.: *Augustine: Ancient though Baptized* (Cambridge: Cambridge University Press, 1994).

Sorabji, R.: *Time, Creation and the Continuum* (London: Oxford University Press, 1983).

4

Berkeley

Lisa J. Downing

George Berkeley's (1685–1753 CE) most lasting philosophical legacies are his immaterialism – the denial of the existence of matter – and his idealism, the positive doctrine that reality is constituted by spirits and their ideas. This is as Berkeley would have wanted it; he clearly viewed the thesis that *esse est percipi aut percipere* (to be is to be perceived or to perceive) as his central philosophical insight, one which would revolutionize philosophy. However, he would be dismayed, if not surprised, to see the extent to which his idealistic system is still commonly regarded as unacceptably counterintuitive. Berkeley was in his own lifetime often dismissed as a skeptical purveyor of paradoxes. Nothing could have been further from his intentions; Berkeley saw his idealism as being reconcilable with common sense and, more importantly, as providing a weapon against both skepticism and atheism. To understand the significance of immaterialism/idealism for Berkeley, it is necessary to fill in more of his historical context.

Berkeley was born in 1685 near Kilkenny, Ireland. After several years of schooling at Kilkenny College, he entered Trinity College, in Dublin, at age 15. He was made a fellow of Trinity College in 1707 (three years after graduating) and was ordained in the Anglican Church shortly thereafter. At Trinity, where the curriculum was notably modern, Berkeley encountered the new science and philosophy of the late seventeenth century, which was characterized by its hostility towards Aristotelianism. Berkeley, however, was never satisfied for long with any received opinions, no matter how up to date; he immediately began to exercise his sharp critical faculties on the works of DESCARTES, LOCKE, Malebranche, Newton, HOBBES, and others. Berkeley's self-description here is revealing:

one thing I know, I am not guilty of. I do not pin my faith on the sleeve of any great man. I act not out of prejudice & prepossession. I do not adhere to any opinion because it is an old one, a receiv'd one, a fashionable one, or one that I have spent much time in the study and cultivation of. (*Philosophical Commentaries*, entry 465)

Berkeley's philosophical notebooks, which he began in 1707 and did not intend for publication, are often styled the *Philosophical Commentaries* because of the fact that many of the entries record his responses to other philosophical texts. The *Commentaries* provide rich documentation of Berkeley's philosophical evolution, enabling the reader to track the emergence of his immaterialist philosophy from a critical response to, most crucially, Locke, Descartes, and the Cartesians.

Berkeley saw Locke and the Cartesians as sharing a commitment to a general picture (with particular qualifications in each case) which we might call representative mechanist materialism. According to this view, there are two sort of beings in the world, spiritual beings (minds) and material beings (bodies). Material beings are mind-independent and conceived mechanistically, as composed of submicroscopic particles fully characterizable in terms of a strictly limited number of (primary) qualities: size, shape, motion/rest, and perhaps solidity. Other apparent (secondary) qualities (color, taste, sound) are not intrinsic qualities of bodies themselves, but are explained in terms of the effects that bodies have on perceivers. In perception, the immediate object of awareness is an idea, a mind-dependent item. However, the sensory idea represents a mind-independent material object to us, thus allowing us to (mediately) perceive the material object which caused that idea.

Berkeley regarded representative mechanist materialism as pernicious in that it was conducive to atheism and led immediately to skepticism. In its commitment to matter, it allowed the existence of something mind-independent, and something which might be thought to be God-independent as well, thus laying the groundwork for the denial of the existence of a Christian God. Although, of course, God does play an important role in the philosophies of Descartes, Malebranche, and Locke, Berkeley no doubt believed that he saw the consequences of materialism in Hobbes and SPINOZA, the "notorious infidels" of the seventeenth century. The tendency to skepticism is perhaps more compelling to the modern reader: the primary/secondary quality distinction entails that our senses systematically mislead us; we mistakenly think that the apple is red in just the way it appears to us to be, while redness *in the apple* is merely a power derived from a particular arrangement of uncolored particles which allows the apple to cause us to have an idea of red. Still more seriously, representationalism seems to open up the possibility of still more grave deception; if we only have immediate access to ideas, what grounds do we have to suppose that they are representative of reality at all? Berkeley saw a strikingly simple solution to these difficulties: abandon matter and construct a metaphysical system from spirits (minds) and their ideas:

> *matter* or *the absolute existence of corporeal objects*, hath been shewn to be that wherein the most avowed and pernicious enemies of all knowledge, whether human or divine, have ever placed their chief strength and confidence. And surely, if by distinguishing the real existence of unthinking things from their being perceived, and allowing them a subsistence of their own out of the minds of spirits, no one thing is explained in Nature; but on the contrary a great many inexplicable difficulties arise: if the supposition of matter is barely precarious, as not being grounded on so much as one single reason: . . . if withal the removal of this *matter* be not attended with the least evil consequence, if it be not even missed in the world, but everything as well, nay much easier conceived without it: if lastly, both *skeptics* and *atheists* are for ever silenced upon supposing only spirits and ideas, and this scheme of things is perfectly agreeable both to *reason* and *religion:* methinks we may expect it should be admitted and firmly embraced. (*Principles*, section 133)

Berkeley provided an initial glimpse of his mature metaphysics in his first important published work, *An Essay Towards a New Theory of Vision*. Most obviously, Berkeley intended this work to address an ongoing debate on the question of how distance is perceived by sight, and indeed the *New Theory* became an influential work in the psychology of vision. Berkeley also, however, sought to establish a conclusion that is directly relevant to his idealism: that the objects of sight and touch are heterogeneous. Berkeley argues that what we see is something ideal, mind-dependent, quite distinct from what we touch (*New Theory*, sections 43–50). Interestingly, he leaves in place the assumption that the objects of touch are mind-independent material objects; he tells us elsewhere that it was beside his purpose to refute this "vulgar error" in a work on vision (*Principles*, section 44).

By 1710, however, Berkeley was prepared to propose and defend his full idealistic system. In the *Treatise Concerning the Principles of Human Knowledge* (1710) and the *Three Dialogues between Hylas and Philonous* (1713), Berkeley lays out his two-sided case for idealism. On the one hand, he conducts a negative campaign designed to demonstrate the incoherence of materialism; on the other, he seeks to show positively the workability of his idealist system. Both the positive and negative programs, while not ultimately conclusive, are compelling and continue to reward detailed philosophical scrutiny.

The main body of the *Principles* opens with a strikingly simple "refutation" of materialism which takes the following form (see *Principles*, section 4):

1 We perceive ordinary physical objects.
2 We perceive only ideas/sensations.
3 Therefore, ordinary objects are ideas/sensations.

Of course, the representative mechanist materialist would respond to this argument by introducing a distinction between mediate and immediate perception, noting that on his view ordinary objects are perceived mediately, while we immediately perceive only ideas, thus avoiding the conclusion. In effect, Berkeley devotes much of the rest of the *Principles* to pointed criticism of the sort of representationalism that permits this response. Most importantly, he argues that because an idea can only be like another idea, we cannot suppose that ideas represent material objects by resemblance. Nor can the thesis that ideas represent material objects in virtue of being caused by them be defended, since "they [the materialists] own themselves unable to comprehend in what manner body can act upon spirit, or how it is possible it should imprint any idea in the mind" (*Principles*, section 19).

In addition, Berkeley devotes the introduction to the *Principles* to an influential attack on Lockean abstract ideas, arguing that abstract, general ideas cannot be formed in the way Locke sometimes seems to suggest, by stripping away particularizing features of ideas of particulars, leaving an intrinsically general idea. Rather, in Berkeley's view, what serve us for general ideas are simply ordinary ideas of particulars, used in a general way. Berkeley saw his anti-abstractionism as fueling his attack on materialism, for he held that we cannot abstract ideas of shape from ideas of color in the way that the materialists' primary/secondary quality distinction seems to require, nor can we "distinguish [i.e. abstract] the existence of sensible objects from their being perceived, so as to conceive them existing unperceived" (*Principles*, section 5).

Berkeley's positive program is for the most part concerned with showing that, despite the absence of matter, according to his view "there is a reality, there are things, there is a rerum Natura" (*Philosophical Commentaries*, entry 305). Berkeley's reality is constituted by spirits and their ideas. Physical things, or bodies, are congeries of ideas. The order of nature consists in the regularities amongst our ideas, and is guaranteed by the goodness of God (himself a spirit), who causes our ideas of sense. Thus the scientist (or natural philosopher, in Berkeley's day) studies the order of ideas, the grammar of nature. A distinction between real things and imaginary ones (*chimeras*) can be made in terms of the vividness and orderliness of the ideas which constitute real things. Berkeley's system is heavily dependent on God for its workability, but it is worth noting that Berkeley and his contemporaries would have counted this as a virtue of the theory, rather than a defect. Idealism exhibits our dependence, as finite minds, on the infinite mind, and coheres beautifully with the oft-quoted biblical phrase, "in him we live and move and have our being."

Despite Berkeley's acutely critical response to Locke and the Cartesians, his most profound intellectual debts are clearly to them. In particular, Berkeley's emphasis on the centrality of sensory experience in knowledge acquisition is strongly shaped by Locke and has led to his being grouped with Locke and Hume under the rubric of "British Empiricism." This classification, however, should not be permitted to obscure the considerable influence of Descartes and, especially, Malebranche on his thought.

Berkeley was dismayed by the reception of his immaterialist philosophy, and in fact composed the *Dialogues* in an effort to gain a broader audience for his views. His disappointment, however, did not discourage him from further philosophical work. In 1720, while completing a four-year tour of Europe as tutor to a young man, George Ashe, Berkeley composed *De Motu*, a tract on the philosophical foundations of mechanics. In this essay, he critiques the dynamic (force-based) physical theories of his time, particularly Leibniz's and Newton's, and develops and elaborates his philosophy of science. In doing so, he highlights some of the philosophical sources of resistance to Newtonianism and proposes an intriguing solution: an instrumentalist interpretation of Newton's theory as an excellent calculating device, the use of which should not be thought to commit us to the existence of forces.

After his continental tour, Berkeley returned to Ireland and resumed his position at Trinity until 1724, when he was appointed Dean of Derry. At this time, Berkeley began developing his scheme for founding a college in Bermuda. He was convinced that Europe was in moral and spiritual decay, and that the New World offered hope for a new golden age. Having secured a charter and promises of funding from the British Parliament, Berkeley set sail for America in 1728, with his new bride, Anne Forster. They spent three years in Newport, Rhode Island, awaiting the promised money, but Berkeley's political support had collapsed and they were forced to abandon the project and return to Britain in 1731. While in America, Berkeley composed *Alciphron*, a work of Christian apologetics directed against the "freethinkers" whom he took to be enemies of established Anglicanism. *Alciphron* is, however, also very much a philosophical work, and is a crucial source of Berkeley's views on language, which include an interesting critique of the Lockean semantic thesis that every meaningful word must stand for an idea. Berkeley argues here that the purposes of language include the guiding of action, that this may be accomplished without each word suggesting an idea, and that language which successfully guides action is thereby meaningful.

Shortly after returning to London, Berkeley composed the *Theory of Vision, Vindicated and Explained*, a defense of his earlier work on vision against a published attack, and the *Analyst*, an acute and influential critique of the foundations of Newton's calculus. In 1734 he was made Bishop of Cloyne, and thus he returned to Ireland. It was here that Berkeley wrote his last, strangest, and best-selling (in his own lifetime) philosophical work. *Siris* (1744) has a threefold aim: to establish the virtues of tar-water (a liquid prepared by letting pine tar stand in water) as a medical panacea, to provide scientific background supporting the efficacy of tar-water, and to lead the mind of the reader, via gradual steps, toward contemplation of God. Although Berkeley retains the basics of his idealism in *Siris*, neo-Platonic influences produce a work of a very different tone from that of the *Principles* and *Dialogues*. Nevertheless, *Siris* remains a crucial source for understanding Berkeley's attitude toward the natural philosophy of his day.

Berkeley died in 1753, shortly after moving to Oxford to supervise the education of his son George, one of the three out of seven of his children to survive childhood. Despite the mostly uncomprehending response accorded to his metaphysical views by his contemporaries, his influence on Hume and Kant was considerable, his critique of his predecessors continues to shape our understanding of them, and his idealism is one of the enduring positions on the map of Western philosophy.

Bibliography

Writings

Philosophical Commentaries (1707–8), in *Philosophical Works*, ed. Michael Ayers (London: Dent, 1975).

An Essay towards a New Theory of Vision (Dublin, 1709), in *Philosophical Works*, ed. Michael Ayers (London: Dent, 1975).

A Treatise concerning the Principles of Human Knowledge (Dublin, 1710), in *Philosophical Works*, ed. Michael Ayers (London: Dent, 1975).

Three Dialogues between Hylas and Philonous (London, 1713), in *Philosophical Works*, ed. Michael Ayers (London: Dent, 1975).

De Motu (London, 1721), in *"De Motu" and "The Analyst": A Modern Edition with Introductions and Commentary*, trans. and ed. Douglas M. Jesseph (Dordrecht: Kluwer Academic Publishers, 1992).

Alciphron: or the Minute Philosopher (London, 1732), in *The Works of George Berkeley, Bishop of Cloyne, volume 3*, ed. A. A. Luce and T. E. Jessop (London: Thomas Nelson and Sons, 1948–57).

The Analyst (Dublin and London, 1734), in *"De Motu" and "The Analyst": A Modern Edition with Introductions and Commentary*, trans. and ed. Douglas M. Jesseph (Dordrecht: Kluwer Academic Publishers, 1992).

Siris: A Chain of Philosophical Reflections and Enquiries Concerning the Virtues of Tar-water (Dublin and London, 1744), in *The Works of George Berkeley, Bishop of Cloyne, volume 5*, ed. A. A. Luce and T. E. Jessop (London: Thomas Nelson and Sons, 1948–57).

Further reading

Atherton, Margaret: *Berkeley's Revolution in Vision* (Ithaca, NY: Cornell University Press, 1990).

Berman, David: *George Berkeley: Idealism and the Man* (Oxford: Clarendon Press, 1994).

Jesseph, Douglas M.: *Berkeley's Philosophy of Mathematics* (Chicago: University of Chicago Press, 1993).

Pitcher, George: *Berkeley* (London: Routledge and Kegan Paul, 1977).

Tipton, I. C.: *Berkeley: The Philosophy of Immaterialism* (London: Methuen, 1974).

Urmson, J. O.: *Berkeley* (Oxford: Oxford University Press, 1982).

Winkler, Kenneth P.: *Berkeley: An Interpretation* (Oxford: Oxford University Press, 1989).

5

The Buddha

Peter Harvey

The person known as "the Buddha" (*c.*480–400 BCE) was Siddhattha Gotama (in Pali; in Sanskrit Siddhārtha Gautama). "Buddha" means "Awakened One" or "Enlightened One," and is a descriptive title rather than a name. Gotama lived in north-east India at a time of lively religious and philosophical debate. The prestige religion then was Brahmanism, an early form of Hinduism administered by Brahmins, the upper, priestly class of a fourfold system of sacred classes, and based on a sacred canon of (oral) texts, the *Veda*. Its central ritual was a fire sacrifice, which by the Buddha's day involved animal sacrifice, used to contact one or other deity so as to benefit the sacrificer and his patron. The *Upaniṣads*, composed from around 700 BCE, also sought the *ātman*, the essential Self, which was seen as the "inner controller" of both body and mind, but beyond both, being identical with *Brahman*, the holy power sustaining the universe.

There was also an "alternative" tradition of *samaṇas*, wandering ascetic-philosophers, who rejected the authority of the *Veda*, the pretensions of the Brahmins to be superior, and the efficacy of sacrifice. This group came to include the Buddhists. Their goal was to find true and lasting happiness through a proper understanding of the nature of reality and an appropriate response to it. Apart from the Buddhists, some were Materialists, who denied any form of survival after death, including reincarnation, which Brahmanism had come to believe in. The Materialists sought a life of simple, balanced pleasures. The Sceptics denied the possibility of human beings gaining knowledge of ultimate matters. The Ājīvakas believed in reincarnation but denied that living beings could affect how they were reborn: it was all in the hands of blind "destiny." Lastly, the Jains believed in reincarnation according to the nature of one's karma – action – (as in Brahmanism) and emphasized ascetic self-deprivation so as to purge the *jīva* – the life-principle or soul – of accretions which kept it within the cycle of reincarnations.

Gotama was born the son of an elected aristocratic ruler of a small republic, later swallowed up by one of the expanding kingdoms of the day. Though brought up in comfort, in his twenties he came to ponder on human frailty – ageing, sickness and death – and was inspired by the sight of a calm *samaṇa* to renounce his well-off life, to live off alms, and become a religious seeker of the "unborn, unageing, deathless." After six years of trying yogic trance and then a determined course of ascetic self-deprivation, he came to develop his own path. One night, when aged around thirty-five, he is said to have finally become a Buddha, through the power of his own meditation. He first attained progressively refined levels of lucid trance, through careful observation of breathing-related sensations. Once in a state of profound, alert calm, with the mind highly sensitive, he then attained the "three knowledges": the contents of his enlightenment experience. First, he is said to have remembered several hundred thousand of his past lives. Second, to have traced other beings as they died and were reborn, noting that the nature of their rebirth depended on the quality of their karma. Third, he attained insight into the "Four Ennobling Truths" (see below), which brought him liberation from the round of rebirths. He went on to share his insights with many disciples, the more committed of whom were usually ordained in the order of monks or nuns that he instituted. His disciples would practice the path mapped out by him so as to attain similar insights and trans-formations for themselves, which they also used in teaching others.

The Buddha described himself as both an "experientialist" and an "analyst." By the first term, he meant that he looked to neither tradition nor *a priori* reasoning as the source of truth, but to experience, both normal and meditatively based paranormal. On the thesis that he therefore advocated a form of "empiricism," see Jayatilleke (1963) and Kalupahana (1992), with Hoffman (1987) and Harvey (1995b) assessing the thesis. Yet the Buddha was aware that the mind could easily filter out aspects of direct experience, misinterpret it due to preconceived ideas, and jump to unwarranted conclusions from very little experiential evidence. He therefore also emphasized that:

1 The mind must be carefully calmed and refined, by meditation, to get closer to direct experience, unbiased by moods, preferences, fears, and habits.
2 Experience must then be carefully analysed, to discern what its components actually are, and what one can safely conclude from it.

In his disciples, he valued the quality of faith, in the sense of an inspired aspiration to develop admirable qualities seen in others such as himself, but also wisdom, experientially based direct insight which enabled individuals to see the truth for themselves, rather than just accept it from another.

While some (Kalupahana, 1992) have seen the Buddha's theory of truth as a pragmatic one, it is better to characterize it as a correspondence one (with incoherence also seen as one test of falsity). His pragmatic bent comes in as regards what truths he saw as worth teaching to others (Harvey, 1995b). Here, the test was whether such a teaching (a) could in general contribute to people's spiritual development, and (b) was appropriate to the particular situation and psychological/spiritual state of the individual who came to him for discussion or instruction. Some questions he answered directly, some after clarifying their nature, some after a counter-question, but others he set aside unanswered (Woodward, 1933, pp. 53–4). The last are the ten "undetermined questions": is the world finite or infinite, eternal or non-eternal; is the life-principle the same as or different from the mortal body; which is a true statement on an enlightened person after death, that he or she "is," "is not," "both is and is not," or "neither is nor is not"? The Buddha refused to affirm any of the propositions contained in these questions, seeing concern over them as a time-wasting sidetrack from moral and spiritual development. He also rejected the questions as implicitly postulating an essential, unchanging Self that was eternal or non-eternal, finite or infinite like its world, identical with or different from the body, and had some particular destiny after death. As the Buddha saw no evidence for such a Self, he saw questions implying its existence as, in a sense, meaningless (Collins, 1982, pp. 131–8; Harvey, 1995a, pp. 78–95). On the topics of the ten questions, he seems to have seen the world as without any *discernible* beginning, and as going through a series of cosmic cycles; he also talked of thousands upon thousands of world-systems spread out through space. He seems to have accepted some kind of changing life-principle that is primarily mental but usually interdependent with the body (Harvey, 1993, 1995a, pp. 91–5). On the liberated person, he did not accept that such a person was destroyed after death, and he implied that, beyond any rebirth, however subtle, and beyond time, some form of inconceivable liberated state existed (Harvey, 1995a, pp. 227–45).

During the Buddha's day, the idea of a series of lives was a topic of widespread belief as well as of doubt and denial. The Buddha accepted some form of the doctrine as he felt he had experiential evidence for it. He taught that each sentient being had had innumerable past rebirths, which would continue until liberation from this "wandering on" was attained (Harvey, 1990, pp. 32–9). Rebirth could be in either

(a) one of two good destinies – as a human, or as a god in one or other of a range of heavenly rebirths – or (b) one of three bad destinies – as an animal of some kind, as a frustrated ghost, or in a painful hellish realm. Life in all such realms was finite – though the lifespan of hell-beings, and particularly the gods, could be huge – and was followed by some other form of rebirth. Rebirth as a human was seen as a rare and precious opportunity for moral and spiritual growth. The gods were capable of such growth, but their long lifespan meant that they were liable to forget that they were mortal, and so neglect to seek liberation.

Good or bad rebirths were not seen as "rewards" or "punishments" meted out by some divine being. Indeed, the Buddha did not accept the idea of a creator of the world, since the world, and even the gods, proceeded according to natural laws. In the case of rebirth, the determining factor was the quality of a person's action/karma (Harvey, 1990, pp. 39–46). While Brahmanism taught something similar, it tended to be primarily concerned with action which was *ritually* correct or incorrect. The Buddha saw the *moral* aspect of an action as its key factor. He also saw the prime factor in a karma as the impelling will or intention (*cetanā*) behind it (Keown, 1992, pp. 213–18): this is what generates future karmic results. (By contrast, the Jains focused on the overt side of the action.) Action that was motivated by greed, hatred, or delusion, or was intended to harm a being, was seen as unwholesome, and as therefore generating unpleasant karmic results. Action that was motivated by greedlessness (including meditative calm), kindness, or wisdom, or was intended to genuinely benefit a being, was seen as wholesome and as generating pleasant results. Such results included the form of rebirth, certain character traits, and the subjective impact of some events, but it was not held that everything that happened was due to karma (Woodward, 1933, p. 97). A human was seen as a relatively free agent who, while affected by environment and character, could initiate new action not fatalistically fixed by past events or actions.

The Buddha showed a considerable concern for ethics, in the form of the cultivation of wholesome actions or virtues, and the systematic restraint and transcending of unwholesome ones (Harvey, 1990, pp. 196–216). A set of five ethical precepts were given to his disciples. These were undertakings to avoid (a) injuring living beings (as all sentient beings share a dislike of pain and a like of happiness), (b) taking what is not given, (c) sensual misconduct, such as adultery, (d) lying, and (e) intoxication. In the case of monks and nuns, many more training rules were added in order to develop a life of balanced, mindful sense-restraint, including complete celibacy. Keown (1992) gives a good account of Buddhist ethics, arguing for its likeness to Aristotelian virtue-ethics. Harvey (2000) discusses the dynamics of Buddhist ethics as applied to various issues.

For those who were ready to benefit from them, the Buddha taught the Four Ennobling Truths (Harvey, 1990, pp. 47–72), which can be explained as follows:

1 A pervading feature of life is *dukkha*, "suffering" or, more subtly, "unsatisfactoriness." This is seen in: the pain of being born, and of ageing, sickness, and death; stress, anxiety, loss, and sadness; frustration, arising from the fact that things are only ever temporarily as one wants them to be, and often not even that; the fragility of the life of any sentient being, subject as it is to various limitations.

2 A crucial cause for *dukkha* is craving: demanding desire for something more pleasurable, more ego-inflating, less unpleasant. This craving is seen to cause future rebirth, and thus re-sickness etc., to set up situations where frustration is felt (proportional to the strength and number of one's cravings), and to form the basis of conflicts with others.

3 By removing the cause(s) of *dukkha*, *dukkha* can be ended in the realization of *Nirvāṇa*, a timeless, blissful experience which destroys craving and all attachment, hatred and delusion. One who has fully experienced this becomes an *Arahat*, and at death will no longer be reborn. To tread the path to *Nirvāṇa*, a person must first desire it, to help motivate practice, but to finally attain it, everything must be let go of, including *Nirvāṇa* itself.

4 The path to the end of *dukkha* is the Ennobling Eightfold Path, of wisdom (right understanding and resolve), moral virtue (right speech, action, and livelihood), and calm and joyful meditation (right effort, mindful observation of body and mind, and mental unification). These all reinforce one another.

The Buddha advocated that, after calming the mind, a disciple should engage in careful experiential investigation of the processes making up body and mind. He emphasized that everything (except *Nirvāṇa*) was impermanent and subject to change. In the world and persons, he discovered no unchanging substances, physical or mental, just streams of interacting processes or *dhammas*, all of which were limited in various ways, and thus *dukkha*. He saw a human as composed of five "groups" or "aggregates" (*khandhas*) of such processes:

1 "Material form": processes such as "earth" (solidity), "water" (cohesion), "fire" (heat), and "wind" (motion).

2   "Feeling": pleasant, unpleasant, or neutral hedonic tone.
3   "Cognition": the classifying and labeling of sense- or mind-objects, as in recognition and misinterpretation.
4   "Constructing activities": will and various emotions, which give shape to a person's character and destiny.
5   "Discriminative consciousness," or "discernment": awareness of the presence of a sense- or mind-object, and discernment of its parts or aspects, labeled by cognition.

These are all seen to be in a state of constant dynamic flow, with nothing "owning" them. The Buddha held that everything, when carefully examined, can be recognised to be not-Self or non-Self (*anatta/anātman*): not a permanent, substantial, autonomous Self or I (Collins, 1982; Harvey, 1995a, pp. 17–77). This claim is not, as such, a straightforward denial of such a Self, though such a denial *is* implied. Rather, it is an invitation to examine each thing one tends to fondly identify with as "I" – "what I truly and really am" – and, in realizing its changing, conditioned, non-substantial nature, to let go of it, i.e. not be attached to it (which is not the same as pushing it away). This allows the occurrence of the experience of *Nirvāṇa*, which is beyond all attachment and clinging, and totally lacks anything that could be mistaken for a Self.

The Buddha saw the *sense* of "I-ness," the "'I am' conceit" or ego, as real enough, but he regarded it as a conditioned, limited and deluded state, certainly no real Self. Moreover, he saw it as leading to much suffering for oneself and others, being the root of self-ishness. He also accepted what one can call the empirical or conventional "self": the cluster of changing aggregates – including the ego-sense – as described above. He taught that it was good to cultivate the inner strength and integrity of this changing self, and that the undermining of the "'I am' conceit" actually contributed to this. So an *Arahat* is one who has destroyed this conceit, by seeing all as not-Self, yet has a strong, calm, open, balanced empirical self, free of such limitations as craving.

A principle running through much of the above, and said to have been discovered in the Buddha's enlightenment, is that of Conditioned Arising, or Dependent Origination (*paṭicca-samuppāda*). At its most abstract, this principle states that any thing only arises due to factors which condition it, and ceases when these are absent. Only *Nirvāṇa*, being unconditioned, is beyond arising and passing away. This principle of conditionality is applied rigorously to the working of the aggregates and to the working of the Ennobling Eightfold Path, as well as to a detailed analysis of a chain of twelve processes culminating in *dukkha*. This chain includes craving, but also spiritual ignorance, a deep-seated misperception of the nature of reality which persists in overlooking its qualities as impermanent, *dukkha*, and not-Self, thus feeding the craving and clinging that perpetuate *dukkha*.

Just as the Ennobling Eightfold Path is seen as a "middle way" of practice, avoiding the extremes of harsh asceticism and sensual indulgence, so Conditioned Arising is seen as an intellectual "middle way." Thus the world is seen neither as "existing" – in a solid, unchanging way – nor as a "non-existent" illusion; for it does arise as a stream of changing processes. Likewise, an unliberated person neither eternally exists after death, as no eternal Self can be found to exist, nor is annihilated. The truth lies in the middle: a stream of changing processes, particularly those of discriminating consciousness and karmic traces, spill over after death and, with appropriate physical conditions in a mother's womb, help another life to start. Thus Buddhists prefer to talk of "rebirth" rather than "reincarnation," which implies a reincarnated Self/Soul. While some passages of the early texts indicate that the Buddha accepted a between-lives spirit-being (a *gandhabba*; Harvey, 1995a, pp. 89–108), this form of being was still seen as a cluster of impermanent states, and thus as not-Self. As to what "remains" of a liberated person beyond death, some passages suggest it is a radically transformed, objectless, and thus unconditioned form of discriminating consciousness (Harvey, 1995a, pp. 198–245).

Soon after the Buddha died, a monastic council was held to agree on the contents of his teachings, which were to be passed on by communal chanting. Thus was formed the core of the *Vinaya* and *Sutta* collections, on monastic discipline and the Buddha's discourses, respectively. In the two or three following centuries, *Abhidhamma* texts were composed, systematizing and thus interpreting the teachings in the form of intricate analyses of the working of the mind. In the early centuries CE, new texts emerged which heralded the gradual emergence of a new movement in Buddhism, the Mahāyāna. The new texts were attributed by the Mahāyānists to the Buddha, as they held that visionary and meditative experience could still contact him or draw on the wisdom that had informed him. The Mahāyāna saw the earlier teachings as provisional ones, and included in their texts a critique of the early schools, of which there had developed around eighteen (Harvey, 1990, pp. 73–94, 323–4). Of these, only the Theravāda survives today, being found in Sri Lanka, Thailand, Burma, Cambodia, and Laos. The Mahāyāna is found in Tibet, Mongolia, China, Vietnam, Korea, and

Japan. Both strands of Buddhism include strong traditions of textual study of "the word of the Buddha."

Bibliography

Writings

The Buddha did not *write* anything. The existing sources most indicative of his oral teachings are the *Suttas* collected by the Theravādins, in the Pali language: the five *Nikāyas* or "collections," first written down around 80 BCE.

The *Dīgha Nikāya*, trans. M. Walshe as *Thus Have I Heard: The Long Discourses of the Buddha* (London: Wisdom, 1987).
The *Majjhima Nikāya*, trans. I. B. Horner, in three volumes, as *Middle Length Sayings* (London: Pali Text Society, 1954, 1957, 1959). See also Bhikkhu Nanamoli and Bhikkhu Bodhi, *The Middle Length Discourses of the Buddha* (Boston: Wisdom, 1995).
The *Saṃyutta Nikāya*, trans. C. A. F. Rhys Davids (volume I) and F. L.Woodward (volumes II–V) as *Kindred Sayings* (London: Pali Text Society, 1917, 1922, 1924, 1927, 1930).
The *Aṅguttara Nikāya*, trans. F. L. Woodward (volumes I, II, V), and E. M. Hare (volumes III, IV) as *Gradual Sayings* (London: Pali Text Society, 1932, 1933, 1934, 1935, 1936).
The *Khuddaka Nikāya*: fifteen small texts, including (both in verse): the *Dhammapada*, trans. e.g. Nārada Thera, *The Dhammapada* (London: John Murray, 1954); the *Sutta-nipāta*, trans. H. Saddhatissa, *The Sutta-Nipāta* (London: Curzon Press, 1985).

Further reading

Collins, S.: *Selfless Persons* (Cambridge: Cambridge University Press, 1982).
——: "Buddhism in recent philosophy and theology," *Religious Studies*, 21 (1985), 475–93.
Harvey, P.: *An Introduction to Buddhism* (Cambridge: Cambridge University Press, 1990).
——: *An Introduction to Buddhist Ethics: Foundations, Values and Issues* (Cambridge: Cambridge University Press, 2000).
——: "The mind-body relationship in Pāli Buddhism," *Asian Philosophy*, 3 (1993), 29–41.
——: *The Selfless Mind* (London: Curzon Press, 1995a).
——: "Contemporary characterisations of the 'philosophy' of Nikāyan Buddhism," *Buddhist Studies Review*, 12 (1995b), 109–33.
Hoffman, F. J.: *Rationality and Mind in Early Buddhism* (Delhi: Motilal Banarsidass, 1987).

Jayatilleke, K. N.: *Early Buddhist Theory of Knowledge* (London: Allen & Unwin, 1963; reprinted Delhi: Motilal Banarsidass, no date).

Kalupahana, D. J.: *A History of Buddhist Philosophy* (Honolulu: University of Hawaii Press, 1992).

Keown, D.: *The Nature of Buddhist Ethics* (London: Macmillan, 1992).

6

Confucius

David L. Hall

No philosophic or religious visionary, whether PLATO or ARISTOTLE, Jesus, BUDDHA Gotama, or Mohammed, is the peer of Confucius as a focus of cultural significances, a founder of cultural institutions, and a model of ethical behavior. Even today, in a China nominally influenced by Marxism, it is Confucianism which is the foundation of the society and culture.

Confucius (551–479 BCE) was born in the state of Lu, an area which is today the southeastern portion of Shandong province. He lived during the decline of the Zhou [Chou] dynasty (c.1100–256 BCE). Confucius was one of the earliest of the itinerant scholars who would travel among the competing states offering advice to political leaders on the art of rulership. The great frustration of Confucius was that during his lifetime he never achieved real practical influence, whether in his home state of Lu where he was for a brief period police commissioner, or in any of the other states in which he briefly resided. Confucius returned to Lu late in life and served there as a counselor of the lower rank, while he continued teaching a small number of disciples who would later begin the broader transmission of his ideas.

Confucius' vision of the means to social and political harmony was grounded upon the rites and institutions originated by the Duke of Zhou, some five hundred years before Confucius. It was from these institutions, largely due to Confucius' sponsorship, that Chinese civilization was to emerge. The genius of the Zhou feudal system was to make family relations the basis of political loyalties, which meant that the Zhou institutions insured that the feudal lords were not merely vassals, but also blood relatives, of the King they served.

The crucial aspect of this system which Confucius would stress and which has become a part of Chinese society ever since concerns the importance of the family. It is the family that constitutes the context within which the individual becomes who he or she is. Moreover, the state is itself patterned upon the model of the family. One does not, as with Aristotle, move out from the privacy of the family to become a public person, a "citizen"; rather, one is always a member of a family – both of the biological unit into which one is born, and of the political "family" which urges a broader set of allegiances.

The principal source of Confucius' thought is the *Lunyu* [*Lun-yü*] – the *Analects* – which records his life and teachings. The earlier portions of the work contain personal remembrances of Confucius the man, along with accounts of his habits and predilections. The latter portions, particularly the last five of the twenty chapters, were likely produced after Confucius' main disciples had begun their own careers as trans-mitters of the Confucian way. In these chapters, though Confucius remains the focus, the disciples often speak in their own voice.

There are two other important resources dealing with the life and teachings of Confucius: first, the *Zuo* [*Tso*] commentary on the *Spring and Autumn Annals*; second, the *Mengzi* [*Mencius*]. The *Zuo* commentary purports to be a narrative of the court history of the state of Lu until the death of Confucius. The *Mengzi*, which was to become one of the most influential of Confucian texts, was compiled perhaps some one hundred and fifty years after Confucius, and is named for a follower of Confucius who significantly elaborated the doctrines of the Master (see MENCIUS).

For many Western trained philosophers Confucius presents a real puzzle: how is it that a seemingly disconnected array of *obiter dicta* such as that found in the *Analects* could possibly serve as the focal document for the entire Chinese civilization from the Han dynasty until the present day? What are we to make of this Chinese sage who seemingly ignored the important cosmological and metaphysical issues which have exer-cised Western thinkers from the Presocractics to the present and was content to urge a return to the rituals and institutions of the ancient Zhou dynasty, secure in the belief that self-realization and social harmony are the only worthwhile pursuits for a truly *human* being?

There are two issues here. First, can a philosopher really be taken seri-ously if he fails to ask "the question of being" or to make some claim about the ultimate constituents comprising the world, or ignores the necessity to determine how we come to know, and omits any considera-tion of the most responsible method for justifying our beliefs about God, Nature, or Mind? Second, even if we are to accept Confucius simply as strictly a "moral philosopher" in the narrower sense, is there anything of value to be found in a thinker so provincial and backward-looking as he appears to be?

We shall begin with the latter question. Many interpreters of Chinese culture have argued that the conservative nature of Confucian thought is a consequence of its having been born in a highly unstable period. The Chinese, so the argument goes, in contrast to the more speculative Greeks, were compelled to be overly concerned with social order and harmony rather than with a dispassionate search for Truth. But the suggestion that practical and urgent political concerns forced the Chinese to search for the Way (*Dao* [*Tao*]) while we in the West somehow had the luxury to be speculative and to turn our attention to the profounder issues concerning the truth about the nature of things appears, on reflection, to be a bit self-serving. A more pragmatic interpretation seems equally plausible. The quest for Truth may be as much rooted in social and political concerns as is the search for the Way.

Indeed, if we are to appreciate the peculiar character of Chinese philosophical thought, it is advisable to entertain the possibility that the Western and Chinese cultures were significantly shaped by essentially the same motivation – namely, the realization of social harmony. The fact that China was characterized by greater linguistic and ethnic homogeneity than was the West largely determined the broad intellectual and institutional differences between the strategies of the two traditions. In the pluralistic West it was quite natural to look for a harmonizing principle in some transcendent, universalizing, ground or goal; in the more homogeneous China, it was quite natural to avoid transcendent principles such as "God" or "Reason" or the "Laws of Nature," and to seek the harmonizing standard in the immanence of social relationships.

Thinking in this manner will better dispose us to appreciate Confucius on his own terms. We are still faced, however, with a significant obstacle. For if we ask after Confucius' theory of this or that, or if we attempt to search out his doctrines relative to this or that issue, we will certainly be frustrated. In the senses of these terms with which the Westerner is most familiar, Confucius lacks both doctrines and a theory. If we are to understand Confucius, we can do no better than to think of him as saying of his thought what William James said of pragmatic philosophy – "It is a method only." Confucius doesn't have a theory; he has a method, a *methodos* – that is to say, a *"Way."* The question we must ask, therefore, is "What is the Way of Confucius?"

In *Analects* 4/15, we find these words: "My way is bound together with one unifying thread." In that same section, a disciple glosses Confucius' words as follows: "The Way of the Master is doing one's best in using oneself as a measure to gauge others. That is all." "Using oneself as a measure to gauge others" is a translation of *shu*. The standard by which both self-realization and social harmony are to be attained is *shu*, which Confucius himself characterizes in this manner: "Do not impose on others what you yourself do not desire" (*Analects* 15/24). *Shu* is an act of comparison in which one takes oneself as starting point and attempts to discover the desires of others. *Shu* is the "single thread" unifying Confucius' way.

If one is able to act in accordance with *shu*, it is essential that the standard from which one begins – that is, one's self – be one expressive of appropriate moral character. This is but to say that it is essential that one be truly human. The notion expressive of such humanity is *ren* [*jen*]. *Ren* is often translated as "benevolence" or "human-heartedness." This term also alludes to the process of becoming human. "Human-heartedness," in the sense of being fully human and acting most humanely toward others, is a sound enough rendering of *ren*. This is especially so if we recall that the Chinese term for "heart" – *xin* [*hsin*] – names the seat of both thinking and judgment. Indeed, what we often think of as "will" or "intention" is, likewise, included in the notion of *xin*.

The interpenetration of idea, intention, and affect expressed in the notion of *xin* entails the conclusion that thinking is never a dispassionate speculative enterprise, but involves normative judgments which assess the relative merit of the sensations, inclinations, and appetites that interpenetrate our experience of the world and of ourselves. Since appetites and ideas are always clothed with emotion, they are to be understood, more often than not, as *dispositions to act*. As dispositional, thinking and learning are oriented to the practical ends of the moral life. When, for example, Confucius said, "At fifteen my heart and mind were set upon learning" (*Analects* 2/4), he was indicating his commitment to an ethical regimen aimed at self-realization.

Ren, or human-heartedness, suggests a morally cultivated human being with sensitivities and good judgment who is on his way to becoming a fully realized human being. *Ren* is the ground for the practice of *shu*. The single thread which runs throughout Confucius' thinking involves the practice of cultivating one's self through the cultivation of one's relations with others. To be *ren* is to consider others in such manner as always to avoid imposing upon them what one does not oneself desire. To be *ren* is, thus, to act with *shu* in those relationships formed in the process of taking on the responsibility and obligations of communal living.

We are accustomed to think of efforts aimed at moral perfection as involving a struggle between the reason and passion, or between what we believe we ought to do, and an obstreperous will that frustrates the enactment of that belief. Thus, we often say with St Paul, "The good that I would do I do not do, and the evil that I would not do, that I do." In the Chinese tradition there is little such internal conflict involved in ethical development.

If the problematic of unrealized selfhood does not entail the self divided against itself, what *is* the source and nature of the disturbance that the moral discipline is meant to overcome? If it is not referenced primarily within the self, it can only be a disturbance in the relationships which constitute the self in its interactions with others. The unpartitioned self characterized by *ren*, acting toward others in such manner as to avoid imposing upon them what one does not oneself desire, presents the picture of an ethical program defined by interpersonal, rather than intrapsychic, relations. Charting a harmonious path within and among the world of others is a principal task for those who would achieve real humanity. Such an effort leads to a search for the proper way (*dao*).

Dao or "way" is a crucial term for Confucius, occurring more than a hundred times in the *Analects*. Confucius often characterizes *dao* in terms of the inheritance from past generations. In this sense *dao* is the more or less general cultural resource which may be specified in terms of specific individuals or specific ritual forms. The *dao* of a particular person, or a particular social situation, is a specification of this general inheritance. There is a *dao* of music, and of archery, a *dao* of the bureaucrat, as well as a *tian dao* – a way of heaven. But all these ways are resourced in the rituals, actions, institutions, and writings that have survived in the cultural memory. Thus, *dao* is not some specific norm in accordance with which a person acts; rather, *dao* is realized in the performance of appropriate conduct. Indeed, "It is man who extends the *dao*, not *dao* that extends man" (*Analects* 15/29). Thus, the person of *ren* who acts with *shu* is enabled, in his relations with others, to discern the proper way of conducting himself.

Dao is closely related to *de* [*te*], which is often translated as "virtue." *De* may be understood as the power or excellence specific to a particular individual in a particular set of circumstances. As such, *de* is that which focuses the field of significances associated with the generalized *dao* as cultural resource. *De* is what personalizes *dao*.

It is easy enough to conceive how the virtuous person might place his personal stamp upon his interactions with others in those situations relatively untouched by formal expectations, but Confucius is equally concerned to promote the personalization of the ritual activities (*li*) which aid one in following the proper way. Ritual activity (*li*) is resourced in the inherited body of cultural institutions and the pattern of roles and relationships that locate us within community. Since the various roles and relationships constituting the family provide the principal context for becoming fully human, it is essential that these relations be spelled out in some detail. The most important relationships for Confucius are those of father and son and elder and younger brother.

These hierarchical relationships help to establish the grounds for respect within both the biological and the broader political families. Much of the ritual activity (*li*) associated with the Confucian vision is an articulation and elaboration of the duties connected with the complex varieties of family and social relationships. Thus *li* constitute a code of formal behaviors for stabilizing and disciplining our life situations.

The *li* provide a set of mutual expectations that secure relationships. In the strictest of senses, such ritual activities constitute a language. As a code of behaviors considered strictly in itself, it is a *langue* constituting the syntax of social relationships. As performed in particular situations, ritual activity is *parole* – the fullest expression of the sea of dispositions which serve as resource for social interactions. Ritual activity is, thus, a means of communication that both establishes and maintains a viable community.

If *li* are to promote true self-realization, they cannot be considered mere external forms. These cultural norms must be personalized and refined. I must be *this* son to *this* father. The ancestors I honor must be deeply and richly connected to me and to my family. And if in the performance of the rites I am consistently seen to act with *de* – to express intrinsic excellence in all my actions – I may come to serve as a model for others. Once more we return to *shu*, the single thread: it is *shu* which permits one to realize *de* in a sufficient degree to become a model for others. And it is *shu* which allows others to respond to that model.

The most important model in Confucius is the *junzi* [*chün-tzu*] – the "exemplary person." He is to be contrasted with the *xiaoren* [*hsiao-jen*] – the "small person" – who serves as the principal negative model in the *Analects*. The *junzi* is an embodiment of ritual activity, rightly performed. He is one who so focuses the characteristics and possibilities of his tradition as to make them available to others. Thus, he is a source of continuity with the tradition and a model for both personal realization and social harmony. The *junzi* is a central notion in Confucius' vision.

A final word: Zigong, one of Confucius' disciples, complained that "One cannot get to hear the Master's views on human nature and the Way of Heaven" (*Analects* 5/13). But, despite Confucius' reticence to speak on such issues, some statements of his, such as "At fifty I realized the will [*ming*] of heaven [*tian*]," have led many interpreters to speculate on his "cosmological" views.

Most translators of the *Analects* render *tian* as "heaven" and *ming* as "will" or "fate" or "destiny." Each of these translations is confusing, however. Confucius' indifference to strictly cosmological speculations means that his world is to be discussed without recourse to the notion of transcendence. Thus, heaven is intrinsically intertwined with human existence. *Tian* and *ren* are mutually conditioning. Also, *ming* cannot be understood as will or fate or destiny if these have strongly deterministic interpretations. In a world of interacting, interdepending relationships such as Confucius describes, there is nothing that may be said to be wholly determinative of anything else. Though there is still some suggestion of anthropomorphism in the language of the *Analects*, it is best to understand *tian*, like the generalized form of *dao*, as the field of possibilities for human action. And *ming* is not "fate," but the environing conditions which place greater or lesser limits upon the efficacy of human actions. The point here is that in a Confucian world everything, including one's "fate," is negotiable. And the analogical activities involved in the performance of *shu* are the means by which these negotiations are made.

Bibliography

Writings

Lunyu (Peking: Harvard-Yenching Institute, 1932), trans. D. C. Lau, *Confucius: The Analects* (Hong Kong: Chinese University Press, 1992).
Zuozhuan [Zou Commentary] (Beijing: Harvard-Yenching Institute, 1937).
Mengzi (Beijing: Harvard-Yenching Institute, 1941), trans. D. C. Lau, *Mencius* (Hong Kong: Chinese University Press, 1984).

Further reading

Finagarette, Herbert A.: *Confucius: The Secular as Sacred* (New York: Harper & Row, 1972).
——: "Following the 'one thread' of the *Analects*," *Journal of the American Academy of Religion*, Thematic Issue 47 (1979), 373–406.
Graham, Angus: *Disputers of the Tao* (La Salle, IL: Open Court Press, 1989).
Hall, David L. and Ames, Roger T.: *Thinking Through Confucius* (Albany, NY: State University of New York Press, 1987).
Schwartz, Benjamin I.: "Some polarities in Confucian thought." In David S. Nivison and Arthur F. Wright (eds), *Confucianism in Action* (Stanford, CA: Stanford University Press, 1959).
Tu, Wei-ming: *Humanity and Self-cultivation: Essays in Confucian Thought* (Berkeley, CA: Asian Humanities Press, 1979).

7

Derrida

John C. Coker

Jacques Derrida (1930–CE), a leading figure in French post-structuralist philosophy, is renowned for having developed deconstruction. His prolific writings treat both philosophical and literary works, and do so in various ways, of which deconstruction is the most philosophically significant. The following account will explicate what deconstruction involves by sketching some of its strategies and discussing its import for philosophy.

Derrida's early (1967–72) writings deconstruct the philosophy of presence, which includes the metaphysics of presence and logocentric philosophy. The philosophy of presence assumes that there are beings or meanings that are self-identical unities that can, actually or in principle, be presented fully; examples of such unities are PLATO's ideas and FREGE's and HUSSERL's senses. To deconstruct a philosophy of presence involves demonstrating that its theory is developed (and its text is composed) out of terms and distinctions which, though taken by the theory as given or fundamental, are themselves constructs open to interrogation, and which are demonstrably unstable and lack ultimate grounds. Such ultimate grounds have traditionally been sought in the metaphysics of presence.

The metaphysics of presence comprises a kind of ontology where *being* (or truth) has been understood in terms of some *presence*, whether the presence is, e.g. some sort of self-identical being or a meaning, and whether the presence is taken to be immediately *given* (e.g. a sense-datum), or what is given in principle (e.g. an underlying principle of unity) or teleologically (the ultimate end that is to be realized). Grasping such alleged presences is to apprehend what is and is not the truth. For example, DESCARTES both asserts the fully transparent self-presence of one's own mental states and derives a privileged epistemic access for the individual knowing subject, and he alleges that there are *a priori*, given, self-identical innate ideas.

Logocentric philosophy constitutes itself as exemplary of the *logos*, a Greek word whose meanings include reason, speech, rational discourse, and rational accounts (e.g. philosophical and scientific theories). In general, logocentric philosophies assume paradigms of what is rational, reasonable, etc., and correlatively they exclude or marginalize what does not fit their paradigm. For example, logocentric philosophies have often excluded or marginalized figurative language in favor of a purely literal philosophical language, whether actual or idealized. Deconstructions can serve to show how such philosophies, despite their strictures, operate with the very figurative language they profess to exclude or marginalize. Even when not overtly a metaphysics of presence (though often it is), logocentric philosophy nonetheless models itself, its methods, and its standard of rationality on presences, whether these are essences, paradigms, ideas or idealizations, or what it takes as its givens. Methodologically if not ontologically, logocentric philosophy installs categorical distinctions which are often hierarchic binary oppositions, e.g. the "literal/figurative" distinction in logocentric philosophy privileges the former to the exclusion or marginalization of the latter term. Especially in earlier writings, Derrida interrogates (in a manner to be discussed later) the opposition "speech/writing" (with the first term privileged); but other oppositions are no less important, such as "presence/ absence," "identity/difference," "paradigm/instance," "form/matter," and "intelligible/sensible." The privileged term of such distinctions is taken, by philosophers holding the distinction, to be the dominant one and to allocate the proper place or role of the subordinate term. Which distinction is challenged depends on the position being deconstructed; the deconstruction of such distinctions involves a scrupulously close reading of the sort exemplified in Derrida's writings.

In logocentric philosophies assuming the speech/writing distinction, speech, whether interpersonal or in silent soliloquy, has been understood as the primary medium or milieu of thought. It has been taken to be exemplary of language because of its presumed immediacy – one's thoughts are voiced, one's intended meaning can be simultaneously fully expressed and presented to oneself or to one's interlocutor in a present determinate context. Writing has traditionally been accorded the role of a mere but necessary instrumental supplement to speech: writing is a step removed from speech and merely represents it, though preserving by recording it. Moreover, writing has potentially deleterious effects, e.g. a reliance on written records can degrade living memory (see "Plato's Pharmacy," discussing Plato's *Phaedrus*, in *Dissemination*). Also, a text can potentially be removed from its "original" thought and context of utterance, set into other contexts, and thereby may signify at variance with intended meaning. Because of such potentially deleterious effects on both the thinking/speaking subject and meaning, philosophies of presence have relegated writing to a subordinate place and role.

Derrida questions the distinction between what is internal to and belongs to the thinking/speaking subject (e.g. one's own thinking to oneself in silent soliloquy) and what is external to this subject (e.g. the inscription of one thoughts). According to Derrida, the "immediacy" of speech, even in silent soliloquy, is a kind of verbal illusion or a mere idealization, sustaining the myth of a full self-presence of meaning. Instead of being a use of language that wholly and purely expresses or signifies units of meaning, even speech is not wholly self-present. Rather, like writing as traditionally conceived, the meaning of the spoken word depends on reference to other signifiers (significant spoken sounds or written marks), whose meanings in turn are not wholly self-present. *Of Grammatology* and other works interrogate, and explore the implications of abandoning, the idealization of speech. Derrida's discussion in *Speech and Phenomena* of Husserl's phenomenology exemplifies the deconstructive criticism of this idealization and of the philosophy of presence.

Deconstructive criticism includes the strategies of (a) challenging the categorical distinctions of philosophies of presence, by effecting a reversal of the heirarchy in a binary opposition, and then ultimately questioning the basis of the distinction, usually by (b) emphasizing what such philosophies suppress. According to Derrida, Husserlian phenomenology, while allegedly eschewing metaphysical assumptions, nonetheless remains a logocentric metaphysics of presence, for Husserl believes both in the transparency and self-presence of intentional acts and objects and in meaning-essences that are given. In particular, Derrida disputes Husserl's categorical distinction between expressive and indicative signs. According to Husserl, expressive signs alone are meaningful, for they express, and in speech give voice to, meaningful self-present acts of conscious lived experience which are in turn available to pure reflection and description. By contrast, indicative signs, such as written signs (e.g. a reminder note), are only meaningless marks unless ultimately referred back to expressive meaning (e.g. the meaningful act of remembering). Although Husserl admits that expression and indication are *de facto* intertwined in actual communication, he nonetheless retains the distinction *de jure* and buttresses it by alleging that pure expression can occur in silent soliloquy in solitary mental life. Derrida disputes this distinction by arguing, *contra* Husserl, that the entanglement of expression with indication is there from the outset, and that ultimately pure expression remains a mere idealization. For to avoid being merely momentary and evanescent, verbal or pre-linguistically experiential expressive meanings must, as Husserl's own philosophy requires even for silent soliloquy, be reiterable, identifiable, and recallable over time as having the same meaning – and hence must be articulated indicatively. Even in silent soliloquy, thinking and speaking are like writing and revising on the fly; overlooking this fact creates the illusion of presence. Hence, exemplifying the deconstructive phase of reversal (see *Positions*, p. 41), this necessity of reiterability implies that expressive meaning must involve indicative signs from the outset (otherwise, if there were no reiterability, each act of meaning would be utterly singular, and hence would fall short of meaningfulness), and Husserl's distinction founders. This claim is further reinforced by Derrida's critique of Husserl's theory of temporality.

Derrida pursues the deconstruction of Husserl's philosophy by deploying the second strategy of deconstruction, that of stressing what the philosopher suppresses. According to Husserl's own theory of temporality, the living present moment involves traces of both the retained past present and anticipated future. If so, and since according to Husserl the retained past present is continuous with the recollected past, then the "living" present moment is never purely present, but is constituted with traces of a "dead" past. The ideality of a fully present self-identical expressive meaning, and of a pure reflection on and description of present meaningful lived experience, amounts to a mere idealization. The expressive sign and even ideal non-linguistic meaningful experience can no longer maintain a pure self-identity of meaning, but, like indicative signs, are invested with meaning by reference to other signs from which they are differentiated. The distinction between expression and indication is ultimately replaced and displaced by the notion of the "trace" (to be discussed later in more detail).

Derrida's deconstruction of Husserl is one of his most philosophically cogent accomplishments, for its "classical philosophical architecture" (*Positions*, p. 5) constitutes a philosophical critique involving internal criticism which radically questions Husserlian and other phenomenologies that allege to be able to achieve pure reflection and offer fully adequate descriptions of meaningful lived experience. Not all of Derrida's deconstructions have the full force of a standard philosophical critique: in some cases (such as his reading, in *Disseminations*, of Hegel's *Prefaces* with a view to challenging Hegel's speculative philosophy), they explicate complications that the philosophy deconstructed overlooks or represses, but that in principle, on its own terms, it would have to take into account.

Derrida's ultimate alternative to the philosophy of presence can be compared to RORTY's anti-essentialist semantic holism. Rorty maintains that the milieu of meaning, and the model of the mind, is that of a continually rewoven web of sentential attitudes (e.g. I believe (or desire) that *p*, where "*p*" is a place-holder for a sentence). This web is not tethered to some given present reality; even the sentential attitudes in it are contextually individuated (identified and explicated). But context itself is not given and determinate; instead "it is contexts all the way down," inducing a "hall of mirrors" effect, wherein it is always possible to redescribe by recontextualizing a term of a relation by dissolving it into relations among other things, or vice versa (Rorty 1991, p. 100). In this "hall-of-mirrors," a *mise en abîme* of contexts, sentences can be dissolved into patterns of words, but words have meaning only in the context of a sentence. Instead of a web of sentential attitudes, Derrida's semantic system is that of a web of traces. The notion of a "trace" is that of a signifier (a significant sound or mark) whose meaning is never present as such but instead depends on its being interwoven with other signifiers in a web of differentiated and changing relations. Since neither this web nor meaning is ever complete or fully present, and since neither intention nor context nor any semantic atom (a given unit of meaning) fixes meaning, the result is a theoretical indeterminacy, a hall-of-mirrors or *mise en abîme* of meaning and context, allowing for interminable recontextualization. Deconstruction can even be defined (*Limited Inc.*, p. 136) as "the effort to take this limitless context into account" by attending to "an incessant movement of recontextualization," such that "there is nothing outside context." For example (see "White Mythology" in *Margins*), putatively literal terms can be recontextualized and redescribed as metaphorical, and vice versa, thereby calling into question the privilege traditionally accorded to the literal over the metaphorical; likewise, the distinction between text and context is itself open to recontextualization.

   In later writings Derrida offers reflections on justice and law ("The Force of Law"), the gift (*Given Time*), friendship (*The Politics of Friendship*), democracy (*The Other Heading*), and hospitality (*Of Hospitality*) that give an ethical point to deconstruction. All of these ethical notions are set in a paradoxical relation to their ordinary and traditional philo-sophical counterparts. For example, *hospitality* ideally involves welcom-ing, making a hospitable place for and genuinely sharing with others such that, unlike in ordinary hospitality, no one would any longer be master of the house who sets house rules. *Justice*, though requiring the force of law for effectuation, surpasses and holds all positive laws, and also putative rules or principles of justice, open to ongoing interrogation as to their justice.

Bibliography

Writings

Of Grammatology (1967), trans. G. Spivak (Baltimore, MD: Johns Hopkins University Press, 1976).

Speech and Phenomena (1967), trans. D. Allison (Evanston, IL: Northwestern University Press, 1973).

Writing and Difference (1967), trans. A. Bass (London: Routledge, 1978).

Margins of Philosophy (1972), trans. A. Bass (Chicago: University of Chicago Press, 1982).

Dissemination (1972), trans. B. Johnson (Chicago: University of Chicago Press, 1981).

Positions (1972), trans. A. Bass (Chicago: University of Chicago Press, 1981).

Limited Inc., trans. S. Weber and J. Mehiman, ed. G. Graff (Evanston, IL.: Northwestern University Press, 1988).

Of Hospitality, trans. R. Bowlby (Stanford, CA: Stanford University Press, 2000).

Further reading

Kamuf, P. (ed.): *A Derrida Reader: Between the Blinds* (New York: Columbia University Press, 1991). [Includes an extensive bibliography.]

Howells, Christina: *Derrida* (Cambridge: Polity Press, 1999).

Rorty, Richard: *Objectivity, Relativism, Truth* (Cambridge: Cambridge University Press, 1991).

8

Descartes

Georges Dicker

Descartes (1596–1650 CE) is known as "the father of modern philosophy." He holds this exalted position because he broke significantly
from the Aristotelianism and Scholasticism of his day and framed the
main issues that have preoccupied Western philosophy since the seventeenth century. Born into the lesser nobility in a French town that now
bears his name, René Descartes was educated at the Jesuit college of La
Flèche, where he soon came to think that, except for mathematics, most
of the traditional learning was too lacking in certainty to count as
genuine knowledge. He took a degree in law at the University of Poitier,
and joined the army of the Dutch Prince of Nassau as an unpaid gentleman soldier, in order to travel and learn more about the "great book
of the world." His youthful interest in mathematics was rekindled by a
friendship with the Dutch mathematician Isaac Beeckman, and he made
a number of discoveries that led to his laying down the foundations of
analytical geometry. He hit upon the idea of a method for solving all
problems of geometry, and this soon expanded into the idea of a
method for advancing knowledge in all the sciences. On November 10,
1619, while meditating in a stove-heated room in Germany, he was visited
by three prophetic dreams that confirmed his vision of a unification of
all knowledge. His ambition was to develop a complete system of knowledge, whose structure he compared to that of a tree, with metaphysics
as the roots, physics as the trunk, and medicine, mechanics, and morals
as the branches.

In 1628 Descartes emigrated to Holland, where he was to live for
the next 20 years and to write all his important works, moving his residence 13 times but remaining in contact with many other thinkers
through correspondence. By 1633 he had completed a major treatise on
physics, *Le Monde*, but upon learning of Galileo's condemnation by the
Inquisition for advocating the heliocentric theory (which was also part
of Descartes's physics), he suppressed the work. But he did not abandon

his hope of making his work known to the public, and many of his activities from 1633 onward were designed to secure its acceptance. He hoped that if he could provide convincing proofs of God's existence and of the immortality of the soul, as well as a physics capable of improving human life, then theologians as well as scientists would join in supporting his work, and even that it would replace ARISTOTLE's teachings in the schools. To this end, he published in 1637 his *Discourse on the Method*, along with three scientific and mathematical essays; and in 1641 he published his philosophical masterpiece, *Meditations on First Philosophy*, along with six sets of *Objections* written by leading philosophers and theologians of the day, including HOBBES, Arnauld, and Gassendi, and Descartes's own *Replies*. (A seventh set of *Objections* and *Replies* was added in 1642.) In 1644 he published *Principles of Philosophy*, a large treatise that expounds the metaphysics and epistemology of the *Meditations* and a system of physics that was to enjoy favor until it was superseded by Newtonian physics. His other chief works, aside from his voluminous *Correspondence*, include *Rules for the Direction of the Mind* (1628), a careful though not fully mature account of his mathematically inspired method, and *Passions of the Soul* (1649), which gives his fullest account of the interaction between mind and body, and was written partly in response to criticisms of Princess Elizabeth of Bohemia, with whom Descartes had a long and philosophically fruitful correspondence.

In September 1649 Descartes was invited by another royal correspondent, Queen Christina of Sweden, to join her court in Stockholm in order to provide instruction in philosophy. With some reluctance, Descartes went off to Sweden. This proved to be his undoing. The Queen had him come to her palace to give lessons at 5.00 a.m. three times a week during the severe Swedish winter. Descartes, whose health was fragile, and who had a lifelong habit of reading and writing in bed until late morning, caught pneumonia, which took his life on February 11, 1650.

Although Descartes inaugurated "modern" philosophy, at first sight his overall system does not seem particularly innovative. He maintains, as did many other thinkers, that there exists a world comprising inanimate material objects as well as human beings and other living things, created by an all-powerful, all-knowing, and benevolent God. Descartes's profound originality manifests itself, rather, in the criteria that he insists must be met for this general scheme to constitute a body of genuine knowledge rather than mere belief or opinion, in the specific conceptions of material things, human beings, and God that inform the scheme, and in the ways in which these conceptions flow from his criteria for knowledge.

Descartes's fundamental criterion for knowledge is certainty: nothing can be known unless it is absolutely certain. Accordingly, Descartes begins by attempting to doubt all his previous beliefs or opinions, in order to discover whether there are any that he cannot possibly doubt. He notes that although the beliefs he had taken to be the most unquestionable were based on his senses, there are reasons to doubt beliefs derived from this source. First, the senses are sometimes deceptive, and "it is prudent never to trust completely those who have deceived us even once" (AT VII 18; CSM II 12). Second, even sense perceptions had under the best conditions of observation can be duplicated in vivid dreams, so that "there are never any sure signs by means of which being awake can be distinguished from being asleep" (AT VII 19; CSM II 13). Third, and most radically, it seems possible that an all-powerful God might have so created Descartes that he continually hallucinates the entire physical world: "How do I know that [God] has not brought it about that there is no earth, no sky, no extended thing, no shape, no size, no place, while at the same time ensuring that all these things appear to me to exist just as they do now?" (AT VII 21; CSM II 14). Perhaps, he says, God even allows him to go wrong when doing simple arithmetic. To enforce this radical doubt, Descartes deliberately supposes that "not God . . . but rather some malicious demon of the utmost power and cunning" continually deceives him about the existence of the entire physical world, including even his own body.

But even if there were such a deceiving demon, Descartes argues, it would remain certain that he himself exists; for to be deceived, one must exist! Further, the demon could not possibly make him think falsely that he was thinking, for to think that one is thinking is already to be thinking. Thus it is certain that he is thinking, from which it obviously follows that he exists. "I noticed that while I was thus trying to think everything false, it was necessary that I, who was thinking this, was something. And observing that this truth '*I am thinking, therefore I exist*' was so firm and sure that all the most extravagant suppositions of the sceptics were incapable of shaking it, I came to the conclusion that I could accept it without scruple as the first principle of the philosophy I was seeking" (AT VIIIa 7–8; CSM I 127). By this famous argument, generally referred to as "the *cogito*," Descartes claims to show that even if everything else is doubtful, one's own existence, at least as a "thing that thinks," is absolutely certain.

It may be questioned whether the *cogito* is really a proof of one's own existence, because its premise, "I am thinking," already uses the "I" whose existence is supposedly proved in the conclusion "I exist." Descartes's elaborations of the *cogito* in various texts show that he sometimes rests the argument on the view that thoughts are properties that, as properties, must belong to a substance, which he calls "I" or "myself." However, even if this reasoning, which is rooted in the Aristotelian–Scholastic view that properties require a substance to inhere in (and which, in view of this medieval baggage, can be doubted), proved the existence of a thinking substance, it would still not follow that this substance must be oneself or "I." On the other hand, it can be argued in Descartes's defense that despite the fact that the use of "I" in the *cogito*'s premise renders the argument question-begging, and that appealing to the scholastic substance theory cannot salvage the *cogito*, still the mere fact that "I am thinking" entails "I exist" does show that even if all my beliefs about the physical world, including my own body, are doubtful, my existence remains certain: even doubting *my body's* existence is not tantamount to doubting *my* existence. For it still remains certain that I am thinking (doubting); but from this one very meager certainty, it already follows that I exist! So even if the *cogito* is not in the technical sense a *proof* of one's own existence, it does show that even in the face of the extreme, disorienting doubt generated by the deceiving demon hypothesis, one's own existence remains unshakably certain.

In order to extend his knowledge further, Descartes seeks to identify the feature of the *cogito* that renders it so certain. He finds that the only thing that assures him of it is that he "clearly and distinctly perceives" that he thinks and that to think it is necessary to exist. "So I now seem to be able to lay it down as a general rule that whatever I perceive very clearly and distinctly is true" (AT VII 35; CSM II 24). This "clarity and distinctness" criterion of truth is itself not very clearly explained by Descartes, but it may be taken to mean that in rebuilding one's knowledge, it is permissible to use materials of the same kind as those that enter into the *cogito*; namely, (a) contingent statements about one's own thoughts (e.g. "I am thinking"), (b) obvious necessary truths (e.g. "if I am thinking, then I exist"), and (c) the logical consequences of (a)s and (b)s (e.g. "I exist").

But even after extracting his "clarity and distinctness" criterion of truth from the *cogito*, Descartes is not yet willing to use it in rebuilding his knowledge. For although he cannot doubt a clearly and distinctly perceived proposition like "I can't fail to exist while I'm thinking that I exist" or "I can't never exist if I exist now" or "$2 + 3 = 5$" while focusing his attention on it – although, that is to say, he finds presently occurring clear and distinct perceptions to be utterly "assent-compelling" – he has to admit that "it would be easy for [an all-powerful God], if he desired, to bring it about that I go wrong even in those matters that I think I see utterly clearly with my mind's eye" (AT VII 36; CSM II 25). In order to escape from this oscillation between his certainty about each presently occurring clear and distinct perception, and his generalized doubt about the reliability of his cognitive powers and thus of the general principle that whatever he clearly and distinctly perceives is true, Descartes declares that he must first "examine whether there is a God, and, if there is, whether he can be a deceiver" (AT VII 36; CSM II 25).

Descartes accordingly sets out to prove that a non-deceiving God exists, using as materials in his proof only the idea of God that he finds in his mind and a few principles that he regards as necessary truths which are evident by "the natural light," which is the power or cognitive faculty for clear and distinct perception (AT VIIIA 16; CSM I 203). Chief among these principles is that the cause of an idea must have as much reality or perfection as the idea represents its object as having, a principle that Descartes expresses in scholastic terminology by saying that the cause of an idea must have as much "formal reality" as the idea contains "objective reality." (In this principle the term "objective" has nothing to do with objectivity in the modern sense of "unbiased"; rather it pertains to the fact that an idea always has an intentional object which it represents, so that "objective reality" could be paraphrased as "representational reality" or even "informational content." "Formal reality," on the other hand, refers to a thing's intrinsic reality; it is closer to what we would ordinarily mean by "reality" *simpliciter.*) Descartes attempts to derive this principle from a few highly general causal principles, such as that a cause must have as much reality or perfection as its effect. Now inasmuch as the idea of God represents God as an infinite, perfect being, Descartes finds that only a perfect God has as much reality or perfection as his idea of God represents God as having; or, reverting to his scholastic terminology, that only a perfect God has as much formal reality as his idea of God contains objective reality. It follows that the idea of God must have a perfect God as its cause and, hence, that a perfect God really exists. Further, since the "natural light" reveals that deception is an imperfection, it also follows that God is not a deceiver. But if clear and distinct perceptions could be false, then, given their assent-compellingness, God would be a deceiver; so Descartes concludes that whatever he clearly and distinctly perceives must be true. Human error is possible only with respect to propositions that are not clearly and distinctly perceived, and arises when we misuse our free will, by allowing ourselves to affirm or deny propositions that are not clearly grasped by our understanding.

Descartes's argument for God's existence has given rise to the notorious problem of the "Cartesian Circle": if we ask what assures Descartes that the argument is sound, the only possible answer (and the one he in effect gives) is that he clearly and distinctly perceives its premises to be true and its steps to be valid, so that he is using his clarity and distinctness criterion of truth in the very argument that is supposed to establish that it is a reliable criterion. When confronted with this difficulty by the authors of the second and fourth sets of *Objections* to the *Meditations*, Descartes replied that he had never called into doubt present clear and distinct perceptions, but only the reliability of memories of past clear and distinct perceptions. But this "memory defense" does not square with the radical doubt based on the idea that an all-powerful God could, if he wished, easily deceive Descartes even about his clear and distinct perceptions, despite their assent-compellingness. So Descartes scholars have proposed other ways of rescuing him from the "Circle," such as the "general rule defense," which maintains that while Descartes can doubt the general rule that whatever he clearly and distinctly perceives is true, particular clear and distinct perceptions are not merely assent-compelling but also infallible. This, however, runs into the objection that to doubt the general rule is already to admit that clear and distinct perceptions are not infallible – that human reason itself may be unreliable. Perhaps a more satisfactory defense lies in recognizing that Descartes himself insists that his radical doubt of reason is not merely willful or arbitrary but is itself based on reasons, and that Descartes's reason for doubting reason – that there might be an all-powerful God who *therefore* could make even clear and distinct perceptions erroneous – itself uses deduction; so that if this use of deduction is legitimate, then so is the use of deduction leading to the conclusion that a perfect God *would* not deceive.

Even if the "Circle" can be satisfactorily disposed of, Descartes's specific argument for God's existence seems unsound; because it seems false that only a perfect God has as much reality or perfection as a merely human idea of God represents God as having. As Gassendi put it in the Fifth Set of *Objections*: "the human intellect is not capable of conceiving infinity. . . . Hence if someone calls something 'infinite' he attributes to a thing he does not grasp a label he does not understand" (AT VII 286; CSM II 200). In his *Reply*, Descartes says, in effect, that we can conceive *that* God is infinite, but not *how* he is. But (to borrow an example given by Bernard Williams) this response is analogous to a man's saying that he has an idea of some marvelous machine that can turn sand into protein, while admitting that he has no understanding of how it does so. It hardly seems that the informational content of such a schematic, indeterminate idea is so rich that only a machine that can really perform this feat measures up to that content. Likewise, even if the human idea of God is nominally the idea *of* an infinite being, it seems that its content is not sufficiently detailed or determinate that only a being infinite in power, knowledge, and goodness would correspond to it. Rather, it would seem that many things less great than God, such as angels or saints, have as much formal reality as the necessarily inadequate human idea of God contains objective reality.

Descartes, however, also offers another argument for the existence of a perfect God; namely, a modernized version of the "Ontological Argument" invented by Anselm in the eleventh century. Basically, the argument is that a supremely perfect being must, by definition, have all perfections (otherwise how could it be supremely perfect?); but existence is a perfection (since it is better to exist than not to exist); therefore a supremely perfect being – God – really exists. As Descartes puts it: "it is as much a contradiction to think of God (that is, a supremely perfect being) lacking existence (that is, lacking a perfection), as it is to think of a mountain without a valley" (AT VII 66; CSM II 46). This famous argument, which Descartes formulates in several different ways, is vulnerable to Immanuel KANT's objection that in holding existence to be a perfection, it assumes that existence is a property or characteristic – since a perfection, like power or knowledge or moral goodness, is a type of property (one that makes a thing better than it would be without that property). But, Kant argues, existence is not a property; for in saying that a thing exists, one is not describing it in any way. Descartes's argument is also vulnerable to the objection, made by Thomas AQUINAS and urged against Descartes with great clarity by Caterus (author of the first set of *Objections*), that it proves at best only that "the concept of existence is inseparably linked to the concept of a supreme being" (AT VII 99; CSM II 72), but not that there actually exists anything answering to the concept of a supreme being.

Since Descartes's arguments for God's existence are by general consensus unsuccessful, the question arises of what implications this fact has for the rest of his reconstruction of knowledge. One implication is that Descartes's attempts to vindicate his clarity and distinctness criterion of truth by appealing to God's existence and veracity fail; so that if one holds Descartes to his position that the criterion may not be employed unless it is vindicated, then he cannot advance one step beyond the *cogito*. But let us suppose that the criterion is allowed to stand on its own merits. Then it can be argued that one of the remaining major theses of Descartes's philosophy – Cartesian Dualism – can still be plausibly defended, while the other – the existence of the material world – cannot.

Cartesian Dualism holds that mind is a thinking but non-extended substance which is distinct from any matter that may exist, while matter is an extended and non-thinking substance. Sometimes Descartes supports this central doctrine of his philosophy by arguing that since he can doubt the existence of his (or any) body while remaining certain of his own existence, therefore he must be a mind that actually could exist without a body. This "argument from doubt" is unsound, since he could still be a body but not know it. But in his *Sixth Meditation* Descartes gives other arguments, including one that goes essentially as follows: "If I can clearly and distinctly conceive X existing apart from Y, then X can really exist without Y, and if X can really exist without Y, then X and Y must really be two different things. But I can clearly and distinctly conceive the non-existence of my body while affirming my existence as a think-ing thing; which is to say that I can clearly and distinctly conceive myself, as a thinking and unextended thing, existing apart from my body, as an extended and unthinking thing. Therefore, I am really a different thing from my body, and I could exist without it." In the Fourth set of *Objections*, this argument is ingeniously criticized by Arnauld, who uses a geometrical example designed to show that the argument is at bottom no different than the argument from doubt. Descartes attempts, arguably with some success, to refute Arnauld's objection in his *Reply*.

Although Descartes's argument for dualism does not depend essen-tially on his philosophical theology, his attempt to prove the existence of the physical world does. For the main idea of that proof is that since he has an overpowering propensity to believe that his sensory experi-ences are produced by physical objects impinging on his senses, and he has no way to spot that this is not the case, then God would be a deceiver if the experiences were not produced by physical objects; so these objects must exist. Obviously this proof hinges crucially on the existence of a non-deceiving God, and so collapses if Descartes's arguments for God are unsuccessful.

The significance for philosophy after Descartes of his failure to over-come convincingly his own sceptical arguments concerning the physical world can hardly be overstated. Philosophers as diverse as LOCKE, KANT, and RUSSELL have tried to give different, non-theological justifications for the belief in matter; philosophers as diverse as Reid, DEWEY, and WITTGENSTEIN have argued that doubt of the physical world is illegiti-mate, and some philosophers have held that skepticism is unavoidable. The "problem of the external world" that Descartes bequeathed to modern philosophy continues to be debated to this day.

Although Descartes's proof of the physical world fails, his views about the nature of physical things are of considerable interest. He "geo-metricizes" them, by holding matter to be nothing but a substance extended in length, breadth, and depth. The qualities of color, taste, smell, sound, temperature, and even solidity are considered by Descartes to be "secondary qualities" – nothing but capacities in objects to cause experiences of color etc. in perceivers under appropriate conditions; indeed, Descartes, like other thinkers of the period, sometimes simply equates those qualities with the experiences. The exclusion of even solidity from Descartes's concept of matter has many implications. It means that there can be no void, so that in Descartes's physics motion is possible only when one body moves into the place previously occupied by another. It also means that Descartes has considerable trouble distinguishing matter from space, and even one body from another. Ultimately his view is that there is really only one all-encompassing extended substance, of which particular bodies are only properties, and which we might appropriately call "matter-space." To some extent this foreshadows SPINOZA's view that there exists only a single substance that is both extended and thinking, and of which particular minds and bodies are only finite modes.

In contrast to Spinoza, however, Descartes's view of the human mind is profoundly individualistic: there exist as many thinking substances as there are beings who could have the thought "I am thinking, therefore I exist." Thus Descartes's ontology is one in which there are many thinking and unextended substances and a single extended substance. Nevertheless, he also holds that each human mind has a unique relation to that "portion" of extended substance which is the body of the person whose mind it is. Descartes is usually interpreted as holding that this relation is essentially a two-way causal one: a person's body is the one which is under the control of that person's mind, and whose vicissitudes directly affect that mind. This view of the mind–body relation gives rise to the most vexed question of Descartes's metaphysics; namely, how a purely thinking and unextended substance can causally interact with an extended unthinking one. This "problem of interaction," which is powerfully articulated in Gassendi's *Objections* and in Princess Elizabeth's letters to Descartes, has led some recent scholars to interpret him, not without some textual basis, as a quasi-occasionalist who holds that relations between physical and mental events are divinely instituted correlations rather than causal connections. It has also helped to encourage the development of the materialist theories of mind that are in favor today, though Descartes's focus on the apparently non-physical, "inner" aspect of consciousness remains a difficulty for such theories. In any case, the "mind–body problem" to which his system leads, together with the "problem of the external world" that he posed, are among his principal legacies to philosophy.

Bibliography

Writings

Oeuvres de Descartes, 11 volumes, ed. C. Adam and P. Tannery (Paris: Vrin/CNCR, 1964–76). [The standard original-language edition; here, and commonly, cited as "AT" followed by the volume and page numbers.]
The Philosophical Writings of Descartes, three volumes, ed. J. Cottingham, R. Stoothoff, D. Murdoch, and A. Kenny (Cambridge: Cambridge University Press, 1975–91). [The standard English edition; here, and commonly, cited as "CSM" followed by the volume and page numbers.]

Further reading

Chappell, V. and Doney, W. (eds): *Twenty-five Years of Descartes Scholarship, 1960–1984: A Bibliography* (New York: Garland, 1987).
Cottingham, J.: *Descartes* (Oxford: Blackwell, 1986). [Accessible and comprehensive.]
—— (ed.): *The Cambridge Companion to Descartes* (Cambridge: Cambridge University Press, 1992).
Curley, E. M.: *Descartes Against the Skeptics* (Cambridge, MA: Harvard University Press, 1978). [Clear and instructive on many issues.]
Dicker, G.: *Descartes: An Analytical and Historical Introduction* (Oxford: Oxford University Press, 1993). [Accessible and clear, also the basis for the interpretive and critical aspects of this article.]
Doney, W. (ed.): *Descartes: A Collection of Critical Essays* (New York: Doubleday, 1967).
Frankfurt, H.: *Demons, Dreamers and, Madmen: The Defense of Reason in Descartes's Meditations* (New York: Bobbs-Merrill, 1970). [Clear and provocative.]
Garber, D.: *Descartes' Metaphysical Physics* (Chicago: University of Chicago Press, 1992).
Gaukroger, S.: *Descartes: An Intellectual Biography* (Oxford: Clarendon Press, 1995).
Kenny, A.: *Descartes: A Study of His Philosophy* (New York: Random House, 1968; reprinted, New York: Garland 1987). [Concise, incisive, and comprehensive.]
Sebba, G.: *Bibliographica Cartesiana: A Critical Guide to the Descartes Literature 1800–1960* (The Hague: Martinus Nijoff, 1964).
Williams, B.: *Descartes: The Project of Pure Inquiry* (Harmondsworth: Penguin, 1978). [Philosophically very rich and suggestive.]
Wilson, M.: *Descartes* (Boston: Routledge & Kegan Paul, 1978). [Subtle, highly regarded, and authoritative.]

9

Dewey

James Gouinlock

John Dewey's philosophy is both comprehensive and practical. Dewey (1859–1952 CE) sought a synoptic vision of the natural world, including an understanding of how human strivings are situated within it. His purpose was to distinguish the foremost characteristics of natural existence in a manner that would permit human beings to live more effectively and happily. He is one of the great expositors of pragmatism, a philosophy that unites vigorous intelligence and creative action. His thought is consummated in his philosophy of social intelligence or, as he also called it, democracy as a way of life.

Dewey was born in Vermont in 1859 and died in New York City in 1952. His life coincided with the rapid growth, modernization, and urbanization of America, and he hoped that the democratic experiment begun in America could be developed and enriched in a manner to make it suitable for the conditions of modern life. He is widely regarded as one of the most influential framers of democratic ideals in the twentieth century. His voluminous writings are not confined to such issues alone, however. He wrote extensively on all major philosophic questions.

Dewey's account of the nature of things, which he called his naturalistic metaphysics, can be usefully contrasted to the so-called classic tradition in philosophy. Although that tradition has many variations, it is consistently distinguished by the assumption that true being is perfect, eternal, and unchanging. According to PLATO's theory, for example, all natures, as such, are changeless and eternal; and the good life and the good society must be patterned after allegedly perfect and immutable forms. All other existences, according to Plato, constitute an inferior level of reality, marked by change, imperfection, and unintelligibility. In various renderings in the classic tradition, the putatively not fully real has been denoted by such terms as becoming, appearance, or the merely subjective.

Dewey attacked the tradition systematically. He denied the existence of the eternal and unchanging, and he urged that the traits of nature that had been consigned to a kind of unreality were as fully real as anything else. Change itself is both real and universal; that is, all existing things undergo change. Ends do not inhabit a realm of static being; they are continuous with means and undergo variation with them. Generically, the challenge of life is not to conform to some antecedently fixed pattern of conduct, but to learn to live effectively with processes that continuously produce novelty and variation. Accordingly, Dewey's most fundamental charge against the tradition is that it is incompetent to provide direction to the human endeavor to live with the contingencies of change.

A further trait that had been denied objective reality is the qualitative. In modern philosophy, for example, colors, sounds, scents, feelings, and all combinations thereof have been regarded as subjective, as existing within the separate and self-enclosed domain of mind. At the same time, therefore, all our experience is confined to the content of our own minds. All the qualities that we had predicated of objective natural events and had variously denominated with such terms as lovely or disgusting, enjoyable or miserable, admirable or hateful, are now consigned to the exclusively subjective, having no implication for the nature of nature. Hence the dualism of man and nature, each of which is conceived as a separate substance, each possessing properties exclusively within itself. According to Dewey's analysis, however, there are no independent and self-subsistent substances, and all beings are the outcome of some combination of nature's doings. Immediate qualities are a case in point. They are not properties of or within an independent substance. They are features of a complex of relations, coming into existence when a living organism interacts with its environment. The qualities of a painting or a symphony, for example, exist neither within the mind nor as fixed properties of objects apart from any sentient being. Rather, they come into being and out of it, as events transpire. When they do occur, they are objective properties of conjoint processes, and we experience them directly. We are not, then, shut off from the external world by the consciousness of qualitative events. They are our access to the world.

Another vital feature of the natural world that had been obscured by the classic tradition is the occurrence of the disordered and disruptive. Such traits, which Dewey refers to collectively as the precarious, occur repeatedly in everyone's life, and we could not live well without determining their continuities with other natural powers. In the classic vein of thought, such contingencies are regarded as somehow less than fully real, and our hope is to escape them by withdrawing to the eternal and unchanging. On Dewey's analysis, a precarious happening, such as getting a flat tire or being mugged, is not a subjective or otherwise removed form of existence. It is an objective natural event, with which we must deliberately contend.

A most important trait of nature is what Dewey calls a history – a process of qualitative change, more or less complex, having an identifiable beginning and leading to a definite outcome. What in previous philosophies were treated as original and independent entities are analyzed by Dewey as the outcomes of a history. Qualities, as just observed, are such outcomes. Human nature, mind, knowledge, and value, for example, are likewise outcomes of histories. Dewey's views can, indeed, be summarized as the attempt to formulate a metaphysics according to which all phenomena are understood as functions of natural processes, rather than as separate substances or as supernatural beings.

The implications of Dewey's analysis are of great consequence. As remarked above, human nature has been widely regarded as a fixed essence. Dewey regards this belief as not only false but pernicious. The assertions of fixed forms of human nature, he insists, are in fact prejudices advanced by elites to keep people in their place. The correct view of human nature, by contrast, is liberating. Dewey understood it as the outcome of the interaction of the biological organism and its environment, most importantly its social environment. The traits of character and personality that individuals possess are not original properties, but the result of the interaction of highly plastic and relatively undefined impulses with the contingencies of the environment. Accordingly, as we learn the conditions of human growth and development, we may utilize them deliberately to produce individuals well adapted to function productively in the demanding conditions of modern life. As Dewey urged, his view would negate the assortment of classic theories which hold that one's nature is given and fates each of us to occupy a definite and predetermined position in society. The paths of development for any individual are plural and varying; and when the environment is suitably supportive, one's nature and career may progress in virtually any direction. The recent acknowledgment that women are as competent as men to engage in politics, the professions, and commercial life is a validation of Dewey's philosophy.

Education is of the greatest importance in the formation of human nature. In its fullest sense, education is the deliberate attempt to create desirable and effective traits of character, undertaken at home, in school, at work and play, in all manner of human transactions. The principal means of education is not the passive absorption of information, but sharing in overt conduct: engaging in pertinent and constructive forms of practice, intellectual and moral. In school, as a case in point, students would participate in rigorous processes of inquiry and discovery. This is pragmatic, a learning by doing. Such engagement, Dewey believed, forms the very nature of the participant.

Long believed to be an irreducible substance, mind, too, is the outcome of a history. Dewey argued that the formation of mind is a function of shared activity among beings capable of language. The manipulation of objects discloses their functions, which are their meaning. The possession of a meaning is defined behaviorally: a person is prepared to act with a given object in a specific way to bring about a predictable result – as one possesses the meaning of a pencil when he is prepared to use it to write on paper. To come into possession of meanings in this way is to have operative ideas, or *mind*, in at least a rudimentary fashion; but the full development of mind depends upon the acquisition and use of language. Language itself, as a vehicle of communication, arises in situations of "shared use and enjoyment," where the perceived imperatives of concerted action in a specific environment determine the public meanings of vocal and physical gestures. Language is whatever succeeds in bringing about shared activity. With language, we become capable of orderly and expansive acquisition of meanings, and we become capable of manipulating them. Thus mind in its full sense emerges.

An object of knowledge is also the outcome of a history. Discussion of the object as known provides occasion to amplify the nature of Dewey's pragmatism – or *instrumentalism*, as he preferred. Dewey severely criticizes the idea that inquiry is a matter of the intellectual or perceptual contemplation of events. It is, on the contrary, a deliberate process of overt participation with them. One engages in investigation of the natural world either by the intentional management of selected processes to discover what they do under specific conditions and/or by carefully controlling the conditions of observation.

To proceed in any sort of inquiry, determination of the meanings of concepts is the essential beginning. Following Peirce, Dewey held that the meaning of an object is the sum of all the functions that it can enter into with other entities (most notably human beings). As noted above, we learn the meanings of objects by actively manipulating them to see what they can do and by observing their interactions with other conditions. The meaning of a word denoting such an object is the sum of those functions known to us. "Pencil" would be defined operationally, or pragmatically, as an object that performs definite and distinctive functions. The statement, "This is a pencil," makes an implicit prediction about the behavior of the object in question. The truth of the statement is tested by undertaking the prescribed conduct to see if the predicted results in fact occur. This simple example is the paradigm of scientific investigations, wherein the scientist formulates a hypothesis predicting that if experimental conditions are introduced in a determinate way, they will produce distinctive consequences. The hypothesis is tested by introducing the conditions (including those of observation) as prescribed by the hypothesis and observing the results. Scientific practice includes a social dimension: the inquiries of any scientist are checked by other scientists, and no finding is deserving of credence if it is not of a sort that can be tested by others.

Dewey's analysis abolishes the intractable puzzle of the traditional problem of knowledge, which is to ascertain whether a subjective image corresponds to an outer object which cannot itself be an object of perception. According to Dewey, we do perceive objects. Our problem is not whether an inner image corresponds to an outer object. It is to determine how variations in the functions of one or more objects are correlated with changes in other objects. The object of knowledge is not a transcendent form, but a definite relation between specified processes of change. A familiar law of nature, for example, expresses variations in gravitational attraction as a correlation between variations in mass and distance. In contrast to the alleged objects of knowledge of the classic tradition, knowledge of the pragmatic sort reveals how changes actually occur or might occur. We become capable of bringing about deliberate innovation in the course of events by introducing specific variations in it. We are no longer passive onlookers, but intelligent actors.

Neither does the object of knowledge mirror events as they are antecedent to inquiry. Inquiry proceeds by the employment of the concepts and logical distinctions current in a given community of inquirers, and these tools are both selective and open to continued modification or replacement. Knowledge of events, accordingly, is not given by the objects alone. They do not speak for themselves; they can speak only in human accents. Nevertheless, what is known is true – *warranted*, in Dewey's nomenclature – of the object. He defined instrumentalism as the only true realism. The known meanings have been determined by the inquirers' interaction with their subject matter, deploying their logical and conceptual instruments. As with the development of any form of language, the instruments of inquiry are those which have proven themselves in facilitating successful resolutions of problematic conditions. Our beliefs about objects are selective, fallible, and couched in conceptual terms, but the concepts are constrained and refined by what the objects do in controlled inquiry. The human accent is disciplined by the nature of things. All experience is meaning-laden; but these are worldly meanings, and their possession makes it possible to conduct ourselves with reference to the powers and possibilities of the real world. Science is one of the great resources for this venture. Unlike mere opinion, scientific inquiry provides shared knowledge, which is necessary for shared conduct.

The moral life is the focal point of all Dewey's reflections. In this context, his idea of the *construction* of good is especially apt. According to Dewey's assessment, the pertinent demand of any situation is not to conform to an alleged moral absolute, come what may, but to devise a course of conduct that will combine the agencies of the individual and the environment into a unified whole. The powers of the individual are thereby fulfilled. There are numerous possible options, each with its promises and perils. The agent would formulate a plan of action specific to the given conditions, uniting so far as possible the beneficial tendencies of the situation and bringing the energies of the individual and the environment into a unique consummatory whole. This is a scientific process insofar as it requires knowledge of how the constituents of possible histories might be varied in order to bring about the consummatory phase of experience. It is applied science in the sense that novel conditions are introduced into a history in order to determine its outcome. Educators, for example, wishing to make students more alert and industrious, will formulate a hypothesis about how variations in educational conditions will provide the desired results. The hypothesis is a plan of action. The educators' conduct is guided by scientific ideas in that they institute the conditions as the hypothesis proposes; and if the hypothesis is correct, their plan will achieve its desired end.

The good attained is neither static nor permanent. It is challenged by new problems and gives way to new constructions. There is no final end. Rather, Dewey argued, growth itself is the only moral end. The *process* of life, not some ultimate terminus, is where happiness resides. The process is one of ongoing development and refinement of human potentialities, creating harmonies with the environment, most importantly the social environment.

One of the remarkable characteristics of Dewey's philosophy is his unprecedented emphasis on the social quality of the moral life. Moral problems are interpersonal problems. There being no immutable norms of conduct, it remains for individuals to construct goods as a deliberately collaborative process, where plans of action are a consequence of communication and willingness to contribute. This practice is what Dewey alternately calls social intelligence or democracy as a way of life. It can become highly congenial and rewarding, he thought, declaring that "shared experience is the greatest of human goods." It is a practice requiring distinctive virtues, those of intelligence, flexibility, open-mindedness, and cooperativeness. He urged that these habits be practiced in all media of socialization and education so that individuals would learn to practice them in all forms of associated life. It is already a familiar practice in many environments. In associations of friends and equals, for example, it is common that shared practices be determined by a consultative experience. Dewey thought it within the potential competence of human beings to extend such practices beyond the confines of intimate communities. Social intelligence would not bring final human harmony or eradicate uncertainty, disagreement, and failure; yet it would be, he judged, the best instrument so far conceived to promote human concord and happiness.

It is widely acknowledged that Dewey was highly effective in reconstructing the classic tradition in Western philosophy, and that alone is a momentous achievement. Beyond that, it remains to be seen whether it is truly within human capacity to build democratic communities in the manner that he envisioned.

Bibliography

Writings

John Dewey: The Early Works, 1882–1898, five volumes, ed. Jo Ann Boydston (Carbondale, IL: Southern Illinois University Press, 1961–71).
John Dewey: The Middle Works, 1899–1924, 15 volumes, ed. Jo Ann Boydston (Carbondale, IL: Southern Illinois University Press, 1971–83).
John Dewey: The Later Works, 1925–1953, 16 volumes, ed. Jo Ann Boydston (Carbondale, IL: Southern Illinois University Press, 1981–90).

The most important works include the following:

Democracy and Education (1916) (*Middle Works, volume 9*).
Human Nature and Conduct (1922) (*Middle Works, volume 12*).
Experience and Nature (1925) (*Later Works, volume 1*).
The Public and Its Problems (1927) (*Later Works, volume 2*).
The Quest for Certainty (1929) (*Later Works, volume 4*).
Ethics, with James H. Tufts (1932) (*Later Works, volume 7*).
Art as Experience (1934) (*Later Works, volume 10*).
Logic: The Theory of Inquiry (1938) (*Later Works, volume 12*).

Further reading

Campbell, J.: *Understanding John Dewey* (Chicago: Open Court, 1995). [Best general introduction.]

Gouinlock, J.: *John Dewey's Philosophy of Value* (New York: Humanities Press, 1972). [Dewey's moral thought in the context of his naturalistic metaphysics.]

——: *Excellence in Public Discourse: John Stuart Mill, John Dewey, and Social Intelligence* (New York: Teachers College Press, 1986). [Dewey's philosophy of social intelligence.]

Ryan, A.: *John Dewey and the High Tide of American Liberalism* (New York and London: W. W. Norton, 1995). [Dewey's career as a public philosopher.]

Sleeper, R.: *The Necessity of Pragmatism* (New Haven, CT: Yale University Press, 1986). [Dewey's theory of inquiry in contemporary context.]

10

Foucault

Ladelle McWhorter

Michel Foucault (1926–1984 CE) was born in Poiters, France, the second child of Anne Malapert and Paul Foucault. It was expected that he, like his father, would study and practice medicine. The Second World War disrupted education in France, however, and both the war and the occupation had tremendous effects on Foucault. As he stated years later, "I think that boys and girls of this generation had their childhood formed by these great historical events. The menace of war was our background, our framework of existence.... Maybe that is the reason why I am fascinated by history and the relationship between personal experience and those events of which we are a part" (Eribon, 1991, p. 10). Foucault left Poitiers for Paris in 1945 and entered the École Normale Supérieure the following year, finishing in 1951.

Instead of pursuing an academic career, Foucault took a series of cultural diplomatic posts abroad. His biographer suggests that, as a homosexual, Foucault felt stifled by French customs and culture (Eribon, 1991); whatever the reasons, Foucault had no love for France, asserting that tourists "come to France as painters went to Italy in the seventeenth century, to see a dying civilization" (Foucault, 1997, p. 123). But after the 1968 riots, Foucault returned to France to take a post in the newly created university at Vincennes. He remained there until he was called to the Collège de France in 1970, where he became Professor of the History of Systems of Thought. In 1971, with his life-partner Daniel Defert and several friends, he founded the *Groupe d'Information sur les Prisons.* Thus began Foucault's involvement in politics. Through the rest of his life his concerns included prison conditions, refugee resettlement, and gay rights.

Scholars usually divide Foucault's books into two groups, major works and minor works. Minor works include *Mental Illness and Psychology; Death and the Labyrinth* (on Roussel's novels); *Dream and Existence, This is Not a Pipe* (on the painter Magritte); and two "casebooks," compilations of historical material that Foucault gathered while working on the histories of punishment and sexuality: *I, Pierre Riviere, having slaughtered my mother, my sister, and my brother* and *Herculine Barbin: being the recently discovered memoirs of a nineteenth-century French hermaphrodite.* These works, while important, are usually not considered crucial to the development of Foucault's philosophical views. Major works include *Madness and Civilization* (1961); *The Birth of the Clinic* (1963); *The Order of Things,* which catapulted Foucault to fame in 1966; *The Archeology of Knowledge* (1969); *Disciple and Punish* (1975); *The History of Sexuality, volume 1* (1976); and *The Use of Pleasure* and *The Care of the Self* (1984), volumes 2 and 3 of the *History of Sexuality* series.

Scholars frequently divide the major works into two groups as well. Those published before 1970 are labeled "archeological" works, or works that exemplify or elaborate upon Foucault's archeological method of historical and textual analysis, while those published after 1970 are labeled "genealogical" works, or works that exemplify the method of analysis that Foucault adapted from Friedrich NIETZSCHE (which he describes in "Nietzsche, Genealogy, History"). Foucault's central concept in his "archeological" works is that of the "episteme," a broad system of rules for knowledge formation that are immanent, he claims, in all or most of the disciplinary fields of a given historical period. As epistemes shift or break up, it becomes possible to know the world in new ways and impossible to take older ways of conceiving and analyzing the world seriously. Genealogical works, by contrast, do not employ the concept of the "episteme" and do not posit general conditions for all regions of knowledge within one historical epoch. Those works classed as "genealogical" focus on relationships between specific regions of knowledge, institutions, and power. As a result, the genealogical works are less sweeping in their historical and epistemological claims.

Foucault himself does not draw a distinction between "archeology" and "genealogy." In an interview in 1983, he offers a different framework altogether for understanding his writings. Referring to all his major works as "genealogies," Foucault asserts that he has always been interested in subjectivity. He classifies his books in relation to three questions. How do people understand themselves as knowers? How are people subjected in power relations? How do people establish themselves as moral agents? (Foucault, 1997). Each book, Foucault says, takes up one or more of these questions in the context of a particular region of thought, such as psychiatry or medicine.

Foucault never assumes that any of our concepts or ways of understanding the world, including ourselves, are universal or perfectly stable through time. Investigation reveals that even the most basic features of our ways of thinking are historically formed, that there was a time before our particular way of thinking existed. We may believe, for example, that disease has always been conceived as an invasion of the body or that sexuality has always been held to be basic to the personality, but Foucault demonstrates otherwise. Still, opponents might say, there are basic features of the world that we apprehend more or less directly – such as the materiality of our own bodies – that inform our thinking and are common across cultures and ages. Foucault disagrees. "Nothing in man, not even his body, is sufficiently stable to serve as the basis for self-recognition or for understanding other men" (Foucault, 1977, p. 153). Foucault's work on madness, medicine, the formation of social sciences, and sexuality are designed to show that what we take for granted as simple truths about the nature of human bodies, minds, and societies are embedded in complex and historically contingent systems of perception; furthermore, though transformations in the ways people understand themselves can be traced through time, in widely separated epochs the worlds that people experience are vastly different and discontinuous.

Some philosophers have held that, though the world changes drastically through history, the laws of historical change are constant, and they create some kind of progress, a tendency toward greater order or human perfection. Foucault offers no such theory. So-called "laws of history," he contends, are just postulates, which, like all ways of perceiving the world, are subject to change. There is no reason to assume that either society or individuals are on a path of continuous or even intermittent improvement. Changes occur because of shifts in power arrangements, and while these are understandable in retrospect, they are not scientifically predictable.

Critics argue that Foucault undercuts himself when he says there are no constants in thought and experience. They contend that this renders all knowledge-claims relative to history and power, including Foucault's own knowledge-claims about knowledge-claims. Defenders answer that Foucault's general statements (such as the assertion cited above: "*nothing* . . . is sufficiently stable") may be epistemologically problematic, but the genealogical works themselves are not. When Foucault claims that sex as we conceive of it today is not a constant feature of human experience, that neither the Greeks nor the Romans had a concept comparable to our notion of sexuality, his claim is specific enough to avoid any problem of self-referentiality. By demonstrating the historicity of so many of our assumptions about ourselves, though, Foucault's works do support the supposition that there are no universals or constants in human experience.

Foucault is best known for his "analytics of power." He holds that a thorough understanding of power in our society requires abandoning analytical frameworks – e.g. Liberalism or Marxism – that locate power

in state institutions. Power is everywhere, he asserts. To understand subjection as well as resistance and change, we must examine power at the
micro-level – relations between boss and worker, therapist and client,
teacher and pupil, husband and wife. It is at this level that systems of
"power/knowledge" are produced and reproduced and are sometimes
disrupted and overthrown. Power is not something that one person or
group holds while others lack it; power exists only in relation, only in
"exercise." Power relations must be constantly repeated if institutional-
ized dominations are to be maintained. Thus power relations are always
reversible or alterable, which means that the institutions and dominations they support are always vulnerable. Freedom, Foucault insists, is an
ever-present feature of power relations.

Since the mid-eighteenth century, Foucault warns us, however, power
relations have intensified. This is the result of innovations in technolo-
gies of power through the nineteenth century, the most far-reaching of
which Foucault calls "normalization." As populations grew, functionar-
ies needed techniques for managing large groups of people – workers,
soldiers, schoolchildren, etc. At the same time, with industrialization and
the invention of the rifle, the tasks these groups of people had to
perform became more complex. Gradually the new techniques that
various administrators invented came together at a theoretical level in
the idea of development. Individuals develop (skills, physical features,
etc.) along a continuum in response to set stimuli at measurable rates.
This notion gave rise to the idea of norms of development, statistically
significant degrees of accomplishment in relation to given tasks. Norms
in turn made possible the notion of deviance, statistically measurable
differences between people engaged in acquiring a skill or a characteristic. This process of measuring and describing people according to
developmental norms created administrative classification systems that
interpret variations as deviations and render deviating individuals
subject to disciplinary action, therapy, or other forms of forceful inter-
vention. Even those institutions most clearly associated with the state and
the law (such as the judiciary, police, and prison system) are not fully
explicable apart from this concept of normalization, Foucault maintains.
Normalization is the most basic and ubiquitous form that power takes
in the modern world.

In his last works, Foucault takes up the question of how people constitute themselves as ethical beings. His focus in these works is sexuality
and sensual pleasure. He argues that the current belief that sexuality is
a fundamental and inescapable aspect of a human life and that mental
and physical health require that one's sexuality be carefully analyzed,
classified, and managed is the product of a series of shifts in relations

of power that occurred over the last three centuries. Sexual identities (heterosexual and homosexual, for example) are not natural kinds but are, rather, social phenomena constructed in response to shifts in power arrangements in the nineteenth century. The fact that sexual identities and other important features of our existence are historically contingent does not mean, however, that we can change them at will. Historically constructed objects of knowledge are not illusions. They are reality, since reality itself is historically emergent. But as we come to understand various aspects of ourselves and our societies as historically contingent, the power that our current way of thinking exercises over our lives will lessen somewhat, perhaps making it possible to think differently. Foucault, therefore, is interested in what he calls an "aesthetics of existence," self-overcoming (as Nietzsche would term it) or self-creation as a way of life. He advocates a perpetual openness toward the future, toward possibilities and differences as one styles one's existence in accordance with the values and practices one defines at a given moment as beautiful or best. This self-stylization he regards as a kind of self-discipline, which he calls a "practice of freedom." It can counter disciplines imposed upon us by the forces of normalization that pervade our society.

Bibliography

Writings

Madness and Civilization, trans. R. Howard (New York: Vintage, 1965).
The Order of Things (New York: Vintage, 1970).
The Archeology of Knowledge, trans. A. M. Sheridan Smith (New York: Pantheon, 1972).
The Birth of the Clinic, trans. A. M. Sheridan Smith (New York: Vintage, 1973).
Discipline and Punish, trans. A. M. Sheridan (New York: Vintage, 1977).
"Nietzsche, genealogy, history." In D. Bouchard (ed.), *Language, Counter-memory, Practice* (Ithaca, NY: Cornell University Press, 1977).
The History of Sexuality, three volumes, trans. R. Hurley; volume 1, *An Introduction* (New York: Vintage, 1978); volume 2, *The Use of Pleasure* (New York: Pantheon, 1985); volume 3, *The Care of the Self* (New York: Pantheon, 1986).
Ethics: Subjectivity and Truth, ed. P. Rabinow (New York: The New Press, 1997).

Further reading

Eribon, D.: *Michel Foucault*, trans. Betsy Wing (Cambridge, MA: Harvard University Press, 1991).

11

Frege

Hans-Johann Glock

Gottlob Frege (1848–1925 CE) was a German logician and professor of mathematics at Jena. His philosophical importance is twofold. First, he invented modern mathematical logic, which is a major tool of contemporary analytic philosophy; second, he himself employed this tool to great effect in the philosophy of logic and mathematics. The driving force behind his work was logicism, the project of reducing mathematics to logic. Although mathematical propositions are *a priori*, they are not synthetic, as KANT thought, but analytic in the sense of being provable from logical axioms and definitions alone. Logicism seeks to define the *concepts* of mathematics in purely logical terms (including the set-theoretical notion of a class), and to derive its *propositions* from self-evident logical principles.

The invention of modern logic in Conceptual Notation

To pursue this program, Frege had to overcome the limitations of Aristotelian syllogistic logic. *Conceptual Notation* (1879) marks a watershed in the development of logic, because it provides the first complete axiomatization of first-order logic (propositional- and predicate-calculus) and exhibits mathematical induction as an application of a purely logical principle. It is an attempt to realize LEIBNIZ's dream of a *characteristica universalis*, a formal language which would allow us to check rigorously the validity of proofs in any field seeking watertight demonstrations. This formal language abstracts from all features of propositions which are irrelevant to the validity of proofs in which the propositions occur, thereby isolating their "conceptual content," what we nowadays call their logical form.

The basic idea is to analyse propositions not into subject and predicate, like school-grammar and Aristotelian logic, but into *function* and *argument* (Preface). The expression "$x^2 + 1$" represents a function of the variable x, because its value depends solely on the argument we substitute for x – it has the value 2 for the argument 1, 5 for the argument 2, etc. Frege extended this mathematical notion so that functions do not just take numbers as arguments, but objects of any kind. Thus the expression "the capital of x" denotes a function which has the value Berlin for the argument Germany. Equally, a sentence like "Caesar conquered Gaul" can be seen as the value of a two-place function x *conquered y* for the arguments Caesar and Gaul. Accordingly, it is analysed not into the subject "Caesar" and the predicate "conquered Gaul" but into a two-place function-expression "x conquered y" and two argument-expressions "Caesar" and "Gaul."

Frege further extended this idea to propositional connectives and expressions of generality. "All electrons are negative" is analysed not into a subject "all electrons" and a predicate "are negative," but into a complex one-place function-name "if x is an electron, then x is negative" and a universal quantifier ("For all x, . . .") that binds the variable occurring in the function-name. "All electrons are negative" does not claim of the class of electrons that it is negative; it claims of every thing in the universe that *if* it is an electron, it is also negative. Existential propositions ("Some electrons are negative") are expressed through the universal quantifier and negation ("Not for all x, if x is an electron, then x is not negative"). This quantifier-variable notation is capable of formalizing propositions involving multiple generality, which are essential to mathematics. It displays, for example, the difference between the true proposition "For every natural number, there is a greater natural number" ("$(x)(\exists y)$ $y > x$") and the false proposition "There is a natural number which is greater than all other natural numbers" ("$(\exists y)(x)$ $y > x$").

The definition of number in The Foundations of Arithmetic

Foundations (1884) turns to the next challenge facing logicism, providing a definition of the concept of a cardinal number. It starts with a brilliant critique of Kant's view that arithmetic is based on intuition and of Mill's view that it is based on inductive generalizations. Frege's alternative is guided by three principles: (1) there is a sharp difference between what is logical and hence objective, and what is psychological and hence subjective; (2) one must not ask for the meaning of a word in isolation, since words mean something only in the context of a proposition; (3) the difference between concept and object must be heeded. Frege maintains that number statements such as "Jupiter has four moons" ascribe a property not to an *object* but to a *concept*, namely to the concept "moon of Jupiter" the property of having exactly four things falling under it. By a similar token, "God exists" does not ascribe a property (existence) to an object, but to the concept God, namely that at least one object falls under it. Unlike omnipotence, existence is not a "component" of the concept *God* (a feature used to define it), but a "property," which is why the ontological argument fails.

Frege resists the conclusion that numbers are properties of concepts. A number n "belongs" to a concept, but the property of the concept is not n itself, but *having the number n belonging to it*. Instead, he claims that each number is a "self-subsistent, re-identifiable object," on the grounds that numerals are singular terms ("The number 7") and occur in equations; indeed, adjectival occurrences of numerals – "Jupiter has four moons" – can be paraphrased as equations – "The number of Jupiter's moon is four." Our reluctance to accept that numbers are objects, albeit of a non-spatial kind, is due to our inclination to ask for the meaning of terms in isolation (contrary to (2), the so-called context-principle), which leads us to look for a mental image as the meaning of numerals, one of the ways in which we confuse logic and psychology – contrary to (1).

For Frege, anything which is designated by a singular term is an object, and the crucial feature of objects is that they can be identified and re-identified. Consequently, Frege must provide *criteria of identity* for numbers. He defines the concept of number in terms of *numerical identity* ("is the same number as"), relying on an ingenious process of abstraction. A cardinal number is simply that which is identical when two concepts are equivalent, i.e. have the same number of things falling under them. Accordingly, the cardinal number of the concept F can be defined as the extension of the concept "concept equivalent with F." Since the extension of a concept is the class of things that fall under it, this amounts to treating numbers as classes of classes with the same number of members. The number two is the class of pairs, the number three the class of trios, and so on. This definition is *not* circular, since numerical equivalence between classes can be defined without presupposing cardinal numbers, namely through the notion of a *one-to-one correlation*. Two classes are equivalent if each member of the first can be correlated with a different member of the other class leaving none over. Moreover, the classes of which numbers are classes can be defined without using numerical notions like "pair," through purely logical concepts. 0 is the class of classes equivalent to the class of objects which are not identical with themselves, i.e. as a class which contains only the null-class: {ø}. 1 is the class of classes equivalent to the class whose only member is 0: {0}. 2 is the class of classes equivalent with the class whose members are 0 and 1: {0,1}; etc.

Semantic foundations

In a series of seminal articles, Frege turned to the semantic foundations of his system. *Conceptual Notation* oscillated between treating functions as linguistic expressions and their values as sentences, and treating them as what these expressions stand for and their values as "judgeable contents" (what sentences express). "Function and Concept" overcomes this confusion between signs and what they signify. Atomic formulae are composed of argument-expressions or "proper names" and a concept-word or function-name. The argument-expressions are names of objects, the concept-words are names of functions. Concepts are functions which map arguments no longer onto judgeable contents, but onto two newly introduced "logical objects," the True and the False. The value of the function "*x* conquered Gaul" is either the True (e.g. if we substitute "Caesar") or the False (if we substitute e.g. "Alexander"), depending on whether the resulting proposition is true or false. Sentences are *proper names* of either one of these "truth-values." The logical connectives ("~," "&," "∨") by means of which molecular formulae are formed are functions which map truth-values onto truth-values. Negation, for example, is a unary truth-function which maps a truth-value onto the converse truth-value ("*p*" is true iff "~*p*" is false). Finally, the quantifiers are second-level functions which map concepts (first-level functions) onto truth-values; "For all *x*, *Fx*" maps the concept *F* onto the True if *F* holds true for all arguments (as with "*x* is identical with itself"), otherwise onto the False.

Any object can be the argument of any first-level function, and there are no ranges from which arguments have to be taken: "The number 7 is red" is simply false rather than nonsensical. But while Frege does not draw categorial distinctions between objects, he sharply distinguishes concepts and objects. Objects can stand on their own; by contrast, concepts (and functions generally) are "incomplete" or "unsaturated," i.e. require completion by an argument to form a complete whole. The same goes for function-signs: "$2.x^2 + x$" and "*x* conquered *y*" require completion, while the proper names of both their arguments ("2," "8," "Caesar," "Gaul") and of their values (the True or the False) – that is, sentences like "$2.2^3 + 2 = 18$" or "Caesar conquered Gaul" – are self-subsistent. Sentences are proper names because they have no empty places and hence must stand for an object, where by object is simply meant anything which is not a function, i.e. anything designated by a saturated expression.

As a grammatical criterion for distinguishing function-names from proper names Frege specifies the definite article. Yet, by this criterion

(1) "The concept *horse* is a concept" is about an object ("*the* concept …") rather than a concept. In "Concept and Object" Frege accepts this paradoxical consequence, and concludes that (1) is false; elsewhere he suggests that (1) is nonsensical. Either way, we cannot say anything true about concepts. Frege tries to live with this result by talking about the extensions of concepts instead, but this does not solve the problem, since he needs to talk about concepts, if only to distinguish them from objects.

Frege regarded this predicament as a mistake forced on us by language. In fact, he has boxed himself into a corner by basing a semantic distinction between singular terms and predicates on a dubious metaphysical distinction between self-subsistent and unsaturated entities. According to Frege, we cannot refer to concepts by means of terms like "the concept *horse*" because the saturated nature of that term precludes it from referring to something unsaturated like a concept. This view arises out of the untenable idea that concept-words ("*x* is a horse") name unsaturated entities (functions), and that names cannot perform that role because they do not reflect the unsaturated nature of their purported referents. But concept-words do not name entities, they express principles of classification. And unlike the concept-words we use to *express* concepts, the terms by which we refer to them ("the concept *horse*") need not be "unsaturated," i.e. capable of a predicative use.

Frege was concerned only with the logical content of expressions, and not, for example, with their "coloring," the mental associations they evoke. In "On Sense and Meaning" he distinguishes two aspects of the content of signs: their meaning (*Bedeutung*), which is the object they refer to, and their sense (*Sinn*), the "mode of presentation" of that referent. A sign refers to a thing through its sense, and that sense determines its meaning: one and the same meaning can be presented through different senses, but not vice versa. While the ideas individuals associate with a sign are subjective (psychological), its sense is objective. It is what is grasped by different individuals who understand the sign, yet it exists independently of being grasped.

Frege applies this two-tier model of meaning to all types of expressions. The meaning of a sentence is its truth-value; the sense of a sentence is the thought it expresses (what is asserted) by virtue of presenting the truth-value as the value of a function (concept) for an argument (object). The meaning of a proper name is what it stands for, its sense the descriptions through which we identify that bearer. Concept-words express a sense and refer to a concept.

The sense/meaning distinction explains why an identity-statement like "The morning star is the evening star" differs from the trivial "The morning star is the morning star" in being informative. "The morning star" and "the evening star" have the same meaning – Venus – but different senses, since they present it in different ways. It also explains how an expression like "the least rapidly convergent series" fails to refer without being senseless. Any sentence in which such an expression occurs will have a sense – express a "thought" – but lack a meaning, i.e. a truth-value. For the sense and the meaning of a sentence are a function of the senses and meanings respectively of its components. The sense of a name is the contribution it makes to the thought expressed by sentences in which it occurs. Moreover, that thought is given by the conditions under which the sentence is true. According to Frege's followers, therefore, his claim that a sentence means a truth-value amounts to no more than the idea that it has a semantic value, which determines the truth-value of complex propositions in which it occurs, and is itself determined by what its components refer to. However, these compositionalist principles are in tension with the context-principle of *Foundations*. If a word has a content only within the context of a sentence, how could its sense and reference determine the senses and references of sentences in which it occurs? This may explain why Frege never repeated the context-principle after dividing content into sense and meaning.

Basic Laws of Arithmetic

Basic Laws was intended to be the crowning achievement of Frege's work. It uses the symbolism of *Conceptual Notation*, modified by the semantic innovations of the early 1890s, to derive arithmetic from logic along the lines sketched in *Foundations*. The preface to Volume I completes Frege's critique of idealism and psychologism: (1) what ideas we associate with words is irrelevant to their definition (sense); (2) most of our judgements are not about ideas, but purport to describe mind-independent objects; (3) the logical "laws of thought" do not describe how human beings actually think, but prescribe how we ought to think; they are strictly necessary and objective laws of "truth," not contingent psychological laws of "holdings-to-be-true." Thoughts are not private ideas in the minds of individuals, but inhabit a realm beyond space and time. Along similar lines, Volume II criticizes formalism, the view that mathematics is a game played with symbols, on the grounds that mathematical symbols have a content only because they are associated with extralinguistic entities (meanings and senses). *Basic Laws* also formulates a stringent condition on the legitimacy of concepts, namely that they have sharp boundaries. By combining the requirement that a function should be defined for any argument with the law of the excluded middle, Frege reaches the conclusion that for any concept F and any object x, either x is determinately F or it is not. As a result, vague predicates like "is bald" and predicates which are not defined for all objects turn out to be "inadmissible sham concepts."

Frege's system is axiomatic: the truths of logic and arithmetic are deduced from "basic laws" according to specified rules of inference. Logic is concerned with proof: its task is to derive certifiedly true theorems from indubitable axioms. For this reason, Frege's conception of logic differs from contemporary semantic conceptions in two respects. First, the axioms are understood not as analytic consequences of the definitions of logical signs, but as *self-evident* truths which unfold timeless relations between logical entities, and are certified by a "logical source of knowledge." Second, nothing can be inferred from false propositions; all inferences proceed from "asserted," i.e. true, propositions. Every line in Frege's logical system has the form "⊢p," where "p" signifies the thought and "⊢" – the "assertion-sign" – the act of assertion which takes us from a mere thought to a truth-value. The assertion-sign also serves to distinguish the occurrence of a thought when it is not asserted – e.g. the occurrence of "p" in "⊢$(p \supset q)$" – from its occurrence on its own – "⊢p" – when it is (this so-called "Frege point" is ignored by the traditional view that the assertive force attaches to the predicate, which is part of asserted and unasserted propositions).

Frege's impressive system came to grief because it relies on naive set-theory. The definition of the cardinal numbers relies on his Basic Law V: the extension of F = the extension of G if and only if every F is G. This means that for every concept there exists an extension or class having for its members precisely those objects that fall under the concept. But in that case there are classes that have other classes as members, which, as RUSSELL noticed, leads to the paradoxical notion of the class of all classes which are not members of themselves: if that class is a member of itself, it is not a member of itself, and vice versa. When Frege was informed about Russell's paradox, he lost heart for completing the logicist project.

Last writings

As a result of this blow, Frege produced very little between 1903 and 1917. Eventually he became convinced that the whole project of founding arithmetic on logic (including the idea that numbers are classes of classes) was irretrievably undermined by the flaws of set-theory. At the same time, Frege continued to believe in the merits of his function-theoretic logic. In 1918 he started the book *Logical Investigations*, of which the first three chapters were published as articles. The first and most important – "The Thought" – starts out by arguing that the notion of truth is *sui generis* and indefinable. Although Frege is a realist, he rejects the correspondence theory on the dubious grounds that a complete correspondence between a representation and what it represents would be possible only if the two were identical. He goes on to maintain that the bearers of truth are not sentences but their senses – thoughts. One and the same sentence ("I have been wounded") can be used to express either a truth or a falsehood, and a single truth can be expressed by different sentences ("I have been wounded"/"H. J. G. has been wounded"). Unlike the sentences that provide their linguistic "garb," thoughts are imperceptible. Unlike ideas, which are the private properties of individuals, they do not depend on someone having them (they are true or false independently of someone grasping or believing them), and can be shared and communicated between people.

Frege uses these truisms not just to combat psychologism, but also to erect an elaborate three-world ontology (later revived by Karl Popper). Thoughts are "non-actual" – that is, non-spatial, atemporal and imperceptible ("non-sensible") – yet "objective." They inhabit a "third realm," a "domain" (*Gebiet*) beyond space and time which contrasts with the "first realm" of inalienable ideas (individual minds), and the "second realm" of actual and objective material objects. Thus Frege combines a Platonist conception of thoughts – and hence of logic – with a Cartesian conception of the mind (see DESCARTES); as a result he was at a loss to explain how minds can "grasp" thoughts, denizens of a different ontological realm.

Frege's impact on analytic philosophy

Frege's logicist project was unsuccessful, he was relatively unknown in his own lifetime, and his philosophical impact was mediated through Russell, WITTGENSTEIN, and Carnap. Yet at present he is universally recognized as the greatest logician since ARISTOTLE, and perhaps the greatest philosopher of mathematics ever. As a result of Dummett's work, many also regard him as the father of analytic philosophy and its linguistic turn, on the grounds that he viewed logic rather than epistemology as the foundation of philosophy, and pioneered theories of meaning for natural languages.

Frege purged psychology from logic, and his anti-psychologism influenced HUSSERL and Wittgenstein. But he never propounded a general conception of philosophy or declared questions of meaning to take priority over questions of truth and justification. Indeed, his logicism was itself motivated by the epistemological ambition of providing mathematics with secure foundations. Moreover, his conception of the relation between logic and language was explicitly non-linguistic. He regarded language as an indispensable vehicle of thoughts, but only because human beings cannot perceive thoughts without their linguistic clothing. Equally, he conceded that there is a rough correspondence between the structure of thought and that of language, but the task of logic is to analyse thoughts, which are extralinguistic abstract entities. Finally, although Frege showed considerable interest in natural languages, and occasionally relied on ordinary grammar for constructing his formal system, he conceived of the latter not as revealing the hidden logical structure of natural languages, but as providing an *ideal* language for the purposes of science, one which avoids ambiguity, vagueness, referential failure, and truth-value gaps.

At the same time, the notion of such an ideal language had a profound impact on the analytic tradition. Together with Russell, Frege was *the* pioneer of logical analysis. They not only invented a powerful logical system, but also demonstrated its use in tackling philosophical problems. Without that twofold inspiration, the idea of *analysing language* would have remained an empty slogan. Moreover, despite the often outdated framework, many of Frege's semantic insights remain definitive, and his categories and problems continue to shape the agenda of modern philosophical logic. For example, although his remarks on sense and meaning are sparse and often inconsistent, they have significantly influenced contemporary debates about the relation between language and reality, and about the nature of linguistic understanding. Last not least, his philosophical prose is a striking model of how complex problems can be discussed in a way which is clear, profound, and honest.

Bibliography

Writings

The Foundations of Arithmetic, trans. J. L. Austin, 2nd edn (Oxford: Blackwell, 1959).

The Basic Laws of Arithmetic, trans. and ed. M. Furth (Berkeley and Los Angeles: University of California Press, 1964).

Conceptual Notation and Related Articles, trans. and ed. T.W. Bynum (Oxford: Clarendon Press, 1972).

Posthumous Writings, ed. H. Hermes, F. Kambartel, and F. Kaulbach, trans. P. Long and R. White (Oxford: Blackwell, 1979).

Philosophical and Mathematical Correspondence, ed. B. McGuinness, trans. H. Kaal (Oxford: Blackwell, 1980).

Collected Papers, ed. B. McGuinness (Oxford: Blackwell, 1984).

Further reading

Baker, G. P. and Hacker, P. M. S.: *Frege: Logical Excavations* (Oxford: Blackwell, 1984).

Bell, D.: *Frege's Theory of Judgement* (Oxford: Clarendon Press, 1979).

Dummett, M.: *Frege: Philosophy of Language*, 2nd edn (London: Duckworth, 1981).

——: *Frege: Philosophy of Mathematics* (Cambridge, MA: Harvard University Press, 1991).

Kenny, A. J. P.: *Frege* (London: Penguin, 1995).

Sluga, H.: *Gottlob Frege* (London: Routlege & Kegan Paul, 1980).

—— (ed.): *The Philosophy of Frege*, Volumes 1–4 (New York & London: Garland, 1993).

Weiner, J.: *Frege in Perspective* (Ithaca, NY: Cornell University Press, 1990).

12

Hegel

Tom Rockmore

Georg Friedrich Wilhelm Hegel (1770–1831 CE) is one of the few real philosophical giants. It has been well said that he is a modern ARISTO-TLE. His deep learning in many fields, not only philosophy, provides his texts with an unusually encyclopedic character. His thought, like KANT's, constitutes a peak in the history of German idealism, a period often held to be one of the two richest in the philosophical tradition. Hegel's life and times were shaped by the French Revolution, arguably the most important political event of the modern period. The great post-Kantian German idealists – Fichte, Schelling, and Hegel – all came to maturity after this event, whose upheavals were reflected in their theories, above all in Hegel's.

Hegel was born in Stuttgart on April 27, 1770, in the same year as Ludwig van Beethoven, the great German composer, and Friedrich Hölderlin, the equally famous German romantic poet. A precocious child, he was distinguished all his life by an unusual capacity for silent meditation. As a young man, Hegel studied from 1788 to 1793 at the Tübinger Stift, a Protestant seminary in Tübingen, a town near Stuttgart in southwestern Germany close to the border with Switzerland. While at the seminary, he became friends with Schelling and Hölderlin. On finishing his studies, Hegel found a job as tutor in a wealthy family in Berne. In 1796, he found a similar position in Frankfurt am Main. When his father died in 1799, leaving him a modest inheritance, Hegel decided to become a philosopher. He accepted Schelling's invitation to join him in Jena, then the intellectual capital of Germany. There he published his first philosophical text, wrote his dissertation, which, after its successful defense, gave him the right to teach, and composed his first great book, the *Phenomenology of Spirit.*

Hegel remained in Jena until the university was closed by Napoleon's troops after the Battle of Jena. Short of money, he was then obliged to leave the university. He initially went to Bamberg, a small town in

Bavaria, where he became editor of a weekly newspaper, before going on to Nuremberg, where he served as head of a secondary school, or *Gymnasium*, from 1808 to 1816. While in Nuremberg, he wrote the *Science of Logic.* He returned to university life in 1816 by accepting a position at Heidelberg, where he wrote the *Encyclopedia of the Philosophical Sciences* as an aid to his students. He remained there for two years, before going on to Berlin in 1818 to occupy the chair vacated by Fichte. In Berlin he published the *Philosophy of Right,* also as a manual for his students. He died suddenly during a cholera epidemic in 1831, at the age of 61, at the very height of his fame. He is buried in Berlin next to Fichte, one of the two contemporaries (along with Schelling) whom Hegel thought worthy of the name philosopher.

It is common to interpret Hegel's theory immanently; that is to say, mainly or even solely through a study of his writings, including course notes and other texts unpublished during his lifetime. An approach of this kind is probably never sufficient, since all thinkers belong, and react, to the ongoing discussion of earlier and current times. It is especially unwarranted with respect to Hegel, whose theory explicitly depends on his conception and reading of the history of philosophy. Thus it is unlike that of DESCARTES or even Kant, for whom the prior discussion is either subject to error or simply entirely mistaken. Hegel viewed the philosophical tradition as in effect an immense Socratic dialogue in which different thinkers offer contrasting views of knowledge. Since Descartes, numerous thinkers have accepted the Cartesian conviction that we need to start over, as it were, in order to make a true beginning to philosophy. On the contrary, Hegel – like Newton, who claimed to build on the shoulders of giants – held that we cannot avoid building upon the still valid parts of the prior philosophical tradition.

In principle, since Hegel intended to build upon the positive elements in all preceding thought, his own theory can be understood through his reading of any of his predecessors. In practice, the most economical approach to Hegel's theory is through his reading of Kant's critical philosophy, which is the true proximate source of his own position. According to Kant, there can be at most a single true philosophical theory. In the wake of the publication of Kant's *Critique of Pure Reason,* it was widely thought that although he was correct to insist on the need for philosophy to be a science, in his critical philosophy he had failed in this task. With the exception of a few opponents of Kant, most thinkers in the post-Kantian period, including the post-Kantian German idealists, believed that his theory fell short of its aim and needed to be reformulated according to its spirit, not its letter. Fichte's claim that he alone among the post-Kantians had grasped the spirit of Kant's critical philosophy was accepted by the young Hegel and the young Schelling. Hegel's position, which initially arose from his effort to come to grips with Kant's critical philosophy as restated by Fichte and Schelling, was only later extended to come to grips with the entire philosophical tradition.

As its name suggests, Hegel's first philosophical text is devoted to elucidating the "Difference Between the System of Fichte and Schelling" (1801). This early text is unusually important as an accurate indication of a number of characteristic doctrines Hegel later elaborated into his mature philosophy. Hegel, who was always slow to make up his mind, rarely changed it later. This little text on Fichte and Schelling is astonishingly mature for a first philosophical publication. Hegel here regards Kant's critical philosophy as in principle correct, but incomplete, requiring further development in order to complete Kant's Copernican Revolution in philosophy. The proper direction for further development is indicated by Fichte, who, according to Hegel, basically improved the deduction of the categories that Kant only pretended to deduce. Hegel thought Reinhold was correct in suggesting the need to provide a systematic statement for the critical philosophy, but wrong in attempting to found or to ground it. Rejecting what is currently called epistemological foundationalism, Hegel maintains that philosophy has no ground, or first principle in a Cartesian sense of the term. Similarly rejecting the traditional, deductive view of philosophy as linear, Hegel describes it as intrinsically circular. Like Kant, Hegel insists on system as the criterion of philosophical science, which he, unlike Kant, interprets as requiring a structured conceptual unity subtending diversity of any kind. He situates the need for philosophy in difference, or disunity, suggesting that philosophy necessarily plays a synthetic role in unifying the contents of conscious experience.

In the period between his first philosophical publication and the *Phenomenology*, Hegel published several other long essays. His study of *Faith and Knowledge* (1802) takes up the problem of determining the difference between Fichte's subjective philosophy and Schelling's objective philosophy or philosophy of nature (*Naturphilosophie*). In this essay, Hegel explores the supposedly subjective theories of Kant, Fichte, and Jacobi. Kant famously limits reason to make room for faith; for Hegel, the opposition beyond reason and faith expresses the opposition between religion, which precedes the Enlightenment, and reason, which the Enlightenment in principle incarnates. According to Hegel, the vanquished in this battle, which resulted in the victory of reason over religion, is not really religion, and the victor is also not the incarnation of reason. This analysis later became the basis of his famous discussion of the French Revolution in the *Phenomenology*, where Hegel criticizes the Revolution as the self-stultifying result of abstract reason run amok.

Hegel also wrote a long study of natural right that is the first sketch of his last great work, the *Philosophy of Right*. His essay concerns three themes: the scientific study of natural right, its place in practical philosophy, and its relation to the positive science of right, or the law. In place of Kantian morality (*Moralität*), which he regards as overly abstract, Hegel expounds his own rival conception of ethics (*Sittlichkeit*), which is based on the life of the people. Hegel's critique of Kant's view of morality and his exposition of his rival conception of ethics will later occupy an important place in the *Phenomenology*, the *Encyclopedia*, and the *Philosophy of Right*.

Hegel is the author of only four books. The *Phenomenology of Spirit*, his first book, appeared in 1807. If the *Critique of Pure Reason* is the greatest work of the eighteenth century, then this book is perhaps the greatest work of the nineteenth century. Hegel's *Phenomenology* is both the introduction to and the first part of his system of philosophy. The book was written rapidly, under financial pressure – Hegel needed the money – and to safeguard a financial guarantee that it would be completed in timely fashion. According to legend, it was completed toward midnight of the day preceding the Battle of Jena. It presents a phenomenological analysis of the science of the experience of consciousness, and is divided into main sections on consciousness, self-consciousness, and reason. The latter includes a detailed discussion of spirit, Hegel's alternative to the Kantian view of pure reason.

In this book, Hegel addresses a dizzying array of topics centered on a theory of cognition (*Erkennen*) – what would now be called a theory of knowledge, or epistemology – following the path from immediate consciousness, through consciousness and self-consciousness, to a final view of absolute knowing. The notion of spirit (*Geist*) captures Hegel's anti-Kantian claim that knowledge is not the result of pure reason operating on the *a priori* level prior to and apart from experience. Reacting to Kant's effort to elucidate the general conditions of knowledge and experience of objects, Hegel is concerned with knowledge not as prior to but as only resulting from experience. But like Kant he rejects the idea of grasping so-called empirical facts apart from a conceptual framework. According to Hegel, knowledge claims presuppose a shifting conceptual scheme, elaborated (consciously or unconsciously) at a given time and place and by a given segment of the population. In rejecting the Kantian idea of pure reason, Hegel suggests that knowledge depends on spirit, or "impure" reason, which is *a posteriori*, or rooted in experience and arising out of the life of a people. Spirit is manifested in the collective efforts of human beings over the course of recorded history to know their world and themselves. Through this conception of spirit, Hegel can be said to offer a new theory of social justification to replace the Kantian theory of justification through pure reason. Hegel views reason as contextualized and historicized, hence as impure, and he takes the knowing subject to be a real, finite human being. The term "science" is taken to mean rigorous as opposed to ordinary reasoning or even to dogmatic, hence undemonstrated, forms of philosophy. Hegel understands "phenomenology" as the study of what is directly given to consciousness.

According to Hegel, who wishes to avoid presuppositions of any kind, philosophy cannot start with knowledge, or even with a final conception of it. Throughout the book, he is engaged in an undeclared debate with Kant. Following Kant, he insists on a distinction between sensation and perception. His book starts from an analysis of sense-certainty, the immediately given, the lowest and most immediate form of consciousness encountered on a level prior to perception. Although in some ways an empiricist, Hegel like Kant rejects the idea of immediate knowledge derived from experience, a view featured in such English empiricists as LOCKE and Bacon. He further repudiates Kantian empiricism, which is based on a supposed relation between phenomena, regarded as appearances, and independent reality. According to Hegel, we can never examine the relation between our view of a thing – anything – and this thing outside consciousness. He regards knowledge as resulting from a process in which we progressively narrow and eventually overcome the differences between our views of things and the things of which they are the views, *both* of which are contained within consciousness.

Absolute knowing, the end point of the knowing process, is often incorrectly conflated with theological claims about divine knowledge or even with unrevisable perceptual claims. For Hegel, this term refers to a form of knowledge that encompasses, with Kant, the conditions of knowledge of the objects of experience, as well as, going beyond Kant, the conditions under which the real human subject can reach such knowledge. Following Kant's practice, Hegel uses the term "absolute" to designate what is not in any way dependent, hence without presuppositions or assumptions.

Like Descartes and Kant, Hegel insists on the importance of self-consciousness within the epistemological process. Unlike his predecessors, who take self-consciousness as a given, he regards it instead as a historical product arising in and through social interactions among individuals. In this context, Hegel's discussion of the master–slave relation is justly celebrated. ARISTOTLE saw this relation as being justified by the intrinsic differences in mental capacities of the master and slave, whereas Rousseau saw it as reflecting the failure of society to achieve freedom for all its members. In his brilliant reanalysis of this relation, Hegel suggests in effect that it is neither natural, since it is based on economic inequality, nor stable. According to Hegel, this relation tends toward a resolution in which the slave will be seen as the master of the master and the master as the slave of the slave. He further suggests the idea of mutual recognition as a form of social interrelation lying beyond the master–slave relation. His claim that the master–slave relation is inherently unstable has often been taken as pointing toward social revolution.

The *Phenomenology of Spirit* is a controversial study which is regarded differently in different languages and literatures. Some, mainly those writing in English or French, regard it as Hegel's most important book; others, especially those writing in German, hold that it is a mere juvenile work which is superseded in his mature system. Those who discount the lasting importance of the *Phenomenology* routinely emphasize the significance of the *Science of Logic*, Hegel's second book, a huge work that appeared in three installments (1812, 1813, 1816). Hegel finished revising the first volume of this book in 1831, a scant week before his sudden death.

The relation of the *Phenomenology* to the *Logic* is also controversial. The *Logic* is properly understood, not as a new beginning, but rather as continuing the task undertaken in the *Phenomenology*. The latter book was originally to have been followed by a second part on logic and the two concrete sciences of the philosophy of nature and the philosophy of spirit. In fact, the *Logic* grew into a separate book. In the *Phenomenology*, Hegel treads the path leading from immediate consciousness – through such concrete shapes as morality and ethical life, art and religion – to absolute knowing, or the standpoint of philosophical science. Hegel, like Kant, thinks we grasp so-called empirical facts through a categorial framework that, unlike Kant, he believes cannot be deduced. A main concern in the *Logic* is to identify and show the interrelation of the categories composing the conceptual framework of cognition.

The main post-Kantian idealists all believed that Kant failed to deduce the categories and hence fell short of the goal of idealism. Hegel, who accepts Fichte's proposed deduction of the categories as achieving Kant's goal, regards Fichte's transcendental philosophy as authentic idealism. Since the deduction of the categories is central to Kant's critical philosophy, the vast categorial analysis in the *Science of Logic* can be understood as Hegel's effort to bring to a close the effort begun by Kant. The book comes in two volumes and is divided into three parts. The first volume, which treats of objective logic, contains two parts concerning Being and Essence. The second volume, or the subjective logic, is entirely devoted to the theory of the Concept (*Begriff*). Hegel opposes the kind of logic that had held sway from Aristotle to Kant. Kant, who made transcendental logic central to his study of the conditions of knowledge, regarded logic since Aristotle, like geometry since Euclid, as a finished discipline. Hegel rejects the traditional view of logic as abstracting from all content. According to him, logic, which is neither abstract nor without content, is concerned with objective thought, which is the content of pure science, or thought as it takes itself as its object.

In place of the well known idea of logic as a system of rules characterizing the abstract forms of static objects, Hegel offers a system of concrete concepts that take shape and come together according to an internal dialectic. His conception of dialectic, which has only the name in common with the Marxist conception of dialectical materialism, is rarely referred to directly in his writings. But it is constantly presupposed in his idea that concepts in and of themselves develop into other, more encompassing concepts. An example is the famous discussion of Being, Nothing, and Becoming with which the book opens. Hegel argues that when we consider mere, featureless Being as an object of thought, it is Nothing; and we further see that since, on reflection, Being turns into, or becomes, Nothing, Being and Nothing are mediated, or linked, through Becoming.

The *Phenomenology* and the *Logic* are the only books Hegel wrote for his philosophical colleagues. His two other books were both written for his students. When Hegel returned to the university in Heidelberg in 1816, he needed a manual, as was then customary, as an aid for students in his courses. The first of these is the *Encyclopedia of the Philosophical Sciences.*

Kant had strongly insisted on the need for philosophy to be systematic science. Post-Kantian German idealists, including Hegel, were concerned to produce philosophical systems. Throughout his career, Hegel understood philosophy as fully legitimated and as systematically developed. According to him, philosophy must be all inclusive, or encyclopedic, and comprise a whole, or totality, since its parts can only be grasped in terms of the whole. The *Encyclopedia of the Philosophical Sciences* (1817, 1827, 1831), which he quickly composed and later twice revised, was intended as an "official" statement of his philosophical system.

The exposition, which in its final form is divided into no less than 577 numbered paragraphs, remains a teaching manual, and, as Hegel remarked in a letter to Victor Cousin, is no more than a collection of various theses. Even in this long work, on which Hegel labored through-out his university career, there are only hints as to the nature of the famous system.

The idea of an encyclopedia was popularized by the French *Encyclo-pedia*, a semi-popular presentation of science and philosophy edited and written mainly by Diderot and d'Alembert in the mid-eighteenth century. In his own treatise, which only superficially resembles the efforts of the French encyclopedists to assemble all of human knowledge in a single vast work, Hegel utilizes the term "encyclopedia" in at least four senses. First, it is used as an abbreviation of the philosophical sci-ences, of all that was known in his own day; second, it suggests a pre-sentation of this knowledge in the form of a manual directed to students; third, it refers to the official exposition of his system; fourth, it connotes the "circle of knowledge" suggested in the Greek etymology of the word, a conception to which Hegel remained committed in virtue of his view of theory of knowledge as intrinsically circular.

The overall theme of Hegel's *Encyclopedia* is the scientific cognition of the truth. It is divided into the three parts that Hegel originally intended to present in the book that grew into the *Science of Logic*. The so-called lesser *Logic*, the first part of the *Encyclopedia*, presents a severely condensed version of the greater *Logic*, a version which is later than, and which hence can be held to supersede, the earlier work, with two main differences.

First, the very important initial chapter, "With What Must the Science Begin?", is lacking in the lesser *Logic*, which, accordingly, lacks a detailed analysis of the complex, crucial problem of the beginning of science. The problem is how to begin if we need to avoid all presuppositions of any kind and if there is no privileged starting point able to yield certain knowledge that is not itself a presupposition. This issue is especially important for Hegel, who returns to it often in his writings. He is com-mitted to the denial of the Cartesian foundationalist strategy for know-ledge that has long dominated the modern discussion, and he further typically insists that philosophy can make no presuppositions. Here he faces the difficulty of how to begin if one can neither demonstrate nor presuppose an initial proposition. In the greater *Logic*, after careful dis-cussion, Hegel again arrives at the conclusion already reached in the *Phenomenology*, where he suggests that, since there can be no privileged starting point, the proper way to begin is just to begin.

Second, starting with the second edition of the *Encyclopedia* in 1827, there is a very important discussion of the attitudes of thought to objec-tivity, where Hegel provides a systematic analysis of some main views of knowledge in the philosophical tradition. According to Hegel, the first, naive attitude consists in taking mere thought-determinations as fundamental characteristics of things through a direct conceptual grasp of the objects. This attitude corresponds to a dogmatic, or pre-Kantian, philosophy, in short to a theory which, since it is concerned to know its object without raising the question of how it is possible to know anything at all, merely presupposes an answer to this question. In the second attitude, Hegel successively considers forms of empiricism, represented mainly by Locke and by Kant's critical philosophy. In his discussion of immediate knowledge as the third attitude of thought to objectivity, Hegel studies Jacobi's anti-Kantian intuitionism, which stresses the direct grasp of the object as it is. Hegel, who, like Kant, rejects the idea of a direct, intuitive comprehension of the contents of experience, makes conceptual mediation essential to knowledge in the full sense.

The second part of the *Encyclopedia*, the Philosophy of Nature, is a much neglected side of Hegel's thought. It is widely but mistakenly thought that Hegel was ignorant about science and that progress in natural science contradicts his philosophical theory. Kant, who was deeply knowledgeable about natural science, made an important contribution to cosmology. Although less knowledgeable in this area than Kant, in fact Hegel possessed detailed knowledge of the sciences of his day and was critical of such contemporary pseudo-sciences as physiognomy and phrenology. At the beginning of the nineteenth century, when he was writing, the divorce between philosophy and modern science had not yet occurred. There was a long tradition in which philosophers, as recently as Kant and Schelling, had studied the philosophy of nature. Hegel likewise did not make an absolute distinction between philosophy and science. But despite his grasp of contemporary science, Hegel did not always follow contemporary trends. He was sharply critical of Newton, against whom he defended Kepler, as well as of Goethe's theory of colors. He agreed with Kant, against Newton (who held that science was entirely empirical and unrelated to metaphysics), that science required philosophical underpinnings. Hegel insists on a reciprocal relation between physics, which limits, and hence conditions, philosophy, and philosophy, which extends and completes the knowledge gathered in physics.

For Hegel, there are three fundamental sciences: physics, chemistry, and biology. The different levels of nature are irreducible to each other: biology cannot be reduced to chemistry, nor biology and chemistry to physics. Like such modern positivists as the Vienna Circle thinkers, Hegel opts for the unity of science, but he refuses their reductionist tendencies. In insisting on the unity of the sciences, but in rejecting any effort to replace or to substitute one for the others – for instance, to appeal to physics as finally the only real science and the sole source of human knowledge – Hegel is very modern. For instead of simply giving up in the face of modern science, or seeing in it a sort of epistemic panacea, he strives to discern its limits and to integrate it within his wider theory as one approach to knowledge among others. According to Hegel, nature possesses contingency, or real as opposed to mere logical possibility, but nonetheless it does not encompass human freedom. On the contrary, natural necessity or causation is an essential aspect of nature. With respect to nature, the philosophical task consists in understanding the role and limits of causal necessity for cognition.

The Philosophy of Spirit, the third and last part of the *Encyclopedia*, is again concerned with spirit, the general theme of the *Phenomenology*. As we have seen, Hegel proposes his conception of spirit, which draws on the religious tradition and preceding philosophy, to replace Kant's view of pure reason. Hegel affirms that we can only understand cognition from the point of view of spirit, the manifold and developing conscious experiences of real human beings. The *Phenomenology* and the Philosophy of Spirit overlap, but the similarity does not go very far. In comparison with the *Phenomenology*, the Philosophy of Spirit, as befits a manual, is less historical and more systematic. The discussion divides into three parts: subjective spirit, objective spirit, and absolute spirit. In his account of subjective spirit, where Hegel considers the Aristotelian account of the soul, he brings the discussion up to date, discussing anthropology in detail before turning to consciousness and psychology. Objective spirit takes up again and corrects the accounts of right, morality, and ethics found in the *Phenomenology*. Noteworthy here is a discussion of the mutual recognition that extends and completes his famous analysis of the master–slave relation in the earlier work. Hegel brings the *Encyclopedia* to a close with a discussion of absolute spirit, or spirit on the highest, most independent cognitive plane, spirit certain of itself as all reality.

The *Philosophy of Right* (1821), Hegel's last book, written in Berlin, is again a kind of outline or manual designed for students in his courses. This fourth work is composed of no fewer than 360 numbered paragraphs, often accompanied by oral comments whose authenticity is sometimes doubtful. The book as a whole is the further elaboration of earlier discussions of objective spirit. This is the domain in which spirit becomes concrete within the relations of law, morality, and ethical life; that is to say, on the level of the family, in civil society, and in the state. The discussion of right, morality, and ethical life, as well as the family, had initially been presented in the *Phenomenology* and in less historical but more systematic fashion in the *Encyclopedia*. The *Philosophy of Right* includes a preface, an introduction, and three parts concerning, respectively, "Abstract Right," "Morality," and "Ethical Life." Hegel's view of ethics is elaborated here in new accounts of the family, civil society (*die bürgerliche Gesellschaft*) and the state.

The method followed in this treatise is described in the *Encyclopedia* as a progression from the abstract to the concrete. It follows the development of the concept of the will from its realization on the level of formal right (or mere legality) to its most concrete form, which brings together formal right and morality. In the section on Ethical Life, the discussion begins on the level of the family, the most natural and least developed of the manifest forms of right, to take up its exteriorization on the further, more concrete levels of civil society and the state.

The word "right" (*Recht*), which is here used in a legal sense, is normally taken to mean "the totality of rules governing the relations between members of the same society." In *The Philosophy of Right*, Hegel understands this term more broadly to include civil right, that aspect of the concept most closely linked to legal considerations, as well as morality, ethical life, and even world history. In its most general sense, the Hegelian concept of right concerns free will and its realization. Here Hegel follows Aristotle, who thinks that all action aims at the good. It is not sufficient, however, *to think* the good within consciousness; it must also be realized through the transition from subjective desire to external existence so that the good takes shape not only within our minds but also and above all in our lives within the social context.

The Philosophy of Right, in which Hegel presents his political theory, is highly controversial. Since his death, many diverse interpretations of it have been offered. Some commentators see in it a sober and realistic analysis of moral and ethical values and a penetrating criticism of Kantian ethics. Others, particularly Marxists, consider its author to have become by the time he wrote it a reactionary pillar of the Prussian state of the day. According to this interpretation, the old Hegel, who was progressive and even liberal in his youth, became an admirer of the Prussian state, in which he discerned the very goal of history.

The young Hegel famously thought that theory is more important than practice, since ideas tend to realize themselves. When he wrote the *Phenomenology*, he believed that, in the wake of the French Revolution, the world was at a historical turning point, the birth of a new era. When he composed his last book, during the restoration period, Hegel was less sanguine about the prospects for fundamental social change. Although he continued to be interested in concrete social problems, such as poverty and anti-Semitism, he now held, in a famous metaphor referring to philosophy, that the owl of Minerva only takes flight at dusk. It follows that philosophy always and necessarily comes on the scene too late, too late to influence what has already taken place as a condition of its being known. Yet, by inference, a philosophical comprehension of our own time is useful in helping to bring about a better, more rational world.

The literature on Hegel's thought is enormous. At the present we seem to be entering a kind of Hegel renaissance, with books on his thought, particularly in English, appearing very rapidly. Extensive study has been made of his four main books as well as of his lecture notes and writings unpublished during his lifetime. His influence on later philosophy, above all on MARX's theory (which is literally inconceivable without Hegel's), is immense. Hegel's famous analysis of the relation of master and slave in the *Phenomenology* is the conceptual basis of Marx's later analysis of capitalism, and his account of the System of Needs in the *Philosophy of Right* offers a similar basis for Marx's view of economics. Hegel's influence on classical American pragmatism, particularly DEWEY and to a lesser extent Peirce, is clearly decisive. Among many others with deep debts to Hegel we can include KIERKEGAARD, NIETZSCHE, SARTRE and Merleau-Ponty. It is well said that in different ways all the main contemporary philosophical movements can be traced back to Hegel.

Bibliography

Writings

Hegel's Phenomenology of Spirit, trans. A. V. Miller (Oxford: Oxford University Press, 1977).

Hegel's Philosophy of Right, trans. T. M. Knox (London: Oxford University Press, 1977).

Hegel's Science of Logic, trans. A. V. Miller (Atlantic Highlands, NJ: Humanities Press, 1989).

Further reading

Harris, Errol: *An Interpretation of the Logic of Hegel* (Lanham, MD: University Press of America, 1983).

Harris, H. S.: *Hegel's Ladder* (Cambridge, MA and Indianapolis, IN: Hackett, 1997).

——: *Hegel's Development: Toward the Sunlight, 1770–1801* (Oxford: Clarendon Press, 1972).

——: *Hegel's Development: Night Thoughts. Jena, 1801–1806* (Oxford: Clarendon Press, 1983).

Houlgate, Stephen: *Freedom, Truth and History: An Introduction to Hegel's Philosophy* (London: Routledge, 1991).

Pinkard, Terry: *Hegel's Phenomenology: The Sociality of Reason* (New York: Cambridge University Press, 1994).

Pippin, Robert: *Hegel's Idealism: The Satisfaction of Self-consciousness* (Cambridge: Cambridge University Press, 1989).

Rockmore, Tom: *Before and After Hegel: A Historical Introduction to Hegel's Thought* (Berkeley and Los Angeles, CA: University of California Press, 1993).

——: *Cognition: An Introduction to Hegel's Phenomenology of Spirit* (Berkeley and Los Angeles: University of California Press, 1997).

13

Heidegger

Thomas Sheehan

Martin Heidegger (1889–1976 CE) is best known as the author of *Sein und Zeit* (*Being and Time*), published in 1927. The book aims at establishing how being shows up within human understanding. Heidegger offered the provisional answer that our experience of being is conditioned by our finitude and temporality. In a phrase: temporality – i.e. finitude – is what makes possible the understanding of being; or, the meaning of being is time.

Heidegger published only half the book in 1927, the part dealing with human being and temporality. He never produced the rest of the work, but over the next fifty years he did complete the project in other forms. During the 1930s he reshaped some elements of his philosophy without changing its two essential topics: (1) the finite occurrence of being, which he called "disclosure"; and (2) the finite structure of human nature, which he called "Dasein." Understanding how Dasein and the disclosure of being fit together is the key to grasping Heidegger's philosophy.

Heidegger spent his life as a university professor in Germany, first in Freiburg (1915–23), where he abandoned Catholic philosophy, became a protégé of Edmund HUSSERL, and began propounding a radical form of phenomenology. He then taught at Marburg University (1923–8), where his reformulation of the method and tasks of phenomenology found expression in *Being and Time* and led to a break with Husserl. In 1928 Heidegger succeeded Husserl in the chair of philosophy at Freiburg University, where he taught until 1945.

A conservative nationalist, Heidegger joined the Nazi party on May 3, 1933, three months after Hitler came to power. From April 1933 to April 1934 he served as rector of Freiburg University, during which time he enthusiastically supported Hitler and aligned the university with some aspects of the Nazi revolution. His public and private statements indicate that he supported many of the Nazi policies and ideals and that he backed Hitler's war aims well into the Second World War. In 1945 he was suspended from teaching because of his earlier political activities, and he formally retired with emeritus status in 1950. The question of his political sympathies continues to shadow Heidegger's otherwise solid reputation as one of the most original philosophers of the twentieth century.

Apart from philosophy, Heidegger's thought has had a strong influence on such disparate fields as theology (Rudolf Bultmann, Karl Rahner), existentialism (Jean-Paul SARTRE), hermeneutics (Hans-Georg Gadamer), and literary theory and deconstruction (Jacques DERRIDA). The collected edition of his works (his *Gesamtausgabe*, 1975–), will eventually include some eighty volumes, over half of which have already appeared. Most of his works are available in English translation, and the secondary literature on his philosophy is immense and continues to grow. The best study of his work in any language is Richardson (1963), and the most complete bibliography in English is Sass (1982).

The problematic

Contrary to popular accounts of his philosophy, Heidegger's central topic was not "being" but the *occurrence* of being, and more specifically *what causes* the occurrence of being within human experience. Instead of "occurrence" Heidegger speaks equivalently of the disclosure, emergence, unconcealment, truth, or meaning of being. He argues that being does not occur "out there" independent of human beings but shows up only within human experience – analogous to the way that meaning does not occur "on its own" but only within the human sphere. Thus Heidegger's focal topic – *die Sache selbst* as he calls it – was not "being" so much as *what makes being occur within human experience.*

His simple answer to that question was: human finitude, the radical lack-in-being that defines the human essence. That finitude or lack is why human beings are in a state of becoming (temporality); and such temporality is the "meaning" – i.e. makes possible the understanding – of all forms of being. Because this lack-in-being is tautologically "absent" or "hidden," Heidegger's thesis that we understand being only because we are finite can be restated as: *being occurs in our experience only because we are a certain kind of absence.*

That thesis summarizes all of Heidegger's work, and it remained fundamentally unchanged throughout his career. To understand it we must first grasp the distinction between things and their being.

The ontological difference

Heidegger distinguishes between whatever-is (*das Seiende*) and the is-ness (*das Sein*) of whatever-is. He calls this distinction between entities and their being the "ontological difference." An entity, on the one hand, is anything that is or can be, whether it be physical or spiritual, abstract or concrete. For example, God, human beings, socialism, and the number nine are all entities. The *being* of an entity, on the other hand, has to do with the "is" of whatever-is. Clearly the challenge is to find out what "is" (i.e. "being") means for Heidegger.

In one sense Heidegger's ontological difference between entities and their being merely repeats a commonplace of traditional philosophy. The medieval scholastics, for example, had already clearly distinguished between *ens* and *esse*, just as the ancient Greeks before them had distinguished between *to on* and *ousia*. However, Heidegger gives this metaphysical tradition a phenomenological twist. In his usage, the word "being" refers neither to things in the world (= entities) nor to the mere fact *that* such things are (their existence) and are *what* they are (their essence). Nor is "being" a property (e.g. "substance") that things have in and of themselves apart from human beings. Rather, "being" names the *relatedness of things to human interests*, the multiple and changing ways that things can be understood and engaged by correlative human activities. In Heidegger's work, "being" never refers to a single and unchanging "something" standing off by itself, but always indicates an entity's current phenomenal status in correlation with a given human comportment, whether cognitive, practical, aesthetic, or whatever.

The viewpoint here is phenomenological and hermeneutical: the being of a thing is what that thing currently *appears-as* (*phainetai*) within the human sphere, which in turn is based on what it is currently *taken-as* (*hermeneuetai*) by human beings. "Being" names not the metaphysical "is-ness" of things but their phenomenological "presence unto" possible human engagement. In a word, "being" refers to the *significance* or *meaningful presence* that things have for human beings.

Three things follow from this phenomenological understanding of being and distinguish it from the tradition of metaphysics. First, according to Heidegger, entities may certainly have existence regardless of whether human beings are alive or not. However, entities do not have "being" in Heidegger's sense of the term – that is, they do not have significance – apart from some actual or possible relation to human concerns. In fact, without human beings there is no "being" at all. Second, an entity and its being are not two separate realities. Being/significance cannot subsist on its own, separated from entities; rather, it is always the being/significance *of* an entity. Third, although an entity and its being/significance do not occur in isolation, they can be distinguished; and the ability to make this ontological distinction – that is, to know the being/significance *of* any entity – belongs only to human beings. The ontological difference occurs only in the human essence.

Therefore, Heidegger's focal question – "What explains the occurrence of significance within human experience?" – can also be formulated as: "What makes the ontological difference possible?"

Dasein

For Heidegger, the essence of human being consists in "openness," i.e. being the "open place" (the *Da*) where the being/significance of things occurs. This comes out as "Dasein" (human openness as the locus of significance), a technical term that has been carried over into English.

Insofar as human being is *necessarily* open, Heidegger characterizes it as "*thrown*-open" ("thrownness"). We are *a priori* thrust into our existence as a field of possibilities, and we understand whatever we happen to meet by relating it to those same possibilities. In Heidegger's parlance, we understand a thing by "projecting" it in terms of one or another possibility: we take it *as* this or that and thereby understand its significance. Human openness is thus a "thrown projection"; that is, (1) *thrown-open-ness*, as making possible (2) *the projective understanding of the significance of things*. This bivalent structure is called "care" (*Sorge*). Only within the human structure of care does the "being" or "is" of an entity (its significance-as-this-or-that) show up.

Dasein is equally called "being-in-a-world." By "world" Heidegger does not mean a spatio-temporal aggregate of physical entities, such as the universe, or planet Earth. Rather, he means a *unified field of concerns and interests* – such as the "world" of the mother or the "world" of the letter-carrier – which gives meaning to whatever is encountered within that world. In Heidegger's usage, the "world" is the same as the *Da* or open field that defines human being. "Being *in*" the world refers to one's engagement with the meaning-giving concerns and interests that define any such field.

For example, Mrs Smith as a mother lives in a different world from the same Mrs Smith as a letter-carrier. The difference has to do with her distinct concerns and goals (nurturing children versus delivering the mail) and the possibilities and requirements they generate. Each of her worlds is structured as a dynamic set of relations – all of them ordered to her own possibilities and concerns – that lends significance to the entities that Mrs Smith encounters: children in the one case, letters in the other.

What constitutes the essence of all such worlds – what Heidegger calls their "worldhood" – is the significance that accrues to entities by their relationship to Mrs Smith's concerns and interests. But this significance occurs only in correlation with her engagement with those concerns and interests. In short, one's being-in-a-world discloses the being/significance of entities.

As being-in-a-world and living into its possibilities, Dasein understands not just its *own* being but also the meaningful presence of *other* entities, by referring them to those same possibilities. Our primary way of understanding the significance of entities (which is always a changeable significance and not some eternal essence) is by interpreting them in terms of our pragmatic purposes or possibilities. For example, when I use this stone to hammer in a tent peg, I understand the current being of the stone as *being-useful-for-hammering*. This primary, pragmatic awareness of the being/significance of the tent peg is pre-predicative: it requires no thematic articulation (either mental or verbal) of the form "S = P." Rather, it evidences itself in the mere doing of something: I understand the current significance of the stone by *using* it.

Such first-order practical/pre-predicative awareness is what Heidegger designates "hermeneutical understanding." It is made possible by one's being-in-a-world and specifically by one's structure as thrown projection. In turn, as a second-order or reflective activity (a "method"), "hermeneutics" in Heidegger has less to do with the usual meaning of that term – interpreting texts – than it does with revealing, within all forms of human behavior, the often overlooked structure of being-in-a-world that underlies the first-order hermeneutical understanding of entities.

Temporality

In *Being and Time* Heidegger argues that the defining structure of human openness is "temporality" or "time," a uniquely human condition that is not to be confused with linear, chronological notions of time as past-present-future. For Heidegger, temporality connotes becoming, and human temporality entails becoming oneself. Human becoming is a matter of living into one's future, "standing out" (ek-stasis, ek-sistence) into one's possibilities.

The ultimate possibility into which one lives is one's own death: the possibility that ends all possibilities. Human becoming is mortal becoming, not just because we will die at some future date but above all because mortality defines our becoming at each present moment. As Heidegger puts it, human being is always being-at-the-point-of-death (*Sein-zum-Tode*). Thus one's being is radically finite, and it consists in both (a) being already mortal and (b) "becoming" one's mortality, i.e. anticipating one's death. Such mortal becoming is what Heidegger means by human temporality: the finite *presence* that one has by always and of necessity *becoming* one's own death.

Human temporality means being present by becoming absent; and this mortal becoming is the ineluctably finite essence of human being. When I wake up to that fact and accept it (this is what Heidegger calls "resolve"), I become my own "authentic" self rather than living as the inauthentic "anybody" (i.e. nobody) of everyday existence.

Being and Time contends that Dasein's temporality, as the anticipation of death, is what makes possible being-in-the-world and the resultant understanding of being. The argument may be put as follows. Temporality means having one's presence by being already thrown into one's absence (being-at-the-point-of-death). This means Dasein is *a priori* thrown into possibilities, right up to the possibility that ends all possibilities. But being thrown into possibilities entails the ability to have practical knowledge and to engage in purposeful action. And this ability *is* being-in-a-world. Thus Dasein's anticipation of its own death makes possible being-in-a-world and the disclosure of significance. The "meaning" of being – i.e. that which lets being/significance occur within human experience – is time/finitude.

Disclosure

Disclosure as the occurrence of being within human understanding takes place on three distinct levels that run from the original to the derivative: world-disclosure, pre-predicative disclosure, and predicative disclosure.

(1) The most original instance of disclosure is *world*-disclosure, the very opening up of the field of significance – the *Da* or world – in conjunction with Dasein's being-present-by-becoming-absent. (2) In turn, world-disclosure is what allows *entities* to be meaningfully present and to be known and used – first of all, practically and pre-predicatively – within the various worlds of human concern. (3) Finally, world-disclosure and the resultant pre-predicative disclosedness of entities, taken together,

make possible the *predicative* disclosure of entities in synthetic judgments and declarative sentences of the type "S = P." Properly speaking, the term "truth," taken as the correspondence between judgments and states of affairs, pertains only to this third level of disclosure, where reason, logic, and science operate. Heidegger argues that the "*essence* of truth" – i.e. that which makes predicative truth possible – is world-disclosure, which in turn issues in the pre-predicative disclosure of those entities against which predicative judgments must measure themselves if they are to be true.

The basic sense of disclosure (i.e. world-disclosure) is what Heidegger calls "language," by which he does not primarily mean spoken or written discourse and the rules governing it. For Heidegger "language" means *logos* such as he thinks Heraclitus understood the term: the original "gathering" of entities into meaningful presence so as to disclose them as what and how they are. This disclosive gathering happens only insofar as Dasein is itself "gathered" into its own mortality. "Language" in this original sense is what makes possible language/*logos* in the usual sense – human discourse as the activity of synthesizing and differentiating entities and their possible meanings.

Heidegger argues that disclosure in the primary sense of world-disclosure is born of something intrinsically absent and hidden – human finitude – and he calls this state of affairs the "mystery" of being. The point can be quite mystifying until one realizes that Heidegger takes disclosure to be a unique kind of *movement*.

As Heidegger interpreted them, classical philosophy in general and ARISTOTLE in particular understood movement not just as a change within entities but rather as the very *being* of entities that are undergoing change. Taken in this broad sense, movement refers to an entity's anticipation of something absent, such that what-is-absent-but-anticipated determines the entity's present being. For example, if you are studying for a university degree, that still-absent degree, as your anticipated goal, determines your current status as being-a-student. Your current being consists in moving towards the absent-but-anticipated degree.

Heidegger describes the still-absent goal of any such movement as being "hidden" (i.e. not present). But to the extent that it is anticipated, the "hidden" goal, while remaining absent, also becomes quasi-present by endowing the anticipating entity with its current being as "moving towards . . ." Movement is a matter of presence-and-absence: the absent, *qua* anticipated, both (a) remains absent by being still unattained and (b) becomes finitely present by giving the anticipating entity its *raison d'être*, "dispensing" to the entity its being. In short, insofar as an entity is in movement, anticipation of an absence is what "gives" that entity its current presence: *Es gibt Sein.*

This structure of movement is also the structure of disclosure. (1) In the first place, the movement of absence-dispensing-presence is the very structure of Dasein's temporality. Dasein exists by anticipating its final absence; and Dasein's absent/hidden death, insofar as it is structurally anticipated in thrownness and personally anticipated in resolve, determines Dasein's present being as mortal becoming. Thus, the absent goal of temporality gives Dasein its being while itself remaining absent/hidden. (2) Moreover, since Dasein is the sole locus of the disclosure of *all* meaningful presence, Dasein's anticipation of its *own* absence is what discloses the meaningful presence of *any* entity it meets. The disclosure of the being/significance of whatever-is happens only in conjunction with Dasein's mortal becoming. In other words, disclosure and Dasein are but a single movement that issues in being/ significance.

Heidegger gives this single movement of disclosure the name "*Ereignis.*" In German *Ereignis* literally means "event." However, by playing on etymologies Heidegger interprets *Ereignis* as the process of our being ineluctably "pulled" or "thrown" or "appropriated" into openness. This movement of being-opened-up-by-one's-finitude, in such a way that a world of being/significance is engendered and sustained, is what Heidegger means by *Ereignis*, "appropriation." It is one more name for Heidegger's focal topic, namely, that which makes being/significance occur within human experience.

Although the term *Ereignis* emerges in Heidegger's work only in the 1930s, it is related to what he had earlier called thrownness. "Thrown-open-ness" and "being appropriated into openness" are different names for the same ontological fact, i.e. that human being is always already thrust into openness and claimed by its ultimate possibility in such a way that a world of significance is opened up. The structural priority of one's appropriation-by-absence *over* one's projection-of-significance – i.e. the fact that the former makes possible the latter – is what Heidegger calls "the Turn" (*die Kehre*). During the 1930s Heidegger's growing understanding of this structural Turn at the heart of *Ereignis* led him to recast the form and style of his philosophy (without changing its central problematic) in order to emphasize the priority of appropriation-by-absence over projection-of-meaningful-presence. However, this shift in form and style that occurred after 1936 is not to be equated with the Turn. The shift in style took place within Heidegger's writing and teaching, whereas the Turn constitutes the abiding structure of *Ereignis*.

Overcoming metaphysics

Because finitude – the source of the disclosure of being/significance – is intrinsically absent and hidden, it is easily overlooked and forgotten. When that happens, one remains focused on entities and their being/significance, while ignoring the disclosive movement – one's appropriation into openness – which dispenses that being/significance. This focus on the meaningful presence of entities to the exclusion of the absence that dispenses it is what Heidegger calls "metaphysics." It occurs both in one's personal life and in thematic philosophy. In both cases, metaphysics is characterized not by the "forgetting of *being*" (which is virtually impossible, in any case) but by the forgetting of the *disclosure* of being, which occurs because of human finitude.

The goal of Heidegger's philosophy was to overcome the forgotten-ness of disclosure-due-to-finitude by recovering the sense of finitude both in one's personal life and in thematic philosophy. (1) Overcoming the *personal* forgetting of one's finitude is called "resolve" or "resolute-ness," and it issues in "authenticity." (2) The recuperation of the finitude-as-the-source-of-disclosure in *thematic philosophy* is called the "overcoming of metaphysics" (or in an earlier formulation, the "destruc-tion" of metaphysics), and it leads to what Heidegger called a "new beginning."

(1) *In the personal realm.* The act of personally recuperating one's essence as finite is called "resolve," and it issues in "authenticity," being one's true self. Although we are always in the process of mortal becom-ing, we are usually so caught up in the meaningful presence of the enti-ties which we encounter that we forget the finitude and mortality that makes such encounters possible. Heidegger calls this condition "fallen-ness." Nevertheless, in special "basic moods" (such as dread and wonder) we can rediscover our relation to the finitude/lack that dispenses being, the absence that allows for meaningful presence.

In these basic moods we directly experience not just things, or the significance of things, or even the world that underlies such significance. Rather, we experience the very *finitude* that opens up human being, forms a world, and thereby issues in the disclosure of the being/signif-icance of things within human understanding. In contrast to things, the being of things, and even the world that contextualizes such signifi-cance, Heidegger calls this finitude/absence the "nothing." To experi-ence this nothing, he says, is to "hear the call of conscience"; that is, to become aware of one's radically mortal finitude. To flee that call is to live as an inauthentic or fallen self. Alternately, to heed that call by choosing to embrace one's mortal becoming means to overcome one's oblivion of the source of all disclosure of significance and thus to "overcome metaphysics" in one's everyday life.

(2) *In thematic philosophy.* The forgetting of finitude as the source of the disclosure of all significance also characterizes thematic philosophy. Heidegger reads the history of Western metaphysics as a series of epochs in which philosophers elaborated different interpretations of the being of entities – for example, being as *idea* in PLATO, as *energeia* in Aristotle, right down to being as eternal recurrence of the same in NIETZSCHE. Each epoch of metaphysics is characterized by its understanding of the presence of entities and its oblivion of the absence/finitude that makes possible (or "dispenses") that presence. For Heidegger, the last and climactic phase in this "history of being" is our own epoch of technology and nihilism.

Today, Heidegger claims, finitude as the source of disclosure is all but obliterated by the widespread conviction that the significance of entities consists in their universal availability for exploitation. Entities are understood to be, in principle, endlessly knowable by an ideally omniscient reason and totally dominable by a would-be omnipotent will. Here the meaningful presence of entities takes on its most extreme form: it means the unreserved presence and total submission of entities to human manipulation. Heidegger calls this state of affairs "nihilism" because the absence that dispenses meaningful presence – including today's presence-for-exploitation – now counts for nothing (*nihil*).

Nevertheless, finitude as the source of disclosure is never completely obliterated, even when it is overlooked and forgotten. Under metaphysics, Heidegger argues, the hidden giving of being still goes on giving, although in a doubly concealed way: the finite source of disclosure is both intrinsically hidden *and* forgotten. Heidegger thought that a penumbral awareness of this hidden giving could still be found in the classical texts of the great thinkers from the pre-Socratics to Nietzsche. In interpreting those texts, Heidegger attempted to retrieve and rearticulate the barely expressed "unsaid" – that absence is the hidden source of meaningful presence – which lurks within the "said," the philosopher's text.

This is especially true of pre-Socratic philosophers such as Anaximander, Parmenides, and Heraclitus. Heidegger considers them to have been *pre*-metaphysical thinkers insofar as their fragments evidence an inchoate awareness of the hidden source of the occurrence of disclosure, under such titles as *aletheia*, *physis*, and *logos*. He characterizes these archaic Greek thinkers as a "first beginning" of non-metaphysical thought, and he hoped that his own work would prepare for a "second beginning" of non-metaphysical thought. This new beginning would consist in one's turning back to and "entering" *Ereignis* by recollecting the hidden source of disclosure within one's own Dasein. However, while recollection entails overcoming the *forgetting* of disclosure, it does not undo the intrinsic *hiddenness* of finitude. The point, rather, is to allow the hidden source of disclosure both to remain hidden and, as hidden, to empower the world of significance. The way to do that is to accede to one's appropriation by absence.

Heidegger was convinced that the overcoming of metaphysics was less a matter of writing out a new theory of being (a "fundamental ontology" as he once called it) than of personally recuperating one's radical finitude. For a while he apparently thought that not just individuals but also masses of people might achieve authenticity, virtually at a national level. At one point he even expressed the sentiment that the Germans alone, in their essential relation to disclosure, had a mandate to save Western civilization from nihilism.

Finally, however, Heidegger distanced himself from such empty hopes. He came to see the end of metaphysics not as a future achievement of large groups of people, let alone of one race or nation. Rather, metaphysics comes to an end only for individuals – one at a time and without apparent relation to each other – as each one, in splendid isolation, resolutely achieves the "entrance into *Ereignis.*" For all the broad historical sweep of his philosophy, for all the boldness of its call for the "destruction of metaphysics," Heidegger's thought ends where it began, with a call to the lone individual to achieve his or her radical and solitary authenticity: "*Werde wesentlich!*" (GA 56/57, p. 5) – "Become your essence."

Bibliography

Writings

Gesamtausgabe (Frankfurt am Main: Vittorio Klostermann, 1975–). [The collected edition of Heidegger's books and lecture courses. Over forty volumes have been published so far, many of which have been translated into English. Abbreviated as "GA."]

Being and Time, trans. J. Macquarrie and E. Robinson (New York: Harper Row, 1962); another translation by J. Stambaugh (Albany: State University of New York Press, 1996). [Heidegger's most famous work, *Sein und Zeit*, originally published in 1927; GA 2.]

Poetry, Language, Thought, trans. A. Hofstadter (New York: Harper Row, 1971). [Collected essays, including "Origin of the Work of Art."]

On the Way to Language, trans. P. D. Hertz and J. Stambaugh (New York: Harper Row, 1971). [Collected essays on language, all dating from the 1950s; GA 12.]

Early Greek Thinking, ed. D. F. Krell and F. A. Capuzzi (New York: Harper & Row, 1975.) [Essays on the pre-Socratics.]

The Question Concerning Technology and Other Essays, ed. W. Lovitt (New York: Harper Row, 1977).

Nietzsche, four volumes, trans. D. F. Krell and F. Capuzzi, (New York: Harper Row, 1979, 1987). [Lecture courses and notes from 1936 to 1946.]

The Basic Problems of Phenomenology, trans. A. Hofstadter, (Bloomington: Indiana University Press, 1982). [Lecture course, summer, 1927; GA 24.]

The Metaphysical Foundations of Logic, trans. M. Heim (Bloomington: Indiana University Press, 1984). [Lecture course, summer, 1928; GA 26.]

History of the Concept of Time: Prolegomena, trans. T. Kisiel (Bloomington: Indiana University Press, 1985). [Lecture course, summer, 1925; GA 20.]

Kant and the Problem of Metaphysics, trans. R. Taft (Bloomington: Indiana University Press, 1990). [Originally published in 1929; GA 3.]

Parmenides, trans. André Schuwer and Richard Rojcewicz (Bloomington: Indiana University Press, 1992). [Lecture course, 1942–3; GA 54.]

Basic Writings, rev. edn, ed. D. F. Krell (San Francisco: Harper, 1993). [Collected essays. Largely but not entirely overlaps with *Pathmarks*, below.]

Basic Questions of Philosophy: Selected "Problems" of "Logic", trans. R. Rojcewicz and A. Schuwer (Bloomington: Indiana University Press, 1994). [Lecture course, winter 1937–8; GA 45.]

The Fundamental Concepts of Metaphysics: World, Finitude, Solitude, trans. W. McNeill and N. Walker (Bloomington: Indiana University Press, 1995). [Lecture course, winter, 1929–30; GA 29/30.]

Aristotle's Metaphysics θ 1–3, trans. Walter Brogan and Peter Warnek (Bloomington: Indiana University Press, 1995). [Lecture course, summer 1931; GA 33.]

Hölderlin's Hymn "The Ister", trans. William McNeill and Julia Davis (Bloomington: Indiana University Press, 1996). [Lecture course, summer 1942; GA 53.]

Plato's Sophist, trans. Richard Rojcewicz and André Schuwer (Bloomington: Indiana University Press, 1997). [Lecture course, 1924–5; GA 19.]

Pathmarks, ed. W. McNeill (New York: Cambridge University Press, 1998.). [A collection of key essays including "What Is Metaphysics?" "On the Essence of Truth," "Plato's Doctrine of Truth," and "Letter on Humanism"; GA 9.]

Ontology: The Hermeneutics of Facticity, trans. John van Buren (Bloomington: Indiana University Press, 1999). [Lecture course, summer 1923; GA 63.]

Contributions to Philosophy: From Enowning, trans. Parvis Emad and Kenneth Maly (Bloomington: Indiana University Press, 1999). [Translation of Heidegger's posthumously published *Beiträge zur Philosophie: Vom Ereignis*, which dates from 1936–8; GA 65.]

Towards the Definition of Philosophy: 1. The Idea of Philosophy and the Problem of Worldview; 2. Phenomenology and Transcendental Philosophy of Value; with a transcript of the lecture course "On the Nature of the University and Academic Study", trans. Ted Sadler (New Brunswick, NJ: Athlone Press, 2000). [Lecture course, War Emergency Semester, 1919; GA 56/57.]

Introduction to Metaphysics, trans. R. Polt and G. Fried (New Haven, CT, and London: Yale University Press, 2000). [Lecture course, summer, 1935; GA 40.]

Elucidations of Hölderlin's Poetry, trans. Keith Hoeller (Amherst, MA: Humanity Books, 2000). [Heidegger's essays on Hölderlin, first published in 1944 and in an expanded second edition in 1951; GA 4.]

Zollikon Seminars: Protocols – Conversations – Letters, ed. Medard Boss, trans. Franz Mayr and Richard Askay (Evanston, IL: Northwestern University Press, 2001). [Translation of the 1987 German work, which includes texts of Heidegger's occasional seminars from 1959 to 1969 in Zurich and the nearby suburb of Zollikon, as well as records of Heidegger's conversations with psychiatrist Medard Boss, 1961 to 1972, and excerpts from Heidegger's letters to Boss, 1947 to 1971.]

Phenomenological Interpretations of Aristotle: Initiations into Phenomenological Research, trans. Richard Rojcewicz (Bloomington: Indiana University Press, 2001). [Lecture course, 1921–2; GA 61.]

Further reading

Richardson, W. J.: *Heidegger: Through Phenomenology to Thought* (The Hague: Martinus Nijhoff, 1963). [The best study of Heidegger's work in any language.]

Kisiel, Theodore, *The Genesis of Heidegger's Being and Time* (Berkeley: University of California Press, 1993). [The classic account of Heidegger's philosophical development from 1915 to early 1926.]

Sass, H. M.: *Martin Heidegger: Bibliography and Glossary* (Bowling Green, OH: Philosophy Documentation Center, 1982).

14

Hobbes

David Gauthier

Thomas Hobbes (1588–1679 CE) was born prematurely when his mother's labour was brought on by news of the approaching Spanish armada. His uncle financed his education, which culminated in Oxford at Magdalen Hall (a predecessor of Hertford College). After taking the BA degree, he became tutor to the son of William Cavendish, Earl of Devonshire, gaining access to one of England's finest private libraries, and enjoying the opportunity of accompanying his pupil to the Continent. Though his studies focused on the Classics, his growing concern with politics may be discerned in his decision to translate Thucydides' *History of the Peloponnesian War* into English.

In 1628 he was obliged to leave the Cavendish family, becoming tutor to the son of Sir Gervase Clinton. This led to his second Continental tour, during which he fell in love with geometry, taking Euclid's demonstrations to be a model for scientific and political thought.

Rejoining the Cavendish household, Hobbes again visited the Continent in the company of his former pupil's son, making the acquaintance of such leading thinkers as DESCARTES, Gassendi, and Galileo. On returning to England in 1637 he began to develop his own system of thought, planning three works proceeding from *body* to *man* and then to the *citizen*. However, responding to increasingly troubled political conditions, he deferred his enquiry into body, and after circulating his first thoughts on human nature and the state in 1640 as *The Elements of Law*, published the third part of his projected system, *De Cive* (*On the Citizen*), in 1642.

By then Hobbes was in Paris, judging England unsafe for a defender of absolute monarchy. He resumed his work on natural philosophy, giving special attention to the study of optics, which fascinated him. In 1646 he became mathematical tutor to the king's son, the future Charles II, then a fugitive in France. But as the civil war in England turned decisively against the monarchy, Hobbes distanced himself from his royalist connections, while turning his scholarly attention to writing *Leviathan,* the definitive statement of his moral, political, and religious thought. In 1651, the year of its publication, he returned home, swearing allegiance to the new Commonwealth government under Cromwell.

His study of natural philosophy, *De Corpore* (*On Body*), appeared in 1655, followed by the brief *De Homine* (*On Man*) in 1658, divided between optics and a sketch of human nature which added little to the account in *Leviathan.* He became embroiled in two major controversies – on the compatibility of liberty and necessity, which he defended against Bishop Bramhall, and on the possibility of squaring the circle, which he defended against the devastating criticisms of John Wallis.

His last works, published posthumously, were the unfinished *Dialogue between a Philosopher and a Student of the Common Laws of England,* developing his quite original view of law, and *Behemoth,* a history of the civil wars focusing on the question of who, at any given time, held sovereign power. In his later years he returned to the Classics, translating Homer's *Iliad* and *Odyssey* into English verse. He continued his connection with the Cavendish family, dying at their Hardwick estate.

Hobbes's reputation has always rested primarily on his political doctrines. But these are only part of a comprehensive account of scientific method, human nature, morals, sovereignty, law, and religion, whose basic tenets are the following. (Except where otherwise noted, quotations are from *Leviathan.*)

1   Politics, like geometry, is a demonstrable science, and geometry and politics are the only demonstrable sciences, because they deal with what human beings construct.
2   All beings are material bodies, and all life is bodily motion.
3   Each living being, and in particular each human being, desires primarily its own "conservation," i.e. to sustain its life, and secondarily its own "delectation," i.e. to live well.
4   Each human being calls the objects of its desires "good," and of its aversions "evil."
5   Human beings are naturally equal, since the weakest can kill the strongest.
6   Human beings naturally become enemies because: (a) sometimes they desire the same objects ("competition"); (b) anticipating the possibility of desiring the same objects they seek to pre-empt one another ("diffidence"); (c) they demand to be valued by others at the rate they set on themselves ("glory").
7   The natural condition of human beings is therefore one of continual war, "of every man against every man"; in this war nothing is

either just or unjust, force and fraud are the principal virtues, and each person's life is "solitary, poor, nasty, brutish, and short."

8 In this condition of war, each has the right of nature to do whatsoever he judges best conducive to maintaining his own life, even if this extends to taking the life of another person; the unlimited exercise of this right ensures the continuation of war, with its consequent insecurity.

9 Thus it is a law of nature, or command of reason, that each person seek peace, and a second law that to obtain peace, each give up some of the right of nature, provided others do the same.

10 Two (or more) persons mutually and reciprocally give up some of their right by making a covenant among themselves, and it is a third law of nature that human beings keep their covenants, which is the basis of justice.

11 A just person is one whose will is determined by the justice, and not by the apparent benefit, of his or her actions.

12 But since in the natural condition of humankind no one can trust his fellows actually to be just, human beings must covenant to create a commonwealth by instituting a common power able to enforce their covenants and so to ensure peace and security.

13 This common power is the sovereign, whom Hobbes usually assumes to be an individual man but who could be a woman or an assembly of persons, and whose actions must be authorized by covenant of all of his subjects, so that they acknowledge all his acts as their own.

14 In authorizing the sovereign's actions, the subjects also oblige themselves to obey him in whatever ways are necessary to ensure their peace and security.

15 Law is a command addressed to someone obligated to obey the commander, and so the commands of the sovereign are laws to his subjects.

16 All human beings may know that there is a god, or first cause of the universe, who, being omnipotent, has the natural right to rule over his creation.

17 But no one has natural knowledge of what god commands, so that, although it is better to obey god than man, each person must accept the sovereign's interpretation of god's word.

Hobbes's peculiar methodology is summarized in the first tenet. In demonstration, we reason from definitions that specify how we construct the defined objects (such as the circle, in geometry, or the sovereign, in politics), to the properties of these objects that follow from their construction. Hobbes's account of definitions has been much disputed. Sometimes Hobbes seems to treat them as conventions for the use of words, sometimes as self-evident truths. But if definitions express how objects are constructed, they are neither conventions nor self-evident; they state what we are able to do. His view of science has also been disputed. Does he seek a single deductive system beginning with body and ending with the citizen? No, because we do not construct natural bodies, and so could not demonstrate their properties as we demonstrate the properties of geometrical and political bodies.

The second tenet shows that Hobbes is a materialist; even god is corporeal. He is also a mechanist, comparing living beings to automata or self-moving engines – the heart is a spring, the joints are wheels. These natural engines are motivated to maintain their vital motions. He is often interpreted as treating all motivation as aimed at self-preservation, and so as egoistic, which would seem to rule out moral motivation. But Gert (1967) has argued that Hobbes thinks a person may be motivated by benevolence or by justice, and others, such as Hampton (1986) and Kavka (1986), treat him as considering human motivation to be predominantly, but not exclusively, egoistic.

Hobbes's account of "good" and "evil" shows that he is a subjectivist about value. He insists that "these words . . . are ever used with relation to the person that useth them, there being nothing simply or absolutely so," although in the commonwealth, the sovereign is authorized to decide what is good and evil. But although persons disagree about values, Hobbes insists that "all men agree on this, that peace is good, and therefore also the way or means of peace . . . are good." And they agree because individual judgments of good and evil lead human beings to the natural condition of war, which denies them the security and satisfaction they seek. Hobbes's account of the causes of natural conflict, emphasizing the natural distrust ("diffidence") human beings have of each other, and the reasonableness, given this distrust, of "anticipation" – seeking to master others before they master you – is a classic statement of the logic of an arms race, in which each step a person takes toward his or her own security is a greater step toward the insecurity of others. Hobbes seems to represent this behaviour as fully rational, despite its disastrous outcome, but recent critics such as Hampton have insisted that only a measure of short-sightedness can explain how otherwise rational persons would end up in a state of war. Clearly Hobbes raises, even if he does not settle, fundamental questions about the grounds of human conflict.

Hobbes denies that morality is present in the natural condition of war. The one normative idea that he allows is the "right of nature," or liberty each person has to do what he or she thinks best for preservation. We may call this a right to life, but it does not correspond to what we would mean by such a right. For we treat a person's right to life as making a claim on others, corresponding to a duty on their part at least to allow that person to live. But for Hobbes a natural right makes no claim on others; my natural right licenses me to do whatever I can to preserve myself, but leaves you free to take my life, if you can and if you believe you would thereby be more secure.

The laws of nature are rational commands, requiring each person to do what is necessary for his or her preservation – and so to seek peace. Peace requires that each give up some part of his or her natural right – thus we increase our security and well-being by mutually giving up the right to kill one another. Hobbes also speaks of the laws of nature as commands of god, and some scholars, such as Warrender (1957) and Martinich (1992), have argued that they actually oblige persons to obedience only as divine commands. Others, including Gauthier (1969), have argued that for Hobbes, to be under obligation to perform some action is merely to lack the right to omit it, so that in mutually giving up some part of our right of nature, as we are rationally required to do, we create obligations for ourselves, without introducing God as the source of obligation.

The third law of nature, which commands justice or the keeping of covenants, is challenged by the "Foole," who insists that since reason "dictateth to every man his own good," it would not be against reason to break one's covenants "when it conduced to one's benefit." Hobbes replies that, although one may, contrary to expectation, benefit from breaking one's covenant, yet that does not make it reasonable. And, he says, "he which declares he thinks it reason to deceive those that help him" by breaking his covenant when they have already performed, "cannot be received into any society that unite themselves for peace and defence but by the error of them that receive him." In other words, a person who, like the "Foole," denies that he always has reason to be just, is unfit to be member of society, and so must expect to be left in the insecurity of the natural condition of war. Only someone motivated by justice, and not simply by apparent benefit, is truly fit for society. To be just is advantageous, because it makes one fit for society, but in acting justly one does not seek one's advantage. In this response to the "Foole," Hobbes offers an account of how justice and advantage or self-interest are related, which is arguably his most significant contribution to moral theory.

But Hobbes never suggests that human beings are sufficiently rational to learn this lesson without some force to keep them from temptation. "Covenants, without the Sword, are but Words." And so he turns to political theory. All must covenant to confer their rights on some one person or group, who will thereby have the power to compel them to adhere to the ways of peace. This person, the sovereign, must have absolute power, because any attempt to limit him would be both disadvantageous and unenforceable. He may not be opposed by his subjects, or accused of any injustice, because they acknowledge all his acts as their own. The costs of being subject to an absolute sovereign, although real, are small in comparison with the costs of either anarchy, in which sovereign power is absent, or civil war, in which sovereign power is disputed. This part of Hobbes's doctrine has won few adherents. Many would agree that coercive power is needed to maintain peace and order among human beings, but few would allow that such power need, or should, or perhaps even could, be absolute. Perhaps Hobbes's reaction to the instability of his time clouded his judgement.

Although his theory focuses on instituting a sovereign by agreement, Hobbes allows that a sovereign may also arise by conquest, when each vanquished person separately covenants with the victor, offering submission in return for preservation. This account is not altogether consistent with Hobbes's usual insistence that the sovereign is not a party to the covenant instituting him, and so cannot be accused of violating it, but in fact the victor's covenant contains no commitment which he might violate. The vanquished promises obedience so long as he or she is spared, "which obliges not the victor longer than in his own discretion he shall think fit." Hobbes then represents both the relation between servants and their master, and the relation between children and their parents, on the model of the relation between vanquished and victor – a view unlikely to commend itself to believers in "family values."

Hobbes is often considered a forerunner of legal positivism – the view that law is a normatively self-contained system so that the validity of a law is quite independent of its morality. But in treating law as the command, not "of any man to any man, but only of him whose command is addressed to one formerly obliged to obey him," Hobbes clearly departs from positivism. The validity of a law depends on a prior relation of obligation, itself moral rather than legal, between the person subject to the law and its issuer. But Hobbes does not agree with the defenders of natural law who relate legal validity to the moral content of an alleged law, and not merely to the moral authority of its source. Whatever the sovereign commands is law to his subjects.

Hobbes insists that "love of the knowledge of causes" leads a person "of necessity . . . to this thought at last: that there is some cause, whereof there is no former cause, but is eternal, which is it men call God."

Nevertheless, in his own day he was frequently denounced as an atheist, and Curley (1992), among recent scholars, clearly entertains this possibility. There can be no doubt that Hobbes's religious views were unorthodox, and that in founding political authority on agreement among the subjects rather than on the will of God he ran strongly counter to the royalist arguments of his day. He denies that we can have natural knowledge of God's will, and in replying to Bishop Bramhall, explicitly asserts that the laws of nature are the laws of God only when delivered in the word of God, or Scripture, and are not laws, but only "theorems, tending to peace," when known through natural reason. And Scripture is law only as the sovereign's command. So although Hobbes insists that we are subject to God's law, it would seem that this is so only insofar as subjection is commanded by our earthly sovereign. This creates a real difficulty, since Hobbes also wants to insist that the sovereign is bound by God's law – but who then commands him to be subject to it? But problems about religion should not obscure Hobbes's great achievement, in showing how both morality and political society may be understood as rational remedies for the costly conflicts of natural interaction.

Bibliography

Writings

Leviathan (London, 1651), ed. C. B. Macpherson (Harmondsworth: Penguin, 1968); or E. Curley (Indianapolis: Hackett, 1994). [Macpherson retains the original spelling and punctuation; Curley includes translated passages from the Latin version of 1668, where these vary significantly from the original English.]

Man and Citizen, ed. B. Gert (Indianapolis: Hackett, 1991), containing English translations of *De Cive* (1642), and of the chapters from *De Homine* (1658) on human nature.

Further reading

Brown, Keith C. (ed.): *Hobbes Studies* (Oxford: Basil Blackwell, 1965). [A collection of important essays.]

Curley, Edwin: "'I Durst Not Write So Boldly' or, How to read Hobbes' theological–political treatise." In D. Bostrenghi (ed.), *Hobbes e Spinoza, Scienza e politica* [*Hobbes and Spinoza, Science and Politics*] (Naples: Bibliopolis, 1992), pp. 497–593.

Gauthier, David: *The Logic of Leviathan* (Oxford: Clarendon Press, 1969).

Gert, Bernard: "Hobbes and psychological egoism," *Journal of the History of Ideas*, 28 (1967), 503–20.

Hampton, Jean: *Hobbes and the Social Contract Tradition* (Cambridge: Cambridge University Press, 1986).

Kavka, Gregory: *Hobbesian Moral and Political Theory* (Princeton, NJ: Princeton University Press, 1986).

Macpherson, C. B.: *The Political Theory of Possessive Individualism: Hobbes to Locke* (Oxford: Clarendon Press, 1962).

Martinich, A. P.: *The Two Gods of Leviathan* (New York: Cambridge University Press, 1992).

Oakeshott, Michael: "The moral life in the writings of Thomas Hobbes." In *Rationalism in Politics* (London: Methuen, 1962), pp. 248–300.

Peters, Richard: *Hobbes* (Harmondsworth: Penguin, 1956).

Warrender, Howard: *The Political Philosophy of Hobbes* (Oxford: Clarendon Press, 1957).

Watkins, J. W. N.: *Hobbes's System of Ideas* (London: Hutchinson, 1965).

15

Hume

James M. Humber

The particulars of Hume's life (1711–76 CE) are fairly well known, and almost every book-length commentary on Hume's works contains a detailed biography. In briefest outline, the facts are as follows.

David Hume was born in Edinburgh, Scotland, on April 26, 1711. His father, a lawyer and member of the landed gentry, died when Hume was only two. Hume's mother never remarried and appears to have devoted herself to raising David, together with his brother and sister. When Hume was 12 he entered Edinburgh University. (In the eighteenth century it was not uncommon to enter the university at this early age.) After two or three years Hume left the university to begin a period of private study. From 1729 to 1734 he suffered the effects of what today might be called a nervous breakdown. To ameliorate the effects of the disease Hume quit his studies, moved to England and became a clerk to a sugar merchant. The disease was cured, but Hume was fired after four months' employment.

In 1734 Hume moved to France and wrote what is arguably the greatest of his philosophical works, *A Treatise of Human Nature*. The book was not well received, and the only complimentary critique was written by Hume himself, albeit anonymously, in a pamphlet entitled *The Abstract*. After publishing the *Treatise* Hume returned to "Ninewells," his family's country estate in Scotland. While here Hume was denied a professorship at the University of Edinburgh. Powerful members of the Scottish clergy opposed Hume's appointment, arguing that his philosophical views were dangerous to both morality and religion. This was only the beginning of a series of religious attacks that dogged Hume until his death.

From 1745 to the mid-1750s Hume published a number of important philosophical works, the best known being *An Enquiry Concerning Human Understanding*, a shortened and rewritten version of Book I of the *Treatise*, and *An Enquiry Concerning the Principles of Morals*, a revised version of Book III of the *Treatise*. In 1753 Hume was denied a second professorship, this time at the University of Glasgow. In 1763 he became an assistant to England's ambassador to France, and took up residence in that country. In France Hume was considered a celebrity, and was sought out by all the "rich and famous" of Paris. Hume died on August 25, 1776, probably of colon cancer. Prior to his death he arranged for the posthumous publication of *The Dialogues Concerning Natural Religion*, his best known work on the philosophy of religion.

Hume is described by those who knew him as having been kind and moderate, and as being possessed of good humor and wit. He was sociable, loved the drawing rooms of Paris and games such as whist. He was close to his friends, "took a particular pleasure in the company of modest women," and was referred to by the French as "le bon David." At the same time he had an intense dislike of organized religion, was tremendously obese, was given to look at people with a disconcerting "vacant stare," and spoke with a thick Scottish accent. All in all he was a complex individual, and this complexity is mirrored in his philosophical writings.

Perhaps the best word to describe the intellectual climate in Great Britain in the Eighteenth Century is "empiricistic." Broadly defined, empiricism is the doctrine which holds that sense experience is the sole source of human knowledge. Philosophical empiricism expresses itself in a variety of ways; the version of empiricism which dominated British thought in the 1700s exhibited at least three central themes. First, it opposed, and often attacked, rationalism, a philosophical movement which arose on the European continent in the early 1600s (see DESCARTES, SPINOZA, and LEIBNIZ). Unlike empiricism, rationalism was impressed by the fallibility of sense perception, and as a result stressed the importance of rational intuition and demonstrative reasoning in understanding the nature of reality. Second, British empiricism was analytic or reductionistic and closely allied with what, in Hume's day, was called the "new science." The new science – whose origins can be traced from Galileo through Newton – stressed the experimental method and the need to use instruments such as the telescope and microscope to understand the world. These emphases appealed to the empiricists; for they recognized the need to experiment and felt that comprehension of any given phenomenon required not only close scrutinization, but also division of the phenomenon into its simplest parts, which then easily could be understood. Finally, in the religious sphere empiricistic principles were used by some to support "natural religion." In its most extreme form this doctrine rejected revealed theology altogether, and instead stressed the "reasonableness" of religious belief. Basically the claim was that a core of Christian beliefs could be demonstrated by use of the methods employed in the new science. At the very least, proponents said, a close examination of nature revealed an order that bespoke the existence of a divine architect/moral lawgiver.

Traditionally, Hume's philosophical works have been interpreted in two different ways. The first interpretation takes him to be a skeptic. On this view Hume is seen as embracing the principles of his empiricist predecessors, LOCKE and BERKELEY, and then showing that consistent application of these principles inevitably leads to skepticism. In opposition, the second interpretation classifies Hume as a naturalist. On this view Hume's principal purpose is not to support skepticism, but rather to show that there are forces (mostly non-rational forces) in human nature which allow us to escape the paralyzing power of skeptical doubt and so function effectively in everyday life. Passages in Hume's writings can be found to support each of these interpretations.

In addition to the empiricism, skepticism, and naturalism noted above, there are three other elements in Hume's thought which are worthy of mention. First, Hume is much more of an anti-rationalist than either Locke or Berkeley. To be sure, Hume agrees with his empiricist predecessors in holding that rationalism underestimates the role sense perception plays in our understanding of the world. However, he goes even further and argues that reason plays a much smaller role in human life than virtually everybody thinks. Indeed, on Hume's view reason is "subservient" to our emotions and should be viewed as a mere "handmaiden" to the passions. Second, Hume is very much a philosopher of common sense. This is not to say that he thinks common sense (or ordinary language, which expresses our common-sense beliefs) provides answers to philosophical problems. Rather, he is classified as a common-sense philosopher because he holds that philosophical analysis must either accord with common-sense beliefs or be able to explain why its conclusions are at odds with those beliefs. As Hume puts it, "philosophical decisions are nothing but the reflections of common life, methodized and corrected" (*Enquiry Concerning Human Understanding*, p. 162). Finally, Hume is not merely opposed to revealed theology; he also uses the principles of empiricism to launch repeated attacks upon natural religion. These attacks are intended to show that empiricism and the new science provide no support for the tenets of organized religion. On the other hand, it is not clear whether Hume thinks it is unreasonable to believe in God. He explicitly denies being an atheist. However, if he does believe that reason supports belief in a Supreme Being it seems clear that he does not think it supports belief in the all-good, allwise, omnipotent God of Christianity; for he intimates that the whole of natural theology can be reduced to one "ambiguous and undefined" proposition, namely "that the cause or causes of order in the universe probably bear some remote analogy to human intelligence" (*Dialogues*, p. 227).

We have enumerated the principal themes in Hume's thought. What remains is to see how these themes emerge in Hume's discussions of various philosophical issues. We shall examine four such issues; in each case Hume's treatment of the topic is considered seminal.

Causation and the problem of induction

Hume distinguishes all contents of consciousness into two broad classes and then uses this distinction to aid his analysis of the causal relationship. The first group of conscious contents he calls "impressions." Impressions are strong, vivid thoughts; they are "original" in the sense that they are not copied from any antecedent mental acts. Examples of impressions are things such as seeing a tree, tasting an orange, feeling a headache, hating someone. The second sort of conscious contents Hume calls "ideas." These are copied from impressions (or parts of impressions), and as such are less forceful and vivid than their originals. For example, if you remember being angry you have an idea, rather than an impression, of anger. Again, if you use your imagination to form the mental image of a purple cow, that image is an idea and not an impression.

Hume tells us that the human mind must first have impressions before it can form ideas. For instance, a person who has never seen anything purple could not create the image of purple in his or her mind and so could not imagine a purple cow. On the other hand, one who has had impressions of, say, a brown cow and a purple flower could use elements in those impressions to create the imagined idea of a purple cow. Finally, Hume also claims that ideas serve as the meanings for terms in our language, e.g. the idea of a purple cow is the meaning of "purple cow."

Sometimes we use terms whose meanings are unclear; when this happens Hume tells us that we can clarify the ideas which serve as those terms' meanings by identifying the impressions from which the ideas are derived. Using this method Hume soon discovers that some philosophical terms have no meaning at all. For example, some philosophers tell us that the term "material substance" refers to an underlying "stuff" in which physical properties such as color, weight and shape "inhere" or "subsist." However, when we have an impression of any physical object we only perceive the properties of the object and have no impression at all of an underlying "stuff" that supports those properties. Without an impression of an underlying substratum for physical properties we can have no idea of what that support is, and "material substance" turns out to be meaningless.

The discovery that certain esoteric philosophical terms such as "material substance" are meaningless does not bother Hume; for these terms are only used by a few individuals (philosophers) who often claim to be more knowledgable than they are. On the other hand, things are quite different when Hume attempts to clarify the meanings of terms in ordinary language and finds that they appear to lack meaning. For instance, Hume believes that whenever people say "*x* causes *y*," what they mean to assert is "*x* causally *necessitates y*," or "given *x*, *y must* occur." However, when Hume attempts to find the impression that gives rise to the idea of causal necessity he becomes frustrated. We all believe, for example, that fire causes (necessitates) heat. But when we examine any fire all we find is that fire and heat occur together; we see no bond, link, or tie connecting the two events so that we can be assured that wherever one exists the other also must be. In short, we have no impression of any necessary connection linking fire (the cause) to its effect (heat), and so no idea of any such connection. If this is so, though, it appears that we cannot know the expression "fire causally necessitates heat" is true, for we do not know what "causally necessitates" means. Moreover, Hume believes that what is true of fire and heat is true of all instances of cause and effect conjunctions; in no case do we have an idea of a necessary connection linking cause to effect. And if this is so, we cannot be sure that *any* assertion of the form "*x* causally necessitates *y*" is true.

Hume's insistence that we are aware of no necessary connections linking causes to effects gives rise to another problem. Whenever we make inferences beyond what we remember and what is given to our present experience we make use of what is called inductive reasoning. Inductive inferences assume that the future will be like the past. For example, when we tell a child never to put his or her hand in a fire we assume that future fires will be hot, just as all past fires have been. We could justify both the assumption that the future will be like the past and the inductive inferences that rest upon this assumption if we knew there were necessary connections between causes and effects that made it impossible for these events to be separated. However, Hume believes we have no such knowledge. Now if this is true – if we are not aware of anything in causes that necessitates their effects – we cannot know that the future will be like the past and our use of induction would seem to be without rational justification. This problem – the problem of justifying inductive inferences – is known as the problem of induction; it is directly traceable to Hume.

Hume's philosophical conclusions concerning causation are clearly at odds with common sense; for ordinarily we assume that we are not speaking nonsense when we say that causes necessitate their effects, and we believe that induction is a justified inference procedure. At the same time, Hume is a common-sense philosopher; thus he finds the opposition between common sense and philosophical analysis problematic and he feels the need to explain how such an opposition could arise. Ultimately, Hume's explanation is psychological. Although we never perceive any real connections between causes and effects, what we do see, Hume says, are repeated cause–effect conjunctions, e.g. experience shows that fire and heat are *constantly conjoined*. Furthermore, repeated perceptions of causal conjunctions produce a habit in our mind such that whenever we think of one element in a conjunction we are determined by habit to think of the other, e.g. when we think of a fire we automatically think of heat. Mental habits of this sort link our thoughts of various objects and events. (Specifically, they link the ideas of those objects and events that we believe are causally related.) For Hume these habits also serve as the impressions which give rise to our idea of causal necessity. On Hume's view, then, although we do not know that any event in the world is *really* linked to another, we believe that various events are inseparably bonded because mental habits have connected the *thoughts* of those events in our minds. Moreover, given our belief in causal necessity, we are naturally predisposed to use induction and to think that it is a justified inference procedure.

Hume's psychological explanation for our belief in causal necessity has been subjected to numerous attacks and it seems fair to say that no contemporary philosopher accepts the theory. On the other hand, Hume's claim that we have no knowledge of causal necessity is still taken seriously, and the problem of induction continues to stir debate. These are no small legacies, and if they were Hume's only contributions to the philosophical literature they would assure him a place of importance in the history of philosophy.

Personal identity

Hume's analysis of personal identity parallels his analysis of causality in a number of ways. First, just as Hume thinks that it is commonsensical to believe in causal necessity, so too he thinks that common sense leads each of us to believe that we are single, unitary beings (i.e. persons or selves) who maintain personal identity over time. Second, as with causality, when Hume seeks to find an impression that could serve as the basis for an idea of a self that remains essentially unchanged throughout life, he fails. Using introspection and looking "inward," Hume discovers only a stream of successive thoughts or perceptions; e.g. he could be aware of seeing a piece of cake at time t, wanting the cake at t_1, tasting the cake at t_2, etc. When Hume experiences successive thoughts of this sort he tells us that he is aware of each as distinct, different and separable from all others. Thus, introspection would seem to give Hume an impression of himself as a succession of discrete, individual perceptions rather than an impression of himself as a single, unified entity. Moreover, just as we have no impression of an underlying material substance in which physical properties subsist, so too, Hume insists, we have no impression of an unchanging, mental substance in which successive thoughts reside. Thus, Hume cannot appeal to the notion of an invariable, thinking substance to explain our belief in personal identity. In the end, then, Hume's conclusions concerning the self and personal identity, like his conclusions concerning causation, are at odds with common-sense belief.

As was the case with his analysis of the causal relationship, Hume feels the need to explain why nevertheless we believe in personal identity. And as was the case with causation, Hume's explanation is psychological. First, Hume claims that we get our idea of identity, in general, by continuously viewing an unchanging object, e.g. by staring at a picture on the wall. Next, Hume says, when we introspectively review thoughts in our mind we find that remembered ideas resemble the impressions from which they are derived and that "our impressions give rise to their correspondent ideas; and these ideas in their turn produce other impressions" (*Treatise*, p. 261). In short, Hume's claim is that our thoughts exhibit the relationships of resemblance and causation. Furthermore, when we introspect and review our successive thoughts Hume says that these relationships cause our review to proceed by a "smooth and easy transition." This "smooth and easy" action of thought is very similar to the experience we have when we continuously view an unchanging object. Given this similarity, we confuse the two mental acts. That is to say, when we review our successive thoughts we think we are perceiving a single, invariable object (i.e. a self that maintains its identity over time), when in fact we are aware of nothing more than a bundle of related perceptions. Obviously, if this analysis is correct, belief in personal identity is belief in a "fiction," albeit an explicable fiction. And this is precisely what Hume concludes.

Despite the obvious similarities between Hume's examination of the causal relationship and his analysis of personal identity there is one very significant difference. In the "Appendix" to the *Treatise* Hume reviews his explanation for our belief in the fiction of personal identity and unequivocally rejects it (*Treatise*, pp. 633–6). However, Hume is not at all clear as to why he is dissatisfied with his explanation, and Hume scholars have puzzled over this issue for centuries. At the same time, philosophers of mind continue to struggle with the problem of personal identity. In large measure, they have Hume to thank for their labors.

Miracles

While many in Hume's day were impressed by the claims of natural religion, Hume attacked the movement. Perhaps the most ingenious and widely discussed of Hume's attacks upon natural religion occurs in Section X of the *Enquiry Concerning Human Understanding*. There Hume attempts to demonstrate "that a miracle can never be proved, so as to be the foundation of a system of religion" (p. 127). Hume's argument is subtle, and subject to various interpretations. Luckily, our purposes in this chapter do not require that we examine these differences, and we shall focus our attention only on those themes in Hume's argument which provoke little by way of interpretive controversy.

The position which Hume is seeking to attack in Section X of the *Enquiry* claims that we can prove miracles exist and then use the existence of these events to establish the truth of Christianity. Hume's principal argument against this position relies upon a distinction he had earlier drawn in the Enquiry between "proofs" and "probabilities." For Hume, a proof is an argument from experience which allows for no doubt because there is no opposition in the empirical evidence. For example, we have a full proof that snow is cold because all snow that anyone has ever felt has been cold. On the other hand, we have only probable knowledge when there is some opposition in our experience. For instance, if Sue finds that she gets a headache eight out of every ten times that she drinks gin, it is only probable that Sue will get a headache when she drinks gin.

Given the distinction between proofs and probabilities, Hume then claims that a wise person proportions her or his belief to the evidence. For example, a wise person expects snow to be cold "with the last degree of assurance," and if Sue is wise she will be exactly 80 percent "assured" that drinking gin will give her a headache.

The next step in Hume's argument is to use the distinction between proofs and probabilities to weigh the evidence for and against the existence of miracles. As Hume sees things, it is human testimony that provides the support for belief in miracles. Of course, we all know that human testimony is not always true; people lie, are mistaken about their perceptions, etc. At best, then, the evidence for a miracle's occurrence can never amount to anything more than a probability. On the other hand, Hume claims that miracles, by definition, are violations of natural law. (For example, if I jump from a tall building and survive because I land in a pool of water, this is not a miracle. However, it would be a miracle if I survived because I did not fall, but rather walked on air.) Further, Hume insists, laws of nature are always supported by experience that is *totally uniform.* (We would have no "law of gravity," for instance, if all unsupported objects were not observed to fall.) Thus, whenever anyone testifies to having seen a violation of a law of nature (i.e. a miracle), the uniform experience supporting the law provides a complete proof that the testimony is false. At the same time, we have only probable support for the testimony's truth. In these circumstances a wise person will weigh the evidence on both sides of the issue, proportion his or her belief to the evidence, and refuse to believe in the miracle's occurrence. Obviously, if this analysis is correct, belief in miracles is always unjustified, and we cannot appeal to the existence of such events to prove the truth of any system of religion.

Ethics and moral judgment

Books have been written on Hume's ethics, and in this essay we can do little more than highlight certain "central themes" in Hume's moral philosophy.

First, while virtually all moral theories in Hume's day were normative, Hume's theory is empirical or descriptive. (A normative theory lays down norms for behavior; it tells people what they ought and ought not to do, regardless of their feelings on the matter. On the other hand, an empirical theory analyzes our use of moral terms, and describes how moral judgments are actually made in everyday life.)

Second, given his descriptive approach to ethics, Hume arrives at a number of conclusions that are at odds with the philosophical mainstream. For instance, in opposition to most moral theorists Hume does not believe that moral judgments are directed principally toward actions. Rather, he holds that moral judgments are concerned primarily with traits of character, and that if actions are judged morally right or wrong this is only because they are viewed as "signs" indicating the virtuous or vicious nature of a person's character.

Another area in which Hume's ethical views differ markedly from the majority concerns the role he believes reason plays in moral judgment.

Unlike most, Hume thinks reason plays a very small part in moral judgment. For Hume, reason judges either matters of fact or relations. Now to be sure, moral judgment must begin with some description of the facts and the relations between and among those facts. However, on Hume's view, a complete description of such a state of affairs would include no evaluative statements, i.e. all of the propositions describing the state of affairs would assert what "is" or "is not" the case, and none would assert that something "ought" or "ought not" to be. Now, given such a description Hume does not believe that we could logically infer any moral conclusions from it. Still, people do make moral judgments. Thus Hume concludes that some other faculty than reason must be responsible for moral judgment. In the end Hume's view is that passion serves as the basis for moral judgment, and that judgments of this sort simply report our feelings about a person's character and actions. This position is known as "moral subjectivism."

Subjectivists hold that moral assertions can accurately or inaccurately reflect our feelings; hence, assertions of this type can be true or false. Hume would seem to accept this view; however, there is another sense in which Hume is not a classical subjectivist. Most versions of subjectivism hold that moral evaluations are akin to judgments of taste. On this view moral judgments can vary from person to person, and there simply is no way, ultimately, to adjudicate disputes in moral assessment. Hume rejects this view. As Hume sees things, differences in moral judgment can arise from either of two sources. First, people can understand the facts and the relations among those facts in totally different ways, and this can give rise to different feelings (i.e. different moral judgments). For Hume, disagreements of this sort can be eliminated by reaching a proper understanding of the facts. (Thus, although Hume is a subjectivist, he nevertheless believes that reason has an important – albeit subservient – role to play in ethics. Specifically, reason "paves the way" for proper moral judgment by presenting the observer with a correct understanding of the facts and their relations.) Second, Hume believes that moral judgments can be skewed by self-interest, personal preferences and other idiosyncratic influences. Indeed, from the Humean perspective, assertions that reflect only one's personal feelings and biases are not really moral judgments at all. (For example, if self-interest alone prompts one to say "John is virtuous," Hume would deny that this is a moral judgment.) For Hume, moral judgments must be made from a "general" or "non-personal" perspective, and so reflect feelings that arise from emotional "principles" such as benevolence and sympathy, which, Hume believes, *all* humans share. Moreover, Hume believes that it is possible to overcome our personal biases and that when this happens all humans will experience the same emotive response. In the end, then, Hume believes that it is possible to reach agreement in our moral evaluations. All that is required is that evaluators: (a) have a correct understanding of the state of affairs that is being judged; and (b) "cut through" their personal feelings to get at those emotive principles that are common to all humanity.

One final point concerning Hume's moral theory warrants mention. When Hume examines those character traits to which we commonly give our approval and disapproval he concludes that they all share one of two characteristics in common, i.e. they are either useful or agreeable to oneself or others. Moreover, Hume believes this proves that what he called the "monkish virtues" – humility, celibacy, fasting, silence, solitude, and the like – are not truly virtues, for they are not "useful or agreeable." Given this view, it is not surprising that the Scottish clergy would bear Hume some animus.

The above examination of specific topics in Hume's philosophy indicates only some of the ways in which his thought has affected Western philosophy. Not mentioned, for example, is Hume's influence upon Immanuel KANT, the German philosopher credited with bringing about a change in philosophy comparable to the Copernican Revolution in science. Kant admits that he was awakened from his "dogmatic slumbers" by reading Hume's works, and without Hume it is unlikely that Kant's genius would fully have manifested itself. Also, Hume's influence on the philosophy of religion extends far beyond his analysis of miracles. Indeed, Terence Penelhum, a distinguished Hume scholar and philosopher of religion, describes Hume's *Dialogues* as "beyond any question the greatest work on philosophy of religion in the English language" (Penelhum, 1975, p. 171). Certainly, no one who has read Hume's *Dialogues* would attempt to prove the existence of a theistic God by arguing that the order in the universe requires the existence of such a divine being. Finally, Hume probably has had a greater influence upon twentieth-century British and American analytic philosophy than any other philosopher in the seventeenth and eighteenth centuries. For example, Hume's work contributed to the rise, in the 1930s, of the philosophical movements known as logical positivism and emotivism. Furthermore, Hume's influence continues to be illustrated by the *way* in which contemporary analytic philosophers practice their trade. These individuals have a mistrust of grandiose metaphysical schemes, a penchant for careful logical analysis, a desire for clarity of expression, and a refusal to disregard in their entirety the beliefs of common sense as expressed in everyday discourse. In all of this one cannot help but detect the footsteps of Hume.

Bibliography

Writings

The Philosophical Works of David Hume, four volumes; Volumes 3 and 4, *Essays Moral, Political and Literary*, ed. T. H. Green and T. H. Gross (London: Longmans, Green, 1875).

Abstract of a Treatise of Human Nature, ed. J. M. Keynes and P. Sraffa (Cambridge: Cambridge University Press, 1938).

Dialogues Concerning Natural Religion, ed. N. K. Smith (London: Thomas Nelson & Sons Ltd, 1947).

The Natural History of Religion, ed. H. E. Root (Stanford, CA: Stanford University Press, 1967).

Enquiries Concerning the Human Understanding and Concerning the Principles of Morals, ed. L. A. Selby-Bigge, rev. P. H. Nidditch (Oxford: Oxford University Press: 1975).

A Treatise of Human Nature, ed. L. A. Selby-Bigge, rev. P. H. Nidditch (Oxford: Oxford University Press, 1978).

Further reading

Ardal, P.: *Passion and Value in Hume's Treatise* (Edinburgh: Edinburgh University Press, 1966).

Capaldi, N.: *Hume's Place in Moral Philosophy* (New York: Peter Lang, 1989).

Flew, A.: *Hume's Philosophy of Belief* (London: Routledge & Kegan Paul, 1961).

Fogelin, R.: *Hume's Skepticism in the Treatise of Human Nature* (London: Routledge & Kegan Paul, 1985).

Mossner, E.: *The Life of David Hume* (Oxford: Oxford University Press, 1980).

Norton, D.: *David Hume: Common Sense Moralist, Skeptical Metaphysician* (Princeton, NJ: Princeton University Press, 1982).

Noxon, J.: *Hume's Philosophical Development* (Oxford: Oxford University Press, 1973).

Penelhum, T.: *Hume* (London: Macmillian Press, 1975).

Smith, N. K.: *The Philosophy of David Hume* (London: Macmillan Press, 1949).

16

Husserl

J. N. Mohanty

Edmund Husserl (1859–1938 CE) was born in Prosonitz, Austria, on April 8, 1859. He studied mathematics and philosophy in Leipzig, where he attended lectures by Wundt, then in Berlin, where among mathematicians Weierstrass and among philosophers Paulsen influenced him most, and finally in Vienna, where he finished his PhD in mathematics under Königsberger in 1883. For some time he worked in Berlin putting together Weierstrass's lectures on Abelian functions. During the years 1884–6, he studied with Brentano upon the recommendation of his lifelong friend Masaryk (later to be the President of Czechoslovakia). If Weierstrass imparted to him "the ethos of (my) scientific thinking," Brentano's influence made him opt for philosophy as his life's undertaking. Eventually, Brentano sent him to Halle to habilitate with his former pupil Carl Stumpf. He habilitated in 1887 with a work on the concept of number, after which he remained in Halle as *Privatdozent* up until 1901, when he got his first Professorship in Göttingen. In Halle he became a friend of Cantor, while in Göttingen he enjoyed the friendship of Hilbert. Both mathematicians influenced, in different ways, his thinking. Husserl taught in Göttingen until 1916, when he accepted a chair in Freiburg. After retirement in 1928, he continued to live in Freiburg until his death in 1938.

The books Husserl published during his lifetime are: *Philosophie der Arithmetik* (1891), *Logische Untersuchungen* (1900), *Ideen zu reinen Phänomenologie und phänomenologische Philosophie* (1913), *Formale und transzendentale Logik* (1929) and *Cartesianische Meditationen* (1931). Besides, the lectures he gave in Vienna and Prague in the 1930s were put together posthumously in a volume known as *Die Krisis der europaischen Wissenschaften und die transzendentale Phänomenologie* (1954). Some of his later writings on logic were edited by Ludwig Landgrebe in a volume entitled *Erfahrung und Urteil* (1948). However, these constitute only a fragment of the manuscripts he left behind, which, in order to be spared destruction during the Nazi era, were moved by Father van Breda, a former student, to Louvain, Belgium, where the Husserl Archive was founded by him. The Archive has now brought out more than 25 volumes of Husserliana, including the *Nachlass*, as well as new editions of earlier published books and papers.

Philosophy of mathematics

Husserl's original philosophical interest was in mathematics, especially in the concept of number. In developing a concept of number, he takes cardinals as fundamental. Since ordinals relate to series and series can be taken as ordered sets, cardinals which relate to sets are taken to be more primary. Analysis of the concept of number presupposes an analysis of the concept of multiplicity. Numbers are best regarded as determinations of an indeterminate concept of multiplicity. The concrete phenomena with which one begins are of course determinate objects. But such objects may be taken completely arbitrarily, i.e. without any constraint as to the specific nature of the objects. Any group of entities can be unified into a totality. A totality is formed by an act of collective combination. This act of combination does not result in a new content in addition to those combined. Neither is combination belongingness to one consciousness, nor does it involve a Kantian sort of synthesis of the contents combined (see KANT). Unlike other relations, the relation of combination is independent of the specific natures of the contents; nothing of this relation is to be found among the contents. Every relatum can be freely and unrestrictedly varied, the relation remaining the same.

The concept of number arises through abstraction exercised upon a concrete totality formed by collective combination. Since the determinate nature of the contents can be freely varied, interest focuses upon the totality, while the contents combined are considered merely as any content, each one as some one. "Something" can be said of any thinkable content. Without the concept of something, there can be no number concept. Thus the totality (redness, this pencil, the moon) yields, by abstraction, the set (something, something, something). The latter yields the determinate concept of three.

Husserl rejected FREGE's definition of number in terms of equivalent classes for reasons which he later concedes were not good enough. He also rejects Frege's view that number statements are about concepts, i.e. answers to the question "How many ϕs?" Contrary to Frege, Husserl held that anything whatsoever can be counted; any set of objects, however heterogeneous, can form a multiplicity. Although espousing an empiricistic theory of the genesis of number concepts, i.e. an account whereby these concepts arise out of concrete intuitions, Husserl nevertheless held that not all numbers, certainly not the very large ones, can be intuited. In the latter cases, our concepts of numbers are said to be symbolic in the sense that they are necessarily mediated by signs. Without such sign-mediated, or "inauthentic," presentations of numbers, and so without symbolic operations, arithmetic as a science would not be possible. Calculation consists in deriving signs from signs in accordance with rules within a system of signs.

The theory developed by Husserl in the *Philosophie der Arithmetik* was misconstrued and wrongly criticized by Frege as being psychologistic. What Husserl was in fact giving was an epistemological theory of the origin of our number concepts. A projected second volume of the work did not appear. Husserl abandoned the project as he moved toward a more axiomatic understanding of the nature of mathematics and began to understand the domain of mathematics to be a "definite manifold" defined through a system of axioms.

During the years 1896–1903, Husserl seems to have worked intensively on philosophy of space and geometry, yet another project which was later abandoned. But he did arrive at certain distinctions which were to have influence on his later thinking. He distinguished between four different concepts of space: the space of everyday life, the space of pure geometry, the space of applied geometry, and the space of metaphysics. Space of pure geometry was said to be an idealization of everyday space. He also held at this time, not unlike Frege, that geometry cannot be completely formalized, that the Euclidean manifold (in the formal sense) is not yet concrete space, and that the three-dimensionality of space cannot be logically deduced.

Philosophy of logic

Husserl's contribution to philosophy of logic may be listed under the following headings: refutation of logical psychologism, the idea of a pure logic, the idea of formal ontology, the thesis regarding the threefold stratification of formal logic, and a new conception of transcendental logic.

In the "Prolegomena to a Pure Logic" (1900), Husserl launched a wide-ranging attack on psychologism as a theory of logic and on forms of relativism which, on his view, are consequences of psychologism. The psychologism he attacks is the theory that the essential foundation of logic lies in empirical and naturalistic psychology. Husserl's arguments against such a view fall into two main groups. In the first place, he insists on the radical difference between the necessary, in Husserl's terminology "ideal," laws of logic and the empirical generalizations, and so probable laws, of psychology, in fine between the ideal and the real orders of being. No logical law, he insists, entails the existence of persons or the way their minds work. Second, the relativistic consequences of psychologism – be it individual or specific relativism – are just incoherent, both theoretically (logic, being the theory of any theory whatsoever, cannot be founded upon another theory, i.e. psychology) and pragmatically (relativism cannot assert its own truth). The rejection of psychologism leads Husserl to the conception of pure logic, whose domain is the sphere of meanings (again, in Husserl's terminology, ideal meanings), which include concepts, propositions, syllogisms, and theories, to the exclusion of mental acts such as beliefs, assertions, denials, and inferring. Contrary to Frege, he did not use the normativity of logic to criticize psychologism, but argued that every normative discourse presupposes a theoretical discourse, from which it follows that normative logic presupposes a pure theoretical logic.

An important part of Husserl's conception of logic is a thesis regarding the threefold stratum of formal logic. Formal logic, he held, should begin with a pure logical grammar which lays down the rules determining possible forms of meaningful composition of meanings and of meaning-modifications, as well as purely syntactical categories. Built up on this foundation is the second stratum, i.e. the logic of non-contradiction, called by Husserl the logic of consequence, and also pure apophantic analytic, to which the fundamental ideas of "analytic consequence," "analytic necessity," and "analytic contradiction" belong. The third stratum is the logic of truth, where for the first time the predicates "true" and "false" are introduced.

Husserl also distinguishes between three different attitudes one can bring to bear upon logic: first, the formal apophantic attitude, then the ontological attitude, and finally the subjective or transcendental attitude. The second yields a formal ontology, i.e. a theory of forms of any object whatsoever. The last gives rise to transcendental logic. Transcendental logic is concerned with the intentional acts which make possible such logical objects as proposition, syllogisms, and logical forms such as conjunctions. Husserl's transcendental logic is not a relapse into the psychologism which he had so vehemently rejected. Psychologism for him, as for Frege, was a part of naturalism. The transcendental attitude requires that the entire naturalistic attitude be put under "brackets," and the various intentional acts which make possible the constitution of logical objectivities be brought to systematic evidence.

Husserl also distinguishes predicative judgment and its logic from pre-predicative experience with its own logic. In *Experience and Judgment,* he shows how forms of judgment such as truth-functional operators like negation, conjunction, disjunction, and "if–then" arise out of pre-predicative negation, conjunction, disjunction, and "if–then."

Consciousness and intentionality

Logic and mathematics provided Husserl with his first access to the transcendental domain of constituting subjectivity. Following his teacher Brentano, he totally rejected the empiricistic picture of consciousness as consisting of data, i.e. ideas or images, and understood its nature in terms of intentionality. However, he took over Brentano's important concept with some modifications. He began with admitting non-intentional elements within consciousness, such as sensations which he called *"hyle."* In the course of time, however, he realized that this was a remnant of his earlier empiricistic prejudices, and he replaced these elements with *deeper levels of intentionality than the intentionality of thoughts.* By "deeper levels of intentionality" are meant such phenomena as the way sensory presentations of "now" recede back into the "no more" while yet carrying with them their temporal horizons, and the way the *given* points to the not-given, etc. Besides, Brentano's two-termed analysis of intentionality (act → object) was refined by him into a three-termed structure: act → meaning → object. Since the object of an intentional act may or may not exist, what is essential to an act is not the existence of an object but the meaning that it necessarily has as its correlate. We may therefore place the existence of the object under "brackets" – and so also the world as the totality of objects – thus neutralizing our belief in existence, yet retaining all the essential structures of consciousness. This reduced or purified consciousness would still have its object, it would still be *of* such and such object – only now of the object placed within quotation marks, as it were, i.e. with the correlate sense (*Sinn*) or meaning. Thus we have the central structure of consciousness:

(1) To every intentional act (or noesis), there belongs a correlative sense (or noema). The noema is an ideal entity, not individuated by either time or belongingness to the mental life of an ego, whereas the act is individuated by both. Thus numerically distinct acts may have an identical noema. The correlation expressed in (1) therefore is a many–one correlation. For many interpreters of Husserl, this correlation *is* consciousness.

A noema is constituted by conferring meaning upon a datum or *hyle*. The intentional act is never merely presenting something; it is also at the same time bestowing meaning on it. Thus, we have:

(2) One and the same object may be presented in different acts as having different meanings, i.e. through different noemata. One can then say, following Husserl, that the identity of an object is constituted by a "synthesis of overlapping" of these many noemata. The overlapping contents must have an identical X as the bearer of those predicates. As long as there are such overlapping predicates, and an identical X (within the noemata), the *sense* of identity of the object is maintained.

Two other features must be added to the above two:

(3) Every act, as well as its object, is presented within a *horizon*. Thus, even if an act of perceiving presents an object that is being perceived, the act belongs to the horizon of an ego's mental life, just as the object is presented as belonging to a spatial and temporal horizon.

The horizon consists of intentional references beyond the central core figure, references which are prefigured and form the background of the figure, and which can be actively pursued and explicated. The explication of the implicit horizonal intentionalities is called intentional explication.

(4) Consciousness is characterized by its own intrinsic temporality. Much of Husserl's work, perhaps some of his best, consists of descriptions of the temporality of consciousness. Here also, he begins by "bracketing" all transcendence – including cosmic, physical, and historical times – and focuses on the temporality of the reduced pure consciousness. He begins by pointing out that this temporality does not consist of a series of "now"-points, as though each perishing "now" were succeeded by another. If this were so, he asks, how would our idea of the past be possible? Even memory, being a present remembering and so occupying a "now"-point, cannot deliver to us our original sense of the past. The "now" must then have an opening towards the past and an opening towards the future. Each "now" must be surrounded by a temporal horizon, a grip on the just-elapsed past and an anticipatory hold on the yet-to-come. As a "now" recedes into the past, it recedes with its entire horizon. The three – primordial now-impression, protention, and retention – together form the concrete living present. Each of these undergoes iterated modifications such as retention of retention of retention. The originally presented time is then "presentified" (*vergegenwärtigt*). It is in this process of "inner time consciousness" that all objective time structures have their origin.

Husserl's thesis of intentionality, especially the concept of "noema," has, in recent times, been subjected to various interpretations. An older line of interpretation recognized the phenomenological bracketing, leading to the discovery of the noema, in the Gestalt psychologists' rejection of the constancy hypothesis, and it took the noema, especially the perceptual noema, to be the perceived precisely as it is perceived. Other interpretations demonstrate the relevance of Husserl's thinking for contemporary analytic philosophy. Some see in the concept of "noema" a Frege-like *Sinn*, only extended over the entire domain of experience and not restricted to linguistic signs. A still more recent interpretive attempt starts with the idea of horizon as consisting of possible lines of development implicit in every experience, and goes on to construe the process of experiencing as involving at every point a selection out of many possible worlds. All these interpretations demonstrate the fertility of Husserl's ideas.

Transcendental phenomenology

Husserl thought of himself as a transcendental philosopher, despite his basic differences from Kant. Most importantly, he rejected the Kantian distinction between phenomena and noumena. Fundamental to his version of transcendental philosophy, known as transcendental phenomenology, is the methodological procedure called reduction or *epochē*, of which there are three varieties: the eidetic, the phenomenological, and the transcendental. The first, eidetic reduction, "brackets" the question of existence and attempts to focus on the essence (of a class of entities under investigation or of an individual) by using a procedure which Husserl called "eidetic" or "imaginative" variation. The second, phenomenological reduction, "brackets" the existence (or non-existence) of the object of an intentional experience, and focuses upon the experience itself with its correlative noema. The third, transcendental reduction, more appropriately called the *epochē*, "brackets," "suspends," and "neutralizes" (i.e. does not make any theoretical use of) the belief in the world, including all interpretations of it, interpretations handed down by the sciences, religions, or metaphysical systems. The resulting purified life of consciousness will then be shown to be the origin of objectivities, or rather the place where all objectivities are "constituted."

What are said to be constituted are not things, but meanings. It is not the material thing, e.g. this table on which I am writing, which is constituted in consciousness. Such a position would amount to a sort of idealism – a mundane idealism – which Husserl rejected. What are constituted are instead predicate-senses such as "material object," "living animal," or "person," which originate from, i.e. derive their meaningfulness from, certain rule-governed types of experiences. These experiences alone make it possible to meaningfully, and sometimes truly, ascribe these predicates to what is presented "over there."

During his Freiburg years, Husserl developed what is known as genetic phenomenology, where meanings were traced back, through a process of intentional explication (i.e. developing the implicit horizonal implications), to their original constitution in history. The paradigmatic example of this work remains the way he shows, in the *Krisis*-book, the origin of the mathematical interpretation of nature (including its secondary qualities) by Galileo. This use of history may suggest that we are back in the natural world. Some critics of Husserl, including DERRIDA, think that this is in fact so. Others distinguish between the mundane history and transcendental history, meaning by the latter history of consciousness, which includes history of constitution of meanings.

Also during this period, especially in the *Krisis* lectures, the idea of the life-world as the foundation of meaning of the sciences comes to the forefront, and the constitution of the life-world – with its twin senses of the perceived world and the cultural world – becomes the focus of transcendental phenomenology.

Since the project of constitution-analysis was to be able to recover the full meaning of constituted entities, Husserl realized that transcendental philosophy must be able to recover the full sense of the idea "world-in-itself." This task requires transcending the "purified" experience of any one person, the reflecting ego, and recovering the sense "other ego" and so the sense of "intersubjectivity." In the famous, but much misunderstood and criticized, "Fifth Cartesian Meditation," he tried to demonstrate how a reflecting ego, starting with a methodological solipsism, i.e. without presupposing belief in other egos, can nevertheless arrive at the sense "other ego." To be sure, he was not trying to prove the existence of other egos in the face of solipsism (just as he never sought to prove the existence of material things in the face of phenomenalism), nor was he concerned with how we know other minds. He was trying to solve a problem that is more fundamental than these two: namely, how is it possible, starting with one's own experiences, to find within that domain any motivations for ascribing the sense "other ego" to something presented in it?

Finally, there is Husserl's continuing preoccupation with the idea of the ego (or *Ich*, I). Starting in the first edition of the *Logische Untersuchungen* with a Humean sort of bundle theory, Husserl soon came to recognize that the intentional acts must have their point of origin, their subject-pole, in a pure ego (*reines Ich*). When the full conception of a transcendental ego as the totality of the subjective life of an I, recovered after the *epochē* as the constitutive source of all meanings, came into its own, the pure ego was recognized as only one component of the transcendental ego. The transcendental ego was often represented as a Leibnizian monad – but with windows and a history of its own. The full transcendental ego is not, however, an entity numerically distinct from the empirical ego; it is the same ego, only now stripped of the naturalistic interpretations to which we subject it. An intentional act such as my seeing the tulips in my garden is empirical insofar as it is inserted into the causal nexus of nature and inner biography of a biological organism that is me, but it is transcendental insofar as – as an intentional act with its own correlative noema "those tulips over there" – it confers sense on what is presented, and thus is a part of consciousness's world-constituting activity.

Husserl's thinking was criticized, from within the phenomenological movement, by his realist followers who opted for an essentialistic realism, and by the existential–hermeneutic followers who, led by HEIDEGGER and Merleau-Ponty, found his thinking tied too much to the primacy of the logical and to the idea of a transcendental ego. But the fecundity of his thinking is borne out by the many fields of enquiry in which his ideas have been enormously fruitful: in sociology, religious studies, anthropology, literary criticism, aesthetics, political philosophy, and ethics to mention just a few.

A final assessment of Husserl's philosophy still waits to be made in the light of his complete *Nachlass*, both published and unpublished.

Bibliography

Writings

All of Husserl's published works are now in the series *Husserliana*, edited by the Husserl Archive, Louvain. The main works in English translation are given below.

Formal and Transcendental Logic, trans. D. Cairns (The Hague: Nijhoff, 1969).

The Crisis of the European Sciences and Transcendental Phenomenology: An Introduction to Phenomenological Philosophy, trans. D. Carr (Evanston, IL: Northwestern University Press, 1970).

Experience and Judgment, trans. J. S. Churchill and K. Ameriks (Evanston, IL: Northwestern University Press, 1973).

Cartesian Meditations, trans. D. Cairns (The Hague: Nijhoff, 1977).

Logical Investigations, 2nd edn, trans. J. N. Findlay (London and New York: Humanities Press, 1977).

Ideas Pertaining to a Pure Phenomenology and to a Phenomenological Philosophy, Book I, trans. Fred Kersten (The Hague: Kluwer, 1982).

Further reading

Bell, D.: *Husserl* (London and New York: Routledge, 1990).

Bernet, R., Kern, I., and Marbach, E.: *An Introduction to Husserlian Phenomenology* (Evanston, IL: Northwestern University Press, 1993).

Dreyfus, H. (ed.): *Husserl, Intentionality and Cognitive Science* (Cambridge, MA: MIT Press, 1982).

Farber, M.: *The Foundations of Phenomenology* (Cambridge, MA: Harvard University Press, 1943).

Mohanty, J. N.: *Edmund Husserl's Theory of Meaning*, 3rd edn (The Hague: Nijhoff, 1976).

——: *Phenomenology, Between Essentialism and Transcendental Philosophy* (Evanston, IL: Northwestern University Press, 1997).

Ströker, Elisabeth: *Husserl's Transcendent Phenomenology* (Stanford, CA: Stanford University Press, 1993).

17

James

Michael H. DeArmey

The stature of William James (1842–1910 CE) as a major philosopher in the Golden Age of American philosophy (1870–1930) is firmly established on the basis of his philosophical psychology, his development of pragmatic epistemology and its application to a wide range of theoretical issues, his analysis of religious experience, and his defense of an experiential and pluralistic metaphysics.

A large inheritance enabled Henry James Sr and Mary Walsh James to provide their older sons, William and Henry, with security and a sterling education. The father, freed from a fixed occupation, moved his children from one tutor or school to another according to his perception of their developing interests. Exercising almost no daily parental control, he let the attraction of new cities and new ideas occupy their attention. But in this setting William James's development as a thinker was protracted and painful. As he approached thirty, he had no career, having cast aside his medical degree (1869) as pretentious. Still dependent on his parents, he had no prospects for a family of his own. He began to be haunted by the possibility that heredity had cast him to be like his father, carefree and careerless. His depression reached suicidal proportions in the early 1870s. Once recovered, he settled into a position of instructor of anatomy and physiology at Harvard. In 1874 he established the first experimental laboratory in psychology. A series of philosophical and psychological papers published over a twelve-year period were the basis for his magnum opus, *The Principles of Psychology*, which appeared in 1890. The 1890s also witnessed the publication of his two controversial essays on faith, "The Will to Believe" and *Human Immortality*. In the first decade of the twentieth century he produced six major works: *The Varieties of Religious Experience, Essays in Radical Empiricism, Pragmatism, The Meaning of Truth, A Pluralistic Universe*, and *Some Problems of Philosophy*. He died in 1910 from a heart condition originating years earlier from hiking in the mountains.

Freedom of the will

The year 1870 was central to James's development as a thinker. His struggle in overcoming depression was bound up with his philosophical activity: reflection on the defense of free will in the writings of the French philosopher Charles Renouvier, and stimulating discussions at a newly formed philosophy club in Cambridge. James's 1884 essay, "The Dilemma of Determinism," is a defense of freedom of the will, the leading ideas of which were formed in the year 1870.

Reading Renouvier led James to develop the idea that neither freedom of the will nor determinism is provable. Whatever action one chose, the determinist would insist that, given antecedent conditions, no other alternative was possible. The defender of free will would insist that within the act of choosing are indeterminate possibilities, and that the choice once made is not epiphenomenal, but a necessary condition of the action. Each side employs different metaphysical postulates about possibility. On what grounds does one choose between postulates in philosophy? Consequences, both logical and practical, are decisive. Logically, on the postulate that we live in a deterministic world, science itself would have no more rational or truth-bearing status than voodoo or numerology. What one believes would be the end product of cellular and other physical causation, and if what one asserted to be true happened to be true, this would be due to good fortune rather than rational insight. So unrestricted determinism is self-defeating.

Unacceptable practical consequences also flow from determinism. A determinist must hold that not only are occurrences of wrongdoing and misery evil, but the immense line of antecedent conditions which produce them are equally evil. A determinist is logically unable to regret such evils, for regret involves the idea that something ought not to be, and ought-to-be makes no sense in a universe in which what happens cannot happen otherwise than it does. If the determinist holds that regret is an error, then the error is still another evil necessitated by antecedent conditions. Nor could a determinist logically say that one ought not to regret. So the determinist must be a pessimist. James notes that the determinist's only avenue of escape from this conclusion is the position that evil is instrumentally good in promoting knowledge of it (a gnostic form of determinism), or good in generating life's excitement and adventure (a romantic form of determinism). But in either form the construal of evil as good allows for moral indifference, for no matter what one does, one promotes the good.

Pragmatism

In 1870 three philosophers and three attorneys formed a regular discussion group to examine "the tallest and broadest questions." Christened "the Metaphysical Club," in defiance of the positivism of that period, their discussions gave birth to pragmatism (from the Greek word for action, πράγμα), the only philosophical movement indigenous to the United States. One of the attorneys, Nicholas St John Green, a Benthamite utilitarian, promoted Alexander Bain's definition of "belief" as that which a person is prepared to act upon. This held sway in the discussions and became the *leitmotiv* of pragmatism. At this time Darwinian evolution was very much in the air, and club members connected belief to habit. They regarded habits as adaptive modifications of instinctive tendencies, thus linking cognition to its organic base. They set about looking for the future practical consequences of propositions and terms, in opposition to the reigning philosophical strategies of tracing ideas to their origins in experience (classical British empiricism), or developing their logical connections (rationalism on the continent). Another club member, Oliver Wendell Holmes Jr, developed the pragmatic or predictive theory of law, defining "law" as how the judges will rule in court. It was Charles S. Peirce, however, who developed the general pragmatic maxim employed by the group: consider what practical effects a conception has; then our conception of these effects is the whole of our conception of the object.

The pragmatic method was not identified publicly as "pragmatism" until 1898, when James delivered a sobering and beautifully styled address at Berkeley, "Philosophical Conceptions and Practical Results." For the pragmatist, he states, there cannot be a difference which does not make a difference in either experience or conduct. To illustrate this claim that theoretical differences must make a practical difference, James cites the clash between theism and scientific materialism. Suppose the world were to end today. Then whatever value the world has would receive our thanks, and it would not matter whether the agency responsible for this value be God or atoms shifting about in the cosmic weather. But if the world has a future, and hence consequences for our practice, then theism and materialism differ sharply. Theism posits that God will not let the great values perish, whereas for materialism everything is doomed to entropic death.

This essay also illustrates the pragmatic method by considering the debate between monists and pluralists. Practically, what does the universe's oneness mean to you? How do you act towards its oneness? The pragmatic method requires an experiential analysis of this concept: oneness might mean continuous passage from part to part (any hiatus or unbridgeable chasm, such as one mind knowing another, would entail pluralism); it might mean susceptibility to being collected (but we can neither physically collect the universe, nor conceptually collect it without loss of richness in detail); the universe's oneness might mean generic sameness, but there seem to be differences in kind (e.g. number, blue, explosion). Finally, the universe might be one in the sense that all its parts have a common origin; oneness in this sense does indeed practically function to guide scientists to look for earlier antecedent conditions, but even here it is not clear that plural origins, with a subsequent mingling of causalities, could not perform the guiding role.

In 1906 James gave the Lowell Lectures at Harvard, published in 1907 as *Pragmatism: A New Name for Some Old Ways of Thinking*. Here James sets out pragmatism as a theory of truth. Pragmatism identifies truth with the function of linking experiences in successful ways. Unlike the correspondence theory, which identifies truth as copying or representing reality, pragmatism identifies truth as agreement with reality. Truth as agreement means that acting on the proposition leads to successful action, successful adaptation to the environment. Thus, there are no eternal or absolute truths. Ultimately, concepts and propositions are ways of "handling" the flow of experience.

Critics of pragmatism claimed that it could not account for truths about the past. They complained that in some cases false beliefs would "work" just as well to fulfill our purposes. Critics such as Arthur O. Lovejoy argued that James failed to distinguish the logical consequences of a proposition from the consequences of believing a proposition.

Philosophical psychology

Acclaimed at the time as the greatest book ever written on human nature, James's *The Principles of Psychology* (1890) was the product of twelve years of writing and research. Written from a strictly positivistic point of view in the attempt to found psychology as a natural science, it incorporates 100 years of research in the biological sciences. This material shows how the life of mind is conditioned by the body. In order to correlate mental states with bodily conditions, James found it necessary to correct previous distortions of "mind," and his brilliant descriptions of the "stream of thought" profoundly affected all subsequent philosophical discussion.

James's first task is to define the subject matter of psychology. But immediately he finds metaphysical and epistemological considerations intruding and disrupting the positivistic program. Psychology does not study sticks or stones, but conscious or minded beings. But what and where are these? I know that I am conscious, but how do I know that other beings are? James's attempt to answer these questions involves comparing non-minded activity with the quite different behavior of living things. Air bubbles, rising in the tank of water, stick to a submerged pane of glass. The frog, however, encountering the glass, varies its behavior until it finds its way around it and up to the surface. Romeo, encountering a wall separating him from Juliet, uses his wits to get over it. In experience, then, the criterion for mindedness is a teleological one: the pursuit of future ends and variable means to reach these ends. This criterion thus expresses the basis in human nature for pragmatism and the pragmatic method, for, as noted above, these employ reference to future practical conduct.

On the difficult topic of mind and body, James's positivistic program leads him to attempt an empirical parallelism of mind and body. As a science, psychology is restricted to the correlation of mental states and bodily conditions. Ultimate questions about causation are left to metaphysics. James's "Dilemma" essay, it will be recalled, argues that the attempt to establish or prove causation in regard to choice is self-defeating. So the parallelism of *Principles* is a corollary of his deepest philosophical commitment. Whether a psychologist were to write a deterministic or indeterministic psychology, this would be the psychologist's personal choice, and no part of psychology construed as a natural science. However, it must be asked whether such a parallelism can be consistently maintained. If mind is by nature selective, if the criterion for mindedness is the choice of means to attain an end, does not this capacity to vary the means impute causality to mental states? That this parallelism becomes problematic is indicated by James's not infrequent use of the language of "seeming." For example, the terminus of willing is not an idea altering brain cells; the terminus "seems to be" the idea itself. Again following the lead of Renouvier, James holds that sustained attention to an idea expels contrary and inhibiting ideas by drawing together its fringed associates. One gets out of bed on a wintry morning, not by thinking of the cold floor or the warm blanket, but by exclusive attention to the day's tasks and rewards.

The most famous chapter of *Principles* is "The Stream of Thought." Its description of the five characteristics of consciousness undermined both classical British empiricism from LOCKE to Mill and idealism from KANT to Royce. The first characteristic of thought is that it is always personal, i.e. owned. The separateness of minds is the most absolute breach in nature. Second, thought is continuously changing, no state of consciousness occurring twice. What is experienced twice is the same object. Differences in circumstance, time of day, mood, age, and the flow of interpretation affect thinking. Third, consciousness is experienced as continuous, having gaps in neither time nor quality. The waking person immediately connects to the same drowsy one who earlier got under the covers. The peal of thunder is not experienced as a qualitative break; what is experienced is thunder-following-silence. Differences in the rate of change are represented by what James calls substantive and transitive states of consciousness. Substantive states are states in which thought rests on some object or logical conclusion. The transitive portions are the barely discernible feelings in the interstices of thought. Fourth, relations such as from, between, by, and tendency, direction, etc., are experienced. Overlooking these relations, empiricism leads to skepticism. Idealism, also not finding relations in experience, posits their construction by the intellect. But experience, carefully examined, shows that every substantive thought is swimming in a pool of relations, which James calls the fringe or horizon of thought. The fifth characteristic of thought is that it incessantly welcomes or rejects, i.e. it is selective.

The chapter on the self develops the first characteristic of thought, its personal form. James's theory of the self incorporates dipolarity. There is an "I" and a "Me," each of which is necessary to the other. The "Me" is objective and comprises the objects to which one has emotional attachment. There are material, social, and spiritual aspects of the "Me." One's emotions wax or wane as these objects prosper or fail. The "I" is the present thought, and it performs all the functions of the soul or ego. As a reality, the "I" is activity; as felt, it is just the feeling of muscular contractions in the head. Continuity and sameness of self over time are interpreted as the present thought appropriating the "Me" (objects) of the passing thought. The "Me" contains marks of ownership from one's own body, and nascent or incomplete purposes which temporally extend into the new present thought. Only a dipolar account of self can provide for that blend of sameness and difference which characterizes our lives.

It is to be noted that the role of emotions in connecting the "Me" to the "I" does not figure in James's famous theory of the emotions. On that theory, sometimes called the "peripheralist" or "James–Lange" theory, emotions are viewed as felt bodily changes. That emotions are essentially expressions of care, expressions of the moral life, is central in establishing the "Me" in the chapter on the self, but this centrality vanishes in the chapter on emotions. To say, as James does in the chapter on the emotions, that we are sad because we cry (and by implication that we are joyous because we laugh), would make our friends and other components of the "Me" objects which happen to cause certain physiological changes. No doubt it is true that they do produce these changes, but it is only because we first and foremost care about these objects.

James is able to relate his theory of the self to the possibility of human immortality. The stimulation of our sensory organs makes the brain pervious to and productive of sights and sounds. What if certain conditions such as those found in religious conversion or mysticism lower the threshold even more, allowing the transmission of something extraordinary? An explanation of this type of religious experience would be that the earthly bodily self and its experiences might be preserved as the "Me" of a higher "I," a more expansive self. Religious experience might then be the marginal awareness of this greater being who appropriates narrower, earthly selves. The experience of such a higher self is a central theme running through personal accounts of religious experience. James is thus able to say, in one of those curious philosophical assertions, that whoever possesses the possessor possesses the possessed.

Radical empiricism

About 1895 James began to work in earnest on the undeveloped empiricism latent in his use of the pragmatic method and appearing in his psychology. The result he named "radical empiricism." Radical empiricism is the requirement that the terms of philosophical discussion be definable by experience and that nothing experienced be omitted. It is the radical requirement that everything in philosophy be reconstructed without benefit of those unifying or supporting, yet unexperienced, entities famous in metaphysical works: substances, egos, souls, absolutes, matter, categories. For the radical empiricist, all there is is "pure experience," or the pure phenomena. This is the primary datum of philosophy. Pure experience is prior to the subjective/objective or mental/physical distinction. That distinction is antedated in human history by pre-reflective experience, and is, moreover, only one way of several ways to reflectively analyze experience. Pure experience refers to the multirelational nature of objects. The same object, say a bed, can enter into many different contexts. The bed can be an item in the history of the room, a percept in a person's stream of thought, a place of ethical concern for the hospital patient, etc. The relations within pure experience are both conjunctive and disjunctive, meaning by this that a bit of pure experience is bound up in discernible ways with other portions of pure experience, but independent in other, also discernible, ways.

The doctrine of pure experience is a fresh approach to the impasse reached in philosophy over certain persistent problems. Indeed, Bertrand RUSSELL, describing James's position as "neutral monism," called it one of the great contributions to metaphysics. Whether an object like the bed is over there or in consciousness depends on the bed's matrix of relations. The impasse over the nature of consciousness is founded on the claim that we have direct awareness of something called "consciousness" or "subjectivity." For the radical empiricist there is no awareness of consciousness *per se*, only the awareness of objects and bodily activities.

A portion of pure experience may enter into any one of four fields: the personal stream, identified by fringe and bodily movement; the field of meanings or Platonic ideas, static and defined by logical relations; the field of value, identified by relations of worth, fitness, obligation, etc.; and the field of nature, quantitatively defined as measurable spatio-temporal change.

Religious experience

The Varieties of Religious Experience is a trail-blazing examination of the kinds of experience that fund religious institutions, rituals, and language. Although "religion" is a collective term for the variety of religions, which may contain no common essence, the focus of all religions is centered upon common features of the human predicament. These features include evil, suffering, death, incompleteness, and fragility. Religious experience involves the claim that there is something "more" beyond the ragged mundane world, and that this "more" is redemptive.

Broadly speaking, there are two types of religious response to the negative features of human life. There is the once-born person, whose healthy-minded religious spirit ignores evil, squeezes the good out of everything, and thankfully makes his way through life. In America, Ralph Waldo Emerson and Walt Whitman exemplify the once-born. The religiosity of the twice-born person is more sophisticated. The person who seriously confronts the misery of the world may become a sick soul. Personal humiliation, a perception of the soiling and tainting of natural goods, despair, and renunciation are its typical stages. Rebirth or conversion stems from a process of "incubation" in the fringe or subconscious of the sick-souled person. Values and beliefs get rearranged, with a corresponding shift in the center of personal energy. Truths half-noticed or ignored may come together. The result, which may be sudden, is a new vision, a more inclusive view, in which the world is disinfected.

Conversion is not the property of a particular religion. Indeed, it may not involve religion at all. James notes that one may be converted in the same fresh-air manner to moralism, patriotism, atheism, even to revenge and avarice! At its height, if its sickly roots are deep enough, conversion may lead to the saintly life. As a type, saintly persons are humanity's best example of moral courage.

Religion as a whole, despite the evils it produces in its institutional forms, facilitates our survival in a world permeated by contingency and sheer bruteness. A fitting way to assess Religion, and a fitting signature for James's philosophy: ye shall know them by their fruits.

Bibliography

Writings

The Works of William James, 19 volumes, ed. Frederick H. Burkhardt, Fredson Bowers, and Ignas Skrupskelis (Cambridge, MA: Harvard University Press, 1981–8).

Further reading

Bjork, Daniel W.: *William James* (New York: Columbia University Press, 1988).

Corti, W. R. (ed.): *The Philosophy of William James* (Hamburg: Felix Meiner, 1976).

DeArmey, Michael H., and Skousgaard, Stephen (eds): *The Philosophical Psychology of William James* (Washington, DC: Center for Advanced Phenomenological Research and University Presses of America, 1986).

Flower, Elizabeth, and Murphey, Murray G.: *A History of American Philosophy*, two volumes (New York: G. P. Putnam's, 1977).

Ford, Marcus Peter: *William James's Philosophy* (Amherst, MA: University of Massachusetts Press, 1982).

Kuklick, Bruce: *The Rise of American Philosophy* (New Haven, CT, and London: Yale University Press, 1977).

Levinson, Henry Samuel: *The Religious Investigations of William James* (Chapel Hill: University of North Carolina Press, 1981).

Linshoten, Hans: *On the Way toward a Phenomenological Psychology: The Psychology of William James*, trans. Amedeo Giorgi (Pittsburgh, PA: Duquesne University Press, 1968).

Lovejoy, Arthur O.: *The Thirteen Pragmatisms and Other Essays* (Baltimore, MD: Johns Hopkins University Press, 1963).

Myers, Gerald E.: *William James: His Life and Thought* (New Haven, CT: Yale University Press, 1986).

Perry, Ralph Barton: *The Thought and Character of William James*, two volumes (Boston and Toronto: Little, Brown, 1935). [A Pulitzer Prize winning and unsurpassed biography and commentary.]

Reck, Andrew J.: *Introduction to William James* (Bloomington, IN, and London: Indiana University Press, 1967). [Clear commentary with representative selections.]

Smith, John E.: *America's Philosophical Vision* (Chicago and London: University of Chicago Press, 1992).

Wiener, Philip P.: *Evolution and the Founders of Pragmatism* (Cambridge, MA: Harvard University Press, 1949).

Wild, John: *The Radical Empiricism of William James* (Garden City, NY: Doubleday, 1965). [Examines James in relation to existentialism.]

Wilshire, Bruce: *William James and Phenomenology. A Study of the Principles of Psychology* (Bloomington, IN, and London: Indiana University Press, 1968).

18

Kant

G. Felicitas Munzel

Life and times: revolutions of the world order

The frequent claim that his philosophy *is* his biography, together with the acknowledged enduring scope of the influence of his thought, an influence held to consist in nothing less than the entire history of philosophy since Kant, effectively asserts that Immanuel Kant (1724–1804 CE) remains very much a vital presence for our world today. His life began inauspiciously, born April 22, 1724 into the humble life of a harness maker's family, in Königsberg, Prussia (today's Kaliningrad, Russia). Baptized "Emanuel" ("God with us"), he was the fourth of nine children (of whom four died in early childhood). The story of his rise to such philosophical prominence, arguably even greater today than at the time of his death on February 12, 1804, may be told as one of an acute mind responsive to the upheavals of the world order on every front during the eighteenth century, revolutions that ushered in our own world order. Thus told, the story takes seriously (with Cassirer) Goethe's observation about the reciprocal relationship for Kant of thought imparting its form to life, while itself bearing the characteristic stamp of that life.

A synoptic overview of the historical, political, social, economic, educational, cultural, and scientific events and persons on the eighteenth-century world stage might well begin with nature's own cataclysmic event, the 1755 Lisbon earthquake, followed by a tidal wave and fire that completed the destruction of most of the city and claimed a reported 30,000 lives. The effect on a humanity already grappling with questions of its status in relation to God and the universe – a status already put in question by the emerging sciences, especially the astronomy of Copernicus, Galileo and Kepler – led many to challenge whether this world is, as LEIBNIZ believed, the "best of all possible worlds." The elder Goethe describes in retrospect the impression of the earthquake on his mind as a child: "not only had nature, both in the unleashing of its forces, and in the plundering, murder, assault and battery carried out by some of the survivors against the others, asserted its seemingly limitless despotism, but God, the Creator and Sustainer of heaven and earth, presented in the profession of the first article of faith as so wise and merciful, had proven Himself, in that He allowed the death and destruction of the just and the unjust alike, to be on no account a fatherly figure." Goethe's struggle to come to terms with the contradiction between what he had been taught and his actual life experience was made all the more difficult because the wise and learned could not agree on the way in which one should regard such an event as the Lisbon earthquake. The bitter interchange between Voltaire and Rousseau on the subject exemplifies this disagreement. Kant, who had touched on the "utter indifference of the universe toward the fate of the individual" in his *Universal Natural History and Theory of the Heavens* (published in 1755), responds with three essays in 1756 exploring the natural causes of earthquakes and rejecting the notion of moral causes attributed to it by many of his contemporaries. In his *Only Possible Basis of Proof for Demonstrating the Existence of God* (1763) he revisits these issues.

With regard to the whole realm of modern mathematical as well as empirical experimental science, Kant is conversant with the theories and technology of his time well beyond his well known critical engagement of Newton. Both the physical and emerging life sciences (for example, the issue of organic generation) attract his attention. In an age of technological inventions as diverse as the steam engine, pioneering work in electricity, the celsius thermometer, fountain pen, and hot air balloon, Kant draws on these innovations in the course of his lectures; for example in his 1775–6 anthropology lectures he explains human visual perception by appealing to magic lanterns, the forerunners of modern projectors. Yet early on he also sounds a warning note: the Prometheus of the modern age, the specialist in any one of these endeavors, must in order to avoid being a one-eyed cyclops be first and foremost educated in practical wisdom, the second eye needed for the affairs of life.

In addition to the scientific and technological revolutions in the laboratories of Europe, the age is confronted with the goods and news brought home by the continuing voyages of discovery. The African Native, American Indian, and South Sea Islander pose a challenge to human self-understanding, now cast in terms of what the human being is as a natural species. In 1775 Kant publishes his essay "On the Different Human Races." The political convulsions of this age of colonialism, slave trade, and ongoing wars include the Seven Years War, the American Declaration of Independence in 1776, and the French Revolution.

Kant's most explicit philosophical response to these social and political events is made in relation to the French Revolution, but his 1793 essay on eternal peace, for example, outlines fundamental articles for a republican constitution which are receiving renewed attention today in the analysis of issues of globalization. Events at the political, social, and economic levels are also reflected in the literary and philosophical works of the age. Kant's writings (again especially his anthropology lectures) are replete with references to the authors of his own and preceding times. Milton's *Paradise Lost* is cited as an example of the sublime, while Shakespeare is credited as being one of the best sources for instruction in human nature. Modern natural law theorists such as Grotius and Pufendorf are also familiar to Kant, as are, of course, the philosophical writings of the tradition and of his contemporaries, the latter including Christian Wolff, Alexander Baumgarten, Jean Jacques Rousseau, David HUME, and Moses Mendelssohn (with whom Kant corresponded).

A revolution connected with all of the other changes, one that was momentous for the age, was the pedagogical reform movement pervading the long eighteenth century in all its spheres: philosophical, literary, educational, political, social, and popular. In the previous centuries, human instruction in the well ordered life, a life in right relation to God, had rested on the divine authority of the Word promulgated through the tradition of the Church. Education had been traditionally subsumed under either theology or philosophy. With the modern world's shift in political power and structures from ecclesiastical to secular authorities, with the challenge of modern empirical, experimental science to Scholastic and Aristotelian metaphysics and logic, with the economic changes that fostered the restructuring of social classes, the questions familiar from the Platonic dialogues take center-stage. Who is the educator? Who shall educate the educator? How is a moral- and civic-minded citizenry to be cultivated? In its self-understanding, in its very conception of the meaning of "Enlightenment," Kant's age was a pedagogical century. As expressed in the words of Isaac Iselin, an avid supporter of the Philanthropist education reform movement, "The task of the new education was to be the achievement of a happy human race; this striving lends the character of philanthropy to the Age of Enlightenment and makes it a pedagogical age." Early histories of the period agree that Enlightenment philosophy was in fact tightly and necessarily bound up with the striving for the reform of the entire system of education. As is clear from Diderot's essay on the definition of an encyclopedia and from d'Alembert's introduction, the *Encyclopédie* was itself conceived as a massive work to help educate the general public, to foster knowledge, truth, and virtue all at once. It was these

French philosophes who voiced the elements which have come to be popularly identified with "Enlightenment," the anti-institutional and anti-religious elements, the impatience with authority and classical authors.

It was the founding of the new educational institute in Dessau in 1774, the Philanthropin, which evoked Kant's own earliest and most explicit public entry into the education reform debate. His reading of Rousseau's *Emile, or On Education* a decade earlier had, on his own testimony, "set him straight" about what constitutes the true dignity of humanity, namely not the advance of knowledge by scholarly inquiry as he had himself believed, but instead the "restoration of the rights of humanity." This objective is articulated in Kant's mature moral thought as that pedagogical method which facilitates the self-consciousness and efficacy of the moral law in the individual. The program of study of the Philanthropin was based on Lockean (see LOCKE) and Rousseauian principles, and Kant gave it his enthusiastic, unequivocal, and unwavering support, calling upon the citizenry of Europe to inform themselves about and give their support to this new school and its "true method of education." Some of the basic principles of that education (principles shared by other reformers) may be summed up as follows. It was axiomatic that instruction should proceed in accordance with nature (that is, in agreement with the capacities and aptitudes of human nature). Pedagogy was essentially teleological: its goal was the perfection of humanity. To make progress toward the realization of human destiny was at once to make progress in enlightenment. So the education called for enlightening human beings (not merely training or mechanically instructing them). Such cultivation and the production of morality, even if there was evil in human beings, was affirmed as the greatest and most difficult, but indispensable, task of humanity. A primary focus of the task was to train teachers. Kant encouraged these goals and in one of his letters to the school's directors states what he regards as the chief role and importance of education: "the only thing necessary is not theoretical learning, but the *Bildung* of human beings, both in regard to their talents and their character."

Kant's position on education, and his heartfelt affirmation (in his lectures on both anthropology and pedagogy) that it consisted in nothing less than humanity's most important task, seems to have been informed not only by the writings and efforts of his contemporaries, but also by the contradictory elements in his own upbringing and education. Famously, his lifelong memory of his schooling at the Pietist institute, the *Collegium Fridericianum,* from 1732 to 1740 was one of horror. Its curriculum was derived from the ideas of August Hermann Francke, a

Pietist educational reformer whose pedagogical principles rested on discipline, supervision, protection, and labor. Kant was admitted to the *Fridericianum* under the auspices of Franz Albert Schulz, who, with the support of Kant's mother, had been providing religious instruction to the older siblings. Schulz modified the Pietist teachings with the philosophical ideas and methods of Christian Wolff, and reportedly the mainstay of the *Fridericianum's* education was Latin. It was here that Kant first came to appreciate the Latin authors cited throughout his writings (including Cicero, Horace, Juvenal, Seneca, Lucretius, Sextus Empiricus, and others). Nonetheless, the discipline was also spiritual, a scrutiny of the heart emphasized under Pietist teachings and executed through the prayers, devotional exercises, sermons, and catechizations which filled the curriculum. The overall experience, in other words, was wholly contrary to the self-sufficiency in thinking and autonomy of will which would form the basic tenets of Kant's philosophy.

The Pietism he witnessed in his home gave Kant a different perspective. For his parents and their example of consideration and love for others, even their opponents, which impressed him deeply as a boy, Kant maintained lifelong praise, respect and gratitude. He averred that those people who were serious about Pietism were actually virtuous and pious, possessing the highest human qualities of calm, serenity, and inner peace undisturbed by any passion.

If his home life gave him the basic experience of moral dignity, the city of Königsberg provided Kant with a nascent cosmopolitan outlook. The capital of East Prussia, it was the seat of government institutions and a Prussian garrison, but perhaps even more importantly, it was a Baltic port that served as an international trading center connecting East Europe and Russia with the rest of Germany, Scandinavia, and England. It attracted people from various backgrounds and so Kant had the opportunity to be exposed to many different cultures. Kant himself, in his anthropology lectures, used Königsberg to illustrate his point that genuine knowledge of human nature was obtained first through one's interactions in one's own community and that without this basis travel abroad was of limited value.

The university in Königsberg, the Albertina, was one of the larger of the 28 German universities of the day and the only one in East Prussia. During his studies at the Albertina (1740–6), Kant's intellectual independence manifested itself in a number of ways. Despite his straightened circumstances, Kant did not undertake his studies with an eye to professional training, be that theology or a civil service post, opting instead to go wherever his self-professed "intellectual curiosity" would lead him and essentially studying the *humaniora* (mathematics, natural sciences, theology, philosophy, and Latin literary classics). His choice of study signals (for Cassirer) the "freer, humane form of education to whose acceptance Kant's philosophy would come to contribute so decisively." Four years after entering the university, Kant began work on his first treatise, *Thoughts on the True Estimation of Living Forces...* (published 1747). In its introduction, an early passage echoes the spirit of ARISTOTLE's assertion that one must honor truth more than one's friends. Kant declares he is honored to call the "great masters of our knowledge" (such as Newton and Leibniz, whom he challenges in the work) his "opponents," that "it is not without benefit to place a certain noble trust in one's own powers," and that "nothing will prevent me from following this path which I have laid out for myself." In short, Kant's philosophical spirit had survived the oppression of the *Fridericianum* and was well on its way to its public expression and development. The passage also heralds the role the mature philosopher would play in relation to Enlightenment thought, at once a participant in its advancement and a critical voice calling into question the varying schools of thought of his time, and hence subjecting "Enlightenment" to a self-examination. Whether Cartesian, Leibnizian, Spinozistic or Wolffian rationalism, whether Lockean empiricism, BERKELEY's idealism, Holbach's materialism, or Humean skepticism, all would be submitted to critique.

After leaving the Albertina in 1746, Kant spent seven years as a private tutor, returning to Königsberg in 1754. The following year his *Universal Natural History and Theory of the Heavens* appeared, and he completed first his *Magister* (with his essay "Succinct Exposition of Some Meditations on Fire") and then his *Habilitation* (with his essay "A New Exposition of the First Principles of Metaphysical Knowledge"). He remained at the Albertina, refusing offers to go to Erlangen (in 1769), to Jena (in 1770), and to Halle (in 1778). In 1770 he received his appointment as Professor of Logic and Metaphysics, a post he carried out until 1796 (as well as assuming the administrative functions of dean and rector – the equivalent of president of the university – several times). His inaugural dissertation on the occasion of his appointment was the essay "On the Form and Principles of the Sensible and the Intelligible World." During his nearly half-century of teaching, Kant accumulated an astounding record in number and range of courses: in addition to yearly courses in logic and metaphysics, he taught physical geography (a course he initiated at the university in 1770 and offered annually thereafter), anthropology (offered every winter semester starting in the academic year 1772–3), moral philosophy, natural law, mathematical physics, philosophical encyclopedia (a kind of history of ideas), natural theology, and pedagogy. Kant belongs to a select group of modern philosophers who worked as professional teachers (and in fact is the first one unless Christian Wolff is included in the list). Kant's own testimony about his life and work as a teacher is remarkable. In a 1778 letter to his former student Marcus Herz, Kant states that the "main purpose of his academic life," which he "at all times keeps before him," is "to cultivate good characters," a point he reaffirms in 1789 (again to Marcus Herz) in his statement that he is consoled he has not lived in vain, because Herz is an example of the fact that he has succeeded in "cultivating some individuals, even if but a few, to be good human beings."

Critical philosophy

In light of Kant's intellectual development, it is not surprising to find him distinguishing between "scholastic" and "cosmopolitan" forms of philosophy, contrasting the philosophy of the schools and a philosophy for the world. In its scholastic conception, philosophy's purpose is to secure the logical perfection of cognition; it is viewed as a science whose aim is limited to achieving a systematic unity of cognition. As a cosmopolitan concept, philosophy is a science of relating all cognitions to the essential purposes of human reason. At stake in this distinction are (among other things) the conception, role, and fate of reason itself in human culture and history, its striving for knowledge, and its function in human life.

Reason was under attack during Kant's time. Rousseau had pointed to the objection (which would become ever more strident in the course of the *Sturm und Drang* movement, later in NIETZSCHE and beyond) that the rational activity pursued in the name of being "master and possessor of nature" (as both DESCARTES and Bacon expressed it) would ultimately be destructive of the arts and sciences, of the very civilization which is its product. And there were purely philosophical assaults on reason. Hume's skeptical analysis undercut the possibility of universal and necessary knowledge, hence undermining not only the Aristotelian sense of "science," but also the objective validity of knowledge in modern science, of mathematics and physics as universal and necessary propositions. Moreover, the conception of reason in the empiricist ethics of the seventeenth and eighteenth centuries was inadequate to account for and justify the possibility of moral insight. Early modern philosophy thus confronted what continues to be seen as its two "most intractable problems," the "simultaneous vindication of the principle of universal causality and of freedom of the human will." Above all, the metaphysically ultimate question of the absolute, therefore the question of the ultimate meaning of reality and of human existence, was denied a legitimate, cognitive resolution.

Kant's so-called Critical Philosophy – as embodied in his famous three *Critiques* (the *Critique of Pure Reason*, the *Critique of Practical Reason*, and the *Critique of Judgment*) – can be seen as an effort to set limits to the use of reason but at the same time to demonstrate, within these limits, the legitimacy of reason and the genuine possibility of human knowledge. This Critical Philosophy was a long time coming. In his so-called "silent decade" (1771–81), beyond the essay on the different human races and the brief articles in support of the Philanthropin, no publications appeared, only repeated promises about the impending results, made especially in letters to Marcus Herz. The complete plan of the philosophical investigation Kant undertook was outlined as four problems: (1) What can I know? (metaphysics). (2) What ought I to do? (moral philosophy). (3) What may I hope? (philosophy of religion). (4) What is man? (anthropology). When his work focused on the first question, the *Critique of Pure Reason* (which Schopenhauer would come to acclaim as "the most important book ever written in Europe") was the result. It appeared in 1781 and was met even by Kant's friends and colleagues with lack of comprehension at best and condemnation at worst. It would take several years (and a second edition in 1787) for Kant's star of fame to rise.

To put the "intractable problems" on a fresh footing, Kant conceives a new philosophical approach which he labels "transcendental critique." It consists in a self-examination into reason, into the conditions of the possibility of experience and cognition; that is, into the conditions of the possibility of mathematics, physics, metaphysics, and morality as sciences. The essence of the approach sets Kant decisively apart from the Greek inquirer in the following way. The immediate object of inquiry is no longer the metaphysical object, the object as it is *in itself*. The focus is instead on the human inquirer and the mind. As Cassirer has well articulated it, we are to understand the question of metaphysics more profoundly through examining its source in our understanding. Philosophical wonder here takes the very capacity to wonder as its object of inquiry. This is also arguably the most profound sense in which it *is* true to say that Kant's philosophy is his biography. Kant, who described himself as an "inquirer by nature," is asking by what right he is the seeker, how he may or may not legitimately proceed in his essential nature as an asking being. Before we can proceed, reason's credentials must be established, and limited. It is easy to see how and why Kant's fundamental reformulation of the philosophical question left his initial readers gasping. The question itself had to be changed, from one of what we know to one of how knowledge is possible. Kant's turn to the self, to the inquirer, constituted nothing less than another revolution, now in the very order of inquiry. It is only in this manner, he argued, that we can establish a new footing for any and every sphere of inquiry, from mathematics, to the physical and life sciences, to morality, aesthetics, history, law, and religion – all of which Kant himself went on to examine in the light of his transcendental, critical turn.

The steps of this process of examining reason before itself as its own tribunal begin with Kant's call for a "Copernican Revolution" in how philosophical inquiry proceeds. It is to be freed from the methods of both mathematical rationalism and scientific empiricism (the conflict between these two in philosophy being nothing less than a "scandal"). The new point of departure is the cognizing subject itself and the fundamental insight that *a priori* cognition (cognition independent of experience) of things is only possible with regard to what we ourselves, as cognizing subjects, contribute to these objects of experience. What we can know with strict universality and necessity are (and only are) the conditions that the mind places upon all experience. Put another way, the subject, the mind, is not first informed by the object; rather, it first gives form to the object. Objectivity *per se*, the very status of being an object, is due to the processes of human sensibility and understanding in relation to given empirical data. Even the objects of geometry and mechanics owe their form as spatial and temporal objects to these processes.

Human cognition consists in two equally contributing parts, sensible intuitions (sensations) and the contributions of the mind. The mind structures the sensible intuitions in terms of the mind-contributed forms of space and time, and it organizes or synthesizes these spatial and temporal intuitions in terms of the twelve categories of the understanding. The categories correspond to the twelve logical functions of judgment; Kant groups them under the four headings of quantity, quality, relation, and modality. Whereas in Aristotelian logic and metaphysics the categories are constitutive of things in themselves, and human perception and grasp of an object consists in a process of abstracting the form from the thing given, in Kant the forms of sensibility and understanding are the organizing principles of empirical sense data and first determine the sense data into objects perceptible by the mind. The process of judgment, by which the mind organizes and synthesizes its experience into objects, is called determinant judgment. Among these organizing principles are the categories of causality and substance. Hence all experience will be the experience of enduring things causally related and connected to one another. Scientific principles of the empirical world, including the principle that all events have causes, may thus be known with certainty because they are based on the universal and necessary forms which first make the experience of that world possible. In this way, Kant claims that Hume's skepticism concerning the law of causality is overcome.

Since the valid employment of the forms of space and time and the categories of the understanding is limited precisely to intuitable sense data, Kant's solution for the possibility of knowledge in the natural sciences does not apply to anything transcending our sense perception. Any attempts to know the objects of the natural universe regarded as what they are in themselves rather than as what they are for us, or to know immaterial objects such as a final cause of all things (theological idea), the totality of the natural world (cosmological idea), or an absolute subject (psychological idea), are doomed to failure. It is true that reason gives us ideas of such transcendent objects, but it cannot provide us with knowledge of them. Kant demonstrates reason's impotence in this regard through his articulation of the antinomies of pure reason. Arguments equally valid from the standpoint of formal logical principles may be put forth for contradictory claims about the transcendent realm, for example, for the proposition that everything in nature is wholly determined, and for the proposition that there is freedom from causality, a *causa sui*. These antinomies (contradictions) into which reason typically falls in previous interminable metaphysical disputes result from the fundamental error, on Kant's analysis, of assuming that cognition is of the things in themselves, the noumena, instead of realizing that cognition can only be of the way things are for us, of things as appearances or phenomena. The distinction between phenomena and noumena allows there to be coherent, scientific explanation of phenomenal events of the world occurring in causally determined chains, while still making room for the possibility that a whole series of such events may have an additional, albeit unknown, cause at the noumenal level of things in themselves. The ideas that reason provides us of a final cause, the totality of the universe, and an immaterial self or ego are interpreted by Kant not as objects of knowledge, not as concepts constitutive of objects, but as heuristic notions that set tasks for inquiry. The idea of a totality of nature and reason's striving for an account of such, for example, may be legitimately employed in scientific inquiry only in a regulative function to urge forward such inquiry in a perpetual quest for ever greater comprehension.

While correcting for the basic source of error in inquiry, the solution thus far not only does not satisfy the metaphysical eros, the striving of reason in those most important matters of God, freedom, and immortality, it strikes down the traditional ontological proof of the existence of God. With no capacity for intuiting the immaterial, the categories of the understanding here cannot be given any "material" to organize into a cognizable object. A logical analysis of the meaning of the concept of God, as omnipotent, omniscient, omnibenevolent, does not logically entail existence. The actual existence of anything is ascertained only by intuiting it. Moreover, even if it can be shown (as Kant thinks he has done) that freedom is not impossible in conjunction with a causally determined world, pointing to freedom's possibility is still a long way from establishing its actuality. For Kant, any possible satisfaction attainable by the human inquirer in these matters can only be gained through a moral route, through asserting the primacy of practical (moral) over theoretical reason. We can only have a moral basis for certitude in these urgent interests of reason.

The development of this moral avenue is begun by Kant in the Doctrine of Method of the *Critique of Pure Reason,* and it is continued in the Dialectic of the *Critique of Practical Reason* and in the discussion of teleological judgment in the *Critique of Judgment.* In his moral philosophy Kant again overturns the traditional order of inquiry. Instead of first ascertaining the end, the ultimate good to be achieved, and then seeking the means and motivations to secure it, Kant focuses on the form of the morally good will, its judgments and actions. What does this good will, the only thing good without qualification, consist in, and how it is achieved? Understanding the good will is the basis upon which the moral end, the highest good, is first conceived and sought as a purpose of human life. The highest good is defined by Kant as the synthetic unity of perfect virtue and complete happiness. Achieving it is a task to be undertaken by human action at the individual and collective social and political levels.

The ultimate realization of the highest good lies, however, beyond simply human power. Humanity does not possess the requisite control over nature to guarantee the achievement of happiness in proportion to the level of virtue attained, nor can the human will be transformed into a "holy one" in this finite and mortal life. The demonstration of the possibility of achieving the highest good, as Kant shows in the *Critique of Judgment,* relies on the "ought, therefore can" formulation basic to moral judging. Since the unity of perfect virtue and happiness ought to exist, it therefore can exist. But how? The answer is that the reality of God and immortality alone make it possible. "Since practical pure reason commands us to use this concept in order to achieve that purpose [the highest good in the world], we must assume it as possible [to realize]. This commanded effect, together with the sole conditions conceivable by us under which [achieving] that effect is possible, namely, the existence of God and the immortality of the soul, are matters of faith. . . . Faith . . . is reason's moral way of thinking in assenting to what is not accessible to theoretical cognition. It is the mind's steadfast principle to assume as true what we must necessarily presuppose as a condition for the possibility of [achieving] the highest moral final purpose, and to assume this because of our obligation to this final purpose." Thus it is through a grasp of what is required morally that we can have reason to believe in the reality of God and immortality. The right of the seeker to affirm the truth of the existence of what is of utmost importance to the human being and human reason, in the wake of the findings of critique which close the door permanently to theoretical cognition in this regard, relies on moral insight and a claim to the consistency of moral duty.

The fundamental premise of Kant's moral thought is the consciousness of the moral law inherent to practical reason. Awareness of the moral law is a fact of reason. In the ordinary human understanding's expression of and demand for "ought," in its passing of moral judgment, in its ability to affirm not only that it can reject sensual claims in favor of the preservation of life, but that it can even sacrifice the latter in favor of a morally upright choice, in other words, in the experience of ordinary human life, Kant finds the manifestation of the fundamental human consciousness of the moral law. This consciousness in fact informs human choice-making in the lives of simple and hardworking peoples (the model of his parental home and its surrounding Pietist community likely forms the backdrop to this observation). The philosophical task, as Kant defines it in his *Groundwork of the Metaphysics of Morals*, is to clarify the moral law, the fundamental principle of morality, to articulate it, separate it out from the muddle of empirical desires, conventions, religious practices, and the like, and to provide it with a philosophical defense against those schools of thought which doubt or even deny its reality. It is a task especially important for moral instruction, since in moral education, in character formation, the objective is to facilitate the clear consciousness of the fundamental moral principle and to lead to its resolute adoption as the supreme criterion in moral judgment. Where such resolute adoption takes place, the human agent is morally self-legislating, or autonomous. The rational agent gives the rational law unto itself. When judgments and decisions are heteronomous instead of autonomous, they are determined by factors external to the agent's reason, whether these factors come from instincts, needs, feelings, or circumstances and other persons. An agent's heteronomous actions fail to achieve moral worth. Human dignity rests on the achievement of moral character, a life of moral worth (and not on progress in scientific advances, as some strains of Enlightenment thought held).

Kant gives several different formulations to the moral law or supreme principle of morality, which he calls the categorical imperative. As Allen Wood has explained these, "Kant's argument is progressive, with the later formulations constituting ever more adequate expressions of the supreme principle of morality. To insure the unity of the principle he is seeking, Kant formulates the moral law first in terms of a certain kind of principle (a categorical principle or universal law), then in terms of a value to be esteemed, respected, and furthered (humanity as an end in itself), then in terms of its ground in the rational will which legislates universally, recognizing no authority except its own autonomy, and finally as the allness or totality of the system of ends expressed in the formula of the realm of ends." The first expression of the moral law is to act only on those maxims or principles that one could will to be a universal law. The second expression is to respect persons as ends in themselves and not only as means to further self-interest. The third is to act only on those principles that one can will or legislate oneself as a rational, autonomous agent, and the fourth is to act always as a member of a kingdom or system of persons conceived as ends in themselves. The concept of duty defines our relation as finite beings of desire and need to the moral law; duty is what we must do, despite frequent desires to the contrary. Our motivation to moral action arises from reason itself, as moral feeling or respect for the law.

Kant's anthropology lectures help to give a clearer sense of his conception of how the *a priori* principle of morality becomes efficacious in human life. There are three levels to his discussion, corresponding to three distinct questions: (1) what we ought to do, or the articulation of the objective moral principle, the categorical imperative to act only on those maxims which one can will to be a universal law; (2) what we are able to do and how we can be brought to do it, or the anthropological investigation into human nature to ascertain its capability of fulfilling what is required of it, of ascertaining what human beings, as freely acting beings, can and should make of themselves; and (3) what we actually do, as documented in the historical record and in such writings as biographies, which provide the empirical information which can be used in moral education both for taking advantage of certain human characteristics and for safeguarding against others. A concrete fulfillment of the teleology of human reason, of relating all cognitions to its essential purposes, requires the social and political organization of the state that is in accord with the moral law and the highest good and so provides its citizens with conditions conducive to their moral self-development (as indicated in such essays as Kant's 1795 *Toward Eternal Peace*, and 1784 "Idea for a Universal History with a Cosmopolitan Intent").

The place of the *Critique of Judgment* in Kant's program of philosophy may be seen in terms of further steps in the analysis of the seeker's relation to the world. This relation is exhausted neither by cognitive, scientific inquiry nor by our moral choices and actions, but contains as well our human aesthetic capacities, our ability to take pleasure in the beautiful, the feeling of the sublime, and reflective, teleological judgment in regard to purposes in nature. For Kant, such considerations are not irrelevant even for the moral and theoretical domains. Indeed, the third *Critique* affirms the mediating role of reflective judgment between nature and freedom, with a resulting unity of the two different orders.

One of the important results of Kant's inquiry is to distinguish aesthetic judgment as a form of rationality in its own right – that is, distinct from theoretical cognition or moral judgment – and so with its own principles, ones that free it also from convention or fashion. In that it is free also from interest in the existence of the object, it is a pure aesthetic judgment of taste unaffected by the private interests which the actuality of the object and its possession might impact. The feeling of the sublime corresponds with the elevation of soul which the moral being as a creature of sense feels in relation to a nature omnipotent with regard to it. As in the case of moral feeling, in aesthetic reflection we turn from outside to reflection upon ourselves within, and in this turning we come to feel an appreciation for who and what we are and to feel the very dignity of our essential nature. Just as in the move from the starry heavens above to the moral law within, an entirely different domain of existence comes into view for us. That nature is seen as purposive, as ordered and teleological, is important not only for realizing reason's moral purposes, but for the life sciences, for the biological investigations emerging in the eighteenth century.

Kant's dictum was that what can and should be learned is not so much philosophy, as to philosophize. What we need to do is not to absorb schools of thought as subjectively historical, as facts reported to one, but instead to "practice reason's talent in the adherence to all its universal principles . . . reserving always the right of reason to examine these principles themselves with regard to their sources and either to confirm or reject them." This is how the educator-philosopher would want his work read. His critics were immediate, including Herder (his former student), Herbart (the successor to his Chair in Königsberg), and HEGEL. That both critics and proponents have actively continued to this date underscores a repeated observation among his commentators: the problems he addressed, from the question of metaphysics, to the epistemological foundations of science, to the possibility and nature of moral agency, remain unavoidable for the modern thinker.

Bibliography

Writings

Kant, Immanuel. *Kants gesammelte Schriften,* ed. Preussischen Akademie der Wissenschaften (Berlin: Walter de Gruyter, 1900–). For English translations, see the *Cambridge Edition of the Works of Immanuel Kant* [introductions prepared by the editors are helpful]. See also *Kant: Political Writings,* ed. Hans Reiss, in the *Cambridge Texts in the History of Political Thought,* 1970, reprinted 1996.

Further reading

Allison, Henry E.: *Kant's Theory of Taste: A Reading of the Critique of Aesthetic Judgment* (New York: Cambridge University Press, 2000).
——: *Kant's Transcendental Idealism: An Interpretation and Defense* (New Haven, CT: Yale University Press, 1983).
Ameriks, Karl: *Kant and the Fate of Autonomy: Problems in the Appropriation of the Critical Philosophy* (New York: Cambridge University Press, 2000).
Cassirer, Ernst: *Kant's Life and Thought,* trans. James Haden (New Haven, CT: Yale University Press, 1981). Originally published as *Kants Leben und Lehre,* 1918 reprint (Darmstadt: Wissenschaftliche Buchgesellschaft, 1977).
Guyer, Paul: *Kant and the Experience of Freedom: Essays on Aesthetics and Morality* (Cambridge: Cambridge University Press, 1993).
Höffe, Otfried: *Immanuel Kant,* trans. Marshall Farrier (Albany: State University of New York, 1994).
Makkreel, Rudolf A.: *Imagination and Interpretation in Kant: The Hermeneutical Import of the Critique of Judgment* (Chicago: University of Chicago Press, 1990).
Munzel, G. Felicitas: *Kant's Conception of Moral Character: The "Critical" Link of Morality, Anthropology, and Reflective Judgment* (Chicago: University of Chicago Press, 1999).
Wood, Allen W.: *Kant's Ethical Thought* (Cambridge: Cambridge University Press, 1999).
Zammito, John H.: *The Genesis of Kant's Critique of Judgment* (Chicago: University of Chicago Press, 1992).

19

Kierkegaard

George J. Stack

Søren Kierkegaard (1813–1855 CE) was a Danish religious thinker, philosopher, and important contributor to Danish literature. His insistence on the priority of individual existence, subjective reflection, choice, and responsibility make him the earliest contributor to the philosophy of existentialism. His dynamic concept of the self, as well as his passionate defense of religious faith, had significant influence on leading theologians and major thinkers in continental philosophy in the twentieth century.

The youngest son of Michael Pedersen Kierkegaard (a prosperous businessman who immersed himself in a guilt-ridden pietism), Søren studied theology at the University of Copenhagen, but was far more interested in philosophy. Kierkegaard eventually was awarded a master's degree in theology and ordained a minister. However, he never took a position as pastor and survived on the inheritance his father had left him.

Aside from his close relationship with his father, the other significant personal relationship in his life was with Regina Olsen, a 17-year-old girl to whom he became engaged. A year later, Kierkegaard suddenly broke off the engagement. He probably did so because he thought himself psychically unfit for marriage and "too old" for such a lively young girl. And, no doubt, he realized that his ambitious literary projects would consume his limited energies, leaving little time or energy for Regina. In his *Papers* he simply wrote that "If I had had more faith, I would have married Regina."

In the mid-1840s Kierkegaard became the butt of a satirical newspaper, the *Kosar*, to such an extent that he was scorned and ridiculed by many. He took this as a form of imposed suffering and as an indication of the cruelty of "the crowd."

Soon after completing his master's thesis, *The Concept of Irony* (1841), Kierkegaard produced an astonishing number of remarkable works in a short time. These writings were presented under different pseudonyms which served to depict a variety of "life-views" or perspectives. His pseudonymous works were *Either/Or* (1843), *Fear and Trembling* (1843), *Repetition* (1843), *Philosophical Fragments* (1844), *The Concept of Anxiety* (1844), *Stages on Life's Way* (1845), *Concluding Unscientific Postscript* (1846), *Crisis in the Life of an Actress* (1848), *The Sickness unto Death* (1849), and *Training in Christianity* (1850). Kierkegaard considered these writings as "poetic" and "indirect communications." At the end of *Concluding Unscientific Postscript* he announced that "Magister Kierkegaard" was the author of these pseudonymous works.

A series of ethical and religious writings were published coeval with the pseudonymous works. These were in the form of "direct communications," in contrast to the "indirect communication" of the poetic–aesthetic writings. The ethical discourses were consonant with Kierkegaard's view that, as he put it in his *Papers,* "no authentic existence is possible without having passed through the ethical." In the religious discourses, *Works of Love* (1847), *Christian Discourses* (1848), *The Lilies of the Field and the Birds of the Air* (1849), *For Self-examination* (1851), and *Judge for Yourself* (1851–2), Kierkegaard presents incisive commentaries on central themes in what he called "NT theology" or the New Testament principles he thought were reduced to clichés in official "Christendom." In these lucid discourses he passionately defended the core values of "primitive Christianity."

In a series of newspaper articles and pamphlets (including his own publication, *The Moment*) Kierkegaard unleashed polemics against the values of "the present age" and against "Christendom" or the official Danish state church in which he claimed genuine Christianity could no longer be found. Most of these critiques were gathered together in *Attack Upon Christendom* (1854–5).

In his earliest thinking Kierkegaard was under the influence of a pervasive Hegelianism (see HEGEL). His magister's thesis (which was equivalent to a doctoral dissertation) showed this influence by its reliance on Hegel's language and categories. Even so, he managed, in an ironic way, to undermine Hegel's deification of "the Universal" by focusing on the subjectivity of SOCRATES' ethical existence.

The rationalist metaphysics of Hegel is criticized (most tellingly in *Philosophical Fragments* and *Concluding Unscientific Postscript*) for a number of reasons. In Kierkegaard's view Hegel's system was comprised of a catena of bloodless abstractions which virtually effaced individuals. It defended a pantheism that absorbed everything into the "Absolute Spirit." Hegel treated Christianity as a historical phase in the evolution of spirit and incorporated it into his rationalist philosophical system, thereby annulling it as a religion that required deep faith and embraced the "absolute paradox" that an eternal being came into existence in temporal history. Finally, Kierkegaard argued that Hegel's theory that all transitions are necessary dialectical movements erased human freedom and justified whatever happens in the world. Indeed, Hegel had said that "The history of the world is the judgment of the world." In *Philosophical Fragments* Kierkegaard emphasized the non-necessity or contingency of every transition from possibility to actuality. The centrality of possibility in the thought of HEIDEGGER and SARTRE is indebted to its importance in Kierkegaard's concept of existence.

Kierkegaard said that he started with "the Socratic." This meant he began his thinking, in opposition to Hegel's stress on what is universal, with Socrates' standpoint of subjective individuality. It was from Socrates' critical analyses that Kierkegaard garnered support for his doubts about objective certainty. As a "corrective" to his age (which valued system over the individual), he recalled individuals to a sense of their value and the importance of their ethical existence. In his insistent defenses of ethical responsibility and religious faith Kierkegaard accentuated "the intensification of subjectivity," the cultivation of "inwardness."

In his first major published work, *Either/Or*, Kierkegaard portrayed a purely aesthetic, amoral, hedonistic way of life. This "stage of life" is the most common because its aim is the maximum enjoyment of life, the pursuit of pleasure as the sole goal of life. The papers of a character called "A" express the range of aesthetic life from the civilized enjoyment of art to the cynical, erotic pursuits described in "The Diary of a Seducer." The internal dynamics of the aesthetic sphere of existence erode the integrity of the self and tend to lead to boredom, despair, madness, or a self-destructive narcissism. The desire for an eternalized moment of enjoyment eludes the aesthetic personality and psychic emptiness haunts the repeated attempts to attain an illusory life of uninterrupted pleasure. The letters of the character Judge William criticize "A" and stress the importance of impassioned choice, continuity, genuineness, and responsibility. His views point to a turn toward the constructive possibility of the ethical stage of existence.

The highest, most complete "sphere of existence" in what Kierkegaard calls "the dialectic of life" is the religious. In *Concluding Unscientific Postscript*, Socrates's individual existential ethics of subjectivity is presented as a transition to a "leap of faith" beyond the limits of reason. Kierkegaard describes two forms of religious life: a natural, immanent religiousness and a religion of transcendence such as Christianity that embraces the paradox of the God-man, Christ, and requires a passional faith "beyond reason" in what is "objectively uncertain." Faith is a subjective, passionate belief in a transcendent divine being whose existence is, for reason, a possibility. In *Philosophical Fragments*, the "absolute paradox" that God, an eternal being, entered time and human history is presented in a series of sophisticated arguments designed to lead the reader to an understanding of the essence of Christian faith.

Our "potentiality-for," our capacity to change our lives and commit ourselves to an integrating constructive goal (*telos*) by means of significant choice, is central to Kierkegaard's concept of freedom. In *The Concept of Dread* he probes the question of original sin and why Adam and mankind in general fall into sin. In doing so, he presents an acute psychological analysis of anxiety (*Angst*) which distinguishes it from fear. Anticipating later thinkers, he sees that fear has a definite object, but anxiety is experienced in the face of nothing whatsoever or "the nothingness of possibility." The state of anxiety is doubly paradoxical since it is "a sympathetic antipathy" *and* "an antipathetic sympathy." The biblical account of the "fall" of Adam is given an interpretation that has never been surpassed. It is Adam's innocence in relation to the divine command not to eat the fruit of the tree of knowledge of good and evil, as well as his freedom, that generates a debilitating anxiety that leads to his fall. Our capacity for choice, then, discloses an "anxious freedom" in relation to our unique existential possibilities. That we experience anxiety when confronted with significant choices (particularly between good and evil) testifies to our freedom.

In *Fear and Trembling*, Abraham's willingness to obey the divine command to sacrifice his son Isaac demonstrates a faith that goes beyond the limits of moral law insofar as it requires "a teleological suspension of the ethical." Kierkegaard dramatizes the limits of social ethics in order to show the distinction between religious faith and ethics, as well as the stringent demands and dangerous temptations of religious passion.

Moods are emphasized in Kierkegaard's writings because they are "determinations of subjectivity." In *The Sickness unto Death*, various forms of despair are described as significations of spiritual states. The aesthetic life ends in unconscious despair and the limits of ethical existence are tied to the limits of finite, relative goods. The cure for the despair haunting finite existence is religious faith. The "eternal validity" of the person is sustained by the "power that created the self." The ultimate choice by which we may be redeemed is that of a dependence on the transcendent being or "Absolute Subject" and an acceptance of our guilt "before God," a personal relation to the divinity.

In the posthumously published *The Point of View of My Work as an Author*, Kierkegaard claims that his entire project, from his earliest writings, was "dialectical" and concentrated on the question of how to become a Christian. Thus, he saw himself as a religious author whose entire task was to recall would-be Christians to the discipline, passion, and vitality of their faith. He offered a radical re-examination of what it means to "become a Christian," using his rhetorical and analytical skills to disclose the limits of reason and open the door to faith.

In his *Papers* Kierkegaard says that one of his goals was to create difficulties, to "jack up the price of existence" because it had become too cheap in "the present age." He desired to save Christian existence from indifference and suffocation by Christendom by iterating the strenuous and demanding requirements of authentic Christianity. The faith he offers is not mild. It proclaims itself "heterogeneous" in relation to worldliness and to our natural tendencies. As a *telos* or goal of existence, it demands what he calls in *Repetition* (and elsewhere) a "willed repetition" of choice, an intensification of existence, a resoluteness, and persistent striving. In his depictions of both Socratic ethical subjectivity and genuine Christian existence he makes "existence," in the strict sense, the goal toward which we ought to strive. And existence itself, like so much he discerned in human life, is inherently "paradoxical."

Kierkegaard, in his lonely battle against depersonalization, anonymous public opinion, and mass consciousness became what he wanted to be known as: "that individual." His influence, as he suspected, was postponed until the twentieth century. After he was stricken with a spinal disease and taken to a hospital, a representative of the Danish state church visited him and wanted to administer last rites to him. He is supposed to have said, with typical sarcasm, "I have no need of the ministration of a civil servant."

Bibliography

Writings

Concluding Unscientific Postscript, trans. David F. Swenson (Princeton, NJ: Princeton University Press, 1941).

Stages on Life's Way, trans. Walter Lowrie (Princeton, NJ: Princeton University Press, 1945).

Attack Upon Christendom, trans. Walter Lowrie (Princeton, NJ: Princeton University Press, 1946).

Either/Or, two volumes, trans. David F. Swenson, Lillian M. Swenson, and Walter Lowrie (Garden City, NY: Anchor Books, 1959).

Philosophical Fragments, trans. David F. Swenson (Princeton, NJ: Princeton University Press, 1962).

The Point of View of My Work as an Author, trans. Walter Lowrie (New York: Harper & Row, 1962).

178 *George J. Stack*

Journals and Papers, ed. and trans. Howard V. Hong, and Edna H. Hong (Bloomington, IN, and London: Indiana University Press, 1967–78).

The Concept of Anxiety, ed. and trans. Reidar Thomte and Albert B. Anderson (Princeton, NJ: Princeton University Press, 1980).

The Sickness unto Death, trans. Howard V. Hong and Edna H. Hong (Princeton, NJ: Princeton University Press, 1980).

Fear and Trembling and *Repetition*, ed. and trans. Howard V. Hong and Edna H. Hong (Princeton, NJ: Princeton University Press, 1983).

Further reading

Collins, James: *The Mind of Kierkegaard*, 2nd edn (Princeton, NJ: Princeton University Press, 1983).

Diem, Hermann: *Kierkegaard's Dialectic of Existence*, trans. H. Knight (Edinburgh and London: Oliver and Boyd, 1959).

Elrod, John W.: *Being and Existence in Kierkegaard's Pseudonymous Works* (Princeton, NJ: Princeton University Press, 1975).

Hannay, Alastair: *Kierkegaard* (London and Boston: Routledge, 1982).

Malantschuk, Gregor: *Kierkegaard's Thought*, trans. H. V. Hong and E. H. Hong (Princeton, NJ: Princeton University Press, 1971).

Price, George: *The Narrow Pass: A Study of Kierkegaard's Concept of Man* (New York: McGraw-Hill, 1963).

Stack, George: *Kierkegaard's Existential Ethics* (1977); repr. (Brookfield, VT: Ashgate, 1992).

Thomas, J. H.: *Subjectivity and Paradox* (New York: Macmillan, 1957).

Thomas, Josiah: *Kierkegaard* (New York: Knopf, 1973).

20

Laozi

Chad Hansen

Laozi [Lao Tzu] (dates uncertain; speculation ranges from from 600 to 200 BCE) is, we assume, the author of the *Daode Jing* [*Tao Te Ching*], the most beloved and widely translated Chinese philosophical text. The figure of Laozi has always been shrouded in mystery. The mystery deepens the more we discover about the texts. Tradition regarded Laozi as CONFUCIUS' (sixth century BCE) teacher and the "founder" of Daoism; the "doubt tradition" movement in modern China gave influential arguments for dating the text to the middle "Warring States" period (fourth century BCE). The discovery of a first-century BCE version of the text suggests that the text was in flux over a long period of time. A. C. Graham has argued that the text probably became important only after ZHUANGZI [CHUANG TZU] died (*c*.295 BCE). Scholars in China, on the contrary, have reverted to the traditional dating, placing Laozi before Confucius. Many scholars, however, dismiss Laozi as mythological or use his name as shorthand for "the author(s) of the *Daode Jing*."

The interpretation of the text is complicated by its disputed history and, thus, is even more controversial. There are now over 100 different translations and close to 2,000 commentaries in Chinese. Traditional views are that Laozi inspired Zhuangzi and they together formed a philosophical school known as "Daoism" which inspired a later religion of the same name. Until recently, scholars mostly thought the religion was a distortion of the philosophy, but some now argue that the text emerged first from a religion that worshiped the Yellow Emperor along with Laozi (known as Huang-Lao).

We obviously cannot consider all the interpretations here and our interest is more philosophical than religious. We can justify our focus whichever historical story we tell, since, as Graham's analysis stressed, it was *The Zhuangzi* that introduced Laozi into Chinese philosophical discourse. Whatever the dates and origin of this text, Laozi first meant to Chinese philosophy what the school of Zhuangzi first found of interest in it. We will look for the philosophical theory that will best justify Zhuangzi's interest and explain the traditional genealogy. And we will leave open whether the religious reading came later than the philosophical one or preceded it.

We should note that religious interpretations dominate the extant translations. They reverse our strategy here and make the interpretation of Zhuangzi conform to the theory that he was a religious disciple. According to this interpretation, Laozi and later Zhuangzi had some mystical experience – an experience of the indescribable oneness of everything. They changed the meaning of "*dao*" ("*tao*") from "guiding instructions" and used it to refer to a divine being (on the model of Buddha or mystical creator-God).

Besides the empirically dubious claims about the mystical experiences and the meaning change, the religious interpretation of the text faces serious difficulties.

1   The mystical reading, "there is a *dao* which language cannot describe," describes that very *dao* and is incoherent on its face. Elaborating further on that *dao*, as religious readings take the texts to do, is hard to motivate.

2   If we take seriously the claim that language cannot talk about *dao*, it must rely on a theory of what language can do as much as it does on the concept of *dao*. We can study that philosophy of language with no threat of incoherence (especially since ordinarily *dao* refers to a linguistic object, namely prescriptive discourse). If we can explain the content and character of Laozi's text using its linguistic theory alone, our approach will undermine any remaining motivation to postulate the mystical experience and accuse Daoists of changing the meaning of the key term in their critique of Confucianism.

Let us start, then, with the historical account in *The Zhuangzi*. It names Shen Dao [Shen Tao] as a forerunner of Laozi. Shen Dao's slogan was "abandon knowledge; discard self." "Knowledge" meant knowledge of some moral *dao*. He used the notion of a "*Great Dao*" to refer to the actual course of world history. You *will* follow it; you need no knowledge of *dao* (guides) to follow the *Great Dao*. "Even a clod of earth, cannot miss the *dao*," he concluded.

The Zhuangzi account distances both Laozi and Zhuangzi from Shen Dao. The narrator says "[Shen Dao's] is a *dao* (guide) that cannot *dao* (guide)," and characterizes it as a *dao* (guide) for the dead, not for the living. The point is that "what will be will be" has no implications for action. Whatever we do will accord with *Great Dao*, but knowing that does not help one decide what to do. Zhuangzi implicitly diagnosed a deeper paradox in Shen Dao's views. Since it is telling us to do something, Shen Dao's slogan is itself a bit of guiding knowledge. So, if we follow it, we disobey it. If we follow Shen Dao's prescription, we do what the prescription itself says not to do. Laozi, however, not only tolerated this paradox, he replicated it.

We can understand Laozi, then, as accepting the paradoxical "abandon knowledge" *spirit* of Shen Dao, but rejecting the fatalism. Something like the *Great Dao* does surface sporadically in the *Laozi*, but it is not the focus of his theory. He may have tolerated the paradox on the grounds stated in his first line: "No *dao* (guide) that can *dao* (guide) is a constant *dao* (guide)." Shen Dao's is a *constant dao* (i.e. natural or not dependent on changeable convention) but it cannot guide. Any *dao* (guide) that can is changeable.

That famous opening line is followed by a less noticed parallel – "Any name that can name is not a constant name." This signals that *dao* denotes linguistic items – systems of guiding discourse. Laozi is skeptical of the reliability of a discourse *dao*. The skepticism rests on the conventional (hence changeable) nature of language. No discourse-based instruction will guide reliably in all circumstances because the terms used do not mark distinctions reliably. The contrast of the natural and the conventional pervades the text.

How does this line of thought lead to the "abandon knowledge" conclusion? What motivates it is the goal of freedom from social control. Laozi treats (prescriptive) knowledge as based on language. Accordingly, knowledge consists of arbitrary, historically "accidental" social systems of making distinctions, guiding desires, and acting. Laozi then justifies "abandon knowledge" as a way to recover our natural, authentic, spontaneous human impulses.

Chinese language theories call all characters *ming* (names). Adjectives and common nouns alike have a scope – they "pick out" a range of reality and exclude the rest. Words are "names" of their "range of stuff." Learning a name for X means learning how to make a distinction between X and non-X. We cannot claim mastery of the word "cat" if we call spiders "cat." We thus learn X and *fei*-X (not-X) together as a single socially shared way to make a distinction. Laozi implies that in learning to apply a distinction and classify things in one way rather than another, we are being socialized into an inherited social design.

Much of this approach to language is common in ancient China. What Laozi adds is that society shapes our desires via words and distinctions. We will not count as having mastered the distinction between beautiful and ugly if we prefer the ugly. Acquiring a "sophisticated" taste molds our desires and shapes our choices and action.

Artificial desires increase strife, first because social structures expand the number of desires and second because the acquired desires are more competitive than natural ones. We would not *naturally* desire things, for example, simply because they were rare. Socially instilled desires motivate a thirst for status and power. Our natural desires are few and simple.

Finally, the desires lead to *wei* (action) – a term at the center of Laozi's famous *wu* (lack)–*wei* (deem:act) [non-action] slogan. Language books teach that the word *wei* (do:deem) has two meanings – "to act" and "for the sake of." Hence, the standard elaboration of Laozi's slogan is that we should not act *deliberately or purposefully*. We could motivate this conclusion by using Buddhist or Western psychology (i.e. desires get in the way of reason), but it is hard to explain why Laozi would recommend being careless or random in action. He has no concept of reason and treats some desires (for sex, food, leisure, etc.) as acceptable.

Wei (do:deem) has another meaning that explains the slogan better in a Chinese context. *Wei* is used in the Chinese approximation of belief contexts ("X believes that T is P"). Classical Chinese splits the embedded belief sentence. The (optional) subject (T) comes before the *wei* (do:deem) and the predicate (P) after. The complete form is: "X with regard to T, *wei* (do:deem) [it to be] P."

If we understand *wei* (do:deem) as treating things according to what we deem them to be, we get an insight into Laozi's slogan. It is a corollary of the view that we are to avoid socially instilled distinctions and desires. So, ultimately, we should also avoid action based on our training in linguistic distinctions. The objection is to socialization, not rational purpose or deliberation. Laozi indicates that he senses a paradox in *wu* (lack)–*wei* (deem:act). He also says "lack" *wei* (do:deem) yet "lack not" *wei* (do:deem). The problem is that we have just learned a guiding concept complete with a distinction, a desire, and a proposed course of action. If we are to avoid *wei* we must also avoid avoiding *wei*.

Laozi's slogan replicates Shen Dao's "abandon knowledge" paradox (i.e. "abandon knowledge" is itself a bit of [prescriptive] knowledge). The knowledge in question is still "social guidance," now analyzed as action guided by desires engendered by social distinctions and names. Laozi's motivation is a desire for naturalness, spontaneity, or freedom from social conventions rather than fatalism, but the paradox is in the conclusion, not the motivation. The paradox in *wu* (lack)–*wei* (do:deem) follows a bigger and more interesting circle.

The analysis starts with the concepts of natural/conventional which it treats as a pivotal distinction. Laozi teaches us a potentially controversial way to draw the distinction (i.e. anything based on "language" is conventional). It implicitly encourages a preference or desire for being natural and, finally, based on the names, distinctions, and desires, it recommends an action. Laozi says, "in pursuit of *dao* we daily forget." This forgetting is the *wei* (deem:act) of getting rid of *wei* (deem:act). As long as we do it, therefore, we fail to do it. In urging *wu–wei* we have identified an action, and in striving to avoid it we are doing what it tells us not to.

Zhuangzi abandoned the paradoxical *wu–wei* position, but he accepted the analysis showing how distinctions and desires are "socially constructed." Laozi's paradox vaguely reminds us of the Buddhist paradox of desire (you must desire to rid yourself of desires). However, Buddhist theory indicts especially the *natural* desires. Laozi's stance is more plausibly interpreted as allowing "pre-social" desires. His position tends toward that of the Confucian nativists, such as MENCIUS. If we can "forget" the learned desires arising from language socialization, we will return to nature.

The "new born" child does have desires (for sex, food, comfort, etc.). These and their "purely natural" successors are the desires that underwrite Laozi's "primitive utopia." A suitably reduced system of desires would sustain social life at the simple agrarian village level but would not generate the "unnatural" ambition to travel and expand one's horizons of knowledge.

The social analysis of knowledge (i.e. discourse guidance) is thus accompanied by a conception of innate or natural knowledge (prelinguistic instinct). This partly gives the text its notorious ambiguity and contradictory character. One finds passages in which knowledge, clarity, and sages are ridiculed and their "accomplishments" pictured as viciously relative. Then other passages speak positively of knowledge, clarity, and sages.

One philosophical way of reading Laozi can ameliorate both the paradox and the inconsistency. It also gives a coherent role to interesting stylistic and content features of Laozi's philosophical poem. According to this philosophical approach, we should read the bulk of the text (the political and metaphysical passages) as a heuristic (i.e. leading us indirectly to discover something), and we should distinguish three systems of knowledge. The first system of knowledge consists of conventional guidance or wisdom. Conventional knowledge includes the familiar moral precepts of Confucians (traditionalists) and the systematic utilitarianism of the Mohists (moral reformers). Moralists propose schemes of guidance designed in the hope that everyone in society will learn and follow them. As Laozi noted, these moral systems are based on learning distinctions and using them in choosing actions.

Laozi challenges the assumptions behind this "positive" view partly by exhibiting a system we can call the negative *dao*. We get this *dao* by reversing all conventional moral assumptions. Laozi's strategy shows that for key guiding terms, we can choose exactly the opposite of conventional wisdom. He draws the sayings in this "negative *dao*" from poems, slogans, couplets, and aphorisms collected from many sources (and, as our textual theory suggests, over a long period of editing). The sources include military stratagems, political cynicism, and Shen Dao's monism. We may even count Daoist primitivism itself as a heuristic example of anti-conventional advice.

This negative *dao* is Laozi's famous "*dao* of reversal." Where Confucian or conventional morality normally values *ren* [*jen*] (benevolence), Laozi notes that *tian* [*t'ien*] (nature:heaven) is not benevolent. We normally value activity, dominance, the upper position, strength, and upstanding rigidity. Laozi urges us to see the value of passivity, weakness, the lower position, and receptive yielding. Laozi values dullness over brilliance, ignorance over knowledge, lacking over having, etc.

These reversals link up easily with the emerging *yin–yang*, sexual reproduction cosmology. Laozi emphasizes the importance of the female and "draws sustenance from the mother." He treats the female as the "valley of the world." Further, *yin–yang* also metaphorically explains the importance of water, with its connection to moisture, the lower position, passivity, and overcoming through yielding.

On the metaphysical side, where we normally value *you* (having:being), Laozi points to the utility of *wu* (lacking:non-being). He stresses the usefulness of the emptiness in a cup, a room, and, famously, the hub of a wheel. The knowledge we gain from these "reversals" of ordinary value may be called "negative knowledge." It consists in seeing that the conventional ways of using terms to guide us can be reversed. They are not constant.

However, we cannot coherently take Laozi to allege that his negative *dao* is a constant *dao*. Confucians criticize the "scheming methods" and the disingenuous tone of some of the "negative" advice. Laozi, they charge, urges us to act submissive in order to dominate. He talks of keeping people ignorant, so they can be ruled more easily.

The criticism implies that Laozi surreptitiously clings to the conventional values, e.g. he really aims at domination. We can excuse his doing so if he is trying to make the negative *dao* seem plausible from our present lights. However, there is a deeper objection. Although he reverses the values, he relies on precisely the same conventional terms and distinctions. Is he still committed to a "constant" *dao* based on "constant names"?

The strategical response is to say that the negative *dao* is a heuristic. Its point is to get us to see something else. Thus it defends Laozi against these charges. The moral of the reversal is not simply to replace one normative scheme with another. It calls into question the whole idea of having a scheme in the first place, hence of *any* replacement scheme. Laozi's position might be that the practical "content" of conventional distinctions lies in the evaluative attitude that accompanies them. The conventional assumption is that they guide us correctly. Hence, if they can be reversed, then the scheme of names is not a "reliable" way to carve things up.

This conclusion is somewhat implausible. Names and distinctions that reflect real joints and fissures of the world can obviously guide us in different ways in different circumstances. Water is good when we are thirsty and bad when we are drowning. We can help Laozi's case a little if we assume he understood Mohism well enough to be appealing to its pragmatic analysis of naming. If the justification of a distinction is only pragmatic success, and if we can show that equal success follows from reversing conventional guidance, this will call into question either the distinctions themselves or the strings of guiding discourse using them.

Now, to what guiding system does the heuristic point? What could the third level of knowledge be? Laozi formulates no answer. Part of the genius and appeal of Laozi's philosophical poem is to leave that up to the reader. We can say that it should not simply be an alternative, posited *dao*. It is more likely that Laozi intended to challenge us to make a "philosophical ascent" to a higher level of ethical reflection – to "thinking about thinking." The most plausible point of the *Daode Jing's* analysis would be meta-ethical. It leads us to reflect on the process of proposing rival *daos* for the purpose of guidance.

Its thrust seems to be relativist or skeptical. To say that there is no constant *dao* is to say that any *dao* will rest on some scheme of background distinctions and attitudes. All standards consist of distinctions and attitudes which are themselves subject to revision on subsequent reflection. We may decide that Laozi's point is either that there is no way or there are many ways of asking and answering ultimate normative questions.

We can also see a philosophical role for the religious or mystical reading that dominates translations. The skeptical point of Laozi's analysis of action-guiding distinctions is that there really are none. A mystical answer is practically indistinguishable from the skeptical one. "There is no ultimate criterion of rightness" and "there is an ultimate criterion that says nothing" will be functionally equivalent. Laozi's skeptical overtones emerge in his occasional celebration of "ignorance" or "dullness." There is wisdom in knowing your not knowing and knowing when to stop.

Bibliography

Writings

Lao Tzu: Tao Te Ching, trans. D. C. Lau (Baltimore, MD: Penguin Books, 1963).
Lao Tsu: Tao Te Ching, trans. Feng Gia-Fu and Jane English (New York: Alfred A. Knopf, 1972).
Lao-tzu: Te-Tao Ching. A New Translation Based on the Recently Discovered Ma-wang-tui Texts, trans. Robert G. Hendrks (New York: Ballantine Books, 1989).

Further reading

Graham, Angus: *Disputers of the Tao: Philosophical Argument in Ancient China* (La Salle, IL: Open Court, 1989).
Hansen, Chad: *A Daoist Theory of Chinese Thought* (New York: Oxford University Press, 1992).

21

Leibniz

Nicholas Jolley

Gottfried Wilhelm Leibniz (1646–1716 CE) was a German philosopher and mathematician. The son of a university professor, he was born in Leipzig at a time when Germany was ravaged by the horrors of the Thirty Years War (1618–48); the promotion of peace and reconciliation in many spheres of life was to be one of his dominant concerns. As a boy he was brilliantly precocious, teaching himself Latin and studying the scholarly works in his father's library. He was educated at the universities of Leipzig and Jena, where his studies foreshadowed the direction of his future interests. His bachelor's dissertation, "On the Principle of Individuation," anticipates his later interest in philosophical and logical problems concerning identity; less directly, his doctoral thesis, "On Difficult Cases in Law," anticipates his concern with providing a quasi-legal defence of God's character against the charge of injustice.

On receiving his doctoral degree Leibniz rejected the offer of a university professorship in favor of a diplomatic post at the court of Mainz. From Mainz Leibniz was sent on a mission to Paris, where he was to remain from 1672 to 1676; during this period he not only met leading intellectuals, such as Huygens and Malebranche, but also developed as a mathematician to the point where he discovered the differential calculus (1675). In 1676 Leibniz returned to Germany to accept the offer of a post at the court of Hanover, which he occupied until his death; in addition to his official duties as court librarian and historian, Leibniz acted as an adviser on political issues and technological projects.

In 1686 Leibniz composed the "Discourse on Metaphysics," which he regarded as the first mature statement of his philosophy; a summary of this work was sent to Antoine Arnauld, and an important exchange of philosophical letters ensued. In the 1690s Leibniz sought to engage John LOCKE in correspondence about the teachings of his *Essay Concerning Human Understanding*; Locke's refusal led Leibniz to compose a detailed refutation of the *Essay* entitled *New Essays on Human Understanding* (written 1703–5). When Locke died in 1704, Leibniz suppressed the work, and it remained unpublished until 1765. The one book which Leibniz did publish during his lifetime was *Essays in Theodicy* (1710); this was a response to the fideistic teachings of Pierre Bayle. During the last two years of his life Leibniz corresponded with a disciple of Newton, Samuel Clarke, concerning the nature of space and time and related issues. By this date Leibniz had been (unjustly) accused by Newton of plagiarizing his own version of the differential calculus; as a consequence perhaps the tone of the controversy with Clarke is somewhat acrimonious.

Leibniz's final years were marked by other sources of bitterness. His employer, Elector Georg Ludwig, departed from Hanover in 1714 in order to ascend the British throne as George I, and Leibniz was not encouraged to join the court in London. Although he was now internationally famous, Leibniz spent his final years in relative isolation.

Leibniz is in many ways the exception among the great philosophers of the seventeenth century. First, although as a youth he decided to accept the teachings of the moderns, Leibniz never believed in rejecting the Aristotelian–Scholastic tradition wholesale; instead he was committed to the synthesis of traditional and modern ideas. Secondly, unlike DESCARTES or SPINOZA, Leibniz never produced a definitive statement of his philosophical system; his leading philosophical ideas are dispersed through myriads of letters and short essays such as the "Discourse on Metaphysics" and the "Monadology." Much of Leibniz's best philosophical work remained unpublished at the time of his death, and the definitive edition of his writings is far from complete to this day.

Truth, contingency, and freedom

One of Leibniz's deepest philosophical interests was in the nature of truth. About the time of the "Discourse on Metaphysics," Leibniz propounded a distinctive theory of truth which appears to have important and sometimes disturbing implications for his metaphysics. The theory states that in every true proposition the concept of the predicate is contained in the concept of the subject. This concept-containment theory, as it may be called, stands in contrast to the more familiar theory, deriving from Aristotle, which defines truth in terms of a relation of correspondence between propositions and states of affairs in the world. From his theory of truth Leibniz derives the thesis that every individual substance has a complete concept which contains everything which is ever true of it. Thus, for example, the proper name "Julius Caesar" is not an arbitrary label but expresses a concept which contains such predicates as "crossed the Rubicon."

Although Leibniz holds that his theory of truth is of quite general application, he nonetheless insists that there are two kinds of truth: truths of reason and truths of fact. Truths of the former kind, which include those of logic and mathematics, are said to be necessary; truths of the latter kind, which include singular propositions such as "Julius Caesar crossed the Rubicon," are said to be contingent; although they are true, they might have been false. Leibniz further maintains that the mind of God is the locus of complete concepts, and that thus he alone is in a position to know the truth of singular propositions *a priori.* Ever since Arnauld, critics have found it difficult to see how Leibniz can find room for contingent truths. Indeed, it has seemed to some readers (including Bertrand RUSSELL) that Leibniz should have adopted a Spinozistic necessitarianism. In effect, Leibniz maintains that all true propositions are "analytic" (in KANT's terminology), and it is natural to suppose that analyticity entails necessity; that is, if the concept expressed by the predicate term is contained in the concept expressed by the subject term, the proposition cannot fail to be true. Leibniz was well aware of this problem, but how he proposed to solve it remains a matter of scholarly controversy. It appears, however, that at various times Leibniz proposed different solutions. One such proposal tries to explain contingency in terms of infinite analysis: unlike necessary truths, contingent truths cannot be proved in a finite number of steps. Another proposed solution is that existence is the source of contingency; thus, the proposition "Julius Caesar crossed the Rubicon" is contingent inasmuch as, though his complete concept contains all his predicates, Julius Caesar might not have existed.

As a philosopher in the Christian tradition, Leibniz endeavoured to establish the reality of both human and divine freedom. His ability to solve the problem of contingency is crucial to the success of this endeavor, since he regards contingency as a necessary condition of freedom; a free action for Leibniz is one that is contingent, spontaneous (uncoerced), and intelligent. Critics have complained that Leibniz cannot really succeed in establishing that there are free actions. Intuitively, in the case of a free action, the agent could have done otherwise, and none of Leibniz's analyses of contingency is able to show how this condition of freedom is satisfied.

Theodicy

Perhaps Leibniz's most famous or notorious thesis is that the actual world is the best of all possible worlds. This doctrine provided an easy target for Voltaire's ridicule in *Candide,* but it may be viewed as an intelligible response to problems in philosophical theology. On the assumption that God is essentially good, it is natural to argue that the world which he creates is the best of the alternatives available to him. Skeptics may wonder, however, whether this doctrine is really consistent with the existence of the various evils in our world, such as sin and suffering. In the *Essays in Theodicy* and other writings Leibniz attempts to defend his doctrine against such objections.

Leibniz's doctrine that God freely creates the best of infinitely many possible worlds was developed in large measure as a response to Malebranche. In the *Treatise of Nature and Grace* Malebranche had argued that in his creative activity God is subject to the constraint that his ways must honor him; in particular, God must act through simple, general laws. Although God could have created a better world than the actual one, he would thereby have violated the constraints on his creative activity. From the "Discourse on Metaphysics" onwards Leibniz subtly opposes Malebranche by arguing that simplicity of means is itself one of the criteria for evaluating possible worlds; the best possible world is that which combines maximum richness or variety of phenomena with maximum simplicity of covering laws. Leibniz holds that the actual world satisfies this criterion.

The "variety–simplicity" criterion, as it may be called, is Leibniz's basic standard for evaluating possible worlds; as he himself recognizes, this criterion is a physical one. There appears to be no reason to suppose that the world which satisfies this criterion should be conducive to human happiness; Voltaire's critique of Leibniz may thus seem to be massively irrelevant. This verdict, however, would be mistaken. In "On the Ultimate Origination of Things" Leibniz argues that the world which satisfies the "variety–simplicity criterion" will also be the most morally perfect; that is, the world in which human happiness is at a maximum. Critics have generally been skeptical as to whether Leibniz has a sound argument for this further thesis.

In defending God's character against the charge that he is responsible for the evils of this world, Leibniz makes use of traditional themes; in particular, he accepts the Augustinian thesis that evil is not something positive but the privation of good (see AUGUSTINE). Yet Leibniz also ingeniously deploys some of his more distinctively metaphysical doctrines. For example, he exploits the resources of his complete concept theory to show why God could not have created an improved version of our world in which its evil features were edited out. The basic strategy is to argue that since the complete concept of, say, Mother Theresa contains predicates that relate her to, say, Adolf Hitler, the attempt to delete Hitler from her world would result in a contradiction.

The metaphysics of substances

Leibniz's metaphysics of the actual world is most famous for the theory of monads. But this theory first appears at a relatively late date in Leibniz's philosophical career; indeed, it can be seen as the culmination of his lifelong concern with the nature of substance. Leibniz's thinking about substance appears to go through two main stages, which are represented in the "Discourse on Metaphysics" and the "Monadology."

In the "Discourse" and related writings Leibniz appears to accept a realist, quasi-Aristotelian ontology. According to this account, the universe consists ultimately of corporeal substances, the paradigm examples of which are organisms, such as human beings and animals. Each corporeal substance is constituted by a soul and a body, which in turn consists of other corporeal substances and so on to infinity; here Leibniz's metaphysics draws support from the discoveries made possible by the recent invention of the microscope. The reason why organisms, but not other bodies, qualify as substances is that they alone are endowed with true unity; such unity is conferred by the soul or principle of life. Leibniz is uncertain at this stage whether the soul is a substance in its own right.

Around 1700 Leibniz appears to abandon this quasi-Aristotelian ontology for a more idealist metaphysics; this is the monadology. According to this theory, reality ultimately consists of monads or soul-like entities, simple, partless beings which are thus incapable of being destroyed (except by a miracle). Since they are like souls, monads have no physical predicates, not even spatial position; they are endowed only with perception and appetition (i.e. a dynamic principle by virtue of which monads pass from one perceptual state to its successor). Monads are hierarchically arranged according to the clarity and distinctness of their perceptions. God is the supreme monad; human minds, by virtue of possessing reason, enjoy a relatively privileged status; at the bottom of the scale are "bare monads," whose perceptions are extremely obscure and confused. Although such an idealist metaphysic may appear to leave no room for bodies, Leibniz explains that this is not the case; he does not eliminate bodies, but reduces them to simple substances. Leibniz's considered view is that bodies are aggregates of monads which are misperceived as extended things by human observers.

Leibniz seems to have been led to monadology by becoming convinced that no material being could be a genuine unity and thus qualify as a substance. Nonetheless, there are a number of constants in Leibniz's metaphysical thinking. Throughout his career he is committed to the Identity of Indiscernibles; no two substances are exactly alike, or differ in number alone. Further, Leibniz consistently holds that created substances cannot interact and that they are the causal sources of all their non-initial states. Leibniz explains the appearance of interaction in the world in terms of a harmony pre-established by a benevolent God. The doctrine of pre-established harmony is perhaps best known as a solution to the mind–body problem bequeathed by Descartes, but it is in fact a wholly general thesis.

Leibniz's metaphysics of the actual world is thus dominated by the idea that a substance is a true unity. Arnauld objected that Leibniz appeared to be thereby introducing a conception of substance ungrounded in the philosophical tradition. Leibniz's reply to Arnauld is instructive: the thesis that substance is a genuine unity follows from – indeed, is even equivalent to – the Aristotelian definition of substance as an ultimate subject of predication. Thus although Leibniz moved away from a realist metaphysics, even in his later idealist theory of monads his thought about substance has Aristotelian roots.

The theory of knowledge

Problems in the theory of knowledge were never at the forefront of Leibniz's philosophical concerns. Although Leibniz adopted an idealist metaphysics in his later philosophy, in contrast to BERKELEY he did not reach this position through a concern with the issue of how knowledge of bodies is possible. Further, in contrast to Descartes, Leibniz never took the problem of radical scepticism seriously; in general, he tended to be dismissive of Descartes's treatment of this problem, and he rejected his view that the *cogito* has a unique claim to certainty.

Perhaps Leibniz's main contribution to the theory of knowledge is his defense of the doctrine of innate ideas and knowledge; this defense is most fully developed in the *New Essays*. In this work Leibniz, like Locke, is primarily but not exclusively concerned with the issue of innate propositional knowledge; echoing PLATO's teachings in the *Meno*, Leibniz argues that sense-experience alone cannot explain our knowledge of necessary truths in mathematics. However, it is not always clear in Leibniz's discussion whether what is at issue is the causal question of how necessary beliefs arise in the mind or the epistemic question of how such beliefs are to be justified.

Leibniz's full defense of innate ideas and knowledge draws on one of his most original contributions to psychology, the theory of unconscious or minute perceptions (*petites perceptions*). Like Descartes, Leibniz defends a dispositional version of the doctrine of innate ideas; according to this account, to have an innate idea of x is to have a congenital disposition to think of x, rather than an actual thought. However, Leibniz departs from Descartes by arguing that these mental dispositions are grounded in unconscious activity. Leibniz thus rejects the Cartesian doctrine that the mind is aware of all its contents. Although the theory of unconscious perceptions is psychologically significant, its primary importance to Leibniz is perhaps metaphysical; it enables him to explain how perception is possible even for bare monads.

Partly because he published little in his lifetime, Leibniz's reputation as a great philosopher was slow to develop; his one published book, the *Theodicy*, did not in general exhibit his best philosophical work. Further, in the eighteenth century there was a reaction against the kind of speculative, revisionist metaphysics of which the theory of monads is a leading example; in the same period Leibniz's reputation was also damaged by Voltaire's satire in *Candide*. However, the publication of the *New Essays* in 1765 exerted an important influence on Kant's critical philosophy; the theory of innate ideas is a significant precursor of Kant's doctrine of categories. In the nineteenth century the publication of Leibniz's more technical writings enabled readers to appreciate not only his importance in the development of symbolic logic but also the role of his theory of truth in grounding some of his metaphysical doctrines. In recent years there has been an enormous growth of scholarly and philosophical interest in Leibniz, which has centred above all perhaps on his contributions to the metaphysics of modality.

Bibliography

Writings

G. W. Leibniz: Sämtliche Schriften und Briefe, ed. German Academy of Sciences (Darmstadt and Berlin: Akademie Verlag, 1923–). [The definitive edition of Leibniz's writings, but still very far from complete.]

Die Philosophischen Schriften von G. W. Leibniz, seven volumes, ed. C. I. Gerhardt (Berlin:Weidmann, 1875–90). [The most useful multi-volume edition of Leibniz's philosophical writings.]

Opuscules et fragments inédits de Leibniz, ed. L. Couturat (Paris: Alcan, 1903). [Particularly valuable for its inclusion of Leibniz's writings on logic.]

G. W. Leibniz: Philosophical Papers and Letters, 2nd edn, ed. and trans. L. E. Loemker (Dordrecht: Reidel, 1969). [The fullest one-volume edition of Leibniz's writings in English translation.]

Leibniz: Philosophical Writings, ed. and trans. G. H. R. Parkinson (London: Dent, 1973).

G. W. Leibniz: New Essays on Human Understanding, ed. and trans. P. Remnant and J. Bennett (Cambridge: Cambridge University Press, 1981). [A superb translation.]

G. W. Leibniz: Theodicy, trans. E. M. Huggard (LaSalle, IL: Open Court, 1985).

G. W. Leibniz: Philosophical Essays, ed. and trans. R. Ariew and D. Garber (Indianapolis: Hackett, 1989).

Further reading

Adams, R. M.: *Leibniz: Determinist, Theist, Idealist* (Oxford: Oxford University Press, 1994).

Broad, C. D.: *Leibniz: An Introduction* (Cambridge: Cambridge University Press, 1975). [An excellent introduction to Leibniz's philosophy.]

Couturat, L.: *La logique de Leibniz* (Paris: Alcan, 1901).

Hooker, M. (ed.): *Leibniz: Critical and Interpretive Essays* (Minneapolis: University of Minnesota Press, 1982).

Jolley, N. (ed.): *The Cambridge Companion to Leibniz* (Cambridge: Cambridge University Press, 1995).

Mates, B.: *The Philosophy of Leibniz: Metaphysics and Language* (New York: Oxford University Press, 1986).

Russell, B.: *A Critical Exposition of the Philosophy of Leibniz* (London: Allen and Unwin, 1900). [A controversial but distinguished study.]

22

Locke

E. J. Lowe

John Locke (1632–1704 CE) is perhaps the greatest of all English philosophers. His magnum opus of 1689, *An Essay Concerning Human Understanding*, was the first major attempt to present a systematic empiricist account of human knowledge and understanding, which Locke saw as arising entirely out of the mind's operations upon its ideas of sensation and reflection. Almost equally influential were his two *Treatises of Government* of 1689, the *Second Treatise* expounding his view that all legitimate civil government is founded on a social contract.

Born the son of a minor landowner and attorney from Somerset, Locke was educated first at Westminster School and then at Christ Church, Oxford, where he was awarded the degree of BA in 1656. After graduating, he entered upon an academic career, combining teaching with further study in theology, philosophy, and medicine. In the mid-1660s Locke became the medical adviser and confidant of the Earl of Shaftesbury, a leading Whig politician of the period. This association lasted until a constitutional crisis over the succession to the throne compelled Shaftesbury to flee the country in 1682. These were perilous times for Shaftesbury's associates, and Locke prudently left England for the Netherlands in 1683, returning only in 1689, upon the accession of William of Orange and his wife Mary. The remaining years of Locke's life were more peaceful and prosperous, and although he accepted public office under the new government, most of his time was devoted to writing and study. Besides the *Essay* and the *Two Treatises*, Locke wrote many other works, most notably the *Letter on Toleration* (1689), *Some Thoughts Concerning Education* (1693), and *The Reasonableness of Christianity* (1695).

When the *Essay* first appeared, many of its more conservative readers attacked it as a threat to established religious authority. To these critics, Locke's views about human knowledge – and especially his attack on the doctrine of innate ideas – appeared dangerously skeptical. In fact Locke himself was no enemy to religious faith, adhering to the tenets of his Protestant upbringing throughout his life. Indeed, part of his intention in the *Essay* was to reconcile such faith with empirical knowledge and rational inquiry. Among Locke's earliest philosophical critics, the most famous were BERKELEY and LEIBNIZ, the former hostile to Locke's belief in matter and abstract ideas, the latter especially concerned to defend belief in innate ideas against Locke's objections.

Locke's arguments against innate ideas are presented in Book I of the *Essay*. The doctrine of innate ideas has a history stretching back to PLATO's defense of it in one of his dialogues, the *Meno*. Medieval Scholasticism, taking its lead more from ARISTOTLE than Plato, was sympathetic to empiricism, but by Locke's time Aristotle's influence was waning and neo-Platonism had undergone a revival. Plato's esteem for mathematics and distrust of the senses are echoed in the rationalist thought of this period, not least in the works of DESCARTES, who was a major proponent of the doctrine of innate ideas and thus one of Locke's implicit targets.

Locke's foremost objection to the doctrine of innate ideas is that there is simply no evidence to support it. He contends that the only evidence which *could* support the doctrine would be evidence of universal assent, throughout the human race, to certain principles of a logical, metaphysical, or moral nature. However, even the best candidates for the title of an innate principle, such as the logical laws of identity and of non-contradiction, are *not* in fact assented to by young children and the mentally defective. To say that such people do know the truth of these principles but are unaware of their knowledge struck Locke as being virtually contradictory. If it is pointed out that all children of sound mind do at least assent to these principles upon attaining the age of reason, Locke's reply is that this is perfectly explicable in terms of their *discovering* the truth of the principles for themselves. In short, Locke urges that positing the existence of innate ideas in order to explain certain elements of our knowledge and understanding is otiose, because he believes that an empiricist explanation of all these elements is available in terms of faculties with which the mind must be credited in any case. The remaining three Books of the *Essay* are accordingly devoted to an empiricist theory of concept-formation and knowledge-acquisition.

In recent times, psycholinguists such as Noam Chomsky have revived the doctrine of innate ideas in order to explain the capacity of all human children to learn a language. They remark that children learn their mother tongue rapidly on the basis of degraded and fragmentary linguistic data. Moreover, all human languages appear to share certain universal grammatical principles. It is urged that such facts can only be explained if the grammatical principles in question are tacitly known by all humans beings, as part of their genetic inheritance. This is also supposed to explain why human languages cannot be learnt by animals of other intelligent species. Locke would probably not have been impressed by such claims. He could take comfort from alternative explanations of language-learning that have recently begun to find favor, invoking the idea of neural networks. Artificial neural networks can, for instance, be trained to learn the rules for forming the past tense of English verbs, and acquire mastery of these rules in a fashion which interestingly mimics that of human children (see Bechtel and Abrahamsen, 1991).

For Locke, sense perception is one of the two sole sources of all our ideas, the other being reflection (that is, introspection). Locke's use of the term "idea" is rather broad, sometimes denoting an element in the content of sensory or introspective experience and sometimes an element in the content of thought or imagination. It is crucial to Locke's empiricist program that ideas may be either *simple* or *complex*, with the latter being analyzable as being compounded out of the former. This enables Locke to contend that all of our ideas arise from experience without committing him to the untenable thesis that every idea we have has actually been encountered in experience. Thus, one may have the idea of a unicorn, compounded out of the ideas of a horse and a horn, even though one has never perceived such a creature. Locke officially *defines* an idea as "Whatsoever the Mind perceives in itself, or is the immediate object of Perception, Thought or Understanding" (*Essay*, II, viii, 8). This passage may suggest that, for Locke, ideas are mental *entities* to which the mind is somehow related in an act of perceiving or thinking, rather like the sense-data of some more recent theorists of perception. But other modern theorists of perception reject an "act–object" analysis of sensation in favor of an "adverbial" analysis, and it may be possible to recruit this approach in interpreting Locke. On the adverbial analysis, a sensing of pain or of color is a *mode* or *manner* of sensory awareness without any inner mental object. For example, rather than speak of being aware of a red sensation, an adverbial theorist would speak of sensing "redly." If Locke's theory of ideas can be interpreted in something like this way, he need not be credited with an "indirect" realist theory of perception – that is, a theory which posits inner mental objects as always intervening between the mind and external objects – with all the skeptical implications which such a theory is commonly believed to harbor (see Lowe, 1995, chapter 3).

The distinction between primary and secondary qualities is central to Locke's theory of sense perception. For Locke, a secondary quality, such as redness or sweetness, is just a *power* (that is, a disposition) which a physical object has, in virtue of the primary qualities of its microstructural parts, to produce a certain sensation in us. Accordingly, he holds that our idea of that quality in no way resembles the quality itself as it is in the object. By contrast, he holds that our ideas of *primary* qualities, such as shape, do indeed resemble the qualities in question. Berkeley thought that this doctrine was absurd, famously maintaining that "an idea can be like nothing but an idea." However, Locke's contention may be defensible if it is interpreted as implying, merely, that some sort of structural isomorphism obtains between a primary quality such as squareness and the sense-content which typically represents that quality in our experience (see Lowe, 1995, chapter 3).

Rationalists like Descartes held that the most basic notions in metaphysics, such as those of *causation*, *identity*, and *substance*, were innate ideas. It was important for Locke, therefore, to show how such ideas could arise wholly from experience. He believed that our idea of causal power arose from introspection upon our own volitional initiation of bodily movements in episodes of voluntary action – a view subsequently challenged by HUME. His account of our idea of personal identity, appealing to the conscious memory that each of us has of our own past thoughts and actions, provoked criticism from Butler and Reid, but continues to be widely discussed today. As for the idea of substance, Locke agreed with Descartes that sense perception only reveals to us certain *qualities* of physical things, and not the "substratum" in which such qualities supposedly "inhere." Hence he is driven to say that we do not possess any "positive" idea of substance, but only a "relative" idea of it as "something we know not what" which is necessary for the support and union of a thing's qualities (see *Essay*, II, xxiii, 2). Critics like Berkeley and Hume dismissed this view as feeble, the latter discarding the term "substance" as effectively meaningless. In fact, however, Locke need not be interpreted as contending, absurdly, that a thing's "substratum" is a featureless "something" which exists independently of all that thing's qualities. Arguably, all he means is that the idea of "substratum" is that aspect of our idea of a thing which remains when we *abstract* from the latter all our ideas of its particular qualities: in short, it is our idea of a thing's being a *bearer* of its qualities, considered in abstraction from any particular qualities that it bears (see Martin, 1980).

Book III of the *Essay* is entitled "Of Words." On the question of whether thought precedes language or language thought, Locke clearly favors the priority of thought. For Locke, thinking just *is* the having of ideas, and thus involves our powers of imagination. The purpose of words, he considers, is to be "signs" of ideas, so that the thoughts we engage in privately can be communicated to others (*Essay*, III, ii, 1). Some commentators have taken Locke to be advancing, in effect, a solipsistic theory of meaning, according to which the meaning of a word in any speaker's mouth is just a private idea in that speaker's mind, inaccessible to any other person. But in reality Locke correctly saw that the privacy of ideas need be no barrier to the successful use of language in communication, as is shown by his treatment of the "inverted spectrum" problem (see *Essay*, II, xxxii, 15). The lesson to be drawn from this is that Locke probably never intended "ideas" to play anything like the role that "meanings" do in present-day theories of meaning, in which the "meaning" of a word is understood as something like a rule or convention determining its correct application by users of the language (see Hacking, 1975, chapter 5; Lowe, 1995, chapter 7).

Locke holds that *general* terms are signs of "abstract general ideas." These, he thinks, are created by the mental activity of *abstraction*, in which the distinguishing features of a number of different but similar ideas are disregarded, leaving an idea which possesses only the features which all those different ideas have in common. There is a careless passage in the *Essay* (IV, vii, 9) in which Locke describes the general idea of a triangle as one "wherein some parts of several different and inconsistent *Ideas* are put together." Critics like Berkeley have ridiculed this, but it seems clear that Locke intended to say that abstraction merely *leaves out* those respects in which a number of similar ideas differ. In fact, Locke's abstract general ideas are very much like the "prototypes" posited by many modern psychologists to explain our capacities for categorization and classification (see Lakoff, 1987, chapter 2).

Locke appeals to abstract general ideas in his account of *essence*. He distinguishes, in the case of substances, between *real* and *nominal* essence – the former being the internal microstructural constitution of a substance which is the cause of its observable qualities, and the latter being the abstract general idea by reference to which we *classify* and *name* that substance (see *Essay*, III, iii). In the case of a substance such as *gold*, our abstract general idea would include the ideas of such observable qualities as yellow color, shininess, heaviness, and ductility. Locke thinks that it is impossible for us to classify substances by reference to their *real* essences, because we do not know what those essences are (and certainly this was true in Locke's day, before the development of the modern atomic theory of matter). But he also thinks that, even if we did manage to discover them, this could not be expected to alter our linguistic practices and we would continue to classify substances by reference to their observable, macroscopic characteristics. In this he has been challenged in recent times by Hilary Putnam (1975), who points out that there is a "division of linguistic labour" among speakers of a language, in consequence of which laymen typically defer to experts on the question of the extension of a general term such as "gold." On this view, the term "gold," even in the mouths of those ignorant of chemistry, refers to the element with atomic number 79.

In Book IV of the *Essay*, "Of Knowledge and Opinion," Locke identifies three distinct sources of knowledge: intuition, reason (or "demonstration"), and experience. By *intuition* we know, for example, that black is not white and that a circle is not a triangle (*Essay*, IV, ii, 1). By *demonstration* we can know such geometrical truths as Pythagoras's Theorem, which we can deduce by intuitively certain steps of reasoning from premises which are themselves intuitively certain. (Locke believed – unlike Hume – that *moral*, as well as mathematical, truths may be discovered by reason, a conviction which had important repercussions for his theological and political views.) Finally, by *experience* we can know that physical objects exist and possess certain observable qualities. For Locke, knowledge demands *certainty*, and where that is absent he thinks we have at most only probable belief or opinion. Because of this, Locke thinks that the scope of our knowledge is "very narrow" (*Essay*, IV, xv, 2). Consequently, he believes that we must leave room for *faith*, since the claims of faith can only be conclusively overridden by those of knowledge, not those of mere probable belief. It is important to note that Locke, unlike some more radical empiricists, does not maintain that all knowledge is acquired solely through experience, since he allows that it may also be acquired by intuition or reason, albeit working upon ideas supplied by the senses or introspection. Hence he acknowledges the possibility of *a priori* knowledge even while denying the doctrine of innate ideas and principles.

The greatness of the *Essay* lies not only in its being the first systematic and comprehensive empiricist account of human knowledge and understanding. It also represents the beginnings of the modern science of psychology, offering as it does a wholly naturalistic account of workings of the human mind. Even more significantly, perhaps, the *Essay* represents the beginnings of the modern separation of philosophy and science into two distinct disciplines. Henceforth the role of philosophy would increasingly be seen to be one of providing a critical, self-reflective perspective on the nature of human knowledge, determining its scope and limits by examining its sources in the mind's own capacities of sense and reason. Thus, Locke's philosophy may be seen as anticipating the "critical" philosophy of KANT, as well as the naturalism which characterizes much of today's philosophical thought.

So far we have concentrated on Locke's contributions to epistemology, metaphysics, and the philosophy of mind and language, but mention should also be made of his important contributions to political philosophy, most notably in his *Second Treatise of Government* of 1689. Locke was a social contract theorist, like HOBBES before him, but did not take so gloomy a view as Hobbes did of the "state of nature," in which human beings were presumed to exist prior to the institution of civil government. Locke believed that human beings in the state of nature were governed by the law of nature, and that "Reason, which is that Law, teaches all Mankind . . . that being all equal and independent, no one ought to harm another in his Life, Health, Liberty, or Possessions" (*Second Treatise*, II, 6). Thus he also believed, unlike Hobbes, that private property could exist in the state of nature, with rights of acquisition and transfer. Indeed, Locke's defense of private property lies at the very heart of his political philosophy, since he sees all such property as arising, ultimately, from the fundamental right that all human beings have to ownership of their own bodies and to the fruits of their own labor. Understandably, then, he considered that the chief reason why human beings in the state of nature would give up their natural liberty and institute civil government was in order to secure their property rights and their personal safety. Accordingly, he was opposed to absolute government and recognized the right of subjects to overthrow a tyrannical ruler who arbitrarily seized their property or threatened their lives and liberties. In these views we find anticipations of many of the ideas which inspired the American constitution some hundred years later. Although the notion of an original "contract" as being the foundation of legitimate government was attacked in due course by Hume and others, in Locke's work it can be seen as a semi-fictional device designed to make vivid the thesis that political obligation rests upon the consent of the governed. Contractarian thinking of this sort has seen a revival in recent times in the work of John Rawls and Robert Nozick.

Bibliography

Writings

Because there are so many editions of Locke's writings, references in the text are to chapter and section; but the following critical editions are especially recommended.

An Essay Concerning Human Understanding (1689), ed. P. H. Nidditch (Oxford: Clarendon Press, 1975).

Two Treatises of Government (1689), ed. P. Laslett (Cambridge: Cambridge University Press, 1967).

Further reading

Ayers, M. R.: *Locke*, two volumes (London: Routledge, 1991).

Bechtel, W. and Abrahamsen, A.: *Connectionism and the Mind* (Oxford: Blackwell, 1991).

Chappell, V. C. (ed.): *The Cambridge Companion to Locke* (Cambridge: Cambridge University Press, 1994).

Chomsky, N.: *Language and Mind* (New York: Harcourt, Brace, Jovanovich, 1972).

Cranston, M.: *John Locke: A Biography* (London: Longman, 1957).

Hacking, I.: *Why Does Language Matter to Philosophy?* (Cambridge: Cambridge University Press, 1975).

Hall, R. and Woolhouse, R. S.: *Eighty Years of Locke Scholarship* (Edinburgh: Edinburgh University Press, 1983).

Lakoff, G.: *Women, Fire and Dangerous Things* (Chicago: University of Chicago Press, 1987).

Lloyd Thomas, D. A.: *Locke on Government* (London: Routledge, 1995).

Lowe, E. J.: *Locke on Human Understanding* (London: Routledge, 1995).

Martin, C. B.: "Substance Substantiated," *Australasian Journal of Philosophy*, 58 (1980), 3–10.

Putnam, H.: "The Meaning of 'Meaning'." In his *Mind, Language and Reality* (Cambridge: Cambridge University Press, 1975).

Rogers, G. A. J. (ed.): *Locke's Philosophy: Content and Context* (Oxford: Clarendon Press, 1994).

23

Marx

Allen W. Wood

Karl Heinrich Marx (1818–1883 CE) was born on May 5, 1818 in Trier, son of a Jewish lawyer who converted to Christianity in 1824. After studying law for a year at the University of Bonn, Marx left the Rhineland for the University of Berlin in 1836, where he associated with members of the radical Young Hegelian movement, and switched from the study of law to philosophy. In 1841 he received his doctorate from the University of Jena, for a dissertation on the materialism of Democritus and Lucretius. The accession to the Prussian throne of Friedrich Wilhelm IV in 1840, however, doomed any hopes Marx may have had for an academic career in philosophy, and he turned his talents instead to journalism, editing radical publications in the Rhineland, France, and Belgium throughout the 1840s.

In 1844 Marx began collaborating with Friedrich Engels, the rebellious and self-educated son of a textile manufacturing family with mills in Barmen, Germany and Manchester, England. It was Engels who introduced Marx to both the study of political economy and the working class movement. Marx's manuscripts on political economy (the so-called Paris manuscripts), written in 1844 but not published until 1930, exhibit a brilliant intelligence, trained in Hegelian philosophy (see HEGEL) but influenced by Enlightenment materialism, beginning to articulate radical criticisms of both the capitalist social order and its theoretical self-understanding in the works of economists such as Adam Smith and James Mill. Marx and Engels's first joint publication was *The Holy Family* (1844), a polemical attack on Young Hegelian philosophy, chiefly on the ground of its preoccupation with theological issues and its practical political irrelevance. The following year the two men were in Belgium, where they collaborated on a second polemical treatise, *The German Ideology*. It went unpublished until 1932, but is of decisive theoretical significance because its first part contains the earliest elaboration of the materialist conception of history that was thereafter to be the methodological basis of Marx's study of economics and history.

While in Belgium, Marx and Engels also founded the Communist League, and jointly wrote its famous *Manifesto*, which was published on the eve of the French Revolution of February 1848. The Revolution brought Marx back to Paris, and then to Cologne, where, until the revolution collapsed, he edited the radical *Neue Rheinische Zeitung* in support of revolutionary change in the Prussian Rhineland. After successfully defending himself and his associates in a Cologne court against charges of "inciting to revolt," Marx fled from Prussian territories in 1849 and soon took up residence in London, where (except for a few trips abroad in later years) he was to spend the rest of his life.

The first years in England subjected Marx and his family to a poverty as brutal and bitter as any he was ever to describe in his writings. Three of the six children died of want before 1856, and Marx's own health was to suffer a decline from which he would never fully recover. Despite this, whenever not confined to bed by illness, Marx regularly spent ten hours a day in the British Museum, doing research and writing. After returning home in the evening, he often wrote far into the night. The chief object of Marx's labors was a comprehensive theoretical analysis, economic and historical, of modern capitalism. A preliminary study was published in 1859 under the title *Toward a Critique of Political Economy*. In 1867, the first volume of Marx's *Capital* was finally published. He continued working on the two remaining volumes until his death, but they were never completed. Engels finally edited and published them, in 1884 and 1893 respectively.

Marx was instrumental in founding the International Workingmen's Association in 1864, and guiding it through six congresses in the next nine years, before it collapsed through internal dissension between the followers of Marx and those of Pierre Proudhon, chief among them the anarchist Michael Bakunin. After 1873, Marx's declining health made it harder and harder for him to work or to take an active part in radical politics. He died in London on March 13, 1883.

Philosophy

Marx's interest in philosophical materialism is evident as early as his dissertation. But as a philosopher Marx always remained also in the tradition of Hegelian idealism, which he sought to marry with Enlightenment materialism. From both traditions he derived the idea that philosophy must both comprehend itself historically and engage itself practically in the progressive struggle of humanity. German idealism was concerned with problems of human selfhood, the nature of a fulfilling human life, and with people's sense of meaning, self-worth, and relatedness to their natural and cultural environment. It saw modern culture as a scene of self-alienation, but also as holding out the promise of overcoming this alienation.

In the Paris manuscripts of 1844, Marx begins to see these problems as fundamentally a matter of the social and economic conditions in which people live. Marx's concern with the plight of the modern working class is from the beginning a concern not merely with "material needs" in the usual sense but more fundamentally with the conditions under which human beings can develop their "essential human powers" and "free self-activity." Truly human and fulfilling life activity would be an activity of free social self-expression. This is free because it is self-determined, developing, and expressing their whole humanity, objectifying itself in a world and then comprehending that world as its adequate expression as the "affirmation," "objectification," and "confirmation" of human nature. These conditions are social because it is the nature of human beings to produce both with and for others. A free life activity must be free not only individually but socially; that is, the social relationships it involves must be rationally understood and consciously chosen in light of that understanding. Marx's critique of political economy holds that the scientific understanding of capitalist social relationships systematically mystifies and falsifies their real nature, in a manner corresponding to the illusion, present practically in those relationships themselves, that they result from nothing but the free choice of independent individuals. A free life activity must be predicated on a rational understanding of the social nature of labor in class society, and then on a practical transformation of those relationships from relations of oppression to relations of free association.

Historical materialism

The theory of society and history that Marx offers in this direction is one which posits socially productive activity as the fundamental determinant of social organization and historical change. For the materialist conception of history, the fundamental element determining social organization is the productive powers of a society, and the fundamental determinant of history is the tendency of these powers to grow. Whether historical materialism is a "technological theory of history" depends on how broadly or narrowly we take the crucial idea of "productive powers." Marx indicates, however, that under this heading he understands not only the arsenal of tools and means of production at people's disposal, along with the human skills required to employ them, but also the theoretical knowledge of nature involved in production and even forms of human cooperation, insofar as they play a direct role in productive techniques and the satisfaction of human needs.

Productive powers at a given stage of development determine the nature of human laboring activity because labor consists in the exercise of those powers. A given set of productive powers favors a corresponding set of "material relations of production" – that is, forms of cooperation or division of labor – which are not directly part of them but facilitate their employment to a greater degree than rival relations would do. Productive powers thereby also favor certain "social relations of production," systems of social roles relating to control of the production process and the disposition of its fruits. These relations are the basis of institutions of property. Taken together, the system of social relations of production constitutes what Marx calls the "economic structure of society" characteristic of a given "mode of production." Marx understands history as divided into periods, specifically as a series of distinct modes of production, each with its own characteristic economic structure, social relations of production and consequent forms of property, and distribution of social power.

The materialist theory treats political, legal, and other such institutions as a "superstructure" erected on this economic base. Political institutions reflect the dominant relations of economic power and property, because their function is to enforce those relations. The dominant ideas, conceptions, and intellectual products in a society are erected on the same economic basis. Like political institutions, they reflect and tend to reinforce the dominant economic structures in the society. Marx does not think that economic relations dictate the thoughts that people have, but they do determine which thoughts gain currency and influence, because they select for thoughts which harmonize with existing social relations. And since the dominant ideas also set the conditions of education and research, economic conditions also indirectly determine the direction new ideas and theories may take. Because they are conditioned in this way, and often serve to reinforce social relations which involve systematic self-concealment and mystification, the dominant thoughts also serve to obfuscate and mystify social relations to those who create and participate in them. Insofar as ideas (including religions, philosophies, aesthetic and scientific productions, and so on) perform this function, Marx gives them the name "ideology."

Marx's theory of historical change depends on the fact that the productive powers of society have a tendency to grow over time. As they grow, they alter their relation to dominant relations of production, or the economic structure of society. New powers come to correspond to new relations of production, which would facilitate their social employment or their further expansion. When the powers and relations of production cease to correspond, and come into conflict, this brings about a change in the economic structure of society, as new relations replace old ones. The old or outdated mode of production is then replaced by a new mode of production. An epoch in which such changes are occurring is an epoch of social revolution.

These Marxian ideas have been taken over with little modification by currently popular theories which hold that we are now undergoing a transition from the industrial age to a post-industrial or "information" age, which parallels earlier transitions from the hunter-gatherer to the agricultural way of life, and from agriculture to industry. The chief difference between Marx's theory and the current ones is that Marx emphasizes the role of class relations in the economic structure, and of class struggles in the process of social revolution. Social relations divide people into determinate groups, which share a common situation and common interests with regard to the distribution of social power, property, and control over the production process. These groups are not classes, but they become classes when they organize to promote their shared interests. They then create new, collective interests over and above the shared economic interests which occasioned their formation. At the same time, they create political structures and social ideologies to promote these distinctive collective interests. Thus it is not Marx's view that class movements are nothing but devices for promoting the individual interests of the class's members.

Marx views the struggle between class movements as the mechanism by means of which one mode of production replaces another during an epoch of social revolution. The old mode is one which favors the class interests of one or more dominant classes, while the class interests of other, revolutionary classes is more in line with the social relations of the emerging mode of production, which better corresponds to the state of the growing productive powers of society. Thus Marx sometimes speaks of the new productive powers of society as the "weapons" used by a revolutionary class against the dominant class which it is struggling to replace. This, for instance, is the way in which the *Communist Manifesto* describes the victory of the bourgeoisie over the feudal aristocracy during the rise of the capitalist mode of production.

The theoretical analysis of capitalism

The materialist conception of history is simultaneously a summary of empirical results, a methodological program for empirical research and a device for projecting the historical future. Just as Marx thinks capitalism defeated feudalism through the progress of human knowledge and the growth of social productive powers, so he is convinced that the rapid expansion of productive powers encouraged by capitalism itself will soon outstrip the limited horizon of capitalist social relationships and lead to a class movement whose historic mission is to abolish class differences themselves and achieve universal human emancipation. With this in mind, Marx was engaged simultaneously in organizing the working class and in a theoretical enterprise whose aim was to articulate the internal conflicts in existing capitalist society – such as the problems of under-employment of labor, underconsumption of its products, and the long-run tendency of the rate of profit to fall – so as to put the working class in a position to assume self-conscious rule over social production and thereby fulfill its historic mission. Marx's theory in *Capital* is constructed self-consciously on the model of the systems of the great German idealist philosophers, Fichte, Schelling, and Hegel, especially following the dialectical structure of Hegel's system. It begins with an abstract analysis of capitalist production, grounded on the idea of a product of labor as an exchangeable commodity. Then it works through the determinate variants of commodity production found in modern capitalism, by developing the categories of exchange value, money, capital, wage labor and surplus-value. These conceptions represent social relations of production, which Marx's analysis shows to be grounded on the determinate form that labor assumes given the productive powers found in modern society. In this way, Marx's method in *Capital* both depends on and illustrates the materialist conception of history. In the subsequent volumes (left unfinished at Marx's death and later published by Engels), Marx develops the theory further, encompassing the process through which capital expands itself and the way capitalist surplus value is divided into profit, interest, and ground rent. As in the first volume, Marx tries to show where the capitalist production process generates the conflicts and instabilities he thinks will lead to its downfall, and its replacement by a higher socialist or communist mode of production under the rule of the proletariat or working class.

The death of Marxism

Marx always saw his theoretical activity as vitally connected to the practical struggle of the working class for universal human emancipation. In an early essay (1843), he depicted philosophy as the "head" of the struggle for emancipation, and the proletariat as its "heart." He fought for the acceptance of his ideas within the working class movement because he thought that the success of the working class movement was dependent on its liberating itself from ideological confusions and achieving a correct scientific understanding of the social and historical process in which it is involved. In line with a radical tradition within the modern Enlightenment, Marx was convinced that humanity was on the verge of a radically new way of life, which would be brought about when the scientific understanding achieved by philosophers or intellectuals joined forces with a democratic mass movement.

There is no doubt that Marx was overoptimistic about the accomplishments of working class social and political organization, and about the prospects for transcending capitalism and its oppressive power relations. At a deeper level, along with the rest of the radical Enlightenment tradition, he overestimated the prospects for human emancipation through a mass movement focused on the secular, scientific ideas and theories of philosophers. The late twentieth century witnessed a resurgence, both at a popular level and among intellectuals, of anti-Enlightenment ideas and values, whether these take the form of popular religious fundamentalisms or, among intellectuals and theorists, of a corrosive skepticism directed against the power of reason among intellectuals and theorists. In our age there is renewed trust in those very social and institutional powers that Marx held most responsible for human oppression, and whose defeat he was convinced would be required for human progress. It is questionable, however, how far these historic defeats of Marxism represent an intellectual defeat of Marx's thought or even a permanent decline in its intellectual or political influence. The confident decrees and declarations we hear all around us that Marx's thought is dead and discredited, that socialism has failed, should themselves arouse our suspicion. For they resemble all too closely the very opposite pronouncements which used to be made by dogmatic Marxists in similar tones of infallibility, as though the future of the human race were something already decided, and they had been elected to announce the decision. Too often the historical arrogance stood in inverse proportion to the evidence, and excesses of certainty in theory were nothing but an expression of excesses of unwisdom and inhumanity in practice. But there is no reason to think that the human failings displayed in such conduct are any more characteristic of Marxists than of the adherents of any other set of strongly held views.

With the gain in uncritical confidence in capitalist institutions has come a growing gulf between rich and poor, both within society and between societies, and a deepening oppression of workers on a worldwide scale. The modern economy, for all the changes which have taken place since the mid-nineteenth century, comes more and more to resemble the system of inhuman oppression Marx catalogued and criticized. Even with all the engines of political, economic, and ideological power which have been amassed and deployed by the forces of oppression, it can only be a matter of time until their intemperate triumphalism provokes a significant counter-movement. We of course cannot know what role Marx's thought will play in such a movement, but for now it still remains the chief historical source of the ideas which might fuel resistance to capitalist oppression and the renewed drive toward human emancipation.

Bibliography

Writings

Marx Engels Collected Works (New York: International Publishers, 1975–).

Further reading

Carver, Terrell (ed.): *The Cambridge Companion to Marx* (New York: Cambridge University Press, 1991).
Cohen, G. A.: *Karl Marx's Theory of History* (Princeton, NJ: Princeton University Press, 1978).
Miller, Richard: *Analyzing Marx* (Princeton, NJ: Princeton University Press, 1984).
Wood, Allen W.: *Karl Marx* (London: Routledge, 1981).

24

Mencius

Kwong-Loi Shun

"Mencius" is the latinized name of Meng Ke [Meng K'e], also known as Mengzi [Meng Tzu] (Master Meng), a well known early Chinese thinker. His life is traditionally dated to 371–289 BCE, although recent scholarship indicates that it probably lay entirely within the fourth century BCE. His teachings are recorded in a version of the *Mengzi* [*Meng-tzu*] that was edited, with parts discarded, by Zhao Qi of the second century CE. The text consists of seven books, each in two parts, and each part with a number of passages. ZHU XI [CHU HSI] (1130–1200 CE), a later Confucian thinker, grouped the text along with the *Lunyu* [*Lun-yü*] (*Analects*), which records the teachings of CONFUCIUS (sixth to fifth centuries BCE), and two other early texts – the *Daxue* [*Ta-hsüeh*] (*Great Learning*) and the *Zhongyong* [*Chung-yung*] (*Centrality and Commonality*, or more commonly known as *Doctrine of the Mean*) – to form the Four Books, and regarded them as the basic Confucian texts. The Four Books were used as the basis for civil examinations from 1313 to 1905, and Mencius came to be regarded as the true transmitter of Confucius's teachings, thereby exerting tremendous influence on the later development of Confucian thought.

Mencius lived in a time of social and political disorder. The Zhou [Chou] dynasty (mid-eleventh century to 249 BCE) was in decline, and China was divided into several states that constantly waged wars against each other. Families within states also strove for power, and there was pervasive corruption in government. Different movements of thought emerged, giving different diagnoses of and remedies to the disorderly situation, as well as different proposals about how the individual should live in such times. Confucius had a vision of an orderly society in early Zhou that was sustained by various norms and values. These include the detailed rules of *li* (rites) that govern the interaction between people in recurring social contexts – "*li*," which originally referred to the rites of sacrifice, had come to refer to various rules governing ceremonial behavior (such as funerals and weddings), as well as rules governing the interaction between people related by their different positions within the family and state. The traditional values also include such attributes as filial piety and loyalty, a graded concern for others that differs in nature depending on the social relation others stand to oneself, and seriousness or reverence in one's dealings with others. Confucius believed that the ills of the times resulted from a disintegration of such norms and values, and advocated restoring and maintaining them as a way to bring back order. Individuals should cultivate themselves to embody such norms and values, and Confucius characterized this ethical ideal in terms of *ren* [*jen*] (humaneness) – "*ren*" originally referred either to kindness (especially of a ruler to his subjects) or to the distinctive qualities of certain aristocratic clans, and was used by Confucius to describe this all-encompassing ethical ideal.

Alternative diagnoses of and remedies to the disorderly situation were given by other movements of thought, which posed challenges to the Confucian proposal. MOZI [MO TZU] (fifth century BCE), originator of the Mohist movement, criticized as a waste of resources the *li* practices that the Confucians advocated, such as elaborate funerals and lengthy mourning of parents. Probably seeing this as a criticism of the Confucian idea of graded concern, he attributed the strife and disorder of the times to one's profiting oneself and one's own family and state at the expense of others, and proposed an indiscriminate concern for every individual, family, and state as a remedy. One common objection Mozi encountered was that this idea of indiscriminate concern is impracticable, because it is radically at odds with the actual emotional dispositions of human beings. In response, he argued that indiscriminate concern is itself to one's own interest, and is something easy to practice once one realizes this point. So, for Mozi, public and private interests converge in that it is by attending to the public interest that one furthers one's own interest.

The Yangist movement, one representative of which is Yang Zhu [Yang Chu] (fifth to fourth centuries BCE), diagnosed the problem of the times in terms of the preoccupation with power and external possessions among those in office. The purpose of government is to nourish the nature, or *xing* [*hsing*], of human beings, which for the Yangists consists primarily in living out one's term of life in good health. In striving after power and external possessions, those in office endangered their own lives as well as the lives of their subjects. Order can be restored by each person attending to his or her own nature and not allowing external possessions to harm it, and the ideal ruler is one who has no concern for the throne and the external possessions that come with it. So, the

Yangists also saw public and private interests as converging, though it is by each attending to his or her real interest that the public interest is promoted.

Mencius set out to defend Confucius's ideas against the Mohist and Yangist challenges. He conversed with the rulers of different states to try to convince them to practice the Confucian ideal, had discussions with disciples, and debated with philosophical opponents. Ideas contained in his dialogues and sayings, which are recorded in the *Mengzi*, elaborate on and sometimes go beyond Confucius's teachings.

While still working with key concepts found in Confucius's teachings, Mencius elaborated further on the Confucian ideal by highlighting four ethical attributes. *Ren* (humaneness) emphasizes an affective concern for others that involves both a reluctance to harm others and being moved to actively promote others' well-being. There is a gradation in that one should have special affection for and fulfill special obligations to those who stand in special social relations to oneself. However, unlike the form of gradation Mozi criticized that involves profiting oneself and one's family and state at others' expense, Confucian graded concern is itself regulated by a network of social obligations that involve not engaging in socially unacceptable conduct to benefit those close to oneself. *Li* (observance of the rites), as an attribute of a person, involves a general disposition to follow and a mastery of the details of the rules of *li* that govern people's interaction in recurring social contexts. One should follow these rules with the proper spirit, such as seriousness or reverence, and should also be prepared to suspend or depart from them in exigencies.

The third attribute, *yi* [*i*] (propriety), involves a commitment to do whatever is proper in a situation. The character "*yi*" had the earlier meaning of a sense of honor; as an ethical attribute, *yi* involves one's regarding as beneath oneself what falls below ethical standards, as well as an insistence on distancing oneself from such things even at the expense of gravely undesirable consequences to oneself. The fourth attribute, *zhi* [*chih*] (wisdom), involves an ability to assess what is proper that is sensitive to circumstances and not bound by rigid rules of conduct. General rules, such as the rules of *li* or governmental policies transmitted from the past, are still important, although one should be prepared to adapt or depart from them when appropriate.

Mencius's elaboration on the Confucian ideal is a reaffirmation of the aspects of the Confucian ideal that the Mohists rejected, such as the idea of graded concern and the various practices of *li*. In a debate with Yi Zhi, a Mohist of his times, he pointed out that the main error with Mohist teachings is a mistaken conception of the basis of the ethical life.

The Mohists believed that we can come to endorse an ethical doctrine – such as that of indiscriminate concern – on the basis of supporting arguments, and although our emotional dispositions might not be structured in that direction, we can easily reshape our dispositions in accordance with the doctrine. According to Mencius, this is to regard our ethical life as having "two roots" – our recognition of the validity of an ethical doctrine depends on considerations unrelated to our actual emotional dispositions, while our practicing the doctrine depends on our drawing upon and reshaping the emotional resources we have. Our ethical life should have "one root" in that both the validity of an ethical doctrine and the emotional resources required for its practice have their basis in the actual dispositions that human beings share.

Mencius's view is that human beings already share emotional responses in the direction of the Confucian ideal, and the four attributes described earlier result from nourishing and developing such responses. Everyone would respond with compassion upon suddenly seeing a young infant on the verge of falling into a well, showing that human beings share an affective concern for others. Every young infant demonstrates a special affection for its parents, showing that human beings also share special concern for those close to them, especially family members. *Ren*, as a graded affective concern, results from developing both the general concern for other living things and the special concern for family members. Similarly, the other attributes, *li*, *yi*, and *zhi*, involve developing shared responses such as courtesy and respect for others, a sense of shame, and a sense of right and wrong.

Since the Confucian ideal is itself a development of responses that human beings already share, this accounts for the practicability of the ideal. Furthermore, it follows from such a view that self-cultivation is primarily a process of reflecting on and nourishing the shared ethical responses. Mencius frequently used a vegetative analogy to illustrate this point, comparing self-cultivation to the development of sprouts into mature plants. While teachers can help direct one's attention to the potentials in oneself, everyone has the necessary resources and can become fully ethical by one's own efforts.

In the political realm, Mencius believed that the purpose of government is not just to attend to the material needs of the common people, but also to educate them and assist them in their ethical improvement. Since such improvement is best achieved through the transformative effect of the good character of those in office, those in power should attend to their own self-cultivation. Governmental policies are still necessary, and it is also important to use policies transmitted from the past as a guideline. However, self-cultivation is the ideal basis for the political order both because the primary purpose of government is the ethical improvement of the people, which depends on the cultivated character of those in power, and because instituting the proper policies and properly appropriating past policies require a cultivated character.

Mencius's views about the basis of the ethical life also serve as a response to the Yangist challenge. Agreeing with the Yangist conception of human nature (*xing*) as something that one should nourish and to whose nourishment other pursuits should be subordinated, Mencius argued that we should view human nature in terms of the development of the ethical responses that human beings share, because their development has priority over other pursuits. Even a beggar who is starving to death would disdain accepting food given with abuse, and this illustrates the point that there is something – namely, propriety (*yi*) – to which human beings attach more importance than biological tendencies such as eating, or even life itself. And since human nature is constituted primarily by the development of the shared ethical responses, human nature is good in that it already has an ethical direction. Ethical shortcomings, according to Mencius, are due to a failure to develop such responses, rather than to anything inherently unethical in the human constitution.

Shortly after Mencius's time, another influential Confucian thinker XUNZI [HSÜN TZU] (third century BCE) criticized Mencius's belief that human beings share such ethical responses. Instead, according to Xunzi, human beings are moved primarily by self-regarding desires in the natural state, and strife and disorder result from the unregulated pursuit of their self-interest – this view Xunzi put by saying, in deliberate opposition to Mencius, that human nature is evil. The traditional social arrangements that the Confucians upheld serve to regulate and transform such desires, thereby promoting order and making possible the satisfaction of human desires. Xunzi's version of Confucian thought competed for influence with Mencius's for several hundred years, and Confucian thinkers continued to disagree in their views of human nature – whether it is good, evil, mixed, or neutral, and whether different human beings might have different natures. Later, from the late eighth century onward, more and more Confucian thinkers came to regard Mencius as the true transmitter of Confucius's teachings and to endorse the view that human nature is good. Since the incorporation by Zhu Xi of the *Mengzi* as one of the Four Books, Mencius's view that human nature is good became Confucian orthodoxy, and his teachings continued to influence Confucian thinkers in China up to the twentieth century.

Bibliography

Writings

The Works of Mencius, 2nd edn, trans. James Legge (Oxford: Clarendon Press, 1895).
Mencius, trans. D. C. Lau (London: Penguin Books, 1970).

Further reading

Ames, Roger T.: "The Mencian Conception of *Ren xing*: Does It Mean 'Human Nature'?" In Henry Rosemont Jr (ed.), *Chinese Texts and Philosophical Contexts: Essays Dedicated to Angus C. Graham* (La Salle, IL: Open Court, 1991), pp. 143–75.
Bloom, Irene: "Mencian Arguments on Human Nature (*Jen-hsing*)," *Philosophy East and West*, 44 (1994), 19–53.
Graham, A. C.: "The Background of the Mencian Theory of Human Nature," *Tsing-hua hsüeh-pao* (*Tsing Hua Journal of Chinese Studies*), 6 (1967), 215–71; reprinted in A. C. Graham, *Studies in Chinese Philosophy and Philosophical Literature* (Albany: State University of New York Press, 1990), pp. 7–66.
——: *Disputers of the Tao: Philosophical Argument in Ancient China* (La Salle, IL: Open Court, 1989).
Lau, D. C.: "Theories of Human Nature in Mencius and Shyuntzyy," *Bulletin of the School of Oriental and African Studies*, 15 (1953), 541–65.
Nivison, David S.: "Mencius and Motivation," *Journal of the American Academy of Religion Thematic Issues*, 47 (1980), 417–32.
——: "Two Roots or One?" *Proceedings and Addresses of the American Philosophical Association*, 53 (1980), 739–61.
——: *The Ways of Confucianism: Investigations in Chinese Philosophy* (La Salle, IL: Open Court Press, 1996).
Shun, Kwong-loi: *Mencius and Early Chinese Thought* (Stanford, CA: Stanford University Press, 1997).
Wong, David B.: "Universalism Versus Love With Distinctions: An Ancient Debate Revived," *Journal of Chinese Philosophy*, 16 (1989), 251–72.

25

Mozi

Chad Hansen

Mozi [Mo Tzu] (*c.*490–403 BCE) was China's first true philosopher. Mozi pioneered the argumentative essay style and constructed the first normative and political theories. He formulated a pragmatic theory of language that gave classical Chinese philosophy its distinctive character. Speculations about Mozi's origins highlight the social mobility of the era. The best explanation of the rise of Mohism (the movement influenced by Mozi) links it to the growth in influence of crafts and guilds in China. Mohism became influential when technical intelligence began to challenge traditional priestcraft in ancient China. The "Warring States" demand for scholars perhaps drew Mozi from the lower ranks of craftsmen. Some stories picture him as a military fortifications expert. His criticisms show that he was also familiar with the Confucian priesthood.

The Confucian defender, MENCIUS (371–289 BCE), complained that the "words of Mozi and Yang Zhu [Yang Chu] fill the social world." Mozi advocated utilitarianism (using general welfare as a criterion of the correct *dao* [moral discourse]) and equal concern for everyone. The Mohist movement eventually spawned a school of philosophy of language (called Later Mohists) which in turn influenced the mature form of both Daoism (ZHUANGZI [CHUANG TZU], died *c.*295 BCE) and Confucianism (XUNZI [HSÜN TZU], 298–238 BCE).

The core Mohist text has a deliberate argumentative style. It uses a balanced symmetry of expression and repetition that aids memorization and enhances effect. Symmetry and repetition are natural stylistic aids for Classical Chinese, which is an extremely analytic language (one that relies on word order rather than part-of-speech inflections). Three rival accounts of most of the important chapters survive in *The Mozi.*

The "craft theory" of Mohism helps us explain the distinctive character of disciplined philosophical thought in China. As the Mohists analyze moral debates, they turn on which standards we should use to guide our execution of moral instructions. Mozi's orientation was that the standards should be measurement-like, e.g. like a carpenter's plumb line or square. Measurement-like standards lend themselves to reliable application. Experts do better than novices, but everyone can get good results. He tries to extend this reliability-based approach to questions of how to fix the reference of moral terms. Mozi does not think of moral philosophy as a search for the ultimate moral principle. It is the search for a *constant* standard of moral interpretation and guidance.

Mozi attacks common-sense traditionalism (Confucianism; see CONFUCIUS) as a prelude to his argument for the utility standard. The attack shows that traditionalism is unreliable or *inconstant*. Mozi tells a story of a tribe that kills and eats their first born sons. We cannot, he observes, accept that this tradition is *yi* [*i*] (moral) or *ren* [*jen*] (benevolent). This illustrates, he argues, the error of treating tradition as a standard for the application of such terms. We need some extra-traditional standard to identify which tradition is right. Which should we make the *constant* social guide (*dao*) [*tao*]? For it to give constant guidance, we also need measurement-like standards for applying its terms of moral approval.

Mozi then proposed utility as the appropriate measurement standard for these joint purposes. We use it neither directly to choose particular actions nor to formulate rules, but rather to select among moral traditions. The body of moral discourse to promote and encourage is the one that leads to social behavior that maximizes general utility. How does he justify the moral status of utility itself? He argues that it is the natural preference (*tian* [nature:sky] *zhi* [urge]).

The appeal to *tian* [*t'ien*] thus becomes an important component of Mozi's argument. In ancient China, *tian* was the traditional source of political authority ("the mandate of heaven"). Early Confucianism had "naturalized" *tian* from what many assume was an archaic deity to something more like "the course of nature." Its main characteristic (besides its moral authority) was that its movement was *chang* [*ch'ang*] (constant).

Mozi exploited both the connotations of *tian*'s authority and its constancy. Traditions are variable – they differ in different places and times. If we don't like its traditions, we can flee from a family, a society, even a kingdom. We cannot similarly escape the constancies of nature. Natural constancies thus become plausible candidates to arbitrate between rival traditions. To say a *dao* is constant functions a little like saying it is objectively true.

The constant "natural" urge he identified was a comparatively measurable one – we imagine ourselves "weighing" benefits against harms. Thus, he proposed using the preference for benefit as a reliable, natural standard for choosing and interpreting traditional practices. We count as "moral" and "benevolent" those traditional discourses that promote utility. The natural urge to utility, he says, is like a compass or square. It does not depend on a cultivated intuition or indoctrination.

Society's moral reform takes place when we reform the social *dao* (guiding discourse). People educated in this discourse internalize it, and the resulting disposition is called their *de* [*te*] (virtuosity). (The compound *dao-de* is the standard translation of "ethics.") Our *de* [virtuosity] produces a course of action in actual situations. Whether the course produced by discourse like "When X do Y" is successful or not depends on what we identify as "X" and "not-X" in the situation. For social coordination, we train people to make these distinctions in similar ways. The key to reforming guiding discourse is to reform how we make distinctions, e.g. the distinction between "moral" and "immoral."

Mozi understands the training process in several related ways.

1   We emphasize or make a different set of distinctions the dominant ones – hence we promote different words as disposition guides. For example, he says the ruler should use the word *jian* [*chien*] (universal) and not the word *bie* [*pieh*] [partial]. If he speaks and thinks that way, he will be a more benevolent ruler. Society should make the benefit-promoting words the *constant* words in our social discourse.
2   We reform how we make the distinctions associated with terms that remain the same. For example, we will assign different things to *shi* (right) and *fei* (wrong).
3   We can change the order of terms in the guiding discourse – use it to give different advice.

Notice that Mozi's posture as a moral reformer puts him in an argumentative bind that is related to one faced by utilitarianism (Jeremy Bentham and John Stuart Mill) in the West. He admits he is challenging existing judgments and intuitions. What is the status of the principle he uses in proposing his alternative? How can he make his alternative seem other than immoral to someone from within the tradition he challenges? How can a moral reformer get over the impasse posed by conflicting moral intuitions?

One possibility emerges in another of Mozi's philosophical stories. He uses this story to criticize Confucian pro-family and "partial" moral attitudes. He depicts a conscript leaving his family to make war, and he argues that if the conscript were concerned about his family, he would want those to whom he entrusts them to adopt an attitude of universal concern. He would, Mozi argues, not seek out a person with "partial" moral attitudes. His family-centered, partial moral attitude is "inconstant" in the sense that it leads him to prefer that others have universal rather than partial attitudes. He would achieve his "partial" goals only if the *public* morality were altruistic. Confucian partiality is "inconstant" in that it recommends a public *dao* (guiding discourse) that is inconsistent with it. It cannot consistently recommend itself as the collective social *dao*.

Mozi's analysis shows that Chinese thought has a notion of morality as independent from social conventions and history. However, it ties morality neither to the familiar Western concept of "reason" nor to principles or maxims that function within a belief-desire psychology. Mozi's focus is on the contrasting terms, benefit/harm, not on the sentence "do what maximizes benefit." The concept is a standard against which we measure social discourse as a whole. The standard is not a principle of reason; it is a natural preference distinction. The objects of evaluation are not actions or rules; they are bodies of discourse and widespread courses of action.

The psychological and conceptual structure of Mozi's moral analysis treats human nature as social and malleable. Human malleability derives from our tendency to learn, to mimic, to seek support and approval from those we respect – our social superiors. It derives also from the effect of language on "inner programming."

Mozi promotes *ren* [*jen*] (humanity) as the appropriate utilitarian disposition – the virtue of benevolence. He links it to his choice of universal over partial "love." Mozi acknowledges that instilling universal moral concern requires social reinforcement – official promotion and encouragement. The system that brings this about is described in Mozi's social theory of *shang-tong* [*shang-t'ung*] (agreeing with the superior). Here Mozi gives a familiar justification of a system of authority. It will remind us of Thomas HOBBES's state of nature.

Why, Mozi asks, do we choose ordered society over anarchy – the original state of nature? His description of the latter is of a state of inefficiency and waste. One important difference from the Western parallel is that Mozi sees human beings as naturally moral creatures who disagree on their moral purposes. Prior to society, he says, human beings had different *yi* [*i*] (morality). They end up in conflicts fueled by moral judgments. They cannot agree on what is *shi* (right) and *fei* (wrong). It is clear, Mozi says, that the bad situation arises from the absence of a *zhang* (elder). So [we] select a worthy man and name him *tian-zi* (natural master). He then selects others of worth and creates the governing hierarchy. The hierarchy organizes us to harmonize our *yi* (morality), our use of *shi* (this:right) and *fei* (not-this:wrong). We "report up" what we view as *shi* (this:right) and *fei* (not-this:wrong); if the superior endorses it (*shi*-s it) then we all call it *shi*. If he *fei*-s it, we do too, even if we originally reported it as *shi*.

Another difference from Hobbes is the absence from Mozi's account of any notion of law or retributive punishment. In Mozi's political world, the superior punishes people for failing to join in the utility-preserving system that coordinates attitudes, but not for violating anything like promulgated rules. He "promulgates" only moral judgments, and social agreement is analogous to judicial conformity to precedent and higher court rulings. The judgment that something is *shi* (right) is equivalent to choosing it. Society gains through coordination of behavior and the efficiency of a "constant" *dao* (guiding discourse).

While we harmonize our *shi–fei* judgments with those the ruler, he does not have arbitrary discretion in his assignments of *shi–fei* (right–wrong). He must "conform upward" too, and for the ruler the higher authority is *tian* and the natural standard of utility. Since all human beings have access to that natural measurement standard, ultimately we "conform upward" only when we correctly use the utility standard in judgment. Still, agreement is itself a utilitarian good, so we report up our judgments, and join in the general acceptance of the judgment that comes down.

This difficulty in making the political system coherent illustrates an implicit tension between the reforming utility standard that is accessible to everyone and Mozi's continued need for a traditional social authority. The tension becomes explicit in Mozi's account of three *fa* (measurement standards) for *yan* [*yen*] (language). He lists first the model of past sage kings. Second, he observes the importance of standards to which ordinary people have access "through their eyes and ears." Clear, measurement-like standards can be applied by "even the unskillful" with good results. He lists the pragmatic appeal to usefulness third. While it anchors his reform spirit, he clearly recognizes the importance of historical and traditional patterns in determining correct usage.

Mozi applies his standards in a famous set of arguments concerning "spirits" and "fate." He appeals to what the sage kings and old literature say, what people in general say, using their "eyes and ears" and, most importantly, what effects on behavior will result from saying "spirits exist" versus "spirits do not exist" or "there is fate" versus "there is no fate." Mozi acknowledges that there may be no spirits. Still, he argues, the standards of language all weigh in favor of saying "exists" of them. He characterizes his conclusion as knowing the *dao* (way) of "existence–non-existence." Knowing how to deploy this distinction is knowing to say "exists" of spirits and "does not exist" of fate. We change the content of discourse via making the "exist–not exist" distinction in a particular way.

Mohism died out when the emerging imperial dynastic system promoted a Confucian orthodoxy. Mozi's long-term influence is controversial. Confucian histories treat Mohism as a brief, inconsequential interlude of "Western Style thought." However, his influence arguably shaped Confucian orthodoxy as much as Confucius did. Mozi forced later classical Confucian thinkers to defend their normative theory philosophically, and as a result of his doing so, they adopted his terms of analysis and many of his key ethical attitudes. Paradoxically, the vehicle for the absorption of Mohist ideas was his chief detractor, Mencius, who effectively abandoned traditionalism and constructed a Confucian version of benevolence-based naturalism that was implicitly universal.

Daoism, similarly, grew out of a relativistic analysis of the Confucian–Mohist debate. Arguably, we owe to Mozi the fact that Chinese philosophy exists. Without him, Confucianism might never have risen above "wise man" sayings and Daoism might have languished as nothing more than a "Yellow Emperor" cult.

Bibliography

Writings

The Ethical and Political Works of Mo-tse, ed. Y. P. Mei (London: Arthur Probsthain, 1929).

Further reading

Graham, Angus: *Later Mohist Logic, Ethics and Science* (Hong Kong and London: Chinese University Press, 1978).
Hansen, Chad: "Mozi: Language Utilitarianism: The Structure of Ethics in Classical China," *Journal of Chinese Philosophy*, 16 (1989), 355–80.
Hansen, Chad: *A Daoist Theory of Chinese Thought* (New York: Oxford University Press, 1992).
Mei, Y. P.: *Mo-tse, the Neglected Rival of Confucius* (London: Arthur Probsthain, 1934).

26

Nāgārjuna

Bina Gupta

Nāgārjuna (150–? CE), arguably the most important philosopher of the Mādhyamika school of Mahāyāna Buddhism, lived during the transitional era of Buddhism five hundred years after the BUDDHA's death. This was a time when Buddhist monks began doubting and debating Buddhist teachings and practices. As a result of their inability to reach consensus, Buddhist schools began proliferating. One of the most important literatures belonging to this era is *Prajñāpāramitā*, which literally means "transcendent insight or wisdom" (*Prajñā- + pāram + itā*) but which is usually translated as "Perfection of Wisdom." The principal theme of this work is the notion of *śūnyatā* (emptiness). Nāgārjuna analyzes this notion and develops its ramifications clearly and systematically. Although *Prajñāpāramitā* has been commented upon by both the Mādhyamika and Yogācāra schools of Mahāyāna Buddhism, in time it came to be used synonymously with the teachings of Nāgārjuna.

Buddha had refused to answer any metaphysical questions. He characterized his teaching as *madhyamā pratipad*, the middle way, because it avoids all extremes of being and non-being, self and non-self, self-indulgence and self-mortification, substance and process – in general all dualistic affirmations. Nāgārjuna was puzzled by the Buddha's silence and looked for the rationale behind it. He took the Buddha's silence to mean that reality could not be articulated by any of the metaphysical theses, such as the thesis of permanence and change. Because Nāgārjuna rejected all such metaphysical positions, he thought he was taking a middle position and thus he called his philosophy Mādhyamaka. The followers of this school subsequently came to be known as Mādhyamikas. To the extent that he claimed that he was not taking any metaphysical position at all, his philosophy may also be called *śūnyavāda*.

Nāgārjuna is generally believed to have been born into a Brahmin family in Andhra Pradesh, South India, in 150 CE. Many legends surrounding his name make it difficult to ascertain with certainty what is fact. It is believed that he initially studied the Vedas and other important Hindu texts and eventually converted to Buddhism. Numerous works have been attributed to Nāgārjuna. These works include public lectures and letters to numerous kings, in addition to metaphysical and epistemological treatises that form the foundation of the Mādhyamika school. But there is no doubt that his most important works are *Mūlamadhyamakakārikā* with his own commentary and *Vigrahavyāvartanī*.

The focus of this chapter is Nāgārjuna's *Mūlamadhyamakakārikā* (abbreviated as MMK), *Fundamental Verses on the Middle Way*. It contains 448 verses divided into 27 chapters. The terse and dense nature of these verses continues to generate significant philosophical dialogue up to this day. The central theses of MMK revolve around the notions of *śūnyatā* (emptiness) and *niḥsvabhāvatā* (lack of inherent existence or absence of essence in things). Taking Buddha's doctrine of *pratītyasamutapāda* or conditioned emergence (meaning that all events come into being depending upon preceding conditions) as his point of departure, Nāgārjuna uses a method known as *prasaṅga* or *reductio ad absurdum* to demonstrate that all perspectives about reality involve self-contradiction.

Prasaṅga (reductio ad absurdum)

Prasaṅga is a method of analysis that exposes the inherent self-contradiction of any perspective, thereby demonstrating its absurdity. The analysis consists in showing that the proponent's theses lead to absurdity by using the very same rules and principles accepted by the proponents themselves. Let us examine how Nāgārjuna uses this method to accomplish his goal.

At the outset, Nāgārjuna argues that two possible predications about a putative reality, say an object A, are "A is" and "A is not." The conjunction and negation of the conjunction gives rise to yet two more possibilities: "A both is and is not" and "A neither is nor is not" (*caṭṣkoti* or quadrilemma). This is also known as four-cornered negation. Nāgārjuna analyzes these four alternatives and, by drawing out the implications of each alternative, demonstrates that it is impossible to erect any sound metaphysics on the basis of reason. Let us consider an example. With respect to causation, these four possibilities translate into: (1) a thing arises out of itself, (2) a thing arises out of not-itself, (3) a thing arises out of both itself and not-itself, and (4) a thing arises neither out of itself nor out of not-itself. Nāgārjuna argues that on the first alternative (the Sāṃkhya view) cause and effect become identical. Their identity points to their non-difference. Thus any talk about their being causally related is superfluous. On the second alternative (the Nyāya view) cause and effect become entirely different, and, accordingly, there can be no common ground between the two to make the relation of causality possible. Thus, the second alternative is equally meaningless. He further argues that since the first and the second possibilities are meaningless, the two remaining possibilities that arise out of the conjunction and the negation of the conjunction are equally meaningless.

Nāgārjuna further argues that both the opposing views outlined above (i.e. (1) that the effect, prior to creation, is contained in the cause, and, accordingly is not a new creation, and (2) that the effect is an event, which is totally different from the cause and, accordingly, is a new creation) presuppose that the event which is called cause and the event that is called effect, each has its own *svabhāva* or self-nature. If an event has a nature of its own, it will always have that nature; it will never change. When events have a nature of their own or are ascribed eternal essences, they are either totally identical or totally different. Qualification of the sort "some" or "partially" (i.e. to say that they are partially identical or partially different) is not permissible. In other words, such a self-nature by definition being eternal is free from conditions. Thus it cannot be said to be caused inasmuch as being caused implies conditions; and it therefore cannot be brought into existence.

The point that Nāgārjuna is trying to make is as follows: we have two aspects of a causal relation that are incompatible with each other. One of these aspects is that causation involves dependent origination; the other aspect is that each cause and effect has an eternal essence of its own which is not capable of origination. If we choose the latter, there is no dependent origination; if we choose the former, neither the cause nor the effect could have an eternal essence. If neither of the two has an eternal essence or self-nature, everything becomes conditional. Nāgārjuna argues that when causes and effects are taken as entities with their own self-natures, absurdities arise. Such causes and effects both are and are not entities that exist independently and unconditionally. Causal relations imply not temporal sequence but instead mutual dependence in the sense that a cause is not a cause but for the effect, and the latter is not an effect but for the cause. The conditioned entities such as causes and effects have no essential nature of their own (*niḥsvabhāva*); they are entirely relational.

Śūnyatā (emptiness)

Nāgārjuna makes use of his theory of causal relations and applies it ruthlessly to demonstrate that not only the concepts and the doctrines of the rival schools (permanence, substantial self, etc.), but also the central

Buddhist doctrines (momentariness, *karma, skandhas,* and even the very idea of the Buddha as "having attained thus" [*Tathāgata*]), contain inherent self-contradictions. Every concept, argues Nāgārjuna, acquires meaning only when contrasted with its complement and in that sense every concept implies its own negation. Nāgārjuna examines various metaphysical theories that existed in Indian thought during that time (e.g. the Vaiśeṣika theory that a material object consists of simple atoms; the Sāṃkhya theory that material objects arise out of simple undifferentiated stuff called *prakṛti* or nature; the early Buddhist theory that reality is a process, or, better yet, a series of instantaneous events) and shows that in each of these cases the concepts employed (e.g. of the part and whole, the simple and the composite, permanence and change, undifferentiated nature and differentiated entities) imply their opposites – and to the extent they do, the theses incorporating them cannot be coherently formulated. Since, for example, the concept of a chair is incoherent, the alleged thing chair is also empty, which is to say that it is devoid of self-nature. Thus, for Nāgārjuna, it does not make sense to argue whether things exist or not. Ascribing existence to a thing is only a matter of pragmatic usefulness, not one of attributing ontological reality to it. Accordingly, Nāgārjuna concludes that since no entity can be characterized in itself as having an essence (i.e. being simple, being permanent, being instantaneous, being a whole, or being a part), such putative entities are "empty."

Divergent theories of reality are, on this view, only conceptual constructions (*vikalpa*) in which each construction focuses upon a particular point of view. Thus, in the phenomenal realm there is no absolute truth; truth is always relative to a conceptual system. The phenomenal world has only a pragmatic reality, which is also called conventional reality (*samvṛti*). Conventional truth, however, is not the only kind of truth. There is also the *paramārtha-satya*, i.e. the higher or the absolute truth. The empirical world, according to Buddhist teachings, has only phenomenal, pragmatic, or conventional being (these are used synonymously by the Buddhists); however, from the point of view of absolute truth, the manifold world of names and forms is simply an appearance. Absolute reality transcends the perceptual–conceptual framework of language; it is unconditional and devoid of plurality. It is *nirvāṇa.* Such a truth is realized by intuitive wisdom (*prajñā*). It is non-dual and contentless. It is beyond language, logic, and sense perception.

All this leads Nāgārjuna to assert the paradoxical thesis that *saṃsāra* or phenomenal conditioned reality is not really different from *nirvāṇa;* they are the same (MMK 25, 19–20). In other words, *nirvāṇa* and *saṃsāra* are not two ontologically distinct levels, but one reality viewed from two different perspectives. The distinction between the two, like all else, is relative. The same reality is phenomenal when viewed in the conceptual framework; it is *nirvāṇa* when viewed in itself. Accordingly, *nirvāṇa* is not something that is to be attained, but is, rather, the right comprehension of the *saṃsāra* in which the plurality of names and forms is manifested. Everything is *nirvāṇa*; it is *śūnya*. *Śūnya* is an experience which cannot be linguistically and conceptually communicated; it is quiescent; it is devoid of conceptual construction; and it is non-dual. Even the concept of *śūnya* may be understood from the lower as well as from the higher point of view; from the lower point of view, it signifies lack of self-nature or absence of any substantial reality of its own; from the transcendent standpoint, it signifies the incoherence of all conceptual systems.

Nāgārjuna further argues that no element of existence is manifest without conditions; therefore there is no non-empty element (MMK, 24.19) and whatever is conditionally emergent is empty. He also maintains a three-way relation between conditioned emergence, emptiness, and verbal convention, and he regards this relation as none other than the Middle Way. Thus, (1) conditioned emergence is emptiness; and (2) emptiness and the conventional world are not two distinct ontological levels but two sides of the same coin. To say that a thing is conditionally emergent is to say that it is empty. Conversely, to say that it is empty is another way of saying that it emerges conditionally. What language articulates is the so-called conventional world, which is empty. Nāgārjuna wrestled with the question: "in what sense do words like '*śūnya*' and '*nirvāṇa*' verbally articulate what is incapable of being expressed"? But he accepted the paradox involved to be unavoidable.

In reading Nāgārjuna, it is important to keep in mind that he was neither a thoroughgoing skeptic nor a nihilist. T. R. V. Murti terms *Mādhyamika* dialectic "a spiritual *jujitsu*." He further adds that *Mādhyamika* "does not have a thesis of [its] own." However, to interpret Nāgārjuna as one whose arguments aim only at destruction is to miss the real significance of his philosophy. It is indeed true that Nāgārjuna demonstrates that one can expose self-contradictions in the opponent's arguments without making any claims about what in fact exists, as long as one uses the rules accepted by the opponent. This, however, should not be taken to imply, contrary to Murti's contention, that Nāgārjuna did not have a thesis of his own. In his dialectical method, he rejects the pretensions of reason to know reality. His mode of argumentation does not demonstrate the total inadequacy of reason, because he himself uses reason to demonstrate self-contradictions involved in the opponent's arguments. He shows that everything is conditional in the phenomenal world; that reality transcends both refutation and non-refutation, both affirmation and negation, and hence cannot be captured by discursive reasoning. Reality can only be captured by rising to a higher level, i.e. the level of *prajñā*. In making these assertions Nāgārjuna indeed provides his readers with theses.

Bibliography

Writings

Mūlamadhyamakakārikā of Nāgārjuna, trans. D. Kalupahana (Delhi: Motilal Banarsidass Publishers, 1991).

Further reading

Murti, T. R. V.: *The Central Philosophy of Buddhism* (London: George Allen and Unwin, 1960).

Streng, F. J.: *Emptiness: A Study in Religious Meaning* (Nashville, TN: Abingdon Press, 1967).

27

Nietzsche

Richard Schacht

Friedrich Wilhelm Nietzsche (1844–1900 CE) is one of the most controversial figures in the history of philosophy. He also has become one of its most diversely influential thinkers. He was never an "academic philosopher" either by education or by profession, and his influence in the philosophical community did not begin to be felt until long after his death in 1900, and then was clouded by the travesty of his appropriation by the Nazis. His productive life, moreover, was greatly hindered by debilitating health problems, and was cut lamentably short by a complete physical and mental collapse (from which he never recovered) in 1889, when he was but 44. Yet he left a rich legacy of challenges and contributions to philosophy, the importance and continuing relevance of which are becoming ever more apparent. He sought to revitalize and reorient philosophy, in ways intended to free it from stultifying aspects of its past, and attune it to the demands of the pressing tasks awaiting it.

Friedrich Nietzsche was born on October 15, 1844, and was raised and educated in provincial Saxony (in what is now eastern Germany). His father was a Lutheran pastor in the tiny village of Röcken. Upon his father's early death in 1849, his mother was obliged to relocate with him and his sister to the nearby town of Naumburg. It was during his childhood there that his lifelong loves of music and literature developed and deepened. His precocious scholastic excellence earned him a scholarship to the prestigious classics-oriented academy Schulpforta. While distinguishing himself there in his studies, Nietzsche also avidly pursued his musical interests, becoming a fine pianist and composing a considerable amount of music, including numerous *Lieder* and works for the piano. (His compositional efforts continued through his twenties.)

Nietzsche's university education began in 1864 at Bonn, and continued at Leipzig, focusing upon classical studies. It was in Leipzig that he made two acquaintances that influenced him profoundly: Arthur

Schopenhauer, through his masterwork *The World as Will and Representation*, and Richard Wagner, whose sister was a friend of the wife of one
of Nietzsche's professors. It was though his encounter with Schopenhauer's thinking that Nietzsche's philosophical interests were stimulated
and initially shaped. His relationship with Wagner (which began in hero-
worship, developed into intimacy, and ended in estrangement and
scathing polemic) was intimately bound up with the dramatic changes
that marked the remainder of his personal and intellectual life.

Nietzsche so impressed his professors that he was called to a professorship in classical philology (the study of classical languages and literatures) at the Swiss university of Basel in 1869, at the age of only 24,
before he had even received his doctorate. He resigned a mere ten years
later, however, in 1879, owing both to the deterioration of his health and
to his changing interests. His brief academic career was plagued by
health problems, which were exacerbated by illnesses he contracted
while serving as a volunteer medical orderly in 1870 during the Franco-
Prussian war. This decade was certainly eventful, marked by the publication of *The Birth of Tragedy* (1872) and the four essays making up his
Untimely Meditations (1874–6), and enlivened by his involvement with
Wagner, by whom and whose operatic art *The Birth of Tragedy* was in part
inspired. Yet it ended not only in his abandonment of philology, but also
in his disillusionment with Wagner (for many reasons, including his
growing antipathy to Wagner's anti-Semitism, and his dawning sense that
there was something dangerously pathological about that very art).

Following his early retirement Nietzsche left Basel, and began the
nomadic boarding-house life he was to live for the rest of his active life.
The Nietzsche of this period was the heir of Voltaire (to whom he dedicated his next book, *Human, All Too Human*, in 1878), relentlessly pursuing the project of radical enlightenment. This period also was one of
dramatic intellectual development on his part, in the course of which
he made the transition from classicist, Wagnerian enthusiast and cultural critic to philosopher. In his early writings Nietzsche had looked to
the Greeks and to Wagner for guidance in discovering a way to cultural
and spiritual renewal. He now recognized the inadequacy of his earlier
assessment of the situation and of his first thoughts concerning possible
responses to it, and set about to provide himself with the intellectual
means of improving upon them. Among them were the analytical, critical, and interpretive tools and strategies that came to characterize his
kind of philosophy. He had already begun to address these emerging
concerns in *Human, All Too Human*, a wide-ranging volume of aphorisms
published while he was still at Basel. He continued their exploration in
the further aphoristic works of the rest of what he called his "free spirit"

series, which had begun with that volume: two supplements to *Human, All Too Human* (1879 and 1880), *Daybreak* (1881), and the initial four-part version of *The Gay Science* (1882).

Only six years of productive life then remained to him. During the first three of these six years, moreover, Nietzsche published only his remarkable literary-philosophical experiment *Thus Spoke Zarathustra* (in four parts, 1883–5). All of the other writings he produced, from *Beyond Good and Evil* (1886) to his autobiographical *Ecce Homo* (written at the end of 1888, just prior to his collapse), were written in the remarkable last three years (1886–8). They further included an expanded second edition of *The Gay Science* and *On the Genealogy of Morals* (1887); and *The Case of Wagner, Twilight of the Idols,* and a final diatribe against Christianity, *The Antichrist* (or *Antichristian*, as its title might better be translated), all written – along with *Ecce Homo* – in 1888. Nietzsche's writings from this period also include a great mass of notes in his notebooks, a small selection of which were published in his name after his death under the title *The Will to Power.* The significance of this material is controversial. Much of it is very rough, tentative, and experimental; and it was never intended for publication. Yet Nietzsche did write it; and its interest is enhanced by the fact that it contains much more material relating to some topics than is to be found in the writings he published or completed.

Nietzsche's initial impetus toward philosophy grew out of his deepening concern with a problem going to the very core of our entire Western culture and civilization. It seemed clear to him that traditional ways of understanding ourselves, the world, and value were on the wane. Culturally, they were losing their capacity to convince and sustain; and intellectually, they were proving incapable of withstanding rigorous scrutiny. Indeed, by commanding truthfulness and valorizing a readiness to sacrifice other interests to it, they had sown the seeds of their own destruction. Their demise now seemed imminent.

This was Nietzsche's version of Wagner's tragic-operatic "Twilight of the Gods" ("*Götterdämmerung*," the name of the final part of his celebrated *Ring* tetralogy). As in the Wagnerian case, that demise seemed to Nietzsche to be well warranted as well as inevitable – yet also shattering, even if the absolutes and ideals that we are going to have to do without are only false idols. It is *their* "twilight" in which he believed we now live. (So he punningly entitled one of his last books "*Götzendämmerung*," "*Twilight of the Idols*," signaling both a Wagnerian theme and his own surpassing of the original.) He was deeply concerned about the void that the impending "death of God" (as he came to call it) would leave. By the end of his Basel years he was already convinced that neither modern science and Enlightenment rationalism *nor* modern art and Wagnerian romanticism would be able to fill this void; and this issue gradually came into focus for him as the phenomenon of *nihilism*, the problem of its advent, and the task of its overcoming.

Schopenhauer had proclaimed the "will to live" to be irrational, and life to be pointless striving and suffering; and he had concluded that a life-denying "No" to all "willing" is the course of wisdom. Nietzsche took Schopenhauer's bleak "pessimism" to be but a harbinger of something even more dangerous ("the danger of dangers"): the more radically nihilistic conviction of the utter senselessness and valuelessness of life and the world in general. And precisely because Nietzsche considered it to be an inevitable and powerful temptation in the aftermath of "the death of God," he believed that it would be catastrophic for humanity if no life-affirming antidote to it capable of withstanding all disillusionment could be found. The diagnosis of this predicament, and the quest for such a way out of it, thus became his passion and mission. In *Thus Spoke Zarathustra* he gave expression to the main elements of the reinterpretation and revaluation of human life that were his response to this challenge, in a form intended to make them accessible to anyone in need of such a response and ready for it.

Coming up with such a response was by no means easy for Nietzsche, because he was convinced of the untenability of any disguised as well as overt version of the "God-hypothesis," in all of its religious and metaphysical variations involving the postulation of some sort of absolute reality transcending, underlying, or governing the course of this life and world. And he took their demise (or preclusion) to mean the beginning of the end of all interpretive and evaluative schemes depending upon anything of the kind. His preferred way of disposing of such notions and associated ways of thinking was by way of what might be called their "genealogical subversion." This strategy involves showing that they and their appeal can very plausibly be accounted for in all-too-human terms, and arguing that there is no good reason to suppose there is anything more to them than that – thereby fatally undermining their credibility and viability.

Breaking the grip of such notions upon our thinking, however, requires more than merely providing this sort of critique. It also involves freeing ourselves of our addiction to absolutes, which prompts us to seek others in place of those we have formerly embraced but can no longer take seriously – and which sets us up to be devastated by their absence when we finally comprehend that there are none to be found. Nihilism is the ultimate consequence of this addiction; and so, Nietzsche contends, liberation from this addiction is essential to nihilism's overcoming.

But even that liberation by itself will not be enough. The overcoming of nihilism for Nietzsche further requires the finding of a way and means to a new "affirmation of life" unmediated by any dependence upon transcendence, and in radical contrast to Schopenhauer's condemnation of life and the world as he understood them. It is in this connection that Nietzsche introduces and chiefly employs a number of his most highly charged images. The figure of the "overman," for example, is emblematic of his conception of the qualitative "enhancement of life" (in deliberate contrast to any other-worldly ideal) as the new *this*-worldly locus of value. This image signifies the "affirmation of life" enhanced through the creative transformation and transfiguration of the merely natural, in ways endowing it with artistic worth and aesthetic significance.

Another such image is the idea of "eternal recurrence" – the conception of things forever recurring as they now occur. While Nietzsche experimented in his notebooks with the possibility of taking this idea seriously if construed very literally, it functions for him primarily as a supreme test of one's ability to affirm life and the world *as they fundamentally are* (and will continue to be), rather than as one might wish them to be or become. Can one say Yes to the idea of one's life and everything else recurring eternally? And could one do so even if they were to recur *precisely* as they have occurred? If so, one's affirmation of life would show itself to be dependent upon nothing merely imaginary or ideal, and so secure against all disillusionment.

A further case in point is Nietzsche's concept of "*amor fati*" or "love of fate" (replacing Spinoza's "*amor dei*" or "love of God"). It signifies the attainment of the completely "de-deified" and radically "this-worldly" reorientation of affirmation he envisions. To achieve this "Dionysian" stance involves envisioning all that one is, does, and can become, as a part of a world in which necessity reigns and there are no metaphysical "free wills" – yet (crucially, for Nietzsche) which itself engenders the redeeming possibility of creativity. And it is precisely this saving grace that makes possible the embrace of what is thus envisioned, and so is the key to the Nietzschean notion of a fundamental "life-affirmation" that is beyond all naivete and illusions.

Nietzsche's kind of philosophy is avowedly and unabashedly *interpretive*. Indeed, he contends that all human thought has this character. It always involves selectivity, perspective, and convention, and reflects varying interests and valuations. Philosophical thinking is no exception. It does not follow from this, however, that all interpretations are on a complete epistemic par with each other – namely, that of having *no* genuinely cognitive significance. And Nietzsche is quite clearly convinced that, in at least some contexts, prevailing interpretations can be improved upon, and comprehension can be deepened and refined. This is a significant part of what he calls upon the "new philosophers" he envisions to do, in his "Prelude to a Philosophy of the Future" (the subtitle of *Beyond Good and Evil*); and it is something he himself quite evidently sought to do, with respect to matters as diverse as morality, art, and our own emergent psychological, social, and intellectual human reality.

Perhaps no part of Nietzsche's thought has given rise to more confusion than his thinking with respect to *truth* and *knowledge*. Some of his comments have been taken to amount to a radical repudiation of the very possibility of anything deserving of either name. Yet he also makes much of the importance of truth, truthfulness, knowledge, and intellectual rigor and integrity, in contexts such as those of scientific and philosophical inquiry. At times he makes much of the contingent, artificial, and merely conventional and perspectival character of most of what passes for truth and knowledge in various human contexts, and of the impossibility of coming up with anything that would satisfy the criteria of truth and knowledge to which many philosophers from PLATO to DESCARTES and KANT and beyond have subscribed. On other occasions, however, he draws attention to the problematic character of these criteria, explores alternatives to them, and attempts to give the notions of truth and knowledge a new and more fruitful lease of life, in terms of something like *aptness* and doing (greater or lesser) *justice* to something with ample warrant.

Indeed, while insisting that "truth" and "knowledge" as philosophical purists and absolutists have long conceived of them are myths, Nietzsche came to understand and appreciate that there are many contexts in which it makes good and important sense to retain and employ these notions, notwithstanding all relevant considerations pertaining to contingency, conditionality, conventionality, and perspective. In fact, our ability to shift perspectives actually can enable us to come to understand a good deal about ourselves and our human world. It remains an open question, however, how far such comprehension may be extended, beyond human affairs and into the larger world in which human life goes on. Some phenomena (for example, sports, arts, morals, politics) have the character they do because they have come to be as they are in the course of human events; and so there is no reason to suppose there is anything more to them than we are capable of tuning in on. And in such cases it should be possible for us to attain perspectives that accord sufficiently with them to do something approaching justice to them.

The ubiquity of "perspective" is thus no barrier to the comprehension of what we have made, or to that which is significantly akin to it. And this suffices to reconcile Nietzsche's "perspectivism" with at least a modest (but significant) sort of cognitivism, to which he also shows himself to be committed. Here the notions of humanly attainable truth and knowledge can certainly be salvaged, and significantly employed. The more dubious the supposition of the consonance of attainable human perspectives with the character of some domain, however, the more problematic any ventured interpretation of it becomes.

Nietzsche's proposed interpretation of life and the world in terms of "will to power" is problematic for precisely this reason, as he himself was aware. This has led some to question the seriousness and nature of his commitment to it. Yet he does advance this interpretation, and does so with evident cognitive purport, particularly where human and other forms of life are concerned. He is well disposed to the various interpretations of aspects of life and the world emerging and developing under the aegis of the maturing natural and biological sciences, for example – at least as far as they go. But he contends that the general scientific world-interpretation in terms of dynamic quanta, arrayed in systems and fields of force, is incomplete. And he proposes that it can be improved upon by construing all such phenomena in terms of power-relationships, and by supposing all dynamic quanta to be inherently disposed to enter into such relationships.

"Will to power" is Nietzsche's name for this basic and ubiquitous assertive disposition, typically manifesting itself in *ordering transformation*. The conception of power figuring in this interpretation and hypothesis refers not merely to the more obvious forms of domination and control, but also to a whole range of much more subtle forms of the attainment of mastery and of supremacy. "Power" for Nietzsche is fundamentally a matter of the imposition of some new pattern of "ordering relations" upon forces not previously subject to them. It is one of his more astute psychological insights that frustration in the attempt to achieve one sort of power commonly leads to the development of another, or of alternate forms of competition in which power is both differently won and differently measured. In extending the idea of "will to power" to the interpretation of life and the world more generally, as he clearly was inclined at least tentatively and experimentally to do, he was venturing to be something of a philosophical biologist and cosmologist as well.

It is human life more specifically, however, and our human nature, variability, and possibility, to which Nietzsche devotes most of his attention. In reinterpreting our humanity in a thoroughly naturalistic manner, he contributes significantly to the development of a philosophical anthropology sensitive to its biological, social, and historical dimensions. His common association with Kierkegaard and the existentialists has obscured this importantly different interest and manner of pursuing it. His concern focuses above all on evaluative considerations relating to the quality of human life and its possible enhancement or decline. He considers it imperative, however, to understand the sort of creature we have come to be, in the course of our biological and historical development, in order to know what we have to work with. And this means coming to appreciate both the "all too human" features of ordinary humanity and the more exceptional human possibilities that hold the key to any attainable sort of higher humanity.

While Nietzsche's thinking with respect to our humanity remained tentative and unsystematic to the end, there can be no doubt about its generally naturalistic contours. We are a kind of creature among others that has evolved on this planet, he insists, and have no loftier origin; but we have come to be significantly different from others owing to certain peculiarities in our evolutionary history, in which social factors have played a significant role. All human intellectuality, spirituality, and psychological reality is the result of this process and of the contingencies that have occurred along the way.

Human beings further *differ* in many ways that matter, Nietzsche contends, both by nature and owing to what occurs in the course of their lives, affecting the ways in which their various capacities are (or are not) developed and directed. Human *worth*, for him, is best conceived in terms of the cultivation of abilities that are not shared in equal measure, and more specifically in terms of the attainment of various forms of excellence in which such abilities are employed and expressed, with a premium upon creativity (rather than rationality, morality, individuality or subjectivity). Cultural life is the arena of such activity, with art as its paradigm; and the enhancement of life is fundamentally a matter of its ongoing creative transformation. The distinction Nietzsche draws between "higher" and "lower" forms of humanity is to be understood primarily along these lines, and thus in terms of differences in ways in which human beings *turn out* rather than merely *start out*. The raw materials of Nietzschean "higher humanity" may be biological, and may be unevenly distributed; but the attainment of it depends upon the manner of their cultivation, refinement, and expression.

Nietzsche's "revaluation of values" is thus closely linked to his reinterpretation of life in general and of human life in particular. If there is nothing beyond this life in this world that can serve as a standard or basis for value and value-determinations (as Nietzsche supposes), then value too must be "naturalized," and understood in relation to something having to do with life. Value must reflect the basic character of life, the requirements of flourishing life, the general idea of the enhancement of life, or the sort of thing that the enhancement of life involves – and in Nietzsche's hands it winds up reflecting all of these things at different junctures in his thinking. The basic character of life as "will to power" sets the context for the identification of the artistically conceived enhancement of life as the locus of value, with creativity as its watchword. When Nietzsche undertakes his "revaluation" of things commonly valued either positively or negatively, it is with the question in mind of whether they are not merely life-*preserving* but life-*enhancing* – and if so, for what or whom, in what respects, under what circumstances, and with what larger consequences.

The things Nietzsche subjects to revaluation are numerous and diverse, ranging from Christianity and other religions to various types of art, science, philosophy, politics, morality, and putative virtues and vices. He vehemently attacks Christianity, for example, particularly in the form it was given by St Paul, less for the absurdity of its interpretation of life and the world than for the harmfulness to human flourishing of that interpretation and associated values. He further is convinced that people tend to attach much too much importance to pleasure and pain and to happiness and suffering alike; and that such traits as cooperativeness and pity are commonly overvalued as much as self-assertiveness and competitiveness are underappreciated.

Nietzsche is particularly critical of the sort of "herd-animal" morality that seemed to him to have triumphed in the modern Western world. He takes this type of morality – with its emphasis on conformity, equality, self-denial, and the alleviation of suffering – to owe much in its "genealogy" to the kind of fearful, resentful, leveling "slave morality" that was the natural antithesis to the self-affirming and self-assertive moralities of erstwhile barbarian "masters." He even combatively styles himself "immoralist" and "beyond good and evil" as well as "anti-Christian." But the fundamental thrust of his moral philosophy is not against any and all forms of morality. Rather, it is in the direction of a naturalistic moral theory, advocating moralities sensitive to human differences of circumstances, requirements, and capacities, and attuned to a strongly affirmative conception of human flourishing and "life-enhancement."

Nietzsche's influence upon subsequent European philosophy has been profound. Together with KIERKEGAARD, he was one of the main inspirations of the central figures in German and French existential philosophy (Martin HEIDEGGER, Karl Jaspers, Jean-Paul SARTRE, Albert Camus). Their interest in him focused more upon his repudiation of traditional religious, moral, and metaphysical ways of thinking, however, than upon the naturalistic reinterpretation of human life and approach to evaluative and normative matters to which he himself was inclined.

In the latter respects his lead was followed by others, who sought to mount a philosophical–anthropological counter-movement to existential philosophy (Max Scheler, Helmuth Plessner, Arnold Gehlen) in the second quarter of the century, and some of those associated with the Frankfurt School of critical social theory (Herbert Marcuse, Jürgen Habermas). A radically postmodernist interpretation of his thought also figured importantly in the emergence and development of post-structuralism in France (Michel FOUCAULT, Jacques DERRIDA, Gilles Deleuze, and others). During the last quarter of the twentieth century an appreciation of his thinking began to develop in Anglo-American analytical philosophical circles as well. It is arguable, however, that none of these appropriations has done justice to him, and that his day is yet to come.

Bibliography

Writings

Kritische Gesamtausgabe: Werke, ed. Giorgio Colli and Mazzino Montinari, over 30 volumes to date (Berlin: de Gruyter, 1967–).

The Birth of Tragedy (1872), trans. Walter Kaufmann, with *The Case of Wagner* (1888) (New York: Vintage, 1966).

Human, All Too Human, first published in three installments (1878–80), subsequently in two volumes (1886), trans. R. J. Hollingdale, intro. Richard Schacht (Cambridge: Cambridge University Press, 1996).

The Gay Science (1882; 2nd expanded edn 1887), trans. Walter Kaufmann (New York: Vintage, 1974).

Thus Spoke Zarathustra, first published in four installments (1883–5), trans. Walter Kaufmann, in *The Portable Nietzsche* (New York: Viking, 1954).

Beyond Good and Evil (1886), trans. Walter Kaufmann (New York: Vintage, 1966).

On the Genealogy of Morals (1887), trans. Walter Kaufmann and R. J. Hollingdale, with *Ecce Homo* (New York: Vintage, 1967).

Twilight of the Idols (1889), trans. Walter Kaufmann, in *The Portable Nietzsche* (New York: Viking, 1954).

The Antichrist (completed 1888; first published 1895), trans. Walter Kaufmann, in *The Portable Nietzsche* (New York: Viking, 1954).

Further reading

Clark, Maudemarie: *Nietzsche on Truth and Philosophy* (Cambridge: Cambridge University Press, 1990).

Danto, Arthur C.: *Nietzsche as Philosopher* (New York: Macmillan, 1965).

Hayman, Ronald: *Nietzsche: A Critical Life* (Oxford: Oxford University Press, 1980).

Kaufmann, Walter: *Nietzsche: Philosopher, Psychologist, Antichrist,* 4th edn (Princeton, NJ: Princeton University Press, 1974).

Nehamas, Alexander: *Nietzsche: Life as Literature* (Cambridge, MA: Harvard University Press, 1985).

Schacht, Richard: *Nietzsche* (London: Routledge, 1983).

28

Plato

C. D. C. Reeve

Plato was born in Athens in 428 BCE and died in 347–8. His father, Ariston, was descended – or so legend has it – from Codrus, the last king of Athens; his mother, Perictione, was related to Solon, architect of the Athenian constitution. He had two brothers, Glaucon and Adeimantus, both of whom appear in his dialogue, the *Republic*, as well as a sister, Potone, whose son, Speusippus, was also a philosopher. While Plato was still a boy, his father died and his mother married Pyrilampes, a friend of the great Athenian statesman, Pericles. Thus Plato was no stranger to Athenian politics even from childhood and was expected to enter it himself. Horrified by actual political events, however, especially the execution of SOCRATES in 399 BCE, he turned instead to philosophy, thinking that only it could rescue human beings from civil war and political upheaval and provide a sound foundation for ethics and politics (see *Seventh Letter* 324b–326b).

Plato's works, which are mostly dialogues, have all survived. They are customarily divided into four groups, though the precise ordering (especially within groups) is controversial:

1 Early (alphabetically): *Apology, Charmides, Crito, Euthyphro, Hippias minor, Hippias major, Ion, Laches, Lysis, Menexenus* (some would include *Alcibiades I* and *Theages* in this group).
2 Transitional (alphabetically): *Euthydemus, Gorgias, Meno, Protagoras.*
3 Middle (chronologically?): *Cratylus, Phaedo, Symposium, Republic, Phaedrus, Parmenides, Theaetetus.*
4 Late (chronologically?): *Timaeus, Critias, Sophist, Statesman, Philebus, Laws, Seventh Letter.*

A fifth group consists of works dubiously or spuriously attributed to Plato. Together these works make fundamental contributions to almost every area of philosophy, from ethics, politics, and aesthetics to metaphysics, epistemology, cosmology, the philosophy of science, the philosophy of language, and the philosophy of mind. It is an exaggeration to say that Western philosophy is a series of footnotes to Plato, but it is not an outrageous exaggeration.

Socrates is the central figure in most of Plato's works. In the early dialogues he is thought to be – and probably is – based to some extent on the historical figure (they are often called "Socratic" dialogues for this reason), but in the transitional, middle, and late dialogues, he is thought to be increasingly a mouthpiece for Plato's own doctrines.

Philosophy for Socrates consists almost exclusively in questioning people about the conventionally recognized ethical virtues. "What is justice," he asks, "or piety, or courage, or wisdom?" He takes for granted, it seems, that there are correct answers to these questions – that justice, piety, courage, and the rest are each some definite characteristic or form (*eidos*, idea). He does not discuss the nature of these forms, however, or develop any explicit theory of them or of our knowledge about them. But he does claim that only they can serve as reliable standards for judging whether any given type of action is an instance of a virtue (see *Euthyphro* 6d–e), and that they can be captured in explicit definitions (*Charmides* 158e ff).

Socrates' interest in definitions of the virtues seems to result from thinking of them as "first principles": if one does not know these definitions, he says, one cannot know anything else of any consequence about the virtues (*Hippias Major* 286c–d, 304d–e; *Laches* 190b–c; *Lysis* 212a, 223b; *Protagoras* 361c; *Republic* 354c). Claiming not to know them himself, Socrates also claims to have little or no other ethical knowledge (*Apology* 20c, 21b). These disclaimers of knowledge are often characterized as false or ironical, but ARISTOTLE, an important source of information about Socrates, took them at face value (*Sophistical Refutations* 183^b6–8).

Socrates' characteristic way of questioning people is an *elenchus* (from the Greek verb *elegchein*, to examine or refute). He asks what courage or some other virtue is; the interlocutor puts forward a definition he sincerely believes to be correct; Socrates then refutes this definition by showing that it conflicts with other beliefs the interlocutor sincerely holds and is unwilling to abandon. In the ideal situation, which is never actually portrayed in the Socratic dialogues, this process continues until a satisfactory definition emerges, one that is not inconsistent with other sincerely held beliefs, and so can withstand elenctic scrutiny. Socrates' use of the elenchus thus seems to presuppose that some sincerely held beliefs are in fact true, since consistency with false beliefs is no guarantee of truth and untrue definitions are no basis for knowledge.

The definitions Socrates encounters in his elenctic examinations of others prove unsatisfactory. But through these examinations, which are always at the same time self-examinations (*Charmides* 166c–d; *Hippias Major* 298b–c; *Protagoras* 348c–d), he comes to accept some positive theses which have resisted refutation. Among these are the following three famous Socratic "paradoxes." (1) The conventionally distinguished virtues – justice, piety, courage, and the rest – are all identical to wisdom or knowledge (*Charmides* 174b–c; *Euthydemus* 281d–e; *Protagoras* 329b–334c, 349a–361d). (2) Possession of this knowledge is necessary and sufficient for happiness (*Crito* 48b; *Gorgias* 470e). (3) No one ever acts contrary to what he knows or believes to be best, so that weakness of will is impossible (*Protagoras* 352a ff). Together these three doctrines constitute a very strict kind of ethical intellectualism: they imply that all we need in order to be virtuous and happy is knowledge.

The goal of an elenchus is not just to reach adequate definitions of the virtues or seemingly paradoxical doctrines about weakness of will and virtue; its primary aim is *moral reform*. For Socrates believes that leading the elentically examined life makes people happier and more virtuous than anything else by curing them of the hubris of thinking they know when they do not (*Apology* 30a, 36c–e, 38a, 41b–c). Philosophizing is so important for human welfare, indeed, that he is willing to accept execution rather than give it up (*Apology* 29b–d).

In the transitional dialogues, as well as in some earlier ones, Socrates, as the embodiment of true philosophy, is contrasted with the sophists. *They* are for the most part unscrupulous, fee-taking moral relativists who think that moral values are based on convention; *he* is an honest, fee-eschewing moral realist, who thinks that the true virtues are the same for everyone everywhere. The problem latent in this contrast is that if people in different cultures have different beliefs about the virtues, it is not clear how the elenchus, which seems to rely wholly on these beliefs, can reach knowledge of objective or non-culture-relative moral truth.

In a number of middle and late dialogues, Plato connects the relativist doctrines he attributes to the sophists with the metaphysical theory of Heraclitus, according to which perceptible things or characteristics are in constant flux or change, always *becoming*, never *being*. In the *Theaetetus*, he argues that Protagoras' claim that "man is the measure of all things" presupposes that the world is in flux; in the *Cratylus*, he suggests that the theory of flux may itself be the result of projecting Protagorean relativism onto the world (411b–c). Nonetheless, Plato seems to accept some version of this theory himself (see Aristotle, *Metaphysics* 987^{a}32–4). In *Republic V*, for example, he characterizes perceptible things and characteristics as "rolling around as intermediates between what is not and what purely is" (478a–479d; see also *Timaeus* 52a).

The theory of flux clearly exacerbates the earlier problem with the Socratic elenchus. If perceptible things and characteristics are always in flux, how can justice and the other virtues be stable forms? How can there be stable definitions of them to serve as correct answers to Socrates' questions? And if there are no stable definitions, how can there be such a thing as ethical knowledge? More generally, if perceptible things and characteristics are always in flux, always *becoming*, how can anything *be* something definite or determinate? How can one know or say what anything *is*? Aristotle tells us that it was reflection on these fundamental questions that led Plato to "separate" the forms from perceptible things and characteristics (*Metaphysics* 987^{a}29–^{b}1), as Socrates did not (*Metaphysics* 1086^{b}2–5). The allegories of the Sun and Line in the *Republic* (507a–511e), which divide reality into the intelligible part and the visible (perceptible) part, apparently embody this separation, as does the account of the creation of the universe in the *Timaeus* (especially 51b–e).

Conceived of in this way, forms seemed to Plato to offer solutions to the metaphysical and epistemological problems to which the elenchus and flux give rise. As intelligible objects, set apart from the perceptible world, they are above the sway of flux, and therefore available as stable objects of knowledge, stable meanings or referents for words. As real mind-independent entities, they provide the definitions of the virtues with the non-conventional subject-matter Socratic ethics needs.

Like many proposed solutions to philosophical problems, however, Plato's raised new problems of its own. If forms really are separate from the world of flux our senses reveal to us, how can we know them? How can our words connect with them? If items in the perceptible world really are separate from forms, how can they owe whatever determinate being they have to forms? In the *Meno*, *Phaedo*, and *Phaedrus*, Plato answers the first of these questions by appeal to the doctrine of recollection (*anamnēsis*). We have knowledge of forms through prenatal direct contact with them; we forget this knowledge when our souls become embodied at birth; then we "recollect" it in this life when our memories are appropriately jogged (for example, when we undergo elenctic examination). He answers the second question by saying that items in the world of flux "participate" in forms by resembling them. Thus perceptible objects possess the characteristic of beauty because they resemble the form of beauty, which is itself something beautiful (see *Phaedo* 100c; *Symposium* 210b–211e).

The doctrine of recollection is a problematic doctrine. Among other things, it presupposes the immortality of the soul – something Plato argues for on a number of occasions (see *Phaedo* 69e ff; *Republic* 608d ff; *Phaedrus* 245c ff). But perhaps because recollection is problematic in these ways, he seems to have sought an alternative to it: recollection is not mentioned in the *Republic* or in the late dialogues. This supposed alternative is dialectic, which is also referred to as the method of "collection and division" (*Phaedrus* 265c ff).

Dialectic is introduced in the *Republic* as having a special bearing on first principles – a feature it continues to possess in Aristotle (see *Topics* $101^a37{-}^b4$) – particularly on those of the mathematical sciences. The importance of these sciences in Plato's thought is twofold. First, they provided a compelling example of a rich body of precise knowledge organized into a deductive system of axioms, definitions, and theorems – a model of what philosophy itself might be. Second, the brilliant mathematical treatment of harmony (musical beauty), developed by Pythagoras of Samos and his followers (see Aristotle, *Metaphysics* $987^a29{-}988^a17$), suggested a role for mathematics within philosophy itself. For it opened up the possibility of giving precise definitions in wholly mathematical terms of all characteristics, including such apparently vague and evaluative ones as beauty and ugliness, justice and injustice, good and evil, and the other things of which Socrates sought definitions (see *Republic* 530d–533e, *Philebus* 66a).

The problem Plato found with mathematical science lay in its first principles. Scientists treat these as "absolute starting points" and either provide conceptually inadequate accounts or definitions of them (*Republic* 527a–b) or simply leave them undefined (510c–d). Yet if they are false, the entire system collapses. It is here that dialectic comes in. Dialectic defends these starting points – it renders them "unhypothetical" – not by deriving them from something yet more primitive (which is impossible), but by defending them against all objections (534b–c, 437a). In the process, they undergo conceptual revamping, so that their consistency with one another – and hence their immunity to an elenchus – is revealed and assured. This enables the dialectician to knit them all together into a single unified theory of everything, and so to "see things as a whole" (557c). It is this unified, holistic theory, and not recollection, that is now supposed to provide the philosopher with genuine knowledge (533d–534a).

What one grasps by means of this theory, Plato claims, is the greatest object of knowledge (505a), the form of the good, which seems to be an ideal of rational order or unity expressed in mathematical terms. This mysterious object, which is described as "superior to being in rank and power" (509b), provides the philosopher with the kind of knowledge he needs to design a genuinely good or happy city (the ideal city described in the *Republic*). On a larger scale, it also provides the maker of the cosmos – the Demiurge – with the knowledge he needs to perform his cosmic task (*Timaeus* 29e ff). For even the gods are bound by the objective truths and values embodied in the forms (*Euthyphro* 10a ff).

The emergence to prominence of mathematical science may seem like a major departure from the early dialogues, in which ethics and politics are the near exclusive focus. In fact, as we have seen, it is a deeper probing of the problems raised in those dialogues. Ethics and politics remain central, but Plato has become aware that they need to be treated as component parts of a much wider and deeper philosophical theory.

The *Republic*, which is Plato's single greatest work, offers us a brilliant attempt to articulate that theory in all its complexity. In Book I, Thrasymachus argues that those who are stronger in any society – the rulers – control education and socialization through legislation and enforcement. But, like everyone else, the rulers are self-interested. Hence they make laws and adopt conventions – including linguistic ones – that are in their own best interests, not those of their weaker subjects. It is these conventions that largely determine their subjects' conceptions of justice and the other virtues. Thus, by being trained to follow or obey them, subjects are unwittingly adopting an ideology, a code of values and behavior, that serves not their own but their ruler's interests. That is why Thrasymachus defines justice not as what socialized subjects – like Socrates – think it is (something genuinely noble and valuable that promotes their own happiness), but as what it really is: the interest of the stronger. Because this argument raises the problem for the elenchus we looked at earlier, by representing the beliefs the elenchus must rely on as false or untrustworthy, it cannot be fully answered by elenctic argument. That is why Plato abandons the elenchus and tries to answer Thrasymachus by developing a positive defense of justice of his own (Books II–X).

At the center of this defense is the concept of the philosopher-king, who unites political power and authority with philosophical knowledge of values based on mathematical science and dialectic – knowledge that is unmediated by conventionally controlled concepts and so is free from the distorting influence of power or ideology. What the philosopher-king does is to construct a political system – including primarily a system of socialization and education – that will distribute the benefits of this specialized knowledge among the citizens at large. For there is no question of the knowledge itself being so disseminated; like much expert knowledge in our own society, it is far too complex and difficult for that.

Thus the examined life, which Socrates thought best for all human beings, is now led only by mature adults with scientific and dialectical training (531d ff).

The nature of the system that the philosopher-kings design is based on Plato's psychology or theory of the soul (*psychē*). According to it, there are three fundamentally different kinds of desires: *appetitive* ones for food, drink, sex, and the money with which to acquire them; *spirited* ones for honor, victory, and good reputation; and *rational* ones for knowledge and truth (437b ff, 580d ff). Each of these types of desire "rules" in the soul of a different type of person, determining his values. For people most value what they most desire, and so people ruled by different desires have very different conceptions of what is valuable, of their good or happiness. But just which desire "rules" an individual's soul depends on the relative strengths of his desires and the kind of education and socialization he receives. It is scarcely surprising, in light of these views, that Plato believes that the fundamental goal of ethical or political education is not to put knowledge into people's souls but to train or socialize their desires, turning them around (to the degree possible) from the pursuit of what they falsely believe to be happiness to the pursuit of true happiness (518b–519d).

The famous allegory of the cave illustrates the effects of such education:

Compare the effect of education and the lack of it on our nature to an experience like this. Imagine human beings living in an underground, cave-like dwelling, with an entrance a long way up, which is both open to the light and as wide as the cave itself. They've been there since childhood, fixed in the same place, with their necks and legs fettered, able to see only in front of them because their bonds prevent them from turning their heads around. Light is provided by a fire burning far above and behind them. Also behind them, but on higher ground, there is a path stretching between them and the fire. Imagine that along this path a low wall has been built, like the screen in front of puppeteers above which they show their puppets. . . . Also imagine that there are people along the wall carrying all kinds of artifacts that project above it – statues of people and other animals, made out of stone, wood, and every material. And, as you'd expect, some of the carriers are talking and some are silent. . . . [These prisoners] are like us. . . . They see nothing of themselves and one another besides the shadows that the fire casts on the wall in front of them. . . . And the same is true of the things being carried along the wall. . . . And if they could talk to one another . . . they'd suppose that the names they used applied to things they see passing before them. . . . And if their prison also had an echo from the wall facing them, . . . they'd believe that the shadows passing in front of them were talking whenever one of the carriers passing along the wall was doing so. . . . Then the prisoners would in every way believe that the truth is nothing other than the shadows of those artifacts. (*Republic* 514a–515b)

Now the reason the prisoners are in this predicament is that they, like ourselves, have received none of the education Plato advocates. As a result, they are so tethered by their untrained or unsocialized appetites that they see and desire mere images of models of good things (shadows cast by puppets on the walls of the cave). They are not virtuous to any degree, since they act simply on their whims.

However, when appetites are trained through physical education and that mix of reading and writing, dance and song that the Greeks call *mousikā*, some of the prisoners, i.e. some of *us*, are released from these bonds and are now ruled by their trained or socialized appetites. They have at least that level of virtue required to act prudently and postpone gratification. Plato refers to them as *money-lovers*, since they pursue money as the best means of reliably satisfying their appetitive desires for food, drink, and sex in the long term. They see models of good things (the puppets that cast the shadows). For stable satisfaction of appetitive desires *is* a sort of good. Made especially vivid in the allegory is the pain that moderating appetites involves and the difficulty the newly released prisoners experience in accepting that they are learning to see and experience better things: "When one of them was freed and suddenly compelled to stand up, turn his head, walk, and look up toward the light, he'd be pained and dazzled and unable to see the things whose shadows he'd seen before. What do you think he'd say . . . if we pointed to each of the things passing by, asking him what each of them is, and compelled him to answer? Don't you think he'd be at a loss and that he'd believe that the things he saw earlier were truer than the ones he was being shown?" (515c–d). Our own difficulty in believing in Plato's forms marks another respect in which we are similar to these prisoners.

Further education, now in mathematical science, leads to rule by spirited desires. People ruled in that way are *honor-lovers*, who seek success in difficult endeavors and the honor and approval it brings. They have the true beliefs about virtue needed for success, and hence that greater level of it, which Plato calls "civic" virtue (430c). Finally, education in dialectic and practical city management results in people who are bound only by their rational desires. They are free from illusion, and see not mere images of the good, but the good itself. They are *wisdom-lovers* or philosophers, who have knowledge rather than mere true belief about virtue and so are fully virtuous.

Not everyone is able to benefit, however, from all these types of education; there are some at each stage whose desires are too strong for education to break. That is why there are producers, guardians, and philosopher-kings in the ideal city. That is why, as the citizens of the ideal city, they can cooperate with one another in a just system, where the money-loving producers trade their products for the protection provided by the honor-loving guardians and the knowledge provided by the wisdom-loving kings, rather than competing with one another for the very same goods. Nonetheless, everyone in this ideal system is enabled to travel as far out of the cave of unsocialized desires as education can take him, given the innate strength of those desires. Thus everyone comes as close to being fully virtuous and to pursuing and achieving genuine happiness as he can. It is this that makes Plato's city both an ethical and a prudential ideal, both maximally just and maximally happy.

This conception of the soul and of the education needed to make a person both virtuous and happy clearly involves significant revisions of Plato's Socratic inheritance. Since appetite may not be adequately socialized or habituated it can sometimes overpower reason, resulting in weak-willed action (439e ff). Hence intellectual knowledge of what virtue is and what it requires of us is not sufficient, as Socrates believed, to ensure virtuous action or the happiness it brings; our *desires* must also be appropriately habituated through education and training. Strict intellectualism must therefore be rejected. Moreover, virtue is no longer an all or nothing affair, as knowledge is. True, only the philosopher-kings have the knowledge of the good required for full virtue, but the other citizens do have levels of virtue that are by no means to be despised. These differences notwithstanding, Plato, like Socrates, never doubts that philosophical knowledge holds the key to virtue and so to happiness (473c–e, 499a–c).

Perhaps because of his sense of the depth of the ethical problems Socrates raised, and because mathematical science seemed to offer a new, culturally uncontaminated perspective on them, Plato was able in the *Republic* to think about a host of issues in a wholly fresh and revolutionary way. He argues, for example, that in a just society men and women with the same natural abilities should receive the same education, be eligible for the same social positions, and receive the same social rewards. Somewhat less attractively, he also argues that such a society would have to deny family life and private property at least to its ruling classes (philosophers and guardians), and rigorously censor artistic expression. It is not a totalitarian urge that underlies these prohibitions, however, but a vivid sense of the power of desire and the need to keep it in bounds by reducing temptation.

It is characteristic of Plato's profoundly dialectical cast of mind – revealed by his love of the dialogue form – that no sooner has he laid his full theory before us in all its glory than he begins to criticize it. The best known of these criticisms is the so-called Third Man Argument of the *Parmenides*, a dialogue written soon after the *Republic*. Individual human beings possess the characteristic of being men, say, because they resemble the form of a man, which is separate from them. The form of a man must also possess the characteristic of being a man, just as the form of the beautiful must be beautiful, in order for individual human beings to resemble it. But if the form of a man possesses the characteristic of being a man in just the way individuals do – namely, by resembling a separate form which also possesses the characteristic of being a man – a third man seems to be needed (hence the argument's name). The regress thus begun is infinite and vicious: it apparently shows that nothing can be a man (or anything else) in the way that the theory of forms requires. This is a serious problem. If, however, the *Timaeus* is also one of the later dialogues, as most scholars suppose, then Plato cannot have thought it an insurmountable problem, since he there makes use of the theory of forms once again, adapting it to new explanatory purposes in cosmology.

Moreover, it is not just the theory of forms that Plato continues to submit to reflective scrutiny. Genuine philosophers, of the sort that rule in the ideal city, have knowledge rather than mere opinion. It must be possible, then, to explain what knowledge is and how to achieve it. Plato attempts to provide this explanation, as we saw, first by means of the doctrine of recollection and then by means of science and dialectic. But defending these explanations proves to be no easy task, and the *Theaetetus* seems to raise worries about its success. Moreover, if philosophers have knowledge, while others, the sophists, have false beliefs masquerading as knowledge, it must be possible to think, believe, and utter falsehoods. But the great pre-Socratic philosopher Parmenides argues that this is impossible. To speak or think falsehoods one must speak or think "what is not," but how can one do that when "what is not" is not even there to be thought of or spoken about? Plato wrestles with this argument on many different occasions, especially in Book V of the *Republic* and in the *Sophist*. Maybe we cannot speak or think about what does not in any sense exist, he argues, but that does not mean that we cannot think negative or false thoughts or express negative or false propositions. For when we say or think the negative proposition "Theaetetus is not flying," we are not speaking or thinking of something non-existent, we are thinking about *Theaetetus* (an existing person) and *flying* (an existing characteristic). And what we are thinking about them is that all the (existing) characteristics Theaetetus has are *different* (an existing relation) from *flying*. Similarly, when we think the false proposition "Theaetetus is flying," we are again thinking of existing things, relations, and characteristics, but we are thinking of them as being combined in a way in which they are not in fact combined.

In the *Laws* – Plato's longest work and arguably his last one – he turns again to designing a political system, albeit a second-best one intended to be more attainable by actual states than the ideal system described in the *Republic* (739a–740a). Moral education remains the central business of the system. But political authority is more widely distributed among the citizens, rather than being vested exclusively in the hands of mathematically trained, dialectical philosophers, and the holding of wives, children, and property in common is abandoned.

Plato's views on love – explored in the *Lysis, Symposium,* and *Phaedrus* – have profoundly influenced almost all subsequent thought on the topic, whether in literature or philosophy proper. Love of an individual, he argues, leads to much more abstract philosophical loves: the love of a beautiful person leads to the love of the form of beauty itself (*Symposium* 210a–212b). Sometimes it seems, indeed, that love of the forms actually replaces the love for an individual, who is simply cast aside as the philosopher "ascends" beyond him. But it may be that Plato simply thinks that to love someone is to want the good for him, so that unless one knows what really is good for him – unless one knows the (form of the) good – one cannot possibly love.

Besides writing his dialogues, Plato contributed to philosophy by founding the Academy, arguably the first university (385 BCE). This was a center of research and teaching both in theoretical subjects and in more practical ones. Various Greek cities invited its members to help them in the practical task of developing new political constitutions.

The Academy lasted for many centuries after Plato died. Its early leaders, including his own nephew, Speusippus, who succeeded him, all modified his teachings in various ways. Sometimes, influenced by the early Socratic dialogues, which end in puzzlement (*aporia*), the Academy defended skepticism; at others, influenced by other of Plato's writings, it was more dogmatic, less unsure. Platonism of one sort or another – Middle or Neo- or something else – remained the dominant philosophy in the pagan world, influencing St AUGUSTINE among others, until the emperor Justinian closed the pagan schools in 529 CE. Much of what passed for Plato's thought until the nineteenth century, when German scholars pioneered a return to Plato's writings themselves, was a mixture of these different "Platonisms."

Given the vast span and diversity of those writings and the fact that they are dialogues rather than treatises, it is little wonder that they were read in many different ways even by Plato's ancient followers. In that respect nothing has changed: different schools of philosophy and of textual interpretation continue to find profoundly different messages and different methods in Plato. Doctrinal continuities, discontinuities, and outright contradictions of one sort or another are discovered, disputed, rediscovered, and redisputed. Neglected dialogues are taken up afresh, old favorites are newly interpreted. New questions are raised, old ones resurrected and reformulated. Is Plato's Socrates really the great ironist of philosophy or a largely non-ironic figure? Is Plato a systematic philosopher with answers to give or a questioner only? Is he primarily a theorist about universals or a moralist or a mystic with an otherwordly view about the nature of reality and the place of the human psyche in it? Is the *Republic* a totalitarian work, a hymn to freedom properly conceived, or a *reductio ad absurdum* of the very argument it seems to be advancing? Does the dramatic structure of the dialogues undermine their apparent philosophical arguments? Should Plato's negative remarks about the efficacy of written philosophy (*Phaedrus* 274b–278b, *Seventh Letter* 341b–345a) lead us to look behind his dialogues for his "so called unwritten doctrines" (Aristotle, *Physics* 209^{b}14–15)?

Besides this continued engagement with Plato's writings, there is, of course, the not entirely separate engagement with the problems Plato brought to philosophy, the methods he invented to solve them, and the solutions he suggested and explored. So many and various are these, however, that they constitute not just Plato's philosophy but a large part of philosophy itself.

Bibliography

Writings

The most complete translation into English is *Plato: Complete Works*, ed. J. M. Cooper and D. S. Hutchinson (Indianapolis: Hackett, 1997).

Further reading

Irwin, T. H.: *Plato's Ethics* (Oxford: Clarendon Press, 1995).

Kraut, R. (ed.): *The Cambridge Companion to Plato* (Cambridge: Cambridge University Press, 1992). [The best contemporary introduction to Plato and Plato studies as a whole. Includes a very useful bibliography.]

—— (ed.): *Plato's Republic: Critical Essays* (Lanham, MD: Rowman and Littlefield, 1997).

Nussbaum, M.: *The Fragility of Goodness* (Cambridge: Cambridge University Press, 1986).

Reeve, C. D. C.: *Philosopher-Kings: The Argument of Plato's Republic* (Princeton, NJ: Princeton University Press, 1988).

Vlastos, G.: *Platonic Studies* (Princeton, NJ: Princeton University Press, 1981).

29

Quine

Roger F. Gibson

Willard Van Orman Quine (1908–2000 CE) was among the twentieth century's most important and influential analytic philosophers, placed squarely within the ranks of such towering figures as Bertrand RUSSELL, Ludwig WITTGENSTEIN, and Rudolf Carnap.

Quine was born in Akron, Ohio on June 25, 1908. After graduating from Akron's West High School in 1926, he entered Oberlin College. It was during his freshman year at Oberlin that Quine learned of Russell's mathematical philosophy. Subsequently, Quine majored in mathematics with honors in mathematical philosophy, i.e. mathematical logic. Quine graduated *summa cum laude* from Oberlin in 1930.

In the fall of that same year Quine enrolled as a graduate student in philosophy at Harvard. After completing a two-year PhD at Harvard – where he studied with Clarence I. Lewis and Henry M. Scheffer, and wrote a dissertation entitled *The Logic of Sequences: A Generalization of Principia Mathematica* under the direction of Alfred North Whitehead – Quine was awarded Harvard's Sheldon Traveling Fellowship in 1933. He used the fellowship year to visit Vienna (where he attended meetings of the Vienna Circle), Prague (where he met with Carnap), and Warsaw (where he first met Stanisław Leśniewski, Jan Łukasiewicz, and Alfred Tarski, among other prominent Polish logicians). Quine's Sheldon year was to have a profound and lasting impact on his philosophical development. Upon his return to the United States, he was awarded a three-year fellowship as a Junior Fellow in Harvard's Society of Fellows. In 1936 he was appointed to the faculty of Harvard's philosophy department. There he remained (eventually as Edgar Pierce Professor of Philosophy and Senior Fellow in the Society of Fellows) until his retirement in 1978 at the age of 70.

During his long career (which extended two decades beyond his retirement) Quine lectured worldwide and published numerous journal articles and some 21 books on various philosophical topics, including logic, philosophy of logic, set theory, philosophy of mind, philosophy of language, philosophy of science, epistemology, metaphysics, and ethics. Collectively, Quine's books have been translated into more than a dozen languages. Unquestionably, Quine was the most influential analytic philosopher of the second half of the twentieth century.

Among Quine's more famous publications are his articles "New Foundations for Mathematical Logic," "Two Dogmas of Empiricism," and "Epistemology Naturalized," and his book *Word and Object.*

In "New Foundations," Quine develops a set theory which seeks to avoid Russell's Paradox (i.e. the class of all classes that are not members of themselves is a member of itself just in case it isn't a member of itself), but without relying on Russell's Theory of Types (which proscribed expressions like "the class of all classes that are not members of themselves" on the grounds that they are ungrammatical). Rather, following Ernst Zermelo, Quine drops the presumption that every membership condition determines a class (e.g. the membership condition "the class of all classes that are not members of themselves"). The system of "New Foundations" has generated lively and protracted discussions among mathematicians. A number of relative consistency proofs of the system have been devised, but it has yet to be shown consistent relative to Russell's or Zermelo's systems.

In "Two Dogmas," Quine sets out to repudiate what he takes to be two dogmas of logical positivism, the reigning empiricism at that time. The first dogma is that there is a distinction to be drawn between analytic and synthetic statements. Analytic statements are said to be (roughly) those statements which are true solely in virtue of the meanings of their terms, e.g. "No bachelor is married." Synthetic statements, then, are those that are true, if they are, by virtue of the meanings of their terms *and* how the world is. This distinction between analytic and synthetic statements was of great importance to the positivists since it provided them with a means, consistent with their empiricism, for explaining the apparent necessity of mathematics. Thus, truths like "$7 + 5 = 12$" are necessary because analytic – true by virtue of the meanings of their symbols. However, in "Two Dogmas" Quine attempts to undercut the conviction that the term "analytic" can be significantly applied to statements other than logical truths, like "No unmarried man is married." He does so by advancing a number of considerations designed to show that none of the then-current attempts to character-ize analyticity are successful, and that any further similar attempt is likewise doomed to fail. However, Quine never claimed to have *proved* that there are no analytic truths beyond logical truths.

The second dogma, what Quine calls "reductionism," is the thesis that each individual (synthetic) statement in a scientific theory has associated with it a unique range of confirming experiences and a unique range of infirming experiences. So, each such statement can be tested experientially in isolation from its fellow statements. This dogma also was important to the positivists, since they maintained that, unlike the statements of science, the putative statements of metaphysics, ethics, and aesthetics are incapable of being confirmed or infirmed and are, consequently, cognitively meaningless. In response to this dogma Quine offers a countersuggestion: it is only as a corporate body that the statements of science face the tribunal of experience. In "Two Dogmas" Quine construed "corporate body" here to mean all of science. Later, in *Word and Object*, Quine supplants this radical holism with moderate holism. According to moderate holism, (1) a statement's susceptibility to tests of observation is a matter of degree and some statements (those which Quine calls observation statements) are individually susceptible to such tests, and (2) it is more accurate of current scientific practice to think of significant stretches of science, rather than the whole of science, as the corporate body having observable consequences. Thus understood, Quine's countersuggestion (i.e. holism) purports to be a more accurate characterization of the relation between scientific theory and experience than the positivists' reductionist characterization of that relation. As Quine says, one effect of abandoning the dogmas is "a blurring of the supposed boundary between speculative metaphysics and natural science. Another effect is a shift toward pragmatism" ("Two Dogmas," p. 20).

Judging from what Quine says in "Two Dogmas in Retrospect," if he were to write "Two Dogmas" today, he would say less about analyticity and more about moderate holism. Quine's point here is that the central question of "Two Dogmas" is not, and never was, whether "No bachelor is married" is true solely in virtue of the meanings of its terms, but how an empiricist can best account for the apparent necessity of mathematical truth. If one believes with the Positivists that mathematics is necessary but contentless, then analyticity (if made intelligible) could explain mathematical truth. However, if one believes with Quine that mathematics is not necessary but contentful, then moderate holism could explain mathematical truth as follows: "when a cluster of sentences with critical semantic mass is refuted by an experiment, the crisis can be resolved by revoking one *or* another sentence of the cluster. We hope to choose in such a way as to optimize future progress. If one of the sentences is purely mathematical, we will not choose to revoke it; such a move would reverberate excessively through the rest of science. We are restrained by a maxim of minimum mutilation. It is simply in this, I hold, that the necessity of mathematics lies: our determination to make revisions elsewhere instead" ("Two Dogmas in Retrospect," pp. 269–70). If this account of mathematical truth is accepted, then analyticity (even if made intelligible) is rendered otiose.

In "Epistemology Naturalized" Quine advocates naturalizing epistemology. He does so by offering philosophical arguments and considerations directed against old-time epistemology, i.e. against first philosophy and in favor of its replacement by natural science. On its doctrinal side, traditional epistemology sought to deduce the truths of science from self-evident premises by means of self-evident steps. On its conceptual side, it sought to define body in sensory terms. Quine argues that neither yearning can be fulfilled and, therefore, the traditional epistemological quest should be abandoned. However, he does not urge abandoning epistemology altogether. Instead, he advocates an enlightened persistence in the original epistemological problem – the problem of relating evidence to theory. Quine refers to this enlightened persistence as *naturalized epistemology*. The naturalized epistemologist is enlightened because, having given up the quest for a first philosophy outside of science upon which to ground science, the naturalized epistemologist recognizes the legitimacy of using the findings of science in constructing an answer to the central question of epistemology, namely "How do we acquire our overall theory of the world and why does it work so well?"

Not only does Quine argue in favor of naturalizing epistemology, he also argues in favor of naturalizing empiricism. This latter effort takes the form of scientific arguments, considerations, and speculations concerning how we have acquired our theory of the world. For example, according to Quine, it is natural science that teaches us (a) that whatever evidence there is for science is sensory evidence, and (b) that all learning of the meanings of words must in the end rest on sensory evidence. Respectively, (a) and (b) represent the doctrinal and conceptual sides of the post-positivist, naturalized empiricism that Quine endorses.

Word and Object consists of just 276 pages of text, but the book virtually set the philosophical agenda for analytic philosophers interested in metaphysics, epistemology, and philosophy of language for decades after it was published in 1960. For example, among other things, in *Word and Object* Quine: (1) argues for naturalizing epistemology and empiricism; (2) argues for physicalism as against phenomenalism and mind–body dualism; (3) argues for extensionality as against intensionality; (4) develops a behavioristic conception of sentence meaning; (5) theorizes about the learning of language; (6) speculates on the ontogenesis of reference; (7) explains various forms of vagueness and ambiguity; (8) suggests measures for regimenting language so as to eliminate vagueness and ambiguity as well as to make a theory's logic and ontological commitments perspicuous ("to be is to be the value of a bound variable"); (9) argues against quantified modal logic and the essentialism it presupposes; (10) argues for Platonic realism in mathematics; (11) argues for scientific realism as against instrumentalism; (12) articulates a view of philosophical analysis as explication; (13) argues against analyticity and for holism; and (14) argues against countenancing propositions.

One of the more controversial and widely discussed theses that Quine advances in *Word and Object*, and one connected with his repudiation of propositions, is his thesis of indeterminacy of translation. Imagine a field linguist faced with the job of translating a language of some hitherto unknown tribe, in a situation where there are no pre-existing aids to translation (including no bilinguals). In *Word and Object* Quine refers to the setting of this thought experiment as "radical translation." Suppose with Quine that in this setting the only data the linguist has to go on in constructing his manual of translation is the natives' behavior amid publicly observable circumstances. A rabbit scurries past, and a native utters the one-word sentence "Gavagai." Since the rabbit is salient for both the linguist and the native, or so the linguist supposes, and since the English-speaking linguist would himself utter "Lo, a rabbit," or at least, assent to the query "Rabbit?" under these circumstances, the linguist tentatively translates "Gavagai" as "Lo, a rabbit." Assuming the linguist has translated the native expressions for assent and dissent, the linguist can query the native with "Gavagai?" under various subsequent, publicly observable circumstances. Should the linguist discover that the native would assent to and dissent from the query "Gavagai?" in just those circumstances where the linguist would do likewise for "Lo, a rabbit," then the linguist has acquired good inductive evidence for the correctness of his translation. Thus there is a fact of the matter with respect to the question of whether "Lo, a rabbit" is the correct translation of "Gavagai."

It is important to note, however, that the publicly observable circumstances that license translating the sentence "Gavagai" as the sentence "Lo, a rabbit" do not license translating the term "gavagai" as the term "rabbit." The term "gavagai" (if it is a term) might as well be translated as "undetached rabbit parts." Quine's point is that the publicly observable circumstances that prompt the use of, or assent to, a sentence, even sentences like "Gavagai" and "Lo, a rabbit" which are directly keyed to current stimulation, are insufficient for settling the reference of any terms they may contain. Thus, the same scattered portions of the world which prompt the native to assent to "Gavagai?" could be made up of rabbits, or undetached rabbit parts, or instantiations of rabbit-hood, and so on. In a word, reference of terms is inscrutable.

However, most sentences of a language like English are not tied directly to publicly observable circumstances, as "Gavagai" and "Lo, a rabbit" assumedly are. Thus, translating some native utterance as, say, "Pelicans are our half-brothers" is a much more contextual affair. It involves utilizing what Quine calls analytical hypotheses (i.e. hypotheses that go beyond all possible behavioral data). Quine maintains that the utilization of different sets of analytical hypotheses can issue in differ-ent (i.e. non-equivalent) English translations of the same native utter-ances, translations which may, however, equally facilitate communication with the native. But which one of such a multiplicity of translations is the correct one? Does the native's utterance mean "Pelicans are our half-brothers" or does it mean, rather, "Pelicans are supernatural"? Sup-posing that both translations are consistent with all of the relevant behavioral data, and that both translations facilitate communication with the native, then Quine's indeterminacy thesis claims there is no fact of the matter with respect to the question of which of these non-equivalent translation is the correct one; they are both correct. Thus, Quine does not see the indeterminacy of translation as posing a threat to translation. His claim is not that successful translation is impossible, but that it is multiply possible. The philosophical moral of indetermi-nacy of translation is that propositions, thought of as objectively valid translation relations between sentences, are simply non-existent: "Pelicans are our half-brothers" and "Pelicans are supernatural" may both be correct translations of the same native utterance, but these two English translations do not by any means express the same proposition. Conversely, the hypostatization of propositions as objectively valid translation relations misrepresents the actual practice of translating.

In *Word and Object* Quine explains that in order for a child to master the referential mechanisms of English, the child must learn to use a cluster of interrelated grammatical particles and constructions, such things as plural endings, pronouns, numerals, the "is" of identity, "same" and "other," and so on. He writes: "the contextual learning of these various particles goes on simultaneously . . . so that they are gradually adjusted to one another and a coherent pattern of usage is evolved matching that of society. The child scrambles up an intellectual chimney, supporting himself against each side by pressure against the others" (*Word and Object*, p. 93).

It was Quine's dissatisfaction with this brief and metaphorical account of the child's acquisition of reference which prompted his next major extended work, *The Roots of Reference*. In part three of that book he provides a speculative account of how a child could acquire the referential apparatus of English by a series of grammatical transformations and irreducible leaps of analogy. Quine's account is really an idealization of that process. He takes quantification as found in first-order predicate logic to be an encapsulation of this referential apparatus; thus he speculates on how a child could acquire the idiom of quantification. "By considering what steps could lead the small child or primitive man to quantification, rather than to the less tidy referential apparatus of actual English, we arrive at a psychogenetic reconstruction in skeletal outline. We approximate the essentials of the real psychogenesis of reference while avoiding inessential complications" (*The Roots of Reference*, p. 100). This speculative account of the child's acquisition of reference represents an important step toward answering the central question of epistemology, i.e. the question of how we acquire our theory of the world.

Among Quine's books which appeared after *The Roots of Reference* are *Theories and Things* (1981), *Pursuit of Truth* (1990), and *From Stimulus to Science* (1995). For the most part, all of these develop and/or modify ideas found in *Word and Object*. In 1985 Quine published his autobiography, *The Time of My Life*.

Bibliography

Writings

From a Logical Point of View (Cambridge, MA: Harvard University Press, 1953; 1980).
"New Foundations for Mathematical Logic." In *From a Logical Point of View* (Cambridge, MA: Harvard University Press, 1953; 1980a), pp. 80–101.
"Two Dogmas of Empiricism." In *From a Logical Point of View* (Cambridge, MA: Harvard University Press, 1953; 1980), pp. 20–46.
Word and Object (Cambridge, MA: MIT Press, 1960).
Ontological Relativity and Other Essays (New York: Columbia University Press, 1969).
"Epistemology Naturalized." In *Ontological Relativity and Other Essays* (New York: Columbia University Press, 1969), pp. 60–90.
The Roots of Reference (La Salle, IL: Open Court, 1974).
The Ways of Paradox and Other Essays (Cambridge, MA: Harvard University Press, rev. and enlarged edn 1976).
Theories and Things (Cambridge, MA: Harvard University Press, 1981).

The Time of My Life (Cambridge, MA: MIT Press, 1985).
Pursuit of Truth (Cambridge, MA: Harvard University Press, 1990, rev. edn 1992).
"Two Dogmas in Retrospect," *Canadian Journal of Philosophy*, 21 (1991), 265–74.
From Stimulus to Science (Cambridge, MA: Harvard University Press, 1995).

Further reading

Barrett, R. and Gibson, R. (eds): *Perspectives on Quine* (Oxford: Basil Blackwell, 1990).
Davidson, D. and Hintikka, J. (eds): *Words and Objections: Essays on the Work of W. V. Quine* (Dordrecht: D. Reidel, 1969).
Gibson, R. F.: *The Philosophy of W. V. Quine: An Expository Essay* (Tampa: University Presses of Florida, 1982).
Hahn, L. and Schilpp, P. (eds): *The Philosophy of W. V. Quine* (La Salle, IL: Open Court, 1986).
Hookway, C.: *Quine: Language, Experience and Reality* (Cambridge: Polity Press, 1988).
Leonardi, P. and Santambrogio, M. (eds): *On Quine* (Cambridge: Cambridge University Press, 1995).
Orenstein, A.: *Willard Van Orman Quine* (Boston: Twayne, 1977).

30

Rāmānuja

Indira Carr

Background and influences

Born in a South Indian Brahmin family, Rāmānuja (1017–1137 CE) spent his youth in Conjeevaram and moved to Śrīraṅgam after his initiation into the Vedānta order by his uncle Mahāpūrṇa (a.k.a. Perianāmbi) at Madhurāntakam. He is known in the Indian philosophical tradition for systematizing Viśiṣṭādvaita Vedānta – the school which combines belief in a personal and transcendental God with belief in the non-dual nature of the Absolute (*Brahman*), thus providing an alternative to Advaita Vedānta, which made no room for God (*Īśvara*) or devotion to God (see ŚAṄKARA). The fusion of personal theism and absolutism found in Rāmānuja's philosophy is nothing new. It is found in ancient texts such as the *Bhagavadgītā*, *Viṣṇu Purāṇa*, and the *Bhāgvata Purāṇa*. What is unique about Rāmānuja, in a historical context, is the reintroduction of a realist account of the physical world and the emphasis on religious devotion (*bhakti*) as the route to liberation (*mokṣa*). This was at a time when Śaṅkarite Vedānta – which regarded *Brahman* as the only real, the world an illusion and knowledge (*jñāna*) as the only path for attaining *mokṣa* – had gained widespread popularity in the Indian tradition.

Under Yādavaprakāśa's instruction, Rāmānuja came to appreciate that difference was as much an aspect of *Brahman* as unity, and this insight is reflected in his philosophy of qualified non-dualism (*viśiṣṭādvaita*). However he disagreed with his teacher's view that both identity and difference of *Brahman* are equally real (*bhedābheda*), since to say that *Brahman* was different and not-different at the same time was contradictory. Also, as a realist he felt that pure identity and pure difference were unreal since they were abstractions. Rāmānuja was also influenced by Yāmunācārya's (a.k.a. Āḷavandār) view of God, individual souls, and the physical world as the three real categories.

Rāmānuja worked from within the Southern Vaiṣṇavite tradition – a tradition that regards Viṣṇu as *Īśvara* (Supreme Being) and the devotional poems of the Āḷvārs, collectively known as the *Nāḷāyiradivyaprabandham*, as a Tamil Veda having an authority equal to that of the four Vedas (*Ṛg, Yajur, Sāma,* and *Atharva*) accepted by the Indian orthodox philosophical schools as a source of correct knowledge. As a result of this affinity to Vaiṣṇavism, God, man's relation to God, and religious devotion form the central core of his philosophy. Rāmānuja's major works include *Śrībhāṣya* (Commentary on the *Brahma Sūtras*), *Gītābhāṣya,* and *Vedārthasaṅgraha,* where he examines the doctrine of *bhedābheda.*

The realist

According to Rāmānuja, that which is known has an existence independent of the knower and is in no way dependent on the knower for its existence. In other words, the objects of our experience exist independently of our experience of them. As a realist, Rāmānuja faces, like any other realist, the problem of explaining erroneous perception (e.g. hallucination, illusion, and mirage) and dreams where no objects corresponding to what is perceived are found. How does one explain the apprehension of a sheet of water in the desert when the object corresponding to what is seen does not exist? If all knowledge is of the real, as Rāmānuja claims, then it should be possible to quench one's thirst from the mirage, but this, as we all know, is impossible. Rāmānuja uses the doctrine of quintuplication (*pañcīkaraṇa*) in order to explain that the apprehension of water is real. According to the doctrine of quintuplication, all objects of the physical world are composed of the five elements – earth (*pṛthivi*), water (*ap*), air (*vāyu*), fire (*tejas*), and ether (*ākāśa*) – in various proportions. The mirage therefore contains all the five elements including water, except that water is not the preponderant part of it. And where a shell is seen as silver, the apprehension is real in that what is apprehended is the silver part of the shell. In other words, error is a result of partial or incomplete knowledge. Similarly, where a person dreams of chariots, horses, and lakes, the apprehension is real and private to the individual who dreams. And where a person suffering from jaundice sees a white shell as yellow, that apprehension is once again real since the bile in the visual organ is transmitted along with the visual rays to the object. The yellowness of the conch is not perceived by others since the quantity of bile is minute (*Śrībhāṣya,* 1962 edn, I.1.1, pp. 119–24).

Rāmānuja, it seems, wants to hold on to his realist position even at the cost of providing absurd explanations at times. Presumably, he needs to do this in order to destabilize the Śaṅkarite view of the Absolute as differenceless (*advaita*) and also to strengthen his own view of the Absolute as a unity which is qualified (*viśiṣṭa*).

Absolute (Brahman/Īśvara), soul (cit), and unconscious substance (acit): the three real categories

According to Rāmānuja, *Brahman*, soul (*cit*), and unconscious substance (*acit*) are all ultimate and real. Before we examine the nature of these three reals in Rāmānuja's philosophy, a brief foray into his theory of knowledge is necessary, since his view of the Absolute is linked closely to his epistemological position. Rāmānuja, like the Nyāya and Pūrva Mīmāṃsā schools, accepts two stages in perception – indeterminate perception and determinate perception, where the former is chrono-logically earlier than the latter. According to the Naiyāyikas and the Mīmāṃsākas, in indeterminate perception there is only simple appre-hension or bare awareness, whereas in determinate perception there is discrimination. However, for Rāmānuja there is some differentiation even in indeterminate perception (*Śrībhāṣya*, 1962 ed., I.1.1, pp. 41–2). Accordingly, when a cat is apprehended for the first time it is appre-hended together with its class character, even though the class charac-ter is not recognized. In determinate perception the class character comes to be recognized as common to the whole class. Determinate perception, however, is not the same as recognition (*pratyabhijñā*), as where Sītā observed standing near the bus stop is cognized as the same Sītā seen near the school a few minutes ago. In other words, in deter-minate perception the recognition does not involve the same object but involves the recognition of the object as belonging to a particular class or type.

So for Rāmānuja neither pure identity nor pure difference can be apprehended. From this perspective, the notion of *Brahman* as pure identity – a notion found in Advaita Vedānta – would be meaningless. For Rāmānuja, the Absolute is qualified, i.e. possesses qualities and attributes, not unlike the *Saguṇa Brahman* or *Īśvara* of Śaṅkara. However, for Śaṅkara *Īśvara* is the lower *Brahman*, not the unconditioned *Brahman* which is the Absolute. Rāmānuja views the Absolute as a unity that is qualified and *Īśvara* as this Absolute, and he does not draw a distinction like Śaṅkara between *Brahman* and *Īśvara*.

Other than perception and inference, Rāmānuja accepts valid testimony as a source of correct knowledge. This means that references to *Brahman* as devoid of qualities found in the *Upaniṣads* (e.g. *Taittrīya Upaniṣad* II.1; *Bṛhadāraṇyaka Upaniṣad* III.8.8) need to be explained. According to Rāmānuja these passages only suggest that *Brahman* is devoid of bad qualities, not any qualities at all. Morever, support for the view that *Brahman* possesses qualities is provided by the *Upaniṣads* (*Muṇḍaka Upaniṣad* I.1.9; *Śvetāśvatara Upaniṣad* VI.8; *Śrībhaṣya*, 1962 edn, I.1.1, pp. 26–30).

Besides *Īśvara* (God), soul and unconscious substance are also ultimate and real though dependant on *Īśvara*. They are the body of God and God is their soul. In other words, God is the soul of all the individual souls as well as of nature. Support for this view is provided by Rāmānuja from the various scriptures (*Śrībhāṣya*, 1962 edn, II.1.9, pp. 421–4; I.1.1, pp. 92–5). If *cit* and *acit* are dependent on God, the question that follows naturally is what kind of relationship they have with God. Rāmānuja regards the relation between *Īśvara* and *cit* and *acit* as one of internal inseparability (*apṛthaksiddhi*). This internal relationship is not to be confused with inherence (*samavāya*) of Nyāya, where the relationship is an external one. Unconscious substance and soul are inseparably and internally linked to God, just as substance and attribute are inseparably related.

God, according to Rāmānuja, is the cause and the effect of the world. During dissolution the entire universe is latent within him and during creation the universe becomes manifest. God is transcendent and allpervasive. He is the creator, preserver, and destroyer of the universe. God is also benevolent and merciful and appears in many forms. He also takes animal or human forms (*avatār*) in order to restore righteous order (*dharma*) in the world and protect the good from evil.

As for the soul, it is finite and atomic in size. Numerous in numbers, dependant on God and an attribute of God, souls are regarded by Rāmānuja as independent and capable of exercising free will. The soul is of the nature of bliss, but its blissful nature is obscured due to karmic influences. Only on liberation does it enjoy bliss.

Prakṛti (matter), *kāla* (time) and *śuddhasattva* (pure matter) are the three kinds of unconscious substances and all these are dependent on God. *Acit*, which is uncreated, is the object of pain and pleasure.

Rāmānuja's account of God as possessing qualities like transcendence and benevolence and his view of souls as the body of God are likely to appeal to the religiously oriented. However, there are a number of problems with his account. For instance, it is difficult to understand how *cit* and *acit* can be said to be ultimate if they are dependent on God. If they are related to God in the manner Rāmānuja describes (*apṛthaksiddhi*), it makes their ultimate character even more implausible. The soul, which is dependent on God, is regarded as independent and capable of exercising free will. But how can the individual soul exercise free will when God is the soul of all souls?

Religious devotion and liberation

Knowledge of the true nature of God results in liberation from worldly existence (*mokṣa*) and the enjoyment of bliss in God's presence. Intuitive knowledge of God is obtained only through religious devotion to God (*bhakti yoga*) and by the grace (*prasāda*) of God. As a prerequisite to *bhakti yoga*, an individual has to purify his soul and also understand the true nature of his relationship to matter, such as his body, senses, and the physical world. Purification is obtained through *karma yoga*, i.e. by performing one's duties in a disinterested manner, and understanding of the soul's relationship is obtained by studying the scriptures under a teacher's guidance (*jñāna yoga*). Since an individual can embark on the path of *bhakti* only after the successful completion of *jñāna yoga*, liberation through *bhakti* is available only to the upper castes of Hindu society who can study the scriptures. Influenced by the Āḷvār tradition, Rāmānuja regards total surrender to God (*prapatti*) as another route to *mokṣa* which is available to all regardless of caste or creed. Consistent with his qualified non-dualist view of the Absolute, Rāmānuja holds that the individual soul on liberation shares in the nature of God in enjoying infinite consciousness and infinite bliss, but does not attain identity with God. On release, the soul retains its individuality and shares all of God's perfections other than the all-pervasive nature and creative power.

Conclusion

Rāmānuja's keenness, against a non-dualist background, to retain the real existence of the physical world, his belief in the independent existence of individual souls, and his insistence on making religious devotion to God the only route to liberation make his philosophy unsatisfactory to those looking for logical coherence and clarity. Nonetheless, one cannot but appreciate his move away from the elitism of Advaita Vedānta by making *mokṣa* available to all, regardless of status, by resigning oneself entirely to God. And it is this anti-elitist element that provides a breath of fresh air in a tradition steeped in caste consciousness at all levels. It is therefore easy to see why Rāmānuja became a popular figure in Southern India and was able to convert many to Vaiṣnavism.

Bibliography

Writings

The Vedānta-Sūtras with the Commentary by Rāmānuja [with Rāmānuja's *Śribhāṣya*], trans. George Thibaut (Delhi: Motilal Banarsidass, 1962; first published Oxford: The Clarendon Press, 1904).

Further reading

Comans, Michael: "Later Vedānta." in Brian Carr and Indira Mahalingam (eds), *Companion Encyclopedia of Asian Philosophy* (London & New York: Routledge, 1997), pp. 211–29.
Hiriyanna, M.: *Outlines of Indian Philosophy* (London: George Allen & Unwin, 1932).
Lipner, J.: *The Face of Truth: A Study of Meaning and Metaphysics in the Vedāntic Theology of Rāmānuja* (Albany: State University of New York Press, 1986).
Radhakrishnan, S.: *Indian Philosophy*, two volumes (London: George Allen & Unwin, 1923).
Srinivasachari, P. N.: *The Philosophy of Viśiṣṭādvaita* (Adyar: Adyar Library, 1943).

31

Rorty

Kai Nielsen

Richard Rorty (1931– CE) has stressed his adherence to *antirepresenta-tionalism*, by which he means an account "which does not view knowl-edge as a matter of getting reality right, but rather as a matter of acquiring habits of action for coping with reality" (Rorty, 1991a, p. 1). Rorty is frequently accused of being an antirealist, but that is to confuse antirealism with antirepresentationalism. Both realists and antirealists are representationalists. To be a realist is to believe that most of the kinds of things that exist, and what they are like, are independent of us and of the ways we find out about them. Antirealists deny this. Antirepre-sentationalists, by contrast, reject the very idea that beliefs can represent reality; they are neither realists nor antirealists. They deny that truth is an explanatory property and assert that the correct but platitudinous sentence "'S' is true if and only if S" makes no claim that "S" corre-sponds to anything. They reject the whole antirealist/realist problem-atic, denying "that the notion of 'representation' or that of 'fact of the matter' has any useful role in philosophy" (Rorty, 1991a, p. 2).

Antirepresentationalism, which goes with the perspectivism and con-textualism of pragmatism, rejects the so-called discipline of epistemol-ogy as well as metaphysics. There is no grand Appearance/Reality distinction, as we find in PLATO, DESCARTES, or KANT, for, on an anti-representionalist account, there can be no gaining a glimpse at how things are in themselves. Some allegedly privileged types of vocabulary – say physics – are thought by representationalists accurately to repre-sent reality, while the other discourses are said to be mired in appear-ance. But with the demise of representationalism goes the very idea that there is some determinate way the world is, there to be discovered and accurately represented by some "true philosophy" – perhaps an episte-mology or a philosophy of language (*à la* Michael Dummett) taken as First Philosophy, a philosophical foundation for the rest. Moreover, there is no science or yet-to-be-developed science that is going to be able to step in and do the job – giving the one true description of the world – that philosophy failed to do. There is no sense, if antirepresentationalism is on the mark, in claiming that one vocabulary is "closer to reality" than another. There just are different forms of discourse answering to different interests.

Rorty, consistently with his antirepresentationalism, is a *minimalist* about truth. He rejects correspondence, coherentist, and pragmatist theories of truth. Indeed, he thinks, we should have no *theory* of truth at all, though, given the long history of theories of truth, it is a good idea to have a descriptive account of how "true" functions in our language-games. His minimalist account says that a sentence "S" is true if and only if S. Thus "'The cat is on the mat' is true" if and only if the cat is on the mat. This bare and correct statement of what it means to assert something to be true does not commit one to a correspondence, coherence, or pragmatic theory of truth or indeed to any *theory* of truth at all. It does not say "that behind the true sentence 'S', there is a sentence-shaped piece of non-linguistic reality called 'the fact of S' – a set of relations between objects which hold independently of language – which makes 'S' true" (Rorty, 1991a, p. 4). We do not have any understanding of what it would be for such a correspondence to obtain. But this denial of correspondence must not lead us to think that truth is something we make up or construct. Our linguistic practices do not determine what is true, though we can only *speak* of something being true or false by engaging in the appropriate linguistic practices. That, however, is a different thing from saying our linguistic practices produce truth or make certain things true. However, Rorty also rejects claims made by correspondence theories of truth to a correspondence between language and the world. They require of us the impossible, namely to be able to stand somewhere outside of language and to compare language and the world to see whether they do or do not correspond to each other like a map corresponds to what is mapped or a photograph to what is photographed.

Thought for Rorty, as for Wittgenstein, is inescapably linguistic. There is no having a thought and then finding the words for it. There can be no necessarily private languages. With a language we can, of course, invent another language as in inventing a secret code. But we cannot without already having a language construct a language afresh. There can be no language-less or notation-less thoughts or beliefs. So there can be no standing outside of language and comparing it with the world for fit.

There are, of course, links between our language and the rest of the world, but these links are *causal*, not *epistemological*. Our language, like our bodies, is shaped by our environment. Indeed, our language could no more be "out of touch" with our environment – grandiosely the world – than our bodies could. What Rorty denies is that there is any *explanatory* or *epistemic* point in trying to pick out and then choose among the contents of our language – or of our minds – and then claiming that this or that item "corresponds" to reality in a way some other item of a different type does not, e.g. the claim that all ethical characterizations of our situation are out of touch with reality, while the correct characterizations of physics are not. Moreover, the property truth is neither a normative property giving us criteria for correcting our beliefs nor an explanatory property explaining why we have the beliefs we have or regard some beliefs as justified and warranted and other beliefs not.

When it comes to determining what we are justified in believing and doing, what is needed is as thorough a coherence of beliefs as we can attain, though crucially some of those beliefs will be considered judgments that will be taken to have some *initial* credibility. They are part of our inescapable cultural given. There will be some such givens in all cultures, though the content will vary *in part*. However, there will also be a considerable overlap from culture to culture. But if some of our considered judgments, even our firmest ones, do not fit into a wide coherentist pattern, then they should either be modified until they do fit or be rejected. And this could be true of any of them. None are immune from the *possibility* of rejection. Attaining this pattern of coherence will be a matter of winnowing some of them out but not *holes bolus* trying to throw out all of them or even the bulk of them. We justify one belief in terms of others by weaving and unweaving our web of beliefs until we, for a time, get the most coherent pattern we can forge. But we never escape fallibilism and historicism. What we are justified in believing – taking for true – comes to forging what for a time is the widest and most coherent pattern of beliefs that we can muster. We also need to have an intersubjective consensus concerning this. It is these two things which, Rorty has it, give us the only viable conception of objectivity that we can have or need (Rorty, 1991a, pp. 175–96).

Such a coherentist account is not only antirepresentationalist, but antifoundationalist and holist as well. Foundationalists claim that a belief, to be justified, must either be justified by direct apprehension (observation, rational intuition, or introspection) or be inferentially justified by appeal to such beliefs. Antifoundationalists reject this either by denying that such direct apprehension is possible or by denying that all of our beliefs must be ultimately justified by any of these forms of direct apprehension. Holists take the very identity of a belief to be determined by the web of beliefs of the form of life of the person having the belief, thereby ruling out any form of direct apprehension. There are no basic beliefs yielding certainties or even near certainties on which all the rest of our knowledge and justified beliefs are based. Neither science nor philosophy, nor anything else, can deliver such beliefs. There is no point at which our words or thoughts just represent our sense impressions or atomic facts on which all our other knowledge is based. We have no such simple certainties or foundational knowledge. What we have instead is a fallibilistic, coherentist method of fixing belief replacing epistemology and replacing as well a deductivist model of justification with a coherentist one.

With the abandonment of foundationalism and with it a Kantian understanding of the key task of epistemology, we abandon a classical self-image of the philosopher as someone who stands in some privileged perspective and can tell us in all domains, or indeed in any substantive domain, what counts as genuine knowledge. We give up the deceptive self-conceit that the philosopher can know things that no one can else can know so well. There is no possible transcendental perspective where, independently of some particular social practices and some particular domains, we can say what knowledge is, and correct the ways of science or common sense or our common life by appealing to some conception of superior *philosophical* knowledge which enables us to judge common-sense beliefs and science and give the "real foundations of knowledge."

Bibliography

Writings

Philosophy and the Mirror of Nature (Princeton, NJ: Princeton University Press, 1979).
Consequences of Pragmatism (Minneapolis: University of Minnesota Press, 1982).
Contingency, Irony and Solidarity (Cambridge: Cambridge University Press, 1988).
Objectivity, Relativism and Truth (Cambridge: Cambridge University Press, 1991a).
Essays on Heidegger and Others (Cambridge: Cambridge University Press, 1991b).
Truth and Progress (Cambridge: Cambridge University Press, 1998a).
Against Bosses, Against Oligarchies: A Conversation with Richard Rorty, ed. Derek Hymstrom and Kent Puckett (Charlottesville, NC: Prickly Pear Pamphlets, 1998b).
Achieving Our Country (Cambridge, MA: Harvard University Press, 1998c).
Philosophy and Social Hope (London: Penguin Books, 1999).

Further reading

Bhaskar, Roy: *Philosophy and the Idea of Freedom* (Oxford: Blackwell, 1991).
Brandon, Robert (ed.): *Rorty and His Critics* (Malden, MA: Blackwell, 2000).

Festenstein, Matthew and Thompson, Simon (eds): *Richard Rorty: Critical Dialogues* (Cambridge: Polity Press, 2001).

Malachowski, Alan (ed.): *Reading Rorty* (Oxford: Blackwell, 1990).

Melkonian, Markar: *Richard Rorty's Politics* (Amherst, NY: Humanity Books, 1999).

Nielsen, Kai: *After the Demise of the Tradition: Rorty, Critical Theory, and the Fate of Philosophy* (Boulder, CO: Westview Press, 1991).

32

Russell

Peter Hylton

Bertrand Arthur William Russell, third Earl Russell (1872–1970 CE), was born into an aristocratic English family with considerable political tradition and influence. Both his parents died before he turned four; he was brought up by his paternal grandmother, who seems to have been a rigid and domineering character with a powerful sense of duty. He went up to Trinity College Cambridge in 1890 and studied mathematics for three years before taking up philosophy. The outbreak of the First World War aroused Russell's vehement opposition; his anti-war work led to his dismissal from his position as lecturer at Trinity College in 1916, and to his being jailed in 1918. He was reappointed by Trinity in 1920 but soon resigned. Thereafter he was financially dependent upon sales of books and essays; energy which might have gone into academic philosophy thus went into popular writings. After the Second World War he received the Order of Merit (1949) and the Nobel Prize for literature (1950); he nevertheless devoted much of his time to political activism, in opposition to the establishment. He was motivated by an understanding of the dangers posed by nuclear weapons and, later, by his opposition to the involvement of the United States in Vietnam; in his nineties he again became well known as an anti-war activist.

Russell wrote voluminously, and with astonishing facility, over an immense range of both genres and subjects. It is, however, his philosophical work on logic, metaphysics, epistemology, and related issues which is of lasting value. His writings on these topics from the first two decades of the twentieth century played a large role in setting the tone and framing the questions for what came to be known as "analytic philosophy"; the thought of WITTGENSTEIN and of Carnap, and thus also of many others, is unimaginable without this work of Russell's. This chapter thus concentrates on that period. His work of the 1920s, 1930s, and 1940s, while perhaps less enduring, made important contributions to debates within analytic philosophy, especially to epistemology and the philosophy of science.

In late nineteenth-century Britain the prevailing philosophical tone was set by attempts to assimilate the work of KANT and, especially, HEGEL. These attempts resulted in a variety of views generally grouped under the heading "British idealism"; F. H. Bradley was a leading figure in this movement. A fundamental idea lying behind various versions of idealism is that our knowledge is mediated by conceptual structures and that the (knowable) world is thus in some sense mind-dependent. Another conclusion adopted by many, though not all, idealists was a strong form of *holism*: that the world is not made of up of independent objects standing in relation to one another but is, instead, a single system whose parts can be isolated only at the price of some distortion. According to this view, our knowledge is never of the whole, so nothing we know is fully true – we know merely partial truths. At first Russell accepted the broad outlines of the idealist position. He was, however, far more interested in science, and especially mathematics, than most of those influenced by idealism. He had immensely ambitious plans for a philosophical treatment of all scientific knowledge from a Hegelian point of view; his first philosophical book, *An Assay on the Foundations of Geometry*, was intended to be a part of this project.

Two major shifts in Russell's thought occurred around the turn of the century, one metaphysical and one logical. In metaphysics, he and his younger contemporary at Trinity, G. E. Moore, broke with idealism around 1898, and began to articulate an extreme version of realism. In opposition to idealism, they asserted that the world is made up of objects, each of which is fully real and is completely independent both of our minds and of all other objects – objects are not affected by their relations to other objects, but are merely *externally related* to one another. (The view is thus a form of *atomism*; equally it advocates the philosophical method of *analysis*, which seeks to understand complex wholes in terms of their simple parts, rather than vice versa.) And they postulated that we have a direct cognitive relation, which Russell later called *acquaintance*, to various objects – not only those perceivable by the senses, such as tables and trees, but also, and especially, abstract objects, such as goodness and numbers. Philosophy, as they conceived it, is wholly independent of psychology, and has no particular concern with the human mind.

In logic, Russell encountered Peano at a conference in Paris in August 1900, and set out to understand his logical work. In an astonishingly short time he had not only mastered it but extended it to handle what Peirce and Schröder had called the *logic of relations*. The result was a system of logic dealing not only with inferences involving one-place predicates (such as "... is mortal") but also with those involving relations, i.e. predicates of two or more places (such as "... loves ...", or "... is between ... and ..."). Russell's extension of Peano lacked the clarity and simplicity of the logic which FREGE had (unbeknownst to Russell) produced in 1879; one way or another, however, this part of Russell's logic had the power of what is today called first-order quantification theory, or predicate logic (this is logic which uses variables to generalize about objects, but not about properties of objects). Russell made much of the fact that the new logic deals with relations, which many idealists had not accepted as fully real.

This new logic is crucial for an account of mathematics. To take a simple but important example, the infinitude of natural numbers follows from the following facts: that for every number there is a larger number; that there is at least one number; that no number is larger than itself; and that "larger than" is a transitive relation (i.e. for any numbers, *a, b, c,* if *a* is larger than *b,* and *b* is larger than *c,* then *a* is larger than *c*). The inference from these premises to the conclusion that there are infinitely many natural numbers is obviously correct; the achievement of Frege and of Russell was to treat it within a rigourous system of logic, thereby dispelling some of the mystery surrounding the infinite.

A treatment of the sorts of inferences typical of mathematics does not by itself afford a complete account of that subject. Kant had put forward a view of mathematics as dependent on the forms of our intuition and had thus made it, at least by Russell's lights, mind-dependent. This was precisely the sort of view that Russell wished to combat, and he did so by arguing that the truths of mathematics can all be stated in logical terms and, when so stated, can all be proved by logical means (here too Russell was anticipated by Frege, but his work seems to have been independent of Frege's). This view, known as *logicism,* requires a logic that includes a theory of classes, or some other theory more or less equivalent to what we now call set theory.

In the course of developing a theory of classes, Russell came across what has become known as *Russell's paradox.* It is a natural assumption that there is a class corresponding to each one place predicate (corresponding to the predicate "... is mortal" is the class whose members are exactly those things which are mortal, and so on). Since we have the notion of being a member of a class, we also have the predicate "is not a member of itself"; hence, given the natural assumption, we have the class of things which are not members of themselves. But is this class a member of itself? That is, is the class of things which are not members of themselves a member of itself? Either answer leads to its opposite, resulting in paradox: if it is a member of itself then it is a self-member, and so not a member of the class of non-self-members, i.e. not a member of itself after all; but if it is not a member of itself then it is a non-self-member and so is a member of itself. To avoid this paradox, and others which he saw as related, Russell developed the *theory of types*. According to this theory, entities are of fundamentally different types; what can be said of an entity of one type results in nonsense if we attempt to say it of an entity of another type. In particular, an entity can be a member only of classes immediately higher in type than it is. Sentences which appear to assert or deny self-membership are thus nonsensical. This theory was tentatively put forward in an appendix to *The Principles of Mathematics*, and was developed in "Mathematical Logic as Based on the Theory of Types." It reached its full form in Whitehead and Russell's monumental *Principia Mathematica*, which made out the technical case for logicism in great detail. This work had a profound influence on the progress of mathematical logic, in the hands of Gödel and others; one application of these advances led in turn to the development of computers, and has thus had incalculable practical influence.

Generality, standardly conveyed by variables, is essential to logic and to mathematics. Russell initially hoped to explain generality, and the use of variables, by a theory of what he called *denoting concepts*. According to that theory, a sentence containing a description, i.e. a phrase formed with one of the words "all", "any", "some", "a", and "the", expresses a proposition containing a concept which denotes an object or objects not contained in the proposition. Thus the sentence "All people are mortal" expresses a proposition which contains a denoting concept, *all people*, which in turn denotes all people; the proposition does not itself contain all people. This theory is supposed to explain how the sentence is about all people: it is about them because it contains a denoting concept which denotes them. (The theory is also supposed to explain how a definite description, such as "the man who broke the bank at Monte Carlo," can be part of a sentence which makes sense, even though there is no object which uniquely answers to the description. For the sentence to make sense we need only be sure that there is a proposition which it expresses; the proposition contains the denoting concept, not the supposed man, so its status is unaffected if there is in fact no such man.) Russell's attempt to explain generality in terms of denoting concepts, however, failed, as he himself came to see. The theory of denoting concepts, moreover, proved to be exceedingly complex, and led to formidable difficulties.

Russell thus had every reason to abandon the theory of denoting concepts and to take the use of variables as fundamental, as Frege did. The one obstacle to his doing so was the case of definite descriptions, descriptions formed with "the" which seem to refer to exactly one object. (Frege had taken such phrases as logically primitive.) At some point in 1905 Russell saw how to analyze definite descriptions; this enabled him to discard the theory of denoting concepts completely. The result was his celebrated "theory of descriptions," which analyzes sentences of the form "The F is G" (e.g. "The King of France is bald") as saying: there is an object x which is F, and for every object y, if y is F then $y = x$, and x is G. More briefly: there is one and only one object which is F, and it is G.

The theory of descriptions was immensely important as an example of logical analysis; F. P. Ramsey, in a description endorsed by Moore, called it a "paradigm of philosophy." For Russell it also played an important, though indirect, role in his development of the theory of types. He saw it as a particular case of a more general *theory of incomplete symbols*. Phrases such as "the King of France," which appear to get their meaning by their relation to some non-linguistic entity (whether a monarch or a denoting concept), may, according to this theory, function in quite a different way. Such expressions, according to Russell, "have no meaning in isolation." They are "incomplete symbols": we can explain each sentence in which they occur, but not the phrase itself in isolation. Russell applied this idea to classes, and analyzed expressions which appeared to refer to classes in terms of what he called propositional functions (very roughly, the non-linguistic correlates of expressions containing free variables, such as "x is a prime number"). This helped because he was more willing to suppose that propositional functions are stratified into types than that classes are. According to his new view, we need not assume that there are classes (hence he called it the *no-classes theory*). Symbols for classes make sense in context, because they are defined, in each context, in terms of propositional functions.

Because of Russell's concern to block a whole range of paradoxes, and because of the intricacies of his view of propositional functions, his theory of types is far more complex than would be needed simply to block Russell's paradox. Ramsey showed that a simpler version – now known as *simple type theory* – would suffice for that task (Ramsey, 1925); since that time, Russell's full version has been known as *ramified type theory*. Proving the truths of mathematics from either version of type theory requires the additional assumption, which Russell himself thought could not be justified by logic, that there are infinitely many objects. (Without this assumption we cannot prove that there are infinitely many numbers.) The ramified version also necessitates an axiom – the axiom of reducibility – which is hard to justify except on *ad hoc* grounds. These two points go a long way toward undermining the force of Russell's logicism, even for a sympathetic commentator.

Russell's increasing exploitation of the theory of incomplete symbols marked a partial retreat from his earlier extreme realism. He now accepts that there are many phrases which appear to refer to objects but do not in fact do so. An important example is the so-called multiple relation theory of judgment. According to this view, a proposition is not a genuine entity with which the judging mind is acquainted. There are no propositions in that sense; instead judgment involves acquaintance with a number of entities, and it is an act of the mind which unites them into a judgment. (Russell first considered this view in 1906, and had definitely adopted it by 1909.) An advantage of this theory is that it allows truth to be defined in terms of the existence of appropriate facts. (On his earlier view, truth was an indefinable notion.)

After the completion of *Principia Mathematica*, Russell turned his attention away from logic and mathematics and toward issues raised by our empirical and scientific knowledge. He continued to hold that all knowledge comes via acquaintance, but realized that it is not plausible to think that we are acquainted with the ordinary objects we appear to know. The objects of acquaintance in empirical knowledge, he came to think, must rather be what he called *sense-data* – a certain color which I perceive, for example, or a sound which I hear. For him these were not mental objects but objective entities, directly given to the mind in sense-perception. How, then, do we get from knowledge of sense-data to knowledge of tables and trees, much less electrons and distant stars? Russell's attempt to answer this question exploited the same techniques used in his logicism: talk of ordinary objects was to be analyzed and defined in terms of sense-data and classes of sense-data, and classes of classes of sense-data, and so on. (Russell always attributed this technique of *logical construction* to Whitehead). This idea is most clearly set out in *Our Knowledge of the External World* and in some of the essays in *Mysticism and Logic*; for the most obvious signs of its influence, see Carnap (1928).

Russell began this work on empirical knowledge without having fully articulated the implications of his multiple relation theory of propositions, and its relation to his logic and to his underlying metaphysical views. His work on these topics (now published as volume 7 of *Collected Papers*) was brought to a halt by criticisms from Wittgenstein. Russell never resolved these fundamental problems; his lectures "The Philosophy of Logical Atomism" contain an excellent summary of his views, but leave many problems admittedly unresolved and suggest that their solution may require a more psychological view of meaning. (Wittgenstein's *Tractatus* may be thought of as offering a different kind of solution to these problems – but the solution is a drastic one, involving the abandonment of logicism, and a complete rethinking of the nature of logic.)

Russell's later work in technical philosophy, though perhaps less fundamental than the work we have been discussing, was still of great significance. In 1919 he adopted a view known as "neutral monism," advocated by Mach and by William JAMES. According to this view there are not two kinds of things in the world, the mental and the physical; instead there is one kind of stuff, in itself neither mental nor physical (hence "neutral"). Some arrangements of it are what we call mental, others what we call physical. Thus the mind is not an entity distinct from the rest of the world but is made up of the same fundamental constituents as everything else. Russell's *Analysis of Mind* shows the influence both of that view and of behaviorism; it articulates a psychological approach to issues of belief and meaning. More generally, the book shows a shift from a logical and metaphysical framework towards a naturalistic framework – a shift which might be thought to reach full flower with the work of QUINE. (Much of the discussion of the mental in Wittgenstein's later philosophy can usefully be seen as directed against views that Russell puts forward in this work.) Russell's *Analysis of Matter* is an attempt to come to terms with logical and epistemological issues which he took to be raised by the new physics, especially the theory of relativity and quantum mechanics; an important feature of this work is the idea that we know the structural features of the world, but not its intrinsic nature. In his late sixties he gave the William James lectures at Harvard, published as *An Inquiry into Meaning and Truth*, an investigation of issues in the philosophy of language. His last significant philosophical work was *Human Knowledge: Its Scope and Limits*, which returned to issues of knowledge and its justification. This work is less concerned than Russell's earlier views of knowledge to show that human knowledge is constructed on a foundation of certainty; all our knowledge is, instead, held to be fallible. Empirical knowledge beyond particular facts depends upon postulates, which cannot themselves be derived from experience. (An example: suppose that in all cases where we have observed an A-type event and a B-type event together, we have reason to think that the two are causally related; then, when we observe an event of one of those types alone, it is probable that an event of the other type also took place, unobserved.) The postulates are justified, if at all, by the overall coherence which they bring to our total system of beliefs.

Bibliography

Writings

An Essay on the Foundations of Geometry (Cambridge: Cambridge University Press, 1897).

The Principles of Mathematics (Cambridge: Cambridge University Press, 1903).

"On Denoting", *Mind*, NS, XIV (1905), 530–8. [Very widely reprinted.]

"Mathematical Logic as Based on the Theory of Types", *American Journal of Mathematics*, 30 (1908), 222–62.

Principia Mathematica, with A. N. Whitehead, three volumes (Cambridge: Cambridge University Press, 1910–13).

Our Knowledge of the External World as a Field for Scientific Method in Philosophy (London: George Allen & Unwin, 1914).

Mysticism and Logic and Other Essays (New York: Longmans Green & Co., 1918).

"Philosophy of Logical Atomism," *Monist*, 28 (1918), 495–527; 29 (1919), 32–63, 190–222, 345–80.

The Analysis of Mind (London: George Allen & Unwin, 1921).

The Analysis of Matter (London: Kegan Paul, Trench, Trubner & Co., 1927).

An Inquiry into Meaning and Truth (London: George Allen & Unwin, 1940).

Human Knowledge Its Scope and Limits (New York: Simon and Schuster, 1948).

Logic and Knowledge, ed. R. C. Marsh (London: George Allen & Unwin, 1956) [Contains Russell (1905, 1908, 1918–19), among other essays].

Collected Papers (1983–). [Produced by the Bertrand Russell Editorial Project, based at McMaster University. The project aims to publish all of Russell's writings of less than book length. Ten volumes have been published to date, with various editors; some by George Allen & Unwin, some by Routledge, some by Unwin Hyman.]

Further reading

Carnap, R.: *Die Logische Aufbau der Welt* (Berlin-Schlactensee: Weltkreis-Verlag, 1928); trans. R. A. George, *The Logical Structure of the World* (London: Routledge & Kegan Paul, 1967).

Griffin, N.: *Russell's Idealist Apprenticeship* (Oxford, Oxford University Press, 1991).

Hylton, P. W.: *Russell, Idealism, and the Emergence of Analytic Philosophy* (Oxford: Oxford University Press, 1990).

Pears, D. F.: *Bertrand Russell and the British Tradition in Philosophy* (London: Fontana, 1967).

Ramsey, F. P.: "The Foundations of Mathematics." *Proceedings of the London Mathematical Society*, series 2, 25 (5) (1925), 338–84; reprinted in F. P. Ramsey, *the Foundations of Mathematics and Other Logical Essays*, ed. R. B. Braithwaite (London: Routledge & Kegan Paul, 1931) and elsewhere.

Wittgenstein, L.: *Logische-philosophische Abhandlung* (in *Annalen der Naturphilosophie*, 1921); trans. D. F. Pears and B. F. McGuiness, *Tractatus Logico-Philosophicus* (London: Routledge & Kegan Paul, 1961).

33

Śaṅkara

Brian Carr

Life and writings

Śaṅkara was born in Kaladi, in what is now the modern Indian state of Kerala, during the eighth century CE. There are as yet no firmly established precise dates. In a short life of some 32 years, he wrote (if tradition is right) a very large corpus of works, including commentaries on most of the Hindu *Upaniṣads* (the speculative appendices to the *Vedas*). He traveled widely around India, and is credited with founding important centers of Hindu learning in its four corners. The authenticity of much of the supposed Śaṅkara corpus is a matter of debate, especially since he has commanded very great authority as the major sage of the Advaita Vedānta position.

It is the central aim of this Vedānta school, as interpreters and defenders of the Vedic and Upaniṣadic literature, to establish first a metaphysical monism – as "*Advaita*" (Non-dual) suggests – in which reality (*Brahman*) is not only singular but also featureless, a pure undifferentiated consciousness; and second an epistemology of illusion which explains our failure to appreciate the identity of each apparently "individual soul" (*ātman*) with that single reality. If Śaṅkara's authorship of all the Upaniṣadic commentaries is doubtful, we can at least take as authentic his commentaries on two extremely important texts. The first is Bādarāyaṇa's *Brahmasūtra* or *Vedāntasūtra*, which was itself composed some time between 200 BCE and 400 CE, and Śaṅkara's *bhāṣya* (commentary) on this text contains a philosophy which is rich in ideas and sophisticated in its argumentation.

The second text is the very well known *Bhagavadgītā*, the "Song of the Lord," originally composed during the fifth or fourth century BCE. Śaṅkara's *bhāṣya* on this second text provides an account of the relative positions of the three *yogas* or routes to liberation from the round of birth–death–rebirth (*saṃsāra*) which that text expounds.

Other philosophers of the Vedānta tradition – of whom the most famous are RĀMĀNUJA and Madhva – also composed their own alternative interpretations and defenses of the Vedic and Upaniṣadic literature in the form of commentaries on these two works. Whether Śankara or some other Vedānta philosopher has given the *right* interpretation is of immense importance for Hinduism; whether Śankara's system of ideas can withstand analytic scrutiny as a philosophical system in its own right is of more immediate importance in the context of an emerging Western academic interest in Asian philosophical traditions.

Knowledge of Brahman (reality)

One of Śankara's most striking claims is that there is only one source of knowledge of reality (BSB, I.i.3–4). Most Indian philosophical schools allow a variety of means of access to reality, such as perception, inference, testimony (importantly including that of religious tradition), and analogical reasoning. For Śankara, however, we can come to grasp the existence and nature of reality only through a study and contemplation of the Upaniṣadic texts. All other "means of knowing" are applicable merely to the empirical world, which is utterly different from *Brahman*, reality itself. The *Upaniṣads*, on Śankara's view, are the result of an insight into reality achieved by their composers, and Bādarāyaṇa's *Brahmasūtra* captures these insights in a concise form. In writing his commentary, then, Śankara is himself engaged in the contemplation of the insights of the *Upaniṣads*, and its ultimate soteriological role is to enable its reader to come to a full and proper understanding of reality too. By this understanding, involving no more than a removal of the false picture of reality we labour under, we are offered the route to escaping from *saṃsāra* (birth–death–rebirth) and achieving *mokṣa* (release).

Śankara must acknowledge that it is at least theoretically possible for insight into reality to be achieved without the help of the *Upaniṣads*; for on his account this must have been done by the composers of those texts themselves. Meditation of the kind prescribed in the *Vedas* – *upāsanā* – on the various properties of what Śankara calls "Qualified Reality" (*Saguṇa Brahman*) must of itself be able ultimately to lead to a grasp of the true "Unqualified Reality" (*Nirguṇa Brahman*) or the less gifted of us would have no means at all of achieving it. Such meditation would focus on *Brahman* as manifested as *prāṇa* (vital force), *jyotir* (light), *pañcāgni* (the five fires), and so forth, and most importantly on *Brahman* as manifested as *Īśvara* (God). Moreover, Śankara's position on the inapplicability of perception, inference, and analogical reasoning is open to the obvious objection that all of these must in fact be used in gaining access to the thoughts of the *Upaniṣads'* composers.

The most basic assumption of Śaṅkara's whole approach is that its claim to validity can only be appreciated once the nature of Unqualified Reality has been properly grasped, for then the inadequacy of ordinary "knowledge" and its methods will become apparent. The logical peculiarity of this stance is that until insight has been achieved the truth of the *Upaniṣads'* claims must be taken on trust – an appeal to one of the other standardly recognized means to knowledge, namely "testimony" or "knowledge on authority." Even worse, given that the ultimate knowledge of Unqualified Reality renders all previous knowledge claims at the level of Qualified Reality invalid, consisting of no more than a first faltering step away from the world of ordinary experience, we have a paradox reminiscent of WITTGENSTEIN's claim in his *Tractatus* that the claims in the *Tractatus* are nonsense – albeit important nonsense.

False "knowledge" of self and reality

Śaṅkara must explain how Unqualified Reality can be experienced by us as the complex world governed by causal laws, the world of diverse objects in space and time, and particularly – given his central focus on a rectification of our sense of our own identity – a world in which we distinguish between ourselves and others, and between ourselves as the subjects of experience and the outer world as the object of our experience. That something essentially singular can appear as multiple he illustrates with various suggestive analogies, such as the "space in the pot" and the "sun on water" (BSB, I.i.5; III.ii.19). The space in a pot and the space in a cave are but one space, yet they are conceived by us as individual spaces through the notion of the "limiting adjuncts" of the pot and the cave. And the sun, though itself singular, may be reflected in the water contained in different jars and hence appear multiple. But these are merely analogies, and Śaṅkara must explain precisely how Unqualified Reality appears as our individual selves and the complex experienced world.

The mechanism of false appearance is borrowed from Prabhākara of the Mīmāṃsā school, according to which we falsely see a rope as a snake because we are misled by the similarity of a rope and a snake into mixing up the perceived rope with the remembered snake. The lengthy opening section (BSB I.i.1) of Śaṅkara's *bhāṣya* on the *Brahmasūtra* develops this idea in relation to our misperception of *Brahman* as the individual self (*ātman*). We *are* aware of *Brahman* within ourselves, in as much as we are aware of consciousness – that much, says Śaṅkara, is a common and unquestionable fact of experience. But through our ignorance (*avidyā*) of the real nature of *Brahman* we falsely superimpose as a "limiting adjunct" (*upādhi*) the experienced features of the world consisting in "my body" and "my senses" to arrive at the sense of "my individual consciousness." Just as the ignorance of the fact that a red flower stands behind a translucent crystal leads us to see the crystal as red, so our ignorance is the source of the superimposition (*adhyāsa*) resulting in our conception of the individual self or soul (*ātman*) (BSB, I.i.4; III.ii.14–15).

Śaṅkara says precious little about how the *primary* mistake of seeing *Brahman* in terms of the complexity of objects, including individual bodies and senses, comes about, for his interest is in correcting this particular mistake concerning the *ātman*. But that mistake needs an explanation too. At the very least, his superimposition theory needs a double application, first to produce the complexity of experienced objects, and second to produce the mistake of individual selves. Moreover, we can ask why the ignorance, which is the root cause of all this, exists at all. Where does one's ignorance of the real nature of *Brahman* come from? Though clearly none too happy with the notion, Śaṅkara does invoke the theory of *Māyā*, a Qualified Reality conception of a cosmic force of illusion which has its origins somehow in Unqualified Reality and is the ultimate origin of the individual's ignorance and consequent bondage to the physical world (BSB, I.iii.19).

Refutation of other schools

A good deal of the *Brahmasūtra* and therefore of Śaṅkara's *bhāṣya* is taken up with arguing that the Advaita Vedānta interpretation of the *Upaniṣads* is the correct one. Alternative interpretations of other "orthodox" Hindu schools, such as Sāṅkhya and Yoga, are on the way discarded as distortions of the "obvious" import of various obscure passages in the ancient texts. But then, in *Brahmasūtrabhāṣya* II.ii, Śaṅkara attempts a refutation of Sāṅkhya-Yoga and other major orthodox and non-orthodox schools in a manner ostensibly independent of appeal to scripture and hence independent of the question of the latter's correct interpretation.

Sāṅkhya-Yoga

In fact, since the joint Sāṅkhya-Yoga school has much in common with Śaṅkara's own philosophy, he takes special care to distance himself from it, even at the expense of a somewhat oversimplistic rendering of its claims. On a superficial reading Sāṅkhya-Yoga philosophy can be seen as a simple dualism of mind and nature – knower and known – and Śaṅkara has little difficulty in showing that such a dualism is alien to the *Upaniṣads* and riddled with incoherent ingredients.

The major differences between Śaṅkara's philosophy and that of Sāṅkhya-Yoga, as he sees it, may be summed up as follows (BSB, II.ii.1–10). On his own view, the cause of the diverse world of experience – in the sense of both the material cause and the efficient cause – is none other than *Brahman*. But the operation of a cause in producing its effects is only an *apparent* transformation of the cause (*vivartavāda*) and no new things are ever *really* produced. *Brahman* in its truest sense is without qualities, *Nirguṇa Brahman*. *Brahman* in this sense merely *appears* in the form of *Īśvara* (God) or *Saguṇa Brahman*, which has the fundamental qualities of the world of experience. Finally, *Īśvara appears* to manifest itself in the diversity of objects in that world and in the flux of changes which appear in it. In contrast, Sāṅkhya-Yoga starts with a metaphysical dualism of *Prakṛti*, the experienced world of objects, and of *puruṣa* which experiences it. There is a plurality of *puruṣas* but only one *Prakṛti*; and though the former never really undergo change in their own nature as experiencers, the latter *really* evolves (*pariṇāmavāda*) by a readjustment of its three constituent strands (*guṇas*). The material cause of the world is therefore *Prakṛti*; the efficient cause is *puruṣa*. Such is Śaṅkara's rendering of the story.

The two main arguments developed against the Sāṅkhya-Yoga accounts of material cause and of efficient cause constitute Śaṅkara's case for his own theory of apparent transformation. The first (BSB, II.i.18) is a sophisticated argument concerning the supposed relation of inherence, and the second (BSB, II. ii.7) is a suggestive but less developed argument against interaction between distinct substances.

On the nature of material causation, Śaṅkara at least agrees with Sāṅkhya-Yoga that, in some way, the effect must pre-exist in the cause. The fact that only specific materials can produce specific effects supports this common thesis: curds can only be produced from milk, for example, just as cloth can only be produced from yarns. We need to assume therefore that milk has a special *potency* for curds – that curds are *latent* in the milk. Where Śaṅkara parts company from Sāṅkya-Yoga is in going further and arguing that the effect is *identical* with the cause. Assume that the cause (C), potency (P), and effect (E) are linked by relations of inherence. We have, therefore, two inherence relations to begin with, that between C and P, and that between P and E. But now the relations of inherence involved must themselves be related to their terms – C and P, and P and E – by further relations of inherence, thus starting an obvious infinite regress of inherence relations. The only way out of this regress, argues Śaṅkara, is to reject inherence as a viable relation and replace it with identity. *Ergo* C, P, and E are identical.

Śaṅkara's argument can be criticized from the point of view of contemporary philosophical logic. Inherence gives rise to a regress only if we assume that it can be treated as a third term logically on a par with C, P, and E. Moreover, the ontological status of P seems somewhat different from that of C and E.

Śaṅkara's second argument concerns the nature of efficient causation between fundamentally different kinds of substances. On the Sāṅkhya-Yoga theory, the efficient cause of the evolution of *Prakṛti* is *puruṣa*. But how, asks Śaṅkara, can *puruṣa* and *Prakṛti* come into causal interaction? He considers and easily demolishes two analogies offered by Sāṅkhya-Yoga. On the first, they are likened to a lame yet sighted man riding on the shoulders of another man who is blind yet capable of walking: together they can move about and act in a symbiotic way. But, Śaṅkara points out, the two men obviously have the power of communication, but what sense could we make of communication between *puruṣa* and *Prakṛti*? On the second analogy, they are compared to a lodestone and a piece of iron: the simple presence of the first moves the second. Śaṅkara responds that the mere proximity of *puruṣa* to *Prakṛti* cannot be the cause of movement in the latter, for such proximity is eternal and movement would therefore be unending.

It can be argued that Śaṅkara's case here is weak, on a number of grounds. For one thing, he himself has a similar problem in explaining why *Nirguṇa Brahman* even apparently evolves into the diverse world of experience, and on this issue he offers his theory of *Māyā* as a cosmic force veiling the real nature of *Brahman*. But this theory on the face of it merely restates the problem: why, given the nature of *Brahman*, does *Māyā* evolve out of it? The difficulty of explaining interaction between two distinct types of substances such as those of Sāṅkhya-Yoga seems no greater than the difficulty of explaining the origin of apparent evolution on a strict monism such as Śaṅkara's. And Śaṅkara might, too, be accused of misrepresenting the Sāṅkhya-Yoga account of the evolution of *Prakṛti* by treating it as an interaction of efficient causation. On the contrary, a better model of causation for rendering the theory would be that of final causation, i.e. a teleological model. *Prakṛti* evolves "for the sake of" *puruṣas*, claims the classical *Sāṅkhyakārikā* of Īśvara Kṛṣṇa – so that *puruṣas* may experience the world and so that they may come to appreciate their essential difference from it and thereby achieve *mokṣa*.

Vaiśeṣika

The second orthodox school which Śaṅkara criticises (BSB II.ii.11–17) is the Vaiśeṣika, which adopts a theory of atomism to explain the world we experience. One of his major arguments rests on the inexplicability of order coming about out of atoms in isolation, and hence of atomic combinations coming into being. A second argument concerns the Vaiśeṣika assumption that new properties can emerge out of the combination of atoms, a theory of causation quite opposed to his own theory of apparent change (*vivartavāda*) discussed above. For Śaṅkara, the efficient and material cause of the world of experience is, in his special sense of cause, *Brahman* and not insentient atoms. Yet another orthodox position opposed to Śaṅkara's treats God as merely the efficient cause of the world of experience and not its material cause. God is thus a "mere superintendent," as Śaṅkara puts it, a view which militates against His omnipotence.

Jainism

Śaṅkara also develops criticisms of the major non-orthodox schools, both Jainism (BSB II.ii.33–6) and the various forms of Buddhism. The Jains had developed a carefully integrated set of theories of the multi-faceted nature of reality (*anekāntavāda*), the limited nature of much of human knowledge (*nayavāda*), and the idea of perfect knowledge (*kevala*) to be achieved by the liberated *jīva*. Rather than examining the subtleties of these theories in detail, Śaṅkara chooses to level his attack at one of the most obscure of the Jains' doctrine, the seven-step logic (*saptabhaṅgī*). The motivation for this doctrine in Jainism is clearly to make possible the simultaneous ascription of conflicting predicates without contradiction to one and the same object, by relativizing those predications from different standpoints. Śaṅkara ignores this last condition, and unfortunately renders the Jains' position as allowing for the simultaneous possession by all things of all characteristics – a misdirected criticism which has frequently been rehearsed in later Indian philosophy.

Buddhism

Śaṅkara is equally too quick with his refutation of the various schools of Buddhism (see the BUDDHA) (BSB II.ii.18–32), glossing over the similarities in his own Advaita Vedānta to at least certain aspects of their thinking. The actual indebtedness of Śaṅkara, and perhaps more so his teacher's teacher Gauḍapāda, to Buddhist ideas has always been much debated; but Śaṅkara manages to distance himself from all forms of Buddhism in his commentary on the *Brahmasūtra* by his rendering of those ideas. He divides the tradition into three schools, offering refutations of each in turn: realists (Sarvāstivādins), idealists (Vijñānavādins, or Yogācāras) and nihilists (Sarvaśunyavadins, or Mādhyamikas).

On the Buddhist realist position, the individual is made up of five aggregates (*khandhas*) of momentary ingredients. Apart from the body – which consists of an arrangement of physical atoms of solidity, fluidity, heat, and motion – these are the cognitive, emotional, volitional, and perceptual groups. The individual consists of these alone, being without a permanent *ātman*. Śaṅkara finds it difficult to understand how, on this theory, the arrangement of the momentary ingredients can be held together to form a thinking, perceiving, and acting individual. Second, the momentariness of all ingredients raises the question of how ingredients at one moment can possibly give rise to successive ingredients; for the prior causes have become non-existent before their supposed effects come into being. And, third, on the momentary aggregates theory, it seems impossible to make sense of memory and recognition; for such acts are normally taken to imply the continuity of the experiencer as a vital part of them (BSB II.ii.18–27).

Śaṅkara reports two considerations which have led Buddhists away from this realist position to some version of idealism: (1) objects that existed independently of subjective consciousness would have to be the unperceivable atoms or a logically obscure conglomeration of them which was neither the same nor different from the unperceivable atoms; and (2) the simultaneous appearance of knowledge and its object, which argues for their identity. He finds neither of these considerations convincing, for we have the evidence of our senses that objects exist as perceivable entities, and we can explain the simultaneity in question as simply a consequence of causality (BSB II.ii.28–32). As for Buddhist nihilism, Śaṅkara thinks it suffices to point out that such a position is opposed to all forms of human knowledge.

The route to salvation

Although the *Bhagavadgītā* is a religious work rather than a philosophical text, it makes claims concerning the nature of man, of his spiritual and material aspects, of his social roles, and of his salvation in *mokṣa*, that are a profound stimulus to later philosophical enquiry. The Advaita Vedānta of Śaṅkara is, of course, also an intimate combination of religious and philosophical ideas, and Śaṅkara firmly believes that his position not only is consistent with such religious works but, most importantly, constitutes the only correct interpretation of them. Śaṅkara's commentary on the *Gītā* provides him with the opportunity to argue for this claim at length.

The *Gītā* expounds three routes to salvation (*mokṣa*): *karma-yoga* (the *yoga* of action), *bhakti-yoga* (the *yoga* of devotion) and *jñāna-yoga* (the *yoga* of knowledge). The precise content of these *yogas* is a matter of much dispute, which is hardly surprising given that they are couched in terms of such obscure metaphysical ideas as soul (*ātman*), God (*Īśvara*), embodiment (*saṃsāra*) and salvation (*mokṣa*). What is more, the relationship between the *yogas* is equally obscure. Are they meant to be specific to certain groups of people or are all *yogas* open to all? Are they alternative routes to *mokṣa* that one may choose from at will? Are they perhaps so intimately related that they constitute just three facets of one route? An abundance of alternative answers has been offered to these questions within Hinduism.

Śaṅkara's intention in his commentary on the *Gītā* is to offer a clear rendering of the *yogas* which places them in a simple linear order. The main point of his interpretation is that there is a fundamental division between the ideas of action and of *Brahman*. In the absence of a grasp of the real nature of the latter – of *Nirguṇa Brahman* – we labor under the false impression of an individual self which is the agent in activity and the reaper of the benefits and losses accruing from that activity. When *Brahman* has been appreciated as pure undifferentiated consciousness and we have recognized the idea of our individuality as a mistake, it becomes impossible to function as an agent (BGB introduction, 18.66). Śaṅkara therefore draws a clear contrast between *karma-yoga* and *jñāna-yoga*, between the virtuous path of rites and duties as revealed in the *Vedas* and the path of renunciation of such rites and duties which he takes to be the special message of the *Gītā*.

Karma-yoga, the path which involves activity in accordance with established (Vedic) principles of behavior for the different castes, is meant for social beings (BGB 3 passim). *Jñāna-yoga*, the path which involves the dedicated pursuit of and concentration on *Nirguṇa Brahman* is meant for the asocial, the renunciator of social existence (the *sannyāsin*) (BGB 2 and 7 passim). What of the third path, *bhakti-yoga* – the path of devotion? For Śaṅkara this has a special pivotal role to play, which he explains in terms of mental purification. It is possible to follow the first path, *karma-yoga*, in a selfish way. It is possible to be motivated by a desire for such goals as social esteem, power, and influence, or even the achievement of a lesser kind of spiritual salvation in heaven, conceived of as inhabited by the gods. *Bhakti-yoga* involves a withdrawal of attachment to lesser and selfish ends, and an engagement in duties out of love of Krishna (*Īśvara*). The consequence of selfless devoted activity is the purification of the internal organ (consisting of *cittā*, *buddhi*, *manas*, *and ahaṅkāra* – mindstuff, intellect, mind, and ego). Such purification is a vital step toward the ability to appreciate the real nature of *Brahman* and hence towards the possibility of *jñāna-yoga* (BGB 12 passim). The relative positions of the *yogas* are clear: *karma-yoga* allied to *bhakti-yoga* is the route to be adopted by social beings as a preparation for the renunciation of social existence, and does not of itself lead directly to *mokṣa*; renunciation of social existence is the prerequisite and inevitable concomitance of *jñāna-yoga*, which leads directly to *mokṣa*.

Śaṅkara's account, though clear enough in intention and in outline, faces a number of difficulties. For a start, it could be argued that it fits badly with the structure of the *Gītā* itself, for the nature of *Brahman* is explained to Arjuna by Krishna very early in the text (in chapter 2), even while Krishna is encouraging Arjuna to act according to his caste duty. *Karma-yoga*, too, seems to be much involved with and premised on an appreciation of *Brahman*, since it is through the message that the ordinary consequences of action are of no spiritual value that Krishna attempts to focus on the one important end for Arjuna – *mokṣa*. Indeed, doing duty for duty's sake, or for the sake of *Īśvara*, is the fundamental injunction which is given sense through the point that ordinary human social existence involves a false conception of the nature of the self.

If these were not problems enough, Śaṅkara's rendering of the relation between the *yogas* has to face up to two very important test cases: can it make sense of the *jīvanmukta*, that person who has achieved insight into the nature of *Brahman* yet continues to act within the world as (for example) a teacher, such as Śaṅkara himself. And can it make sense of the very special case of Krishna, who is a manifestation of *Īśvara* and as such appears also to be an actor in an unreal world?

Bibliography

Writings

Brahmasūtrabhāṣya (BSB) [Śaṅkara's commentary on the *Brahmasūtra* of Bādarāyaṇa]. A good translation is *Brahmasūtrabhāṣya of Śrī Śaṅkarācārya*, trans. Swāmī Gambhīrānanda (Calcutta: Advaita Ashrama, 1965).
Bhagavadgītābhāṣya (BGB) [Śaṅkara's commentary on the *Bhagavadgītā*]. A good translation is *Bhagavadgītā with the Commentary of Śaṅkarācārya*, trans. Swāmī Gambhīrānanda (Calcutta: Advaita Ashrama, 1984).

Further reading

Carr, Brian: "Śaṅkarācārya." In Brian Carr and Indira Mahalingam (eds), *Companion Encyclopedia of Asian Philosophy* (London and New York: Routledge, 1997).

Hiriyanna, M.: *Outlines of Indian Philosophy* (Woking: Unwin Brothers, 1932).

——: *Essentials of Indian Philosophy* (London: Allen & Unwin, 1949).

Potter, K. H. (ed.): *Encyclopaedia of Indian Philosophies, volume III, Advaita Vedānta up to Śaṅkara and His Pupils* (Delhi: Motilal Banarsidass, 1981).

Thibaut, G. (trans.): *The Vedānta-sutras with a Commentary by Śaṅkarācārya*, two volumes, Sacred Books of the East Series, 34 and 38, ed. F. Max Muller (Oxford: Oxford University Press, 1890, 1896).

34

Sartre

William R. Schroeder

Jean-Paul Sartre (1905–1980 CE) was a model intellectual for the twentieth century. He was a multitalented thinker who not only created several philosophical systems but also wrote major novels and plays, essays on literary theory and art criticism, and some methodologically innovative biographies. He was awarded the Nobel Prize for literature in 1964, which he declined. In addition, he was the major voice for existentialism, a movement that dominated European thought from 1943 to 1955, and he challenged the dominant theories of his day: refashioning Marxism (see MARX) from within and revising Freud's approach to understanding persons – shifting from a deterministic to a teleological analysis that treats persons as self-constituting agents. He also strove to influence the course of international events through his political analysis and activism, e.g. he opposed the Algerian and Vietnamese wars. Finally, within philosophy he insightfully addressed virtually every issue concerning the nature and everyday life of human beings. Though known for his defense of freedom and human responsibility, his work is perhaps best understood as exploring the relations between individuals and their environments – raw being, nature, technology, the family, other people, groups, and history. He thus offered a complete picture of human life as lived.

His work can be divided into three general periods: existential phenomenology (1934–56), dialectical analysis of groups and history (1957–70), and an exploration of lived historical experience (1971–80).

Life

In 1937–40 Sartre published his first philosophical essays and also his first novel, *Nausea*. He served in the army during the Second World War, but his role allowed him to continue developing his philosophical ideas.

Eventually, he became a prisoner of war – teaching HEIDEGGER's theories to his fellow prisoners. He escaped and returned to Paris, publishing his first major treatise, *Being and Nothingness*, in 1943 and popularizing its ideas in his plays *No Exit* and *The Flies* and the narrative trilogy *The Roads to Freedom* (*The Age of Reason, The Reprieve,* and *Troubled Sleep*). With the liberation, his version of existentialism dominated French thought. In 1945 he founded *Les Temps moderne*, the journal in which many of his essays first appeared. He sketched a preliminary ethics in "Existentialism is a Humanism" and *What is Literature?*

From 1946 to 1955 Sartre wrote several "existential biographies," the most important of which is *Saint Genet*, which examined the relationships between good and evil. Sartre applied his "existential psychoanalysis" in these biographies. Its goal is to discover the subject's fundamental project (the one which integrates all others) and how it changes as the person encounters recalcitrant situations. During the period from 1946 to 1973 Sartre engaged in a long dialogue with Marxism. This effort culminated in his second major philosophical treatise, the *Critique of Dialectical Reason* (1960). In this work he revised his understanding of how individuals are related to the practical world and history, and developed an original understanding of the dynamic structure and historical agency of human groups. The second volume investigates whether history can achieve even partial resolution if it contains ever-present conflicts. Sartre continued his political analysis of contemporary events throughout this period, gradually becoming more active and taking greater risks. His apartment was bombed several times.

His final major project was the 3,000-page *Family Idiot*. Here he analyzed both a particular historical period and the individual development of Gustav Flaubert. This work integrates his previous theories and develops new concepts – expanding his theories of language and writing. Sartre lost his ability to see in 1973, but continued to give interviews, discuss ideas, and have new books read to him. He collaborated with Benny Levi on a final work, called *Hope Now* (1991). Sartre died in 1980; his funeral drew a massive popular procession (of tens of thousands) through Paris, the likes of which has rarely been seen before and may never be seen again.

Existential phenomenology

Phenomenology is the study of the essential structures of experience. Sartre developed an *existential* phenomenology, which describes these structures as they are lived. Sartre initially examined emotions (in

Emotions: Outline of a Theory, 1939), imagination (in *The Psychology of the Imagination*, 1940), and the self (in *The Transcendence of the Ego*, 1937). He claims that emotions are magical attempts to achieve our purposes which abandon the practical requirements of the world. He distinguishes feelings, which are momentary heightened intensities, from emotions, which meaningfully integrate behavior, belief, and fantasy. He also distinguishes feelings from moods, which transcend the moment and require an act of reflective consciousness in order to be produced and sustained (consider the difference between feeling a momentary setback and falling into depression). Because emotions are attempts to magically sidestep practical exigencies and because they are intentional, Sartre claims we are responsible for our emotional lives.

Sartre thinks imagination is a fundamental capacity of consciousness. It transcends the given situation by envisioning alternatives to it. Because the chosen action excludes various alternatives, imagination is a precondition for choice, action, and responsibility. The given facts of the situation can never completely determine or foreclose choices. This means one is responsible for such choices. Sartre also explores the differences between perceiving and imagining: one can learn more from a perceived object by looking, but the imagined object already incorporates one's knowledge of it. Also, the perceived object offers resistance to one's will, while the imagined object can be altered with one's whims.

Sartre completes these early studies with an examination of the psychic self, often taken to be the source of mental states. He distinguishes between pre-reflective and reflective consciousness. Pre-reflective consciousness is directly focused on its object, is absorbed in tasks, and possesses only the most glancing, indirect grasp of itself. Reflective consciousness is a dependent and second-order form, existing only when consciousness attempts to directly observe itself (introspectively or retrospectively). In doing so it synthesizes fleeting, discrete consciousnesses into illusory unities and then assumes these fictions existed prior to its operations. Reflective consciousness thus endows itself with passivity, interpreting consciousness as a result produced by interior "forces." However, there is one type of reflection – which Sartre calls "pure" and on which his entire position is ultimately based – that escapes these illusory fabrications and reveals consciousness just as it is. Most of Sartre's claims derive from this type of purified self-revelation. Sartre demonstrates the import of this pre-reflective/reflective distinction by showing that the psychic self is only a creature of reflective consciousness, that it does not exist in pre-reflective life at all. It emerges only when one attempts to take the other person's viewpoint on oneself – a different way of understanding the experience of reflection. Indeed, the whole panoply of dispositions and inner states people take themselves to possess are merely inventions of *impure* reflection. Sartre also suggests that the causal influence of such states on behavior is illusory. When one makes the transition to purified reflection, these false, self-created unities dissolve, and the contingency and spontaneity of consciousness is revealed.

Sartre summarizes these discoveries in his most famous novel, *Nausea*, which strips away the protective illusions of impure reflection to reveal both consciousness and raw being in their naked states. Typical social roles, accepted values, received traditions, established concepts, and even language itself all conceal the dynamic, self-transcending quality of consciousness and the brute, indifferent superfluity of raw being. Consciousness transcends itself because its past choices never determine its present course; if a project is to continue, it must be rechosen in each situation that threatens it. *Nausea*'s anti-hero, Roquentin, discovers Sartre's radical freedom – the sense that anything is possible – but realizes it is a crushing burden. He also experiences the dissolution of the psychic self, both when the subject of his biographical study refuses to conform to any plausible hypothesis Roquentin can produce and when Roquentin himself abandons his own organizing project (the writing of the biography). This forces him to experience the contingency and spontaneity of his conscious states.

Being and Nothingness extends Sartre's study of the types of consciousness and their relationship with the world, others, and raw being. He contrasts two types of being: a solid, complete, self-identical, self-sufficient type (inert objects) and an empty, incomplete, self-divided type (consciousness) that is parasitic on the first type of being yet transforms it – breaking it into distinct objects and tools by objectifying it. A third type of being mediates persons as they define and use each other; it is the creation of others but nonetheless defines oneself. He calls this one's *being-for-others*. It is an ever-present proof of the other's freedom because it reveals a dimension of oneself and the world (other people) which one cannot ultimately control. One can attempt to influence other people's judgments about oneself in various ways, but there is no guarantee that they will respond appropriately. For Sartre this experience of being objectified articulates the *lived reality* of other persons, which is more basic than one's objectifying *knowledge* of them.

Sartre suggests that the internal division within consciousness produced by reflection is a radicalization of two other internal divisions. The first concerns an ever-present scission in experience resulting from a simultaneous peripheral awareness which accompanies every act of consciousness, and the second concerns lived temporality – the gap between the future goal and the present situation. For Sartre consciousness is always focally consciousness of its object and glancingly aware (of) itself; this supplementary awareness is enough to insure that consciousness can never coincide with itself; a gap (or nothingness) always exists at its heart. Thus, when aware of an object, consciousness is non-focally aware (of) itself as directed toward the object, and thus is divided between its focus and its ancillary grasp of itself. This non-focal aspect of consciousness becomes directed and focal when consciousness shifts into reflection, and then the initial object of the original awareness drops into the periphery; this is just one way in which reflection typically alters (and thus pollutes) the act it tries to clarify. The second split emerges in transcending the present toward the future – opening a distance between the current situation and the goal. When one reaches a goal, then another project emerges and another temporal distance opens. This thrust into the future produces one's lived experience of time's flow.

Sartre develops additional categories for analyzing persons, e.g. "facticity" and "transcendence." Elements of one's facticity are unavoidably given; one need *not* sustain them in order for them to continue, e.g. the fact that one will die, has a past, must be located somewhere, and has specific social definitions. Elements of one's transcendence are chosen, and one must repeatedly sustain them if they are to continue, e.g. one's projects, one's values, one's stance toward the past, one's attitude to death, one's choice to live here rather than elsewhere, and one's response to the social definitions one is given. Persons always transcend the givens of the situation, imagine alternatives, and choose one on the basis of values. Values themselves are chosen and have no objective status. Persons sustain values by committing themselves to the particular actions that realize them.

When people realize the full extent of their freedom and consequent responsibility for their lives, they typically hide this awareness through self-deception (or "bad faith"), which paradoxically denies and asserts the same condition. Sartre explores the types of self-deception. Persons possess both facticity and transcendence. If one denies either dimension, one deceives oneself. If one denies an open future for which one must make choices or a determinate past for which one has responsibility, then one is self-deceived. Similarly, if one takes either factor to function like the other, one deceives oneself. If, for example, one takes the future to be fixed or the past to be completely open to interpretation, then one deceives oneself. Other examples of this duality of facticity and transcendence include the fact that one is a subject for oneself and an object to others, that one is part of nature yet always transcending it, that one exists passively embodied but always uses the body to realize projects. Sartrean authenticity requires that one face and acknowledge this dual condition.

The "look" that other people direct at one creates a social definition for oneself. To others one is "nerdy" or "scrawny" or "impetuous" or "sexy." Though one may dispute such assessments, they have unavoidable social reality. Because the other's judgments and actions define one, one constantly seeks to control those judgments and limit those actions. One can do this two ways: either by constantly dominating others so that they cannot return one's look (confrontation), or by displaying oneself in a way that seduces others to see one as one wants to be seen (assimilation). Neither approach succeeds because other people's subjectivity ultimately cannot be controlled. The very attempt to dominate others reveals their independence either because they can always recover and circumvent one's domination or because they can remain unresponsive to one's seductions.

For Sartre freedom always exists within the limits of a defined situation. These constraints make freedom possible and meaningful. But the situation never determines one's choices. Even the harshest obstacles – gunpoint or prison – do not preclude one's choice of response (one can try to disarm the assailant or escape from prison). In addition, specific choices are usually enrichments of more general choices, which Sartre calls "projects." The project of becoming a teacher requires that one complete a specified program, and this requires that many lower-level projects be pursued. At the highest level are one's fundamental projects; the task of Sartrean psychoanalysis is to discover these and classify them. Sartre thinks people are dimly aware of their fundamental project. Though they may be unable to state it, they can recognize it when stated by others. Sartre seeks to understand action teleologically by referring to its purposes; causal explanations cannot even begin until the goals of the action to be explained are known.

At the end of *Being and Nothingness*, Sartre promises an ethics, one in which authenticity is a central notion. To be authentic involves acknowledging and embracing one's freedom and its implications. Thus, in *The Flies* he suggests three conditions necessary for authenticity: to engage the situation (rather than remaining indifferent to it), to explicitly choose one's responses (rather than enact a choice one does not really endorse), and to sustain responsibility for them in the future (rather than denying or avoiding responsibility). The play's hero, Orestes, exemplifies these conditions dramatically. In "Existentialism Is a Humanism," Sartre suggests that persons bear responsibility for all mankind because, in acting, they offer models for all to emulate. Sartre also stresses that the world is human because no God exists to provide it a transcendent purpose or to offer indubitable support for values. The historical world and the values informing it are created entirely by persons and their choices. He also suggests that persons create themselves through their choices (rather than possessing a predetermined essence) and that abstract rules can never do justice to the situational complexity people confront in practice. Finally, he argues that since freedom is the source of any possible value, it functions as a meta-value, to be respected at all costs.

Sartre continues to elaborate his ethics in *What Is Literature?* and *Notebooks for an Ethics* (published posthumously). He uses the author–reader relationship to clarify the kind of reciprocity he thinks is possible between people. The writer's enterprise appeals to the reader's freedom; the reader must constitute the literary object for it to exist. Similarly, the reader appeals to the constituting freedom of the writer in the process of reading, trusting the author to produce a coherent text. Each maintains a trust in and generosity toward each other. Moreover, writing/reading underline the degree to which each person is responsible for the world simply in disclosing/revealing it. The creativity embodied in writing/reading expresses a more basic creativity operating in perception and action. Sartre wants to extend this model of reciprocity, generosity, and creativity to all social relations and to history. In the two of twelve *Notebooks* that survive, Sartre examines the process of conversion to a more authentic way of life. The central moment in conversion is abandoning the fundamental aspiration to be God (the foundation of one's own freedom) and accepting one's contingency. This forces one to see all values as fallible human creations, rather than as absolutes that haunt and terrorize human activity. Conversion overcomes the alienation into illusory objectifications of ourselves produced by others and our own desperation. It discovers the values of subjectivity: passion, pleasure in the moment, criticism, creation, and generosity. It also has a social element in that it acknowledges that the projects of each make an appeal to the actions of others to maintain and pursue those projects or explicitly indicate their flaws. His ultimate social ideal is a kingdom of ends that is pursued as an historical project, that guides political action, and that is pursued in concert with other agents seeking to sustain the conversion to authenticity each has achieved.

Dialectical analysis of the person–world relation (1956–70)

Sartre's *Critique of Dialectical Reason, volumes 1 and 2*, his second major philosophical system, establishes a more dialectical relation between persons and their environments and examines the preconditions for historical action in the formation of various types of social groups. He also develops the tools through which periods of history can be analyzed in all their complexity. The book is introduced by a long essay, "Search for a Method," which clarifies the progressive–regressive method, which in turn is applied in *The Family Idiot.* The regressive phase analyzes all the complex factors in the historical era to which individuals must respond, while the progressive phase reconstitutes the unity and development of their projects as they negotiate these factors across time. Thus, the method has an analytic moment and a synthetic moment. Important factors in the historical situation include existing traditions and institutions, specific family relations, a distinct level of technology, a class system, and competing ideologies. Each factor offers possibilities for and limits to historical action.

Sartre now interprets human relations with nature, technology, other individuals, and groups on the model of an interchange in which structural features of these "environments" are internalized as the projects of the person are externalized. The world is thus given its character by human action, but human actors are also constrained and shaped by the existing features of the world, many of which were created by past human actions. The contingent features of the current era set limits to historical achievement, but current group actions give direction to future history. Sartre sees no guarantee of historical progress, but in the second volume of the *Critique* he shows that conflict among groups does not necessarily lead to historical stalemate. He thinks people act historically through belonging to groups, and each group creates a social identity for its members through its structures, dynamics, and activities.

Two unique contributions of these books are Sartre's reconsideration of a person's relation to technology and his analysis of group life. Technology is just matter shaped by previous generations' efforts to realize their own purposes, but the resulting tools retain their connections with such purposes so that current people reanimate these past purposes in using the tools, even if they fail to realize this. Unintended consequences of historical action become a central concern for Sartre in these works. In addition, Sartre offers a new ontological analysis of the status of groups. He rejects both the view that groups are mere conglomerations of individuals seeking their own purposes and the view that groups are ontologically distinct organic wholes that have a life of their own that determines the actions of individuals. Instead, Sartre suggests that by participating in a group individuals create/enforce a kind of group identity for themselves and other group members – becoming "common individuals" who willingly adopt the aims of the group and enforce its directives. A genuine group has collectively produced goals, and is distinct from a mere series, in which each person is just one among many numerically related others, e.g. a movie queue or a broadcast audience. Seriality is the zero degree of sociality; genuine groups emerge from this serial condition.

Sartre's philosophical sociology distinguishes four basic types of groups: fused groups, pledged groups, organizations, and institutions. A *fused* group consists of members of a series that spontaneously discover they have a common goal, a discovery often imposed on them by violent threats. The living goal of this group emerges gradually as each person reacts to the tentatively enacted goals of the others; there are no leaders, and the group is short-lived unless its members pledge themselves to one another. The *pledged* group emerges when members explicitly pledge loyalty, take the group's goals as their own, and enforce those pledges on other members. This enforcement function gives the pledged group its unity – generating both fear and brotherhood.

The *organization* emerges when different members of the group take on different functions, which they may perform at a distance from one another. Since each contributes to the group's aims, each has a functional equality. In some respects the organization is the highest achievement of group unity and reciprocity, but it also contains the seeds of the kind of differential authority and inequality that emerges fully in institutions. An *institution* eventually loses its unity and returns into seriality because its leaders objectify the rest of the group, making them mere instruments rather than co-creating subjects. The militant strives to prevent the organization from becoming an institution by reawakening the pacified group members into a more active sense of their roles and responsibilities.

These four types of groups constitute paradigms of group life; every group exists in one of these phases. Sartre thinks most groups arise from seriality, traverse a curve toward full reciprocity, and gradually return into seriality again when leaders and led no longer recognize themselves as having common goals.

For Sartre, history is created by groups of all kinds, at all stages of development. Individuals influence history by participating in various groups. Sartre's topic in the *Critique, volume 2* is whether group conflict typically leads in some direction, however faltering, or whether it leads to stalemate. Individuals, most groups, and history itself all dynamically seek, but never quite reach, full unity. The burden of the second volume is to show that this is true despite conflicts. Sartre initially examines individual conflict (a boxing match), then a small group conflict, and finally a large group conflict (Stalin's relation to his own party). He shows that some unifying direction emerges from each type of conflict. Each group then responds to the general direction arising from that conflict by either opposing or adopting it. Sartre's ultimate goal is a history that is jointly produced by individuals, equally and freely, all of whom authentically choose their actions and sustain each other's choices reciprocally.

Lived experience and history: The Family Idiot *(1971–80)*

Space permits only the most cursory treatment of Sartre's last major book, his most ambitious biographical study, which is about Flaubert. It incorporates all the social and historical elements Sartre examines in the *Critique.* Sartre's goal is to understand not only Flaubert, but also his class and era. He shows how to understand *anyone* if one has sufficient documentation of the person's life. Also, he seeks to clarify Flaubert's general options at each of the crucial junctures of his life in order to better understand his specific choices. He shows how Flaubert responds to each specific configuration in his historical situation – the status of his family, his relation to his parents and brother, the ideology of his class, the novelistic tradition he inherited, etc. He thereby comprehends Flaubert's choice of fundamental project and its concretization in Flaubert's writing practice. He finds the same neurotic structure that governs Flaubert's psyche operating in the collective historical actions of Flaubert's class, and this allows Flaubert to write the defining novel of his age, *Madame Bovary.*

Again Sartre's key claim is that historical agents make themselves out of the conditions that make them, and he continues to use the model of interiorization/exteriorization to understand the dialectical relation between person and world. He shows in some depth how the progressive/regressive method actually works – providing a full analysis of the factors to which Flaubert had to respond (the regressive half), and then reconstructing carefully the dynamic of his responses as they evolved over time (the progressive half). He shows how the ideologies and dynamics of his class position affected his choices and how his choices summarize the fundamental project of his class. In the course of his long study, Sartre creates a variety of new concepts that can further clarify the subtleties of lived experience.

Bibliography

Writings

La Transcendance de l'ego [1936–7] (Paris: J. Vrin, 1965); trans. F. Williams and R. Kirkpatrick as *The Transcendence of the Ego* (New York: Noonday Press, 1957).

L'Nausée (Paris: Gallimard, 1938); trans. Lloyd Alexander as *Nausea* (New York: New Directions, 1959).

L'Etre et le néant (Paris: Gallimard, 1943); trans. Hazel Barnes as *Being and Nothingness* (New York: Philosophical Library, 1956).

Saint Genet: Comédien et martyr (Paris: Gallimard, 1952); trans. B. Frechtman as *Saint Genet: Actor and Martyr* (New York: Mentor Books, 1963).

Critique de la raison dialectique, tome I (Paris: Gallimard, 1960); trans. A. Sheridan-Smith as *Critique of Dialectical Reason, volume 1* (London: New Left Board, 1976).

Les Mots (Paris: Gallimard, 1964); trans. B. Frechtman as *The Words* (New York: Braziller, 1964).

L'Idiot de la famille: Gustave Flaubert de 1821 à 1857, tomes I and II (Paris, Gallimard, 1971), *tome III* (1972); trans. Carol Cosman as *The Family Idiot, volumes 1–5* (Chicago: University of Chicago Press, 1981–94).

Cahiers pour une morale (Paris: Gallimard, 1983); trans. D. Pellauer as *Notebooks for an Ethics* (Chicago: University of Chicago Press, 1992).

Critique de la raison dialectique, tome II (Paris: Gallimard, 1985); trans. Quentin Hoare as *Critique of Dialectical Reason, volume 2* (London: New Left Board, 1991).

Verité et existence (Paris: Gallimard, 1989); trans. A. van den Hoven as *Truth and Existence* (Chicago: University of Chicago Press, 1992).

Further reading

Contat, Michel and Rybalka: *Les Ecrits de Sartre: Chronologie, bibliographie commentée* (Paris: Gallimard, 1970); trans. R. McCleary as *The Writings of Sartre*, two volumes (Evanston, IL: Northwestern University Press, 1974).

Flynn, Thomas: *Sartre and Marxist Existentialism* (Chicago: University of Chicago Press, 1984).

Gerassi, John: *Jean-Paul Sartre: Hated Conscience of the 20th Century* (Chicago: University of Chicago Press, 1989).

Howells, Christina: *Sartre: The Necessity of Freedom* (Cambridge: Cambridge University Press, 1988).

Schroeder, William R.: *Sartre and His Predecessors: The Self and the Other* (London: Routledge & Kegan Paul, 1984).

35

Socrates

John Beversluis

Socrates (470/469–399 BCE), mentor of PLATO and founder of moral philosophy, was the son of Sophroniscus (a statuary) and Phaenarete (a midwife). According to a late doxographical tradition, he followed for a time in his father's footsteps – a claim regarded as apocryphal by most scholars despite the fact that Socrates traces his ancestry to the mythical statuary Daedalus (*Euthyphro* 11b8–9). He also describes himself as an intellectual midwife who, although himself barren, delivers young men of ideas with which they are pregnant (*Theaetetus* 149a1–151d3) – an image generally believed to be Plato's middle-period description of Socrates rather than Socrates' description of himself. The husband of Xanthippe – and later, according to some sources, of Myrto – he was the father of three sons, of whom two were still infants at the time of his death.

By universal agreement, he was uncommonly ugly: flat-nosed, with protruding eyes, thick lips, and a generous girth. He dined simply, bathed infrequently, always wore the same clothes, and went about barefoot – even in the dead of winter. Possessed of remarkable powers of endurance, he could go without sleep for days, outdrink everybody without ever getting drunk, and sustain prolonged, trance-like spells of intense mental concentration. Although later reduced to poverty because of his dedication to philosophy, he was not always poor. Anyone who could spend most of his life as an unemployed intellectual inquirer but still afford to study with Prodicus and to qualify as a hoplite in the Athenian infantry – a rank which required that one be a property-owner and provide one's own weapons – must have had some financial resources to draw on.

Although intimately acquainted with Athenian intellectual and cultural life, he was mightily unimpressed with both. He had little interest in the philosophical ideas of his predecessors, he disputed the alleged wisdom and moral authority of the poets, he expressed deep misgivings about the truth of Homeric theology, he lamented the lack of virtue in public and private life, and he had a low opinion of the sophists who professed to teach it. He had an even lower opinion of the politicians, whom he denounced as panderers to public taste more interested in beautifying the city than in improving the citizenry. Contemptuous of the opinions of "the Many," he was an outspoken critic of democracy and exhorted his hearers to ignore the opinions of the ignorant and to attend only to the moral expert who knows about right and wrong (*Crito* 47c8–d3, 48a5–7). Indeed, among philosophers of classical antiquity, only Plato was more overtly anti-democratic.

Notable for his powerful intellect, he was invincible in argument and, in Xenophon's awestruck phrase, "could do what he liked with any disputant" (*Memorabilia* 1.2.14–16). In *Meno* 79e7–80b2 he is compared to a stingray who numbs people's minds and reduces them to helplessness. In *Apology* 30e1–31a1 he describes himself more positively as a gadfly trying to awaken the great Athenian steed from its intellectual and moral slumber. Despite his reputation as the paradigmatically rational man, willing to act only in accordance with the argument best supported by Reason (*Crito* 46b3–6), he attached great importance to his customary sign (*daimonion*), which gave practical guidance in the form of periodic warnings. He attached comparable importance to dreams and oracles. Indeed, were it not for one particular and well publicized oracular pronouncement, he might never have attracted the attention with which he has been showered for the past 2,500 years.

It seems that his friend Chaerephon had once asked the Delphic oracle whether anyone is wiser than Socrates and had been told that no one is. Astonished by this pronouncement, Socrates had initially tried to refute the oracle by interrogating numerous people with a reputation for wisdom – including the politicians, the poets, and the craftsmen – in hopes of finding someone wiser than himself. But he had failed. This disappointing venture had convinced him that the god was right: no one is wiser than Socrates, albeit only in the modest sense that, unlike these others, he does not claim to know what he does not know. He concluded that he had been given a divine mission to spend his life philosophizing, examining himself and others, convicting them of moral ignorance, and persuading them that they are in the same deplorable epistemic condition as he. For a variety of reasons, catalogued at some length in the *Apology*, Athens retaliated. At the age of 70, he was accused of not believing in the gods of the city, of introducing new gods, and of corrupting the youth. Found guilty, he was sentenced to death by hemlock. Having declined the chance to escape from prison, he was executed in 399.

Since Socrates wrote nothing, our knowledge of him is based wholly on the testimony of others. Anyone who undertakes to write about him must take a stand on the so-called "Socratic problem" generated by the fact that our three major sources of first-hand information – Aristophanes, Xenophon, and Plato – have handed down radically different and unreconcilable portraits. Which, if any, of these very different literary *personae* corresponds to the historical Socrates?

Scattered exceptions aside, most scholars have opted for Plato's portrait. Aristophanes was a comic poet, and his Socrates is an obvious caricature. The *Clouds* is at once a parody of Socrates and a spoof of philosophy, written for laughs rather than as a source of reliable biographical information. Xenophon, on the other hand, was a Socratic apologist. His Socrates is a serious thinker, but he is also something of a bore – an inexhaustible conduit of numbingly predictable and eminently forgettable platitudes. It is hard to understand how so innocuous a person could have attracted the likes of Alcibiades and Critias or why anyone would have bothered to execute him. Plato answers these questions. His Socrates is neither an unabashed clown nor a benign moralizer, but a disturbing philosopher-critic – exactly the sort of person his contemporaries might have judged subversive and worthy of death.

Actually, there is not one Socrates in the Platonic corpus; there are two. The first is concerned almost exclusively with ethics. This is the Socrates of the early dialogues: the *Apology, Crito, Charmides, Euthydemus, Euthyphro, Gorgias, Hippias Major, Hippias Minor, Ion, Laches, Lysis, Protagoras,* and *Republic* I. The second is equally concerned with ethics, but he is also deeply immersed in metaphysics, epistemology, logic, political philosophy, educational theory, and virtually every other area of philosophy. This is the Socrates of the middle dialogues: the *Meno, Cratylus, Phaedo, Phaedrus, Republic* II–X, *Parmenides, Symposium,* and *Theaetetus.* There are, in fact, two "Socratic problems." Unlike the first, which is traceable to the unreconcilable discrepancies between the respective portraits of Aristophanes, Xenophon, and Plato, the second is traceable to the very different but equally unreconcilable discrepancies within the Platonic corpus. Many contemporary scholars have opted for a "developmentalist" solution according to which the views espoused by the Socrates of the early dialogues are those of the historical Socrates, whereas the views espoused by his (in many respects very different) counterpart of the middle dialogues are those of Plato.

Socrates' appearance on the fifth-century Athenian scene marked a radical turning point in the development of Greek philosophy – so radical, in fact, that his predecessors are generically referred to as the *pre*-Socratics. Abandoning cosmological speculation on the ground that its physicalistic and reductionistic explanations ignore the rational determinants of human conduct (*Phaedo* 96a6–99d2), he occupied himself exclusively with practical questions. According to ARISTOTLE (*Metaphysics* 987b1–3, 1078b17–19), Socrates searched for general and universal definitions of ethical terms. The originator of the What-is-F? question – What is piety? (*Euthyphro*), What is temperance? (*Charmides*), What is courage? (*Laches*) – he objected to elucidating moral concepts by appeal to particular cases or commonly held opinions (*endoxa*) and insisted on exact definitions. According to him, any adequate definition of piety must state the common character (*eidos*) possessed by all (and only) pious actions by which they are pious. The same is true of all the other virtues. Insofar as such a definition constitutes the necessary and sufficient conditions governing the application of the term under investigation, it serves as a standard (*paradeigma*) for determining what is and what is not an instantiation of it (*Euthyphro* 6e3–6). Only such definitions enable their possessor to escape from the epistemically unstable and morally precarious state of mind called belief or opinion (*doxa*) and to attain knowledge (*epistēmē*). Aristotle adds that, unlike Plato, Socrates did not ascribe separate existence to these universals (*Metaphysics* 1078b30–2) – a remark which has prompted many scholars to conclude that the historical Socrates did not subscribe to the full-blown Theory of Forms set forth in the *Phaedo* and the middle books of the *Republic*.

Socrates achieved high visibility (and later notoriety) because of the questions with which he afflicted his contemporaries and the arguments with which he refuted them. His instrument of refutation was the Socratic elenchus – from *elenchō*, to examine or refute – that peculiarly Socratic method of argumentation which Aristotle calls "peirastic," in which the interlocutor is refuted "from [his] own beliefs" (*Sophistical Refutations* 165b3–4, *Topics* 100a29–30). The interlocutor asserts a thesis, say, *p*; Socrates thereupon elicits his assent to further theses, say *q* and *r*, and then argues that *q* and *r* entail *not-p*, the negation of the interlocutor's original assertion. Socrates' dialectical purpose is variously interpreted: according to some, he is trying to refute his interlocutor's errors; according to others, he is simply trying to demonstrate inconsistency in his interlocutor's belief-set. Whichever view one adopts, the final outcome is always the same: the interlocutor, confident at first, is inexorably reduced to *aporia* – literally, without passage or a way out. According to (the perhaps overly optimistic) Socrates, anyone reduced to this salutary state of mind will acknowledge his moral ignorance and take up the philosophical quest for the knowledge he lacks.

Plato's early dialogues reflect the Socratic conception of philosophy as a collaborative enterprise – a joint search for moral truth. By a "joint

search," Socrates does not just mean a discussion between two partici-
pants. The dialogues of philosophers like Cicero, AUGUSTINE, Anselm,
and BERKELEY satisfy *that* criterion; but they are not joint searches in
Socrates' sense. In these non-Socratic dialogues, only one participant is
searching for truth; the other participant already has it. The interlocutor plays no vital role in the discovery; he merely provides the occasion
for the philosopher to communicate truth antecedently discovered –
"To deliver a *System*," in a Humean (see HUME) phrase.

Socrates has no system. On the contrary, he disavows all knowledge.
Yet although devoid of wisdom, he is a lover of it – a searcher in search
not only of truth, but also of other searchers. Unlike other philosophers
who employ the dialogue form, Socrates refutes his interlocutors' false
beliefs not in hopes of replacing them with true ones, but in hopes of
replacing them with a desire for true ones. But he will not – indeed,
cannot – supply them himself. His primary task is to convict his interlocutors of moral ignorance and thereby render them fit dialectical part-
ners. The proximate end of philosophizing is not the discovery of truth,
but the realization that one does not have it. The etymological definition of "philosophy" as "the love of wisdom" has become so hackneyed
through repetition that it is easy to forget that it originally meant something important. As a lover of wisdom, the philosopher is distinguished
from all who claim to be wise. Philosophy is search. According to
Socrates, this is not only the best life; it is the only life. The unexamined
life is not worth living (*Apology* 38a5–6). It is in living the examined life,
rather than in enjoying the epistemic benefits which result from living
it, that the highest human happiness is to be found (*Apology* 38a1–2).
The activity of philosophizing is not a *means* to happiness, understood
as an end distinct from philosophizing and contingently connected to
it as a causal consequence; it *is* happiness.

No account of Socrates would be complete without a brief discussion
of his views. Although he disavows all knowledge, certain theses surface,
or are alluded to, so often that commentators have not hesitated to
ascribe them to him. (1) *The soul is more important than the body*. By "the
soul," Socrates does not mean some metaphysical entity distinct from
the body and capable of existing independently of it. (On the subject of
immortality, he remains an agnostic.) The soul is "that in us, whatever
it is, which is concerned with justice and injustice" (*Crito* 47e7–48a1). As
such, it is our most priceless possession and its care our most important
task. (2) *One ought never to requite evil with evil* (*Crito* 49b10–11). Since the
soul is benefited by acting justly and harmed by acting unjustly (*Crito*
47d3–5), one ought never to act unjustly – not even if one has been
treated unjustly oneself. In thus repudiating the *lex talionis*, Socrates

dissociates himself from the typically Athenian view – formally refuted in *Republic* 331e1–336a10 – that justice consists in helping one's friends and harming one's enemies. (3) *It is better to suffer than to commit injustice* (*Gorgias* 474b2–4). Since acting unjustly harms the soul of the wrongdoer, thereby damaging that in him which is concerned with justice and injustice, it is psychologically and morally preferable to endure any amount of unjust treatment than to be unjust oneself. (4) *No one errs voluntarily.* This thesis – the so-called "Socratic paradox" – constitutes the very heart of Socratic intellectualism. Since everyone desires happiness, and since the good is beneficial and the evil harmful, it follows that all desire is for the good, i.e. that no one desires evil recognized as evil, but only because it is mistakenly judged to be good (*Meno* 77b6–78b2). Hence, whoever knows what is good and what is evil will never act contrary to his knowledge (*Protagoras* 352c2–7). In a word, moral weakness (*akrasia*) is impossible; all wrongdoing is the result of ignorance. (5) *The doctrine of the unity of the virtues.* Socrates believed that the virtues constitute a unity – not in the sense that each is identical with the others, but in the sense that they are inter-entailing in such a way that one cannot have any single virtue without having all the others, e.g. one cannot be courageous without being wise (*Protagoras* 360d8–e6).

Socrates' death inspired the *Sōkratikoi logoi* – a collection of ostensibly biographical but, in fact, bewilderingly diverse and discrepancy-ridden "Socratic conversations" that contain such an indistinguishable blend of fact and fiction that even Aristotle despaired of assigning them to a precise literary genre (*Poetics* 1447b8–10). Socrates' views were subsequently championed by the so-called "Socratics," the most important of whom were Antisthenes, Aristippus, and Euclides – the founders, respectively, of the Cynic, the Cyreniac, and the Megarian Socratic "schools." Each focused on one aspect of Socrates' thought to the exclusion of the rest, and each regarded himself as the genuine perpetuator and true heir of his thought.

Bibliography

Further Reading

Benson, Hugh H.: *Essays on the Philosophy of Socrates* (New York: Oxford, 1992).
Beversluis, John: *Cross-examining Socrates: A Defense of the Interlocutors in Plato's Early Dialogues* (Cambridge: Cambridge University Press, 2000).
Brickhouse, Thomas C. and Smith, Nicholas D.: *Plato's Socrates* (New York: Oxford, 1994).

Gower, Barry S. and Stokes, Michael C.: *Socratic Questions: The Philosophy of Socrates and Its Significance* (London: Routledge, 1992).

Gulley, Norman: *The Philosophy of Socrates* (London: Macmillan, 1968).

Guthrie, W. K. C.: *Socrates* (Cambridge: Cambridge University Press, 1971).

Patzer, Andreas (ed.): *Der historische Sokrates* (Darmstadt: Wissenschaftliche Buchgesellschaft, 1987).

Plato: *Early Socratic Dialogues*, ed. Trevor J. Saunders (Harmondsworth: Penguin, 1987). [Contains *Ion, Laches, Lysis, Charmides, Hippias Major, Hippias Minor, Euthydemus.*]

——: *Gorgias*, trans. with notes T. Irwin (Oxford: Clarendon Press, 1979).

——: *Protagoras*, trans. with notes C. C. W. Taylor (Oxford: Clarendon Press, 1976).

——: *The Trial and Death of Socrates*, trans. G. M. A. Grube (Indianapolis: Hackett, 1975).

Santas, Gerasimos: *Socrates, Philosophy in Plato's Early Dialogues* (Boston: Routledge & Kegan Paul, 1979).

Taylor, A. E.: *Socrates* (Edinburgh: Peter Davies, 1932).

Vlastos, Gregory (ed.): *The Philosophy of Socrates. A Collection of Critical Essays* (Garden City, NY: Doubleday, 1971).

——: *Socrates, Ironist and Moral Philosopher* (Ithaca, NY: Cornell University Press, 1991).

36

Spinoza

Genevieve Lloyd

Benedict de Spinoza (1632–1677 CE) has been a figure of some notoriety in the history of Western philosophy. Born in Amsterdam, into a community of Marrano Jews from Portugal, the young Spinoza had an uneasy relationship to both Christianity and Judaism. In 1656, he was excommunicated by the Amsterdam synagogue for unorthodox views on God, prophecy, the human soul, and immortality. He lived a reclusive life, supporting himself through work as a lens grinder, and died of consumption – a death which HEGEL, in his *Lectures on the History of Philosophy*, described as "in harmony with his system of philosophy, according to which all particularity and individuality pass away in the one substance" (Hegel, 1974, p. 254). Spinoza's writings were rejected as atheistic by his early critics. In the next century, especially in Germany, their reception was more ambivalent. His alleged identification of God and the world was caught up in debates about pantheism – the doctrine that God and Nature are identical – and Spinozism became an important strand in the development of Romanticism.

Spinoza's thought had less influence on the development of the dominant streams in modern academic philosophy than that of his contemporary, René DESCARTES. However, more recent philosophy has seen a convergence of interest in Spinoza's philosophy from diverse perspectives. Edwin Curley's excellent translations have made Spinoza more accessible to English-speaking readers, making his insights more readily assimilated into discussion of a range of topics on the agenda of contemporary academic philosophy. For example, Spinoza's treatment of the mind as idea of the body – expressing in thought the same reality that is expressed also as body – has posed important challenges to modern classifications of philosophical views on the mind–body relation. Because Spinoza claims that minds and bodies equally express, in different ways, the same reality, his doctrine cannot be equated with either idealism or materialism. Yet the status of mind and matter as irreducibly different attributes of the same substance – different and equal ways of understanding what is fundamentally the same reality – makes it also difficult to assimilate the doctrine to an "identity" theory, according to which the mental could be defined in terms of the physical. Modern European philosophy has emphasized other aspects of Spinoza's philosophy – highlighting especially his integration of reason, emotion and imagination, and the dynamic character of his treatment of individual existence and of collective power (see especially Deleuze, 1978; Negri, 1981; Montag and Stolze, 1997).

Among Spinoza's early writings are the unfinished *Treatise on the Emendation of the Intellect*, which was included in the works published posthumously in 1677, and the *Short Treatise on God, Man and His Well-being*, which was published only in the nineteenth century. The *Short Treatise* deals with many of the themes of the later and better known *Ethics*, and exhibits the integration of metaphysical and ethical concerns that is a distinctive feature of Spinoza's mature philosophy. His metaphysical views – often startling and apparently outrageous – grew out of his early commentary on Descartes's *Principles of Philosophy*, to which he appended a brief treatment of key doctrines in scholastic philosophy, the *Metaphysical Thoughts*. The *Tractatus Theologico Politicus*, published in 1670, deals with issues of textual interpretation, prophecy, and miracles, as well as more obviously political issues of power and freedom. It was the hostile reception to this work that prompted Spinoza's decision not to publish the *Ethics* during his lifetime.

The *Ethics* was written over an extended period, and commentators – especially Gilles Deleuze and Antonio Negri – have emphasized the significance for the character of this work of its interruption by the more directly political concerns of the *Tractatus Theologico Politicus*. What results is a novel integration of abstract definitions of metaphysical concepts such as *substance, attributes*, and *modes*, with reflection on ideals of freedom, virtue, and the eternity of the mind. Spinoza's other political work, the *Political Treatise*, in which he compares and evaluates rival systems of government, was unfinished at the time of his death.

Spinoza is usually classified as a "rationalist" philosopher – committed to the primacy of pure reasoning in the pursuit of knowledge, and to grounding certainty in deductions from supposedly self-evident definitions and principles. But although much of his philosophy developed out of the work of his fellow rationalist, Descartes, it also incorporates elements from ancient and medieval philosophy – from ARISTOTLE, the Stoics, and Maimonides – as well as from another of his contemporaries, Thomas HOBBES. The diverse range of Spinoza's sources is documented in Harry Wolfson's study of Spinoza. But, as Wolfson stresses, Spinoza creatively transformed his sources into radically new and often unsettling ideas. His originality as a philosopher is expressed in this extraordinary capacity to adapt old concepts and themes to yield new and controversial theses. This is particularly striking in Spinoza's transformation of his Cartesian sources.

Descartes had treated mind and matter as different "substances" – separately existing and divinely created distinct kinds of being. For Spinoza, mind and matter become different "attributes" of the one Substance – different ways in which the one reality can be truly apprehended – and this unique Substance is identified with God or Nature. This God is clearly something very different from religious ideas of a benign Creator who can be held responsible for the existence of the world and for human well-being. Spinoza's God acts not from any free will directed toward ends or goals, but from necessity. A God who acts for the sake of achieving ends, Spinoza argues, would have to be less than perfect; for there would be something which he lacks. The perfect God must express his perfection in the totality of causally connected finite things which make up the world – the total expression of God under the attribute of matter. But this way of construing divine necessity has a further consequence: although finite things depend on God for their existence, the causal relations which connect them with one another to make up the actually existing world must also be necessary. This actual world is the only one possible.

This shift in the concept of God has startling implications for the status of individual human minds. Descartes had of course seen individual minds as causally dependent for their being on God, their Creator. But each mind had its own existence as a separately existing individual substance. For Spinoza, the individual mind becomes just one of many modes – a particular modification of Substance, expressed under the attribute of thought. Rather than standing alone as a separate entity, the mind becomes, as Spinoza provocatively puts it, an "idea" in "the mind of God." Individual bodies are likewise modes of that same God or Substance, expressed as "extension" or matter; and each mind, as an "idea," has such a body as its primary object of awareness.

Spinoza's audacious transformation of the traditional understanding of God and of human minds was central to the hostile reception of his work. His early critics saw his doctrine of the uniqueness of Substance as downgrading God. Although Spinoza insisted that his God was expressed not only as matter and as thought, but also under an infinity of other attributes, he was perceived as committed to reducing the nature of God to that of the material world, and hence as guilty of an atheistic pantheism. Hegel's interpretation was more subtle. Spinozism, he suggested, might be better termed "Acosmism," since it ascribes reality ultimately to God alone: "The allegations of those who accuse Spinoza of atheism are the direct opposite of the truth; with him there is too much God" (Hegel, 1974, pp. 281–2).

Hegel gave eloquent expression to a way of thinking of Spinoza's "monism" which has persisted into more recent commentary. His Spinoza is committed to an all-encompassing wholeness of being, in which individual existence disappears. In Hegel's colourful presentation of the implications of Spinozism, everything particular and determinate is cast into the "abyss of the one identity," where it ceases to be distinguishable from anything else. This view of Spinoza as the philosopher of the abyss is in some ways misleading. Although they are no longer individual substances, particular bodies are distinguished from one another in terms of the preservation of dynamic ratios – different rhythms, as it were – of motion and rest. Finite individuals strive to persist in being as particular proportions of bodily movement. Such striving is for Spinoza their very essence. The existence of individual bodies is enhanced by contact with other bodies – other proportions of motion and rest – which are congenial to them; and they are obstructed by other, less congenial, impinging essences. Minds, as ideas of bodies, also strive to persist as ever clearer articulations of their own bodies as part of nature. This crucial concept of bodily and mental striving – *conatus* – is the basis for Spinoza's development of an ethic centered on the joyful pursuit, individually and collectively, of whatever enhances human self-preservation and thriving.

Some of the most important and vexed interpretative issues posed by Spinoza's philosophy concern his treatment of the relations between "inadequate" and "adequate" knowledge, and especially of the relations between reason and imagination. His treatment of body as an attribute of substance – and hence as of equal metaphysical status to mind – gives imagination, as the awareness of body, a new importance. Both imagination and reason are grounded in the complex structure of the human body, which allows it to retain traces of past interactions with other bodies. This makes it possible for the mind to compare different ideas, grasping what is common to all bodies in ideas that are not tied to any particular body. Such ideas Spinoza calls "common notions": corresponding to what bodies have in common, they can be said also to be common to all minds. So although the awareness of body is the source of the confusions of imagination – when we draw conclusions about the natures of things from the way they affect us when they happen to impinge on our own bodies – it also makes possible higher forms of knowledge that are not tied to the constant presence of the objects known.

There are important connections between Spinoza's treatment of knowledge in the *Ethics* and his political writings. He sees the ideal life of reason as counterpoised to the life of the "multitude," who are dominated by imagination and the passions, especially fear and hope. But the power of reason over imagination and the passions centers on its capacity to understand their operation in individual and social life – including the collective fears and hopes which he discusses in the political works. The understanding of the role of religious ideas in collective life is for Spinoza also closely connected with the concerns of political philosophy. His most important political work, the *Tractatus Theologico Politicus*, includes discussion of prophecy, miracles, and divine law, and of the correct methods for interpreting scriptural texts, as well as of the nature of political institutions. This integration of religious and political themes can be perplexing for modern readers. But Spinoza's concern with understanding the operations of imagination and emotion forms a connecting thread through the apparently disparate topics.

The power of reason to understand and hence transform the operations of imagination and the passions is central also to Spinoza's treatment of human freedom. He sees freedom as residing not in a faculty of free will, able to control the non-rational, but in an understanding of the necessities that govern human beings as part of nature. The belief in human free will is an illusion arising from ignorance of the causes of our actions, and the belief in divine purpose is also an illusion – a retreat, as Spinoza puts it in the appendix to part one of the *Ethics*, to the "sanctuary of ignorance." Belief in a divine will breeds the superstitious belief that everything happens in accordance with a benign providence concerned with human well-being. Belief in human will also misleads us, encouraging us to think of ourselves as somehow exempt from the causal forces that determine the necessities of the rest of the world.

The picture of a world devoid of will and purpose may seem a bleak one. But Spinoza – developing themes from ancient stoicism – reconstructs freedom as understanding and joyfully acquiescing in necessity. The understanding of the passions is also their remedy, taking us from bondage into freedom. For Spinoza the passions are by definition states of passivity – deprivations of power and activity. But to the extent that the mind understands those states of passivity it moves into a greater state of activity; and this for Spinoza is the state of joy. Understanding the passions is the path to freedom and virtue – to a life of active, rational emotion. In the free life of reason, human beings seek their own preservation and thriving, with a joy that by-passes the need for external authority. But because we are unavoidably part of nature, unable to fully grasp the totality of our relations with other things, such ideal freedom can be only imperfectly achieved.

It is a distinctive feature of Spinoza's version of rationalism that he commits himself to a form of knowledge higher than reason. Reason is superior to imagination, but it is itself inferior to what Spinoza calls "intuitive knowledge." This highest form of knowledge is distinguished from reason by its capacity to take things in "in one glance," and by the fact that it understands things in relation to God, the unique Substance, on which they depend. Through intuitive knowledge the mind also comes to an understanding of itself as eternal.

The doctrine of the eternity of the mind unfolds in the concluding sections of the *Ethics*. Some commentators dismiss these sections as impenetrable; others see them as the high point of the *Ethics*, where Spinoza's elaboration of the concepts of *substance*, *attributes*, and *modes* issues in profound insights into the well lived life. These passages illuminate the interactions between reason, imagination, and emotion in Spinoza's version of wisdom. Intuitive knowledge is inseparable from a powerful emotion – the "intellectual love of God." When the mind comes to understand its own status as a modification of God, this transition to greater understanding brings with it a joy that is comprised in God's eternal love of himself. By coming to a fuller understanding of its own finitude, the mind grasps itself as eternal. In that apparent paradox, the concluding sections of the *Ethics* offers a reconciliation of intellect, imagination, and emotion in a unified vision of the mind that undercuts the oppositions – often associated with seventeenth-century rationalism – between reason and supposedly lesser aspects of mental life.

Bibliography

Writings

Descartes' Principles of Philosophy with Appendix, Containing Metaphysical Thoughts (1663). In *The Collected Works of Spinoza, volume I*, ed. and trans. Edwin Curley (Princeton, NJ: Princeton University Press, 1985).

A Theologico-political Treatise (1670), trans. R. H. M. Elwes (New York: Dover, 1951).

Ethics (1677). In *The Collected Works of Spinoza, volume 1*, ed. and trans. Edwin Curley (Princeton, NJ: Princeton University Press, 1985). [Note: the *Ethics* and selections from Spinoza's other works are included also in *A Spinoza Reader*, ed. and trans. Edwin Curley (Princeton, NJ: Princeton University Press, 1994).

A Political Treatise (1677), trans. R. H. M. Elwes (New York: Dover, 1951).

Treatise on the Emendation of the Intellect (1677). In *The Collected Works of Spinoza, volume 1*, ed. and trans. Edwin Curley (Princeton, NJ: Princeton University Press, 1985).

Short Treatise on God, Man and His Well-being. In *The Collected Works of Spinoza, volume 1*, ed. and trans. Edwin Curley (Princeton, NJ: Princeton University Press, 1985).

Further reading

Allison, Henry: *Benedict de Spinoza: An Introduction*, rev. edn (New Haven, CT, and London: Yale University Press, 1987).

Bennett, Jonathan: *A Study of Spinoza's Ethics* (Cambridge: Cambridge University Press, 1984).

Curley Edwin: *Spinoza's Metaphysics: An Essay in Interpretation* (Cambridge: Cambridge University Press, 1969).

——: *Behind the Geometrical Method: A Reading of Spinoza's Ethics* (Princeton, NJ: Princeton University Press, 1988).

Deleuze, Gilles: *Spinoza: Practical Philosophy*, trans. Robert Hurley (San Francisco: City Lights Books, 1988).

Donagan, Alan: *Spinoza* (Chicago: Chicago University Press, 1988).

Gatens, Moira and Lloyd, Genevieve: *Collective Imaginings: Spinoza, Past and Present* (London and New York: Routledge, 1999).

Hegel, Georg W. F.: *Lectures on the History of Philosophy, volume 3*, trans. E. S. Haldane and F. H. Stimson (London: Routledge & Kegan Paul, 1974).

Lloyd, Genevieve: *Part of Nature: Self-knowledge in Spinoza's Ethics* (Ithaca, NY: Cornell University Press, 1994).

——: *Spinoza and the Ethics* (London and New York: Routledge, 1996).

Montag, Warren and Stolze, Ted: *The New Spinoza* (Minneapolis and London: University of Minnesota Press, 1997).

Nadler, Steven: *Spinoza: A Life* (Cambridge: Cambridge University Press, 1999).

Negri, Antonio: *The Savage Anomaly: the Power of Spinoza's Metaphysics and Politics*, trans. Michael Hardt (Minneapolis: University of Minnesota Press, 1991).

Wolfson, Harry A.: *The Philosophy of Spinoza* (New York: Meridian, 1934, 1958).

37

Wittgenstein

P. M. S. Hacker

Ludwig Wittgenstein (1889–1951 CE) was the leading analytical philosopher of the twentieth century. His two philosophical masterpieces, the *Tractatus Logico-philosophicus* (1921) and the posthumous *Philosophical Investigations* (1953), changed the course of the subject. The first was the primary origin of the "linguistic turn" in philosophy and inspired both logical positivism and Cambridge analysis in the interwar years. The second shifted analytic philosophy away from the paradigm of depth-analysis defended in the *Tractatus* and cultivated by logical positivists and Cambridge analysts toward the different conception of "connective analysis," which was a primary inspiration of Oxford analytic philosophy and dominated the third quarter of the century. Wittgenstein is unique in the annals of philosophy for having produced two equally influential, diametrically opposed, philosophies. His work, in both phases of his career, is marked by its originality, subtlety, and stylistic brilliance. By nature an aphorist, he strove to crystallize his thoughts in short and often gnomic remarks of great power, which make considerable demands upon his readers.

Born in Vienna to a wealthy and cultured family of Jewish origin, he studied engineering in Berlin and Manchester. Attracted by the new logic of FREGE and RUSSELL and fascinated by its philosophical implications, he went to Cambridge to work with Russell in 1911. The work he did there marks the beginning of his seven years labour on the *Tractatus*. He served in the Austrian army during the First World War, completing his book while on active service. Convinced that he had solved the central problems with which he had been concerned, he abandoned philosophy and worked as a primary school teacher from 1920 to 1926. The next two years were spent designing and building a mansion in Vienna for his sister. The house, which still stands, is austerely beautiful. During these years, he came into contact with Moritz Schlick, the moving spirit behind the Vienna Circle, members of which had studied the *Tractatus* in detail. The book, and Wittgenstein's conversations with Schlick, Waismann, and more briefly with Carnap and Feigl, exerted great influence upon the evolution of logical positivism.

In 1929 Wittgenstein returned to Cambridge to resume philosophical work. Although he had initially intended to continue working in the vein of the *Tractatus*, he rapidly found deep flaws in his first philosophy. Between 1929 and 1932 his thought underwent profound revolution. He undermined the supporting members of the edifice of his earlier ideas and laid the foundations for his new method and its application both to the range of problems in the *Tractatus* and to the philosophy of mathematics and philosophical psychology. Over the next decade and a half, he consolidated and developed his new ideas, which he communicated in his now legendary classes to his pupils in Cambridge. Through them, and through the circulation of their lecture notes, he revolutionized philosophy at mid-century. He was appointed to a chair at Cambridge in 1939. During the war, he worked first as a hospital orderly in London and later as a laboratory assistant doing research on wound shock in Newcastle. He completed the *Philosophical Investigations* in 1946, but did not publish it. In 1947 he resigned his chair in order to concentrate upon writing. He died of cancer in Cambridge in 1951, leaving behind a voluminous *Nachlass* of some 20,000 pages. The *Investigations* was published in 1953 and was immediately hailed as a masterwork. Over the next decades a further dozen unfinished works and four volumes of lecture notes taken by his students were published.

The first phase of Wittgenstein's career consisted in responding to, and bringing to its zenith, an antecedent tradition of metaphysical and logical reflection upon the relationship between thought, language, and reality. The influences upon him were primarily Frege and Russell, but also Schopenhauer and the two philosopher-scientists Hertz and Boltzmann. Other general cultural influences that he acknowledged were the writings of Karl Kraus, Adolf Loos, Paul Ernst, and Otto Weininger. A later influence was Oswald Spengler. Some of these figures were influential largely in the manner of Rorschach spots – one or two sentences that they had written served Wittgenstein as seeds for the development of his own ideas. The second phase of Wittgenstein's career, which culminated with the *Investigations*, is virtually without precedent in the history of philosophy. It arose, phoenix-like, out of the ashes of the *Tractatus*.

The Tractatus Logico-philosophicus

Two general themes dominate the *Tractatus*. First is the nature of representation, the relation between thought, language, and reality, and the limits of thought and representation. Second is the nature of logic and logical truth. The two are intimately interwoven, since logic is conceived to be a condition of sense. The metaphysical presuppositions of logic are at the same time the metaphysical presuppositions of representation in general. Logic does not presuppose the existence of any logical facts or logical objects, let alone any logical experience, as Frege and Russell supposed. But it does presuppose that names have meanings and that propositions have sense. The meanings of simple (logically proper) names, which are the final residue of logical analysis, are simple sempiternal objects in reality. The sense of an elementary proposition, which is a combination of names in accord with logical syntax and which is logically independent of any other proposition, is the possible state of affairs that the proposition depicts and the existence of which it asserts.

The *Tractatus* opens by delineating a crystalline metaphysics. The world is the totality of facts, not of things. The totality of things (simple objects) of which the world consists constitutes the indestructible substance of all possible worlds. Because the *Tractatus* is a treatise on logic, Wittgenstein gives little clue in the book as to what kinds of items simple objects are – that would belong to a treatise on the application of logic. But it is clear from his notebooks, both before and after the writing of the book, that the kinds of things he had in mind are spatio-temporal points, simple unanalyzable perceptual qualities (minimally discriminable shades of color, sounds, degrees of hardness, etc.) as well as relations. Objects have both form and content. The form of an object consists in its combinatorial possibilities with other objects (a color can concatenate with a spatio-temporal point but not with a sound). The combinatorial possibilities of an object are its internal properties. These determine the ontological category of the object. Different objects that share the same form, e.g. different shades of color, belong to the same ontological category, e.g. color. The actual combinations of an object with other objects, e.g. a shade of color with specific spatio-temporal points, are its external, contingent properties. A possible concatenation of objects constitutes a state of affairs. The obtaining or non-obtaining of a state of affairs is a fact. The totality of positive and negative facts constitutes reality.

A representation of a state of affairs is a model or picture. In it, elements of the picture go proxy for the elements (objects) represented, and their arrangement in accord with conventions of representation represents the arrangement of the items in a possible state of affairs. Such a picture is true (or correct) if things in reality are arranged as it represents them as being. A picture must possess the same logical multiplicity as, and be isomorphic with, what it represents. Propositions are a special case of representation – they are logical pictures. It is of the essence of propositions not merely to be bivalent (i.e. either true or false, as Russell supposed) but to be bipolar – to be capable of being true and capable of being false. This insight lies at the heart of the *Tractatus*. In this way, propositions reflect the nature of what they represent, for it is of the nature of states of affairs that they may obtain or not obtain. An elementary proposition depicts an atomic state of affairs. It consists of simple names, which are the points at which language is connected to reality. The meanings of the simple names are the simple objects in reality for which they go proxy. The logico-syntactical form of a simple name mirrors the metaphysical form of the object in reality that is its meaning. So the logico-syntactical combinatorial possibilities of names mirror the metaphysical combinatorial possibilities of objects. Hence what can be described in language coincides with what is possible in reality. In this sense, the *Tractatus* espouses a form of modal realism. What is metaphysically possible in reality is language-independent, but is necessarily reflected in what makes sense in language. The bounds of sense necessarily coincide with the limits of possible worlds.

Pace Frege, propositions are not names. They do not have a meaning, do not stand for or go proxy for things. Propositions are sentences in their projective relation to the world. They have a sense (or direction); they represent (point towards) a possibility in reality and say that it obtains. A proposition agrees or disagrees with reality, depending on whether it is true or false. It is true if things in reality are as it represents them as being, otherwise it is false. Its sense is independent of whether it is true or false. To understand a proposition is to know what is the case if it is true and also what is the case if it is false, and one can understand it without knowing whether it is true or false. In a proposition, what represents is the *fact* that its constituent names are concatenated as they are. A metaphysics of symbolism informs the *Tractatus*. Only simple names can stand for simple objects. Only relations can represent relations; so in the proposition "*aRb*" it is not "R" that says that *a* stands in the relation R to *b*, but rather *that* "*a*" stands to the left of "R" and "*b*" to the right that says that *aRb*. And only facts (i.e. propositions) represent facts. The sense of a proposition, the state of affairs which it depicts, is a function of the meanings of its constituent names. Sense must be absolutely determinate, as otherwise the law of excluded middle will not apply (and the propositional sign will not express a bipolar proposition). Hence any vagueness in the propositions of ordinary language must be a feature of the surface grammar, which will disappear on analysis. Any indeterminacy must be determinately indeterminate and will be seen to

be so on analysis, which will reveal the proposition in question to be analyzable into a disjunction of determinate possibilities. The essence of the
proposition is given by the general propositional form, which is: "This
is how things are," i.e. the general form of a description of how things
stand in reality. In general, the essence of words is to name objects in
reality, and the essence of propositions is to describe how things stand.

The picture theory of thought and proposition gave a profound
answer to the fundamental problems of the intentionality of thought
and language. When one thinks that a is F, then the object of one's
thought is a – one's thought reaches right out to a and to none other.
One's thought is intrinsically individuated by its content, e.g. that a is F.
If one's thought is true, then it reaches right up to reality, and does not
fall short of what is the case, namely that a is F. What one thinks is precisely what is the case. Hence what one thinks cannot be a mental representation (e.g. an array of ideas in one's mind or an abstract object
such as a Fregean *Gedanke*), for then what one thinks would not be what
is the case if one's thought is true. Nevertheless, one's thought may be
false. But what one thinks (the content of one's thought) remains the
same whether one thinks truly or falsely. So how can one's thought be
identical with what is the case if it is true, and also be independent of
what is the case – if one's thought is false? Furthermore, what one thinks
when one thinks falsely is precisely what is *not* the case. But if what one
thinks when one's thought is false does not actually exist, how can one
think it? It seems that thought predetermines reality "give or take a Yes
or No" – that there is a pre-established harmony between thought and
reality. For if one's thought is true then what one thinks is what is the
case, and if one's thought is false then what one thinks is *that* which is
not the case. Accordingly, thought as it were prepares a mold for reality,
leaving it but two options, to fill it or to leave it empty. What must
thought and reality be like for this harmony to obtain? Further difficulties attend the intentionality of language. One gives expression to
one's thought by a sentence, e.g. "a is F," and the name "a" refers precisely to a and no other, just as the sentence describes precisely what is
the case if what one says is true. But how can mere signs, noises, or marks
on paper represent something? How can one part of reality, as it were,
represent something? How can signs reach beyond themselves and refer
to a long vanished or future object and describe a state of affairs that is
not present and indeed may never obtain?

The modal realist metaphysics of the *Tractatus* and the metaphysics
of symbolism of the picture theory were tailored to resolve this battery
of problems. What is represented by a true proposition is exactly the

same as what is represented by a false one – namely a state of affairs (which may or may not obtain). What is asserted by a true proposition is exactly the same as what is denied by the assertion of its negation. This is possible because the proposition is a picture or model of reality, and internally related to what it represents, i.e. a state of affairs, irrespective of whether things are as it asserts them to be. Precisely because the names of which propositions on analysis consist go proxy for the objects that are their meanings and because their logico-syntactical form mirrors the metaphysical form of the objects, the combination of names in a proposition represents the *possibility* of the objects they stand for being correspondingly combined in a fact. In a proposition a (possible) state of affairs is put together experimentally. So a proposition is literally a model (picture) of a possibility. It is true if the possibility represented obtains, otherwise it is false. This explains how it is that *what* we think is the same irrespective of whether our thought is true or false. It also explains how it is that "p" and "$\sim p$" *represent* the same state of affairs, the former asserting its existence and the latter denying it. An immediate consequence is that negation does not characterize the sense of "$\sim p$," i.e. it does not *characterize* that which is or is not the case and which is represented by "p." It does not stand for something in reality (*pace* Frege and Russell, who conceived of the negation sign as standing for a function or logical object) which is a feature of what is the case. Negation is an operation, not a function. It, as it were, reverses the sense of a proposition. The assertion of "p" expresses agreement with what is represented, i.e. with the state of affairs represented, and says that it obtains; the assertion of "$\sim p$" expresses disagreement with what is represented, and says that it does not obtain. The proposition must *guarantee* the possibility of the fact the existence of which it asserts. It does so by virtue of sharing a logical form with what it represents and by virtue of its constituent names being connected to the constituents of the possibility represented. Whether things are as they are represented as being depends upon whether the state of affairs depicted obtains. The metaphysics of symbolism and the ontology of atomism ensure the harmony between thought, language, and reality. Thought and its expression have a content which is identical with what *can* be the case, and coincide with what is the case if they are true. The correlation of names and their meanings is psychological, effected by acts of meaning by such and such a name *this* ☞ object. We use the propositional sign as a projection of a possible situation. The method of projection is thinking the sense of the proposition, i.e. when we use the propositional sign "p" to say what we think, we think *that p*, so we mean by the sign *the state of affairs that p*, which *is* its sense. So the intentionality of language is extrinsic, derivative from the intrinsic intentionality of mental acts of meaning and thinking.

The logical analysis of propositions must terminate in elementary propositions which are logically independent of each other, i.e. have no entailments. Their truth depends only on the existence and non-existence of atomic states of affairs. Elementary propositions can be combined to form molecular propositions by means of the logical connectives. These devices are not names of logical entities (as Frege and Russell supposed), but truth-functional operators which generate truth-dependencies between propositions. The logical connectives are interdefinable, and can be reduced to the single operation of joint negation. All possible propositions can be generated by means of joint negation of elementary propositions (the thesis of extensionality). All logical relations (of implication, incompatibility, or compatibility) result from the inner complexity of molecular propositions, i.e. the truth functional combination of their constituent propositions. The sense of a molecular proposition is a function of the senses of its constituent elementary propositions. It is determined by the truth functional form of their combination, which fixes the truth conditions of the molecular proposition, i.e. the conditions which the molecular proposition must satisfy in order to be true. There are two limiting cases of truth functional combination, namely tautologies and contradictions. These are the propositions of logic. Since negation is given by the mere bipolarity of the proposition and conjunction by the mere possibility of successive assertion, all the propositions of logic flow from the essence of the proposition as such. Tautologies and contradictions are limiting cases of truth-functional combination inasmuch as they are no longer bipolar. They have no truth conditions, for tautologies are unconditionally true and contradictions unconditionally false. They are well formed but degenerate propositions (in the sense in which a point is a degenerate case of a conic section). A tautology is true under every assignment of truth values to its constituent propositions, so it excludes no possibility; a contradiction is false under every such assignment, so it excludes every possibility. So they are both senseless; they have, as it were, zero sense. They say nothing at all. But this vacuous logical necessity is the only form of expressible necessity. So it cannot be argued that while the empirical sciences investigate the domain of contingent truth, philosophy is an *a priori* science which investigates the domain of necessity. The degenerate truths of logic are not a field in which pure reason alone can attain knowledge about reality, for to know the truth of a tautology is to know nothing about how things stand in reality.

This conception of logical truth was revolutionary. Psychological logicians (e.g. B. Erdmann) had argued that the laws of logic describe the ways human beings are constrained by the nature of their minds to think. Platonists (e.g. Frege) held that the laws of logic describe completely general logical relations between abstract entities which exist in a "third realm." Russell believed that they describe the most general facts in the universe. It was thus held that logic had a proper subject matter of its own, that it was the science of the completely general, and that logical investigation could result in genuine knowledge. The *Tractatus* rejected all these views. The mark of a logical proposition is not, as Frege and Russell had supposed, absolute generality. Logical truths are tautologies, not generalizations of tautologies: either it is raining or it is not raining is as legitimate a logical truth as any, and "(p) $(p \lor \sim p)$" is not even a well formed proposition (since it employs the formal concept of a proposition; see below). Moreover, all the propositions of logic say the same thing, namely nothing. So there is no logical *knowledge* to be attained, merely the transformation of one vacuous tautology into another. But different tautologies exhibit different patterns of internal relations between propositions.

Unlike the vacuous propositions of logic, metaphysical utterances are nonsense – they transgress the bounds of sense. For the categorial concept-words which occur in them – "object," "fact," "name," "proposition," "colour," "space," etc. – are not genuine concept-words but variables which cannot occur in a fully analyzed well formed proposition. They represent the constant form of their values. But what one tries to say by means of the pseudo-propositions of metaphysics, e.g. that space is three-dimensional or that red is a color, is *shown* by features (the forms of the constituent names) of genuine propositions, e.g. that a is located at point x_l, y_m, z_n, or that that point is red. What is shown by a notation cannot be said. Truths of metaphysics are ineffable; and so too are truths of ethics, aesthetics, and religion. Just as KANT circumscribed the limits of knowledge to make room for faith, Wittgenstein circumscribed the bounds of language in order to make room for ineffable metaphysics.

An immediate consequence is that there can be no philosophical propositions, i.e. propositions describing the essential natures of things or the metaphysical structure of the world. So the very propositions of the *Tractatus* itself are condemned as nonsense – as attempts to say what can only be shown. Their role was to lead one to a correct logical point of view. Once that is attained, one can throw away the ladder up which one has climbed. Hence philosophy is not a science. Indeed, it is not a cognitive discipline at all. The results of philosophy are not new knowledge, but philosophical understanding. The future task of philosophy is to monitor the bounds of sense, to clarify philosophically problematic sentences, and to show that attempts to say something metaphysical transgress the bounds of what can significantly be said.

The Philosophical Investigations

The *Investigations* is the precipitate of sixteen years of reflection, which began with Wittgenstein's dismantling of the edifice of the *Tractatus*. He had wanted the book to be published together with the *Tractatus*, so that the two styles of thought could be seen in juxtaposition. The contrast could not be greater. A considerable part of the *Investigations* is concerned explicitly or implicitly with criticizing fundamental commitments not only of the *Tractatus* but also of the whole tradition of philosophical thought of which it was the culmination, and replacing them by a profoundly different conception.

The idea that the meaning of a name is the object it stands for was misconceived. The very idea involves a misuse of the word "meaning," for the meaning of a word is not an object of any kind. There is no such thing as *the* name-relation, and it was misconceived to think that the essence of words is to name something, for words have indefinitely many roles. Although words may be connected to reality in all manner of ways (one may stick a label on a bottle on which is written "Shake before use," wear a name-label on one's lapel, print the name of a book on its cover, hang an "Enter" notice on a door, etc.), none of them determines the meaning of a word; they presuppose it. Words are not connected to reality by semantic links at all. The supposition that they are derives from a misapprehension of ostensive definition, which connects a word with a *sample*, as when one explains what a color word means, e.g. "This ☞ ■ color is black." But the sample invoked is an instrument of language and belongs to the means of representation, not to what is represented. For the ostensive definition does not *describe* anything, but gives a rule for the use of the word "black." It is akin to a substitution rule, for instead of saying "My shoes are black" one can say "My shoes are *this* ☞ ■ color" (employing the sample, ostensive gesture, and phrase "this color" in place of the word "black"). Ostensive definition provides no exit from language. The idea that all words are either definable by analytic definition in terms of necessary and sufficient conditions of application or indefinable was an illusion. There are many different ways of explaining words (e.g. by a series of examples together with a similarity rider, by paraphrase or contrastive paraphrase, by exemplification, by ostension) and not all words are or need to be sharply defined. The demand for determinacy of sense was incoherent, for vagueness is not always a defect and there is no absolute standard of exactness. The terms "simple" and "complex" had been misused, for they are relative not absolute terms, and what is to count as simple or complex must be laid down from case to case. We must not mistake the absence of any criteria of complexity for the satisfaction of the criteria of simplicity. We must recognize the existence of family resemblance concepts, which are united not by characteristic marks (necessary and sufficient conditions of application) but by partially overlapping similarities. In particular, we should note that many central philosophical concepts, such as *proposition, name, language, number,* have no essence, but are family resemblance concepts.

Accordingly, the idea of a general propositional form was illusory, confusing a humdrum propositional variable used, for example, for purposes of anaphoric reference, as in "He told me his tale, said that *that was how things were,* and asked for a loan," with a general form of all propositions. (No one would be tempted to say that the phrase "that's the way the cookie crumbles," which colloquially serves a similar purpose, represents the general form of the proposition.) Propositions have no (non-trivial) common essence, for there are many different kinds of structure which we call "propositions": avowals of experience (such as "I have a pain" or "It hurts"), avowals of intent, ordinary empirical propositions, hypotheses, expressions of laws of nature, logical and mathematical propositions, "grammatical propositions" (in Wittgenstein's idiosyncratic use of this term) which are expressions of rules (such as "red is a color" or "the chess king moves one square at a time"), ethical and aesthetic propositions, and so on. The variegated members of this large family do not possess a shared essence; each kind of case must be scrutinized in its own right. Bipolarity is a feature of an important member of the family, but not a defining property of propositions as such. It was misconceived to suppose that the essential function of the proposition is to describe. For the roles of many kinds of propositions, such as logical and mathematical propositions or avowals of experience or many ethical propositions, are not to describe. Moreover, even when propositions have a descriptive role, one must bear in mind that there are many *logical* differences among descriptions, as is evident when one compares describing a scene with describing the impression of a scene, or describing what one imagines with describing what is the case, etc. Accordingly, it was misconceived to think of logic as flowing from the essential nature of the elementary proposition or as reflecting the logical structure of the world. Tautologies are indeed vacuous. They say nothing, but they are correlates of rules of inference, i.e. truth-value preserving rules for the transformation of propositions. They are autonomous, free-floating, and have no justification, neither ineffable nor effable. But they are held in place by the fact that they are constitutive of what we count as thinking, reasoning, and inferring.

A language is not a calculus of rules together with an array of indefinable names from which all significant sentences (and their truth conditions) can be generated. It is a human institution embedded in a distinctive form of life, grafted upon natural forms of human behavior. It can be elucidated only by attending to the use of words and sentences in the stream of human life. The meaning of an expression is what is given by an explanation of meaning. Explanations of meaning, of a humdrum and familiar kind, explain the use of expressions, and as such constitute rules for the use of the explanandum (at least in the context in question). Hence, too, the meaning of an expression is what one understands when one understands an expression and knows what it means. Understanding is internally related to meaning. It is an ability, the mastery of the technique of the use of an expression. It is exhibited in using an expression correctly, in explaining what it means, and in responding appropriately to its use. These are severally criteria of understanding. Far from making the notion of truth and truth conditions central to the notion of meaning, Wittgenstein made the notions of use, explanation of meaning, and understanding pivotal.

The conception of depth analysis which informed the *Tractatus* is relegated to a minor role. Analysis can yield nothing that is not evident in the practices of the uses of words. For nothing can be hidden in the domain of grammar, i.e. the domain of the rules for the use of words which we follow in our linguistic practices. For there is no such thing as following (as opposed to acting in accord with) a rule with which we are unacquainted. Rules for the use of words are standards of correctness. They are given in explanations of meaning, appealed to in justification and criticism of use, and invoked in teaching. There is an internal relation between a rule and what counts as acting in accord with it (*a fortiori* as following it), which is exhibited in the normative practices of using an expression, evaluating the correctness of its use, correcting mistakes, explaining its meaning, etc. In place of depth analysis, what is requisite for philosophical elucidation is a description of the use of words, of their manifold connections and interconnections with other words, of the circumstances and presuppositions of use, of the consequences of their use and the manner in which they are integrated in human behavior. Such a description, a surveyable representation of the use of a word, will enable one to disentangle the web of the grammar of a word and to resolve philosophical problems.

Concepts are not correct or incorrect, only more or less useful. Rules for the use of words are not true or false. They are not answerable to reality or to antecedently given meanings. Instead, they determine the meanings of words. There is no *semantic* connection between words and world: grammar is autonomous. What appear to be necessities in the world, e.g. that red is a color or that nothing can be red and green all over, are not ineffable metaphysical truths. What we think of as categorial terms (formal concepts) have a perfectly decent use in our language, and can occur in well formed propositions with a sense, e.g. "Red is my favourite color," "Look at the colors of the sunset." What looked like ineffable metaphysical truths, e.g. that red is a color, that space is three-dimensional, that the world is the totality of facts, are no more than grammatical propositions, i.e. expressions of rules for the use of their constituent terms in the guise of descriptions. "Red is a color" is a rule which entitles one to infer from the proposition that *a* is red that it is colored. The proposition that nothing can be red and green all over is the expression of a rule which excludes the form of words "is red and green all over" from use. That the world is the totality of facts is a (misleading) expression of the rule that what we call a description of the world consists of a statement of facts (not a list of things).

The apparent harmony between language and reality, which lies at the heart of the problems of intentionality, requires no pre-established coordination between the logico-syntactical forms of any possible language on the one hand and the metaphysical form of the world on the other. Modal realism is chimerical, for what is logically possible is simply what makes sense, and that is laid down in language. It is correct that the proposition that *p* and the fact that *p* which makes it true are internally related, but internal relations are fixed *in language*. The "harmony" is orchestrated in grammar, in such intra-grammatical articulations as, for example, "The proposition that *p*" = "The proposition which is made true by the fact that *p*," which are simply two different ways of referring to the same proposition. It is correct to say that if one's thought is true then what one thinks is precisely what is the case, but that is not a kind of identity between distinct items, i.e. one's thought and what is the case. It is merely to say that the thought that *p* is the thought which is made true by its being the case that *p* (and made false by its not being the case that *p*) – and that is a grammatical (substitution) rule. Thought and what makes it true make contact *in language*, not between language and reality. Far from the intentionality of language being derivative from the intrinsic intentionality of thought, the intentionality of thought is derived from the intentionality of its linguistic expression, and that resides in the practice of its use and explanation. In general, what appear to be necessary connections in reality or between language and reality are merely the shadows cast by grammar. Metaphysics is not a domain for cognitive investigations in philosophy, but a hall of mirrors which needs to be shattered if we are to see the world and our thought about it aright.

The dominant tradition of philosophy conceived of subjective experience as the foundation of knowledge and language alike. It seems that a person knows how things are with him, that he is experiencing this or that (a pain or a visual impression) immediately and indubitably, but must infer from his subjective experience how things are "outside" him. Hence, it appeared, the private is better known than the public, and mind is better known than matter. Language, it seemed, was rooted in private experience. For the fundamental indefinables of a language seem to be given meaning by association or private ostensive definition connecting words (e.g. names of perceptual qualities, as well as of mental operations, attitudes, and emotions) with experiences. The *Investigations* mounts a full-scale attack upon this venerable conception with a battery of objections known as "the private language arguments."

One's current experience is not an object of subjective knowledge. The ability to avow one's pain does not rest on evidence, nor is it a form of perception. One may know that there is a tree in the quad in as much as one perceives it, but one does not perceive one's perception of it. One does not find out or verify that one is in pain. There is no such thing as being ignorant of whether or doubting whether one is in pain. So saying that one knows or is certain that one is in pain makes no sense either, since there is no possibility of ignorance or doubt to be excluded. To say "I know I am in pain" is either merely an emphatic avowal of pain or a philosopher's nonsense. The idea that the subject enjoys privileged access to his own experience, since no one else can have what he has when, for example, he is in pain, is misconceived. It assumes that the experiences, e.g. pain, of different people are at most qualitatively, but not numerically, identical. But that very distinction applies only to substances, not to experiences. Two people have the same pain if their pains tally in intensity and phenomenological features, and occur in corresponding parts of their bodies. Experiences are not kinds of private property, having an experience is not a relation between a person and an experience, and different people can have the same experiences. The only sense in which experiences may be epistemically private is that one may have a certain experience and neither exhibit the fact nor tell another about it. But if one screams in pain, there is nothing epistemically private about one's pain, and if one tells another what one is thinking, there is nothing one knows which he does not.

The traditional picture of the "inner" was accompanied by an equally distorted picture of the "outer." We often know what another experiences, whether he is in pain or cheerful, what he is thinking or imagining. Our knowledge rests on the evidence of what he says and does, but this is neither inductive nor analogical evidence. Pain behavior is a logical criterion for being in pain. A person's avowal of pain is a *behavioral expression* of pain, which partly replaces the natural pain behavior onto which it is grafted when one learns the use of the word "pain." To say "I think that *p*" or "I intend to *V*" is an expression of thought or intent (not a description of a private episode), and such utterances are criteria for the ascription of thoughts and intentions to others. They are defeasible (e.g. by evidence of insincerity); but if undefeated, then any doubt is senseless and the criteria justify the third-person ascription for which they are grounds.

The behavioral criteria for the ascription of psychological predicates are partly constitutive of their meaning. Psychological predicates are not given their meaning by a private rule, an ostensive definition, in which a subjective experience or impression functions as a private sample. There can be no such thing as a logically private sample. Nor can there be any such thing as a rule which only one person can, logically, follow. A sensation or experience cannot fulfill the role of a sample, for not being perceptible even by the person whose sensation or experience it is, it cannot function as an object of comparison. Nor can there be any criterion of identity for the putative sample, for the alleged sample must be recollected, and there can be no independent criterion of correctness for what one's memory calls up – whatever seems right to one is right, and that means that there is no right or wrong here.

Wittgenstein's reflections in philosophical psychology not only undermine the traditional conception of the "inner" and the "outer," they also transform traditional conceptions of thinking and its relation to language. Language is not a mere vehicle for language-independent thoughts, and sentences are not the mere outward, perceptible garb of thoughts. Intelligent speech is not an outer process of uttering words accompanied by an inner process of thinking. Speaking is not the upshot of a process of translating wordless thoughts into language. What makes speech intelligent, thoughtful, is no accompaniment; in particular, not an accompanying act or process of meaning something by one's words. For meaning something is neither an act nor a process, and what one means is typically what one's words mean. What renders speech thoughtful is the context of utterance, what was said or done before, and what is or might be said or done after, the reasons that the speaker might adduce for what he said and the consequences that he draws. Similarly, understanding is not a process of interpreting dead signs (sounds impinging upon one's eardrums). We no more hear mere sounds when we hear our mother tongue spoken than we see mere patches of color when we look around us. We hear intelligent speech, and experience the meanings of words. Interpretation (unlike deciphering) presupposes understanding, and is called for only when more than one way of understanding is in question. That is *necessarily* the exception to the rule.

The limits of thought are determined by the limits of the expression of thoughts. A dog may think it is about to be taken for a walk, since its behavior can express that expectation, but it cannot now think that it is going to be taken for a walk next week, for only linguistic behavior involving temporal reference can count as the expression of such a thought. The possession of a language not only extends the intellect, it also enlarges the trajectory of the will. A dog can now want a bone, but only a language user can now want to see Naples before he dies. It is not thought that infuses the signs of language with meaning, but the use of those signs in the stream of life.

The conception of philosophy propounded in the *Tractatus* was revolutionary, denying the possibility of any philosophical propositions and doctrines, characterizing the subject as a non-cognitive activity whose aim is the elucidation of propositions by analysis and the curbing of metaphysical pretensions. This conception of the subject is transformed and deepened in the *Investigations*. The notion of ineffable truths that can be shown but not said disappears together with the conception of analysis. But Wittgenstein continued to argue that philosophy is not a cognitive discipline, that there are no philosophical propositions or theses. If there were theses in philosophy, everyone would agree with them, for they would be no more than grammatical truisms – rules for the use of words with which we are perfectly familiar, even if we have to be reminded of them. That we know of others' states of mind on the basis of what they do and say is news from nowhere; the task of philosophy is to disentangle the misconceptions that lead us to think that this is inadequate or impossible, to clear away the misconceptions that prevent us from accepting these rule-governed connections in the grammar of our language that are constitutive of the concepts in question. It is not the task of philosophy to reform the grammar of our language – it leaves it as it is. But that is not a form of philosophical quietism. On the contrary, it recognizes that philosophical problems arise *inter alia* from our existing language, replacement of which would merely mask, and not resolve, the problems. Nor is it a declaration of the impotence or unimportance of philosophy. The problems of philosophy reach as deeply into us as our very language. And their resolution will have profound effects on disciplines, such as mathematics or psychology, which are enmired in conceptual confusion. (Almost half of Wittgenstein's later writings were concerned with the philosophy of mathematics. His philosophy of mathematics has not been discussed in this chapter due to limitations of length.) Wittgenstein's later conception of philosophy is Janus-faced. On the one hand, philosophy is akin to therapy, a cure for the diseases of the understanding, which has a certain affinity with psychoanalysis (but without any analogue of the theoretical commitments of the latter). On the other hand, it is a quest for a surveyable representation of a segment of grammar, which will lay bare the conceptual network. The two are complementary. The task of philosophy is conceptual clarification and the dissolution of philosophical problems. Philosophy cannot add to our knowledge of the world. Its role is to contribute to our understanding of what we do and do not know.

Bibliography

Writings

Werkausgabe, Bände 1–8 (Frankfurt am Main: Suhrkamp, 1989).
Tractatus Logico-philosophicus (London: Routledge & Kegan Paul, 1921, 1961).
Philosophical Investigations, 2nd edn (Oxford: Blackwell, 1953, 1958).
Remarks on the Foundations of Mathematics, 3rd edn (Oxford: Blackwell, 1956, 1978).
The Blue and Brown Books (Oxford: Blackwell, 1958).
Philosophical Grammar (Oxford: Blackwell, 1974).
Remarks on the Philosophy of Psychology, volumes I and II (Oxford: Blackwell, 1980).
Philosophical Occasions 1912–1951 (Indianapolis: Hackett, 1993).

Further reading

Baker, G. P. and Hacker, P. M. S.: *An Analytical Commentary on the Philosophical Investigations. Volume 1, Wittgenstein: Understanding and Meaning* (Oxford: Blackwell, 1980)
——: *An Analytical Commentary on the Philosophical Investigations. Volume 2, Wittgenstein: Rules, Grammar and Necessity* (Oxford: Blackwell, 1985)
Glock, H. J.: *A Wittgenstein Dictionary* (Oxford: Blackwell, 1996).
Hacker, P. M. S.: *Insight and Illusion: Themes in the Philosophy of Wittgenstein*, rev. edn (Oxford: Clarendon Press, 1986; Bristol: Thoemmes Press, 1997).
——: *An Analytical Commentary on the Philosophical Investigations. Volume 3, Wittgenstein: Meaning and Mind* (Oxford: Blackwell, 1990).
——: *An Analytical Commentary on the Philosophical Investigations. Volume 4, Wittgenstein: Mind and Will* (Oxford: Blackwell, 1996).

——: *Wittgenstein's Place in Twentieth-century Analytic Philosophy* (Oxford: Blackwell, 1996).

Hanfling, O.: *Wittgenstein's Later Philosophy* (London: Macmillan, 1989).

Kenny, A. J. P.: *Wittgenstein* (Harmondsworth: Penguin, 1973).

Monk, R.: *Wittgenstein: The Duty of Genius* (London: Jonathan Cape, 1990).

Mounce, H. O.: *Wittgenstein's Tractatus: An Introduction* (Oxford: Blackwell, 1981).

Schulte, J.: *Wittgenstein: An Introduction* (Albany: State University of New York Press, 1992).

38

Xunzi

John Knoblock

Xunzi [Hsün Tzu] or Xun Kuang [Hsün K'uang], who lived between from about 310 to after 230 BCE, made unique contributions to Chinese philosophy in several important areas: the role of music and ritual in government and society; the concept of Nature; the doctrine of the Mind; the theory of names; the argument concerning human nature; and the concept of society and the ideal of the sage.

Music and ritual

An emphasis on *li*, ritual principles, characterizes Ru (Confucian) philosophers generally and Xunzi in particular. His distinctive emphasis on ritual principles is connected with his view of human nature. In his view, the Ancient Kings established the regulations for social and court rites and ceremonies specifically to apportion material goods and both to give expression to and to contain the emotions. In doing so, they followed certain ritual and moral principles which assured that men could satisfy their desires and express their emotions, that the social order would be protected, and that the material goods of society would be conserved. In economic terms, the essential principles of all ritual are: (1) that the desires should be controlled by nurturing and training; and (2) that goods should be unevenly distributed. Xunzi believed that the greatest threat to society was disorder arising out of poverty. To avoid this, the state must assure sufficient goods to satisfy everyone's basic needs. Ritual principles guarantee this; thus, they are "the strength of the state" and the "Way by which the majestic sway of authority is created." Equally important was the need for hierarchy in society. This was founded on the "universally recognized principle" that men of equal rank cannot serve each other. Distinctions of rank and title, disparities of privilege, and different modes of identification by sumptuary tokens contained in ritual principles represent "the highest expression of order and discrimination." In man, frustration results when emotions are not given adequate expression. But allowing the emotions uncontrolled venting may damage life itself. The purpose of ritual forms is to provide adequate expression of joy and grief, but to prevent any excess that may interfere with social order or harm the individual.

When the emotions are stirred by sounds, the body spontaneously expresses them in gestures and facial expressions. This is both a necessary and an inescapable part of our inborn nature. Music gives form to this natural language of sound and movement. But the sounds of music are not sounds originating subjectively from our nature. The impetus for such sounds originates in our mind only when it is stirred by external things. This is part of the Way of Man. Our emotions provide the template for the sounds which give expression to them. When we hear music, our inner mind is directly affected. When the music is profoundly moving, our very character is altered. If goodness is the message of the music, good will be the response; but if it is evil, the response as well will be evil. Every kind of music is reflected exactly in its response.

The effect of music on the inner mind was responsible for the emphasis which Ru philosophers, and later Chinese aesthetes, place on the playing of the zither. The zither could be played in private and music improvised on it was often a vehicle for self-expression. Sensitivity to timbre meant that each note could convey a nuance of the inner mind, which the perceptive listener would notice. From the sage nothing could be hidden in the tone of the voice when one spoke or in the timbre of the music when one played. Musical tones, having their origins in the human mind, ultimately connect humans and the cosmos, just as the shape of a shadow derives from the plane of the three-dimensional object or an echo answers responsively to the uttered sound. Music is more profound than ritual, since it affects our inner states rather than our external conduct. One can force a man to smile, but not to feel joy. Ritual may cause us to act in a certain way, but it cannot cause us to feel in a way consonant with what we do. When music affects our mind, it causes us not only to move in a certain way, but to feel that way as well. The Ancient Kings understood this and placed their highest priority on music. Their concern was not to satisfy the eye and ear, but to influence the mind by regulating our likes and dislikes and by keeping them within set bounds.

View of nature

Xunzi viewed Nature as the impartial and universal power which controls humans and the myriad things. In proposing a morally neutral Nature, Xunzi argues that natural calamities, unusual events, and "ill omens" are not the result of what men do, but are products of the normal operations of Nature. Because they are rare, it is permissible to marvel at them, but because they are part of the "normal" course of Nature, they should not be feared. Xunzi thus explicitly rejects the older notion that the majesty of Heaven/Nature should be feared. Xunzi, in agreement with most of his contemporaries, accepted that Heaven/ Nature "produces" (literally, "bears"), but he denied that Nature acts, seeks, distinguishes, organizes, or perfects what it has produced. These are the tasks allotted to human government headed by a gentleman or sage. While admitting that Nature has its course and its way, Xunzi rejects any notion that Nature engages in purposive action (*wei*) to seek anything. He thus denies to Nature the conscious intentions which the traditional view granted Heaven. Nature, in Xunzi's view, is insensible and unknowing, neither loves good nor hates evil, does not manage, is without intelligence, and is not moved to respond by feelings or affections.

The mind

It is a common human flaw to be obsessed by some aspect of the truth, to pursue double principles, to be of two minds, and to end in hesitation, suspicion, and delusion. For Xunzi, such blindness results from a universal flaw in the operation of the mind. Because the sage understands this flaw in the mind's operations and perceives the misfortune of blindness and being closed to the truth, he weighs all things like a balance. His balance is the Way which the mind alone knows. The mind can know the Way because its inner states mirror the qualities of the Way. The mind is empty, unified, and still, and because of these qualities it can store up memories, consider different things at the same time, and never stop thinking. Emptiness allows entry, unity allows thoroughness, and stillness allows discernment of the Way. Emptiness leads to greatness, unity to purity, and stillness to brightness, which for Xunzi means "understanding" as well. Greatness encompasses all, purity puts everything into its proper place, and discernment enables one to penetrate everything. Thus, a mind of the Way can know the inner laws of order and disorder, can lay out the warp and woof of Heaven and Earth, can tailor the offices of the myriad things, can regulate and distinguish the Great Ordering Principle, and can encompass all that is within space and time.

Rectification of names

Xunzi's program of defining the correct use of names consists of several parts: (1) the names established by the Later Kings; (2) the names of the myriad of objects in the world; and (3) the technical terms of inquiry. The names established by the Later Kings consist of the terminology of criminal law and penal classification of the Shang dynasty, the titles of rank and dignity instituted by the founders of the Zhou dynasty, and the names for the various forms and implements of cultural life contained in the *Rituals*. The last element in Xunzi's program of rectifying names is the definition of technical terms which are employed in analysis of problems of knowledge and value.

The first, and in many respects most important, definition is that of "human nature." When he defines "nature" as "what is present from birth," his definition is intuitively convincing because the concept of nature cannot be conceptually at variance with the concepts of "life" and "birth." Xunzi expands this basic definition of "inborn nature" in several ways. First, he adds those characteristics that are potential but not actual from birth and that, in his description, are produced out of the harmony of inborn nature. Next, he adds those characteristics that involve the sensibilities of the organ responding to stimuli. Finally, the response of the senses to external stimuli is spontaneous, and Xunzi holds that what is done spontaneously, whether involving sense stimuli and responses or something else, is also characteristic of inborn nature. But in addition, he demands that this spontaneity not require any application to learn; this allows him to exclude those things we learn so well that they become second nature to us. Xunzi makes the point that acuity of hearing and clarity of vision cannot be improved by study. After the senses have received stimuli, they are distinguished into six emotional responses. Although the emotions are limitless, the mind by selecting or denying them can act. This process of selection Xunzi calls "thinking."

Xunzi asserts that those qualities found in man that are obtained through learning or mastered through the application of effort are "acquired nature." He distinguishes between inborn nature as "root and beginning, the raw material and original constitution," and the nature we acquire by conscious exertion as "form and principle of order, the development and completion." The process of thinking, which entails selecting among the feelings that Heaven/Nature has given us, is crucial to overcoming original, inborn nature. The application of thinking to human abilities so that they perform appropriate acts is defined as "conscious exertion." "Conscious exertion" is the opposite of what is natural, in the sense of spontaneous actions a person performs without "deciding" or "willing" to do so. The product of "conscious exertion" is a second nature, an "acquired nature." Xunzi distinguishes between two types of "conscious exertions": utilitarian actions occasioned by "legitimate benefits," which he calls "business"; and actions on behalf of the morally good, which he calls "conduct."

Should a new king appear, Xunzi argues, he must generally reform the names. This would necessarily involve not only retaining some old names but also inventing new names. It is thus imperative that any future True King should understand the purpose for having names, the basis of distinguishing the similar from the different, and the crucial considerations for instituting names. A name is not properly assigned to a single reality, and this makes consideration of "logical category, class, kind" crucial. Thus, when we depend on the ear, eye, nose, and mouth, they determine things to be alike in some respects and different in others, so we pick out the most salient characteristics. For instance, when we refer to something as a "bird" we know that it has two feet and wings, and when we refer to something as an "animal" we know that it has four legs and fur.

Man's inborn nature

Xunzi's distinctive claim that human nature is "bad, ugly, evil" flows from his definition of "nature." Xunzi argues that the inborn nature of man is evil on several generally accepted grounds: (1) a love of profit is inborn in man; (2) "dislikes and hatreds" are inborn in man; (3) the desires generated by the senses are inborn in man; and (4) ritual and moral principles were created by the sages; they must be learned and require effort to master. Xunzi also specifically refutes the claim that the fact that man can learn shows that his nature is good, and that the original simplicity and childhood naivete of men is good and that evil results because men lose this nature. "Good" refers to objectively determined relations between things. Following the desires causes "dissolute and disorderly behavior to result, and ritual principles and morality, precepts of good form, and the natural order of reason to perish." "Following one's desire" and "satisfying human needs" are not equivalent terms; thus, what is desirable is not necessarily what is good. Xunzi claims that the harmony produced by social organization enables men to live together and to obtain what they require. We transform ourselves by learning and by conscious exertion. The mind fixes its attention on some goal, devising ways and means to realize it, and effectuating it through the habituation of custom so that the inborn nature is transformed. The habituation of custom modifies the direction of will and, if continued for a long time, the very substance of one's original inborn nature will be altered. Xunzi equates the profound changes that learning creates in our inborn natures to the changes of the butterfly in the chrysalis: "having undergone change, he emerges altered."

The gentleman and the ordinary man share one and the same nature. Every man has the capacity to know and the ability to put what he knows into practice. But having the capacity is not necessarily to realize it. Man's capacities are sufficient to know and act in terms of "humanity" and "morality." If these capacities are used, and improved through practice, effort, and learning, then the "man in the street" can become a sage. But we must not confuse the capacity to know and the ability to act with what we do know and how we do act. It is the former that makes good possible, despite our evil natures; it is the latter that becomes the good we accomplish. Thus inborn nature is "the root and beginning and the raw material and original constitution." Acquired nature is "the form and order, the development and the completion." If there were no inborn nature, there would be nothing for conscious activity to improve; if there were no acquired nature, then inborn nature could not refine itself. It is the union of inborn and acquired nature that makes possible the perfection of man in the form of the sage and the perfection of social order in the unification of the whole world. It is a mistake to conclude that man's inborn nature is good because through conscious exertion we can create an acquired nature that is good.

The need for society

Xunzi argues that by Nature things are inherently unequal. Even before man creates any social distinctions, from Nature there are such distinctions as primary and secondary, young and old, noble and base, male and female. Further, since a great variety of skills are necessary to supply the needs of even a single individual, the differences in the skills that characterize the various occupations naturally result in social differences. When society is built upon such distinctions, each individual recognizes that the "duties and responsibilities" of his "lot" in life are "just" because they are founded on "morality." This accounts for everyone's willingness to accept his position and for the general concord of societies founded on concepts of justice and morality. Such societies seem "good" even on utilitarian grounds, because where there is concord between classes, there is unity, which is the source of strength in a society. Where a society possesses strength, obstacles can be overcome by the unified effort of the society.

Desires, as well as the need to form societies, arise out of man's inborn nature. When a man believes that the objects of his desire can be obtained, it is a necessary and inescapable part of his nature that he will pursue them. If men follow their desires, the inevitable result will be strife and rapacity, violence and predation, and dissolute and disorderly conduct. Thus, although society develops out of man's nature, the result will be not order but disorder, not good but evil. Evil and disorder arise from several causes. Men differ in experience and wisdom and hence differ in regard to what they consider acceptable and moral. Second, the fact that desires are many while things are few means that scarcity occasions conflict over the goods that satisfy desires. Conflict itself exacerbates the problem of scarcity because people then live in alienation from each other and are unwilling to serve each other's needs. Third, differences in strength and intelligence result in the strong coercing the weak and the intelligent intimidating the stupid. Finally, in the absence of rules governing the union of man and woman, there is conflict arising from sexual relations.

Our desires cannot be denied. They dictate that we shall act to obtain objects that will satisfy them, so it is idle to try to reduce the number of our desires. What we must do is guide and moderate them with our minds. What we obtain is never wholly what we desire, and what we avoid is never wholly what we dislike. Everything that we obtain or avoid is a mixture of some qualities we desire and some we dislike. Thus a fundamental role for the mind in pursuing a course of action is determining the relative balance between desirable and undesirable elements in a particular thing. Since a sense of what is right and moral is inborn in man, every man can use his mind to moderate the desires by deeming some things allowable and others not allowable. But, although all men have the same desires and seek the same things, they differ in awareness concerning them. Thus it is necessary for man's original nature to undergo the transforming influence of a teacher and a model so that he will acquire a Way guided by moral principles.

The sage

Xunzi believed that the essence of government was setting aright, rectifying, what was askew. This can be accomplished only by the sage. The sage accumulates moral authority, attracts others to him, and sets the pattern for others who imitate his example. The result is solidarity achieved by attracting others with moral authority and teaching them the proper moral pattern for human relations. Since people willingly imitate the conduct of the sage, the sage king can effect a fundamental change in society. The sage triumphs over his original inborn nature by imposing on it restraints that he then incorporates into ritual principles. This is the expression of his humanity. Others then turn to him as to their home, knowing that the humane man, in seeking to establish himself, seeks also to establish others.

It is not necessary that men be good, or that they display goodwill, or that they do anything other than be subject to the influences of their times. If their times are orderly thanks to a sage king, then they will acquire orderly customs and will be transformed almost immediately. If their times are chaotic, then they will acquire chaotic customs. History confirms this repeatedly. Sages like Yao and Shun could not get rid of men's innate love of profit, but they taught men not to allow it to triumph over their sense of moral duty. Evil rulers like Jie and Zhou Xin could not get rid of men's inborn sense of moral duty, but they caused men's fondness for profit to overcome their love of morality.

Bibliography

Writings

Hsün-tzu: Basic Writings, trans. Burton Watson (New York: Columbia University Press, 1963).
Xunzi, A Translation and Study, three volumes, trans. John Knoblock (Stanford, CA: Stanford University Press, 1988–94).

Further reading

Cua, Antonio S.: *Ethical Argumentation: A Study in Hsün-tzu's Moral Epistemology* (Honolulu: University of Hawaii Press, 1985).
Knoblock, John: "The Chronology of Xunzi's Works," *Early China*, 8 (1982–3), 28–52.
Köster, Hermann: *Hsün-tzu* (Kaldenkirchen: Steyler Verlag, 1967).
Machle, Edward J.: *Nature and Heaven in the Xunzi* (Binghamton: State University of New York Press, 1993).

39

Zhuangzi

Chad Hansen

Zhuangzi [Chuang Tzu or Chuang Chou] (*c.*360 BCE) may have written up to seven chapters (The "Inner Chapters") of *The Zhuangzi* collection. His technical mastery of ancient Chinese linguistic theory in some of these suggests that Zhuangzi studied and thought deeply about semantics. Thinkers of related but distinct theoretical orientations probably wrote the remaining "Outer Chapters." Some of the latter expand on but others contradict themes in the Inner Chapters. They typically draw on literary skills and religion more than linguistic philosophy.

The relation between LAOZI [LAO TZU] and Zhuangzi within Taoism is a growing puzzle. The only verifiable intellectual influence on Zhuangzi was Hui Shi (370–319 BCE), a language theorist. Zhuangzi had a longstanding friendship with the monist dialectician, and he mourned Hui Shi's death as depriving him of the person "on whom he sharpened his wits."

We can view Hui Shi's linguistic theory best against the background of the Mohists' linguistic realism (see MOZI [MO TZU]). The realists said real-world similarities and differences ground the "picking out" that divides the world into thing-kinds. Hui Shi tried to undermine the Mohist's semantic proposal by drawing attention to comparatives. Comparatives also mark distinctions, but it is less plausible that the distinctions are in-the-world. Where we draw a comparative contrast is relative to our purpose and point of view. Whether an ant is large or small varies as we compare it with other ants or other animals. Some of Hui Shi's reported teachings include:

- Heaven is as low as the earth; mountains are level with marshes.
- The sun is both in the middle and descending.
- Natural kinds are both living and dying.
- I go to Yüeh today and arrive yesterday.

For the purpose of understanding Zhuangzi, Hui Shi's key saying strikes at the use of similarity to ground realism:

> The ten-thousand thing-kinds are ultimately alike and ultimately different. Call this the great similarity-difference.

Zhuangzi develops this insight. If we can find a difference between any two things no matter how alike they are, then the basis for distinguishing and grouping is not simple similarity. Similarity, that is, does not justify any *particular* way of dividing reality into "kinds." For each name in our language, we could have evolved conventions that divide the world's stuff up differently.

Hui Shi's relativist sayings, however, conclude with an absolute claim about reality. He tries to refer to "everything" and make a judgment about it from the "cosmic" perspective. He formulates the view typically attributed to Taoists.

> Universally love the ten-thousand thing-kinds; the cosmos is one *ti*. [*Ti* was a technical term referring to the basic parts of any compounded object.]

The Zhuangzi presentation of Hui Shi's views concludes: "He had many perspectives and his library would fill five carts but his doctrine was self-contradictory. His language did not hit his target – the intent to make sense of things." This suggests that Zhuangzi saw Hui Shi as caught in a paradox. Mohist theory had exposed the incoherence of any blanket anti-language (anti-distinction) stance. The Mohists argued both that "'All language is perverse' is perverse" and that rejecting distinctions requires making a distinction. Thus, either denying all distinctions or treating language as distorting reality is incoherent. Zhuangzi probably noticed that Hui Shi's "Everything is one" was an attempt to reject distinctions and thus language.

Zhuangzi himself states the position in his characteristic poetic style: "The cosmos and I were born together; the ten-thousand things and I are one." Then he wonders aloud: "Having already a 'one,' is it possible to say something about it? Having already called it a 'one' can we fail to say anything about it? 'One' and saying it make two. Two and one make three and, going from here, even a skilled calculator cannot keep up with us – let alone an ordinary person."

Skeptical perspectivalism

Zhuangzi's unique philosophical style contributes to his image as an irrationalist. He wrote philosophical fantasy rather than direct argument. Interpreters understandably treat him as a Western romantic, rejecting reason for emotion. Arguably, however, Zhuangzi presents his positions in fantasy dialogues in order to illustrate and practice a pluralist perspective. He puts positions up for discussion, reflects on and then abandons them. He stages these discussions sometimes as imagined conversations among fantasy figures (rebellious thieves, distorted freaks, or converted Confucians), other times as internal monologue. In the fantasy dialogues, Zhuangzi seems to challenge us to identify his voice. Even his monologues typically end with a double rhetorical question in place of a conclusion. "Then is there really any X or is there no X?"

Another key to Zhuangzi's adaptation of Hui Shi's relativism is his treatment of "useful." Everything is useful from some position or other, and there are positions from which even the most useful thing is useless. Things may be useful precisely *in being* useless. Zhuangzi illustrates this latter theme with his famous parables of the huge "useless" tree that, consequently, no one ever chopped down. Pragmatic concerns are always relative to some presumed value.

Zhuangzi develops his perspectivalism without rejecting language. Confucian innatists appealed to a preference for nature over convention to support their anti-language attitudes. Zhuangzi notes that being natural does not require abandoning words. Human speech, from empty greetings and small talk to the disputes of philosophers, is as natural a "noise" as are bird songs. He uses the "pipes of nature" as a metaphor for philosophical disputes. If brooks can go on babbling, philosophers can go on disputating and making distinctions.

Then he considers an objection to his wind metaphor: "Language is not blowing breath; language users have [that (by?) which] they 'language.' What language 'languages,' however, is never fixed." He highlights the indexicality of language to defend this skepticism. His argument deftly exploits a dual use of a core term of Chinese semantic analysis, *shi* – which translators treat sometimes as "this" and other times as "right." First, he fixes the indexical aspect of *shi* in our minds by contrasting it with *bi* [that]. "Is anything really a 'this' or a 'that'?" Then he shifts to the contrast of *shi* and *fei*. *Fei* negates category terms as in "X *fei* (is not a) horse" and, like *shi*, is used alone – to mean "wrong." So *shi* and *fei* together stand for right and wrong use of names of things. Relative to any name, some object will be either *shi* or *fei* (either this is a horse or it is not a horse). This analysis leads to the doctrine that historical, inherited purposes and background knowledge govern naming. The use of *shi–fei* is indexed to our acquired perspective. History and human purpose condition how we divide up and name things in the world. Language marks our perspectives on reality as much as the real joints and fissures in nature.

Zhuangzi focuses on the social perspective, though he sometimes notes differences in perspective within the same person at different times. His main target is the way conflicting attitudes come from using different moral language. He uses the moral debate between Confucians and Mohists as the key example. Utilitarian Mohists say Confucian traditionalism (see CONFUCIUS) is immoral because it leads to bad consequences. Confucians say utilitarianism is immoral because it leads to doing what is wrong. Each criticism presupposes precisely the moral point that is in dispute.

Zhuangzi reflects in places on the perspective of "self," although he is not a subjectivist. Recalling Laozi's emphasis on contrasts, he sees the concept of "self" as based on a contrast with "other." He suggests the deep motive for the "self–other" distinction is that we assume that things like pleasure, anger, sadness, joy, forethought, and regret are held together and governed by something. He observes that these "alternate day and night" and we should give up trying to find a "ruler" of them and merely accept that they are there. Without these "reality inputs" there would be no "self" (i.e. the self is not something separate from them) and without "self," there would be no "choosing of one thing over another." (That is, if there were no such reactions to things, there would not be such a thing as choice and hence no concept of something separate and outside oneself.) He notes the inevitability of our assumption that some "ruler" harmonizes and organizes these feelings into a self, then adds, skeptically, that we never find any sign of it.

Intuitionism

Innatist Confucians do presuppose a "natural ruler" – the moral heart-mind. How, Zhuangzi muses, can it be any more natural than the other "hundred joints, nine openings and six viscera"? Does there need to be a ruler? Cannot each natural organ rule itself or take turns? Identifying one organ as supreme conflicts with the Confucians' intention to take "being natural" as a moral standard.

Zhuangzi observes that all of the organs of the body grow together in encountering and adapting to life. As these do, they are *cheng* [*ch'eng*] (completed) – a term Zhuangzi uses ironically. Any completion, he argues, leaves some defect in its wake. Growth is possible only with some skewing and bias.

Thus, all hearts equally achieve *cheng*. As each grows along with the body, it acquires a pattern of language use – a way of making *shi–fei* judgments about the relation of objects and words. Every person's heart naturally acquires some disposition to these assignments. If *this* acquired heart (the one that grows with the body) is the authority, then Confucian sages have no superior authority over it – hence no superior authority to criticize a fool's attitudes. Confucian innatists assume one pattern of *chen* (completion) is right and they project their historically acquired norm on nature. They assume we need to *cultivate* the *xin* [*hsin*] (heart-mind) so it will give the correct *shi–fei* judgments.

Zhuangzi asks these Confucians how they propose to distinguish a sage's heart-mind from a fool's. The appeal to nature gives us no reason to identify any existing way of cultivating the heart-mind as "right" or "proper." The innatist's attempt to get norms from reality begs the question against rival moral perspectives. Appealing to the sage's insight into nature requires us to distinguish a sage from a fool. Using an acquired insight to make that distinction begs the question against rival moral attitudes, which are equally naturally acquired. Confucian sages are Mohist fools and vice versa!

Zhuangzi's analysis of the *cheng xin* (completed heart-mind) reflects a view found in the *Laozi*. We unconsciously absorb knowledge and moral attitudes in the very process of learning language. Attitudes that seem natural and spontaneous reflect what has become second nature. No innate or spontaneous dispositions survive without being *cheng.* Zhuangzi says that for there to be a *shi–fei* in the heart without its being put there in the process of *cheng* is "like going to Yüeh today and arriving yesterday!"

We can only rank perspectives by assuming some controversial *dao* [*tao*] (moral discourse). Moral direction comes from our *dao*, not from *tian* [*t'ien*] (nature:heaven). Appeals to nature give us no guidance when we confront rival ethical views. Even a judgment that different *daos* are equal in value must (1) be a result of taking some standard for granted or (2) be a misleading way to say "make no judgment." The problem with (2) is that once again it amounts to saying that we should stop speaking or discriminating.

What is the alternative? We naturally (inevitably) do judge and we presuppose some standpoint when we do. Zhuangzi's standpoint is a pluralistic perspective on perspectives. He advocates *ming* (discrimination) but never defines it. *Ming* allows judgments about other viewpoints but it recommends openness and flexibility. Understanding others better may help us improve our own viewpoint *by our existing lights.*

Zhuangzi's perspective is, as he admits, "of a type with the others." We do not need to presuppose that it is an absolute or total view in order to conclude that rival views are partial. His view requires us to appreciate that other outlooks may offer something ours does not. Having limitations need not entail that a perspective is wrong or worthless.

Zhuangzi's focus is more epistemological than metaphysical. He suggests occasionally that there might be a fantastically adept and successful *dao* (e.g. that one might reach the point of being able to endure fire, cold, lightning, and wind). This fantasy presupposes there is an actual world with real features which some *daos* interact with better than others do (given the standards of success we use in appreciating the fantasies).

Skepticism versus dogmatic monism

The linguistic nature of Zhuangzi's analysis is even more pronounced when he responds to the Mohists. He notes that their term of analysis, *ke* [assertable], is relative to a language. Different and changing usage patterns constitute rival conventions. Each convention generates a language and a viewpoint. Single schools of thought may split, and disputing factions may combine again. Any language people *actually speak* is assertable. Any moral discourse for which there is a rival is (from that rival standpoint) not assertable.

Zhuangzi hints that the confidence we have in the appearance of right and wrong in our language is a function of how fully we can elaborate and embellish it. How well can we continue on with our way of speaking? To argue for a point of view is to spin it out in detail. The ability to expand and develop a point of view encourages the illusion that it is complete. The seemingly endless disputes between Mohists and Confucians arise from their highly elaborated systems for assigning "is this" and "not this." As we saw, each can build hierarchies of standards that guide their different choices. They come to consider the errors of rivals to be "obvious."

Zhuangzi introduces *ming* (discrimination) again in discussing the relativity of language. In the same section he imagines an "absolute" viewpoint – the axis of *daos*. We extrapolate back up our historical path to the "axis" from which all began. At the "axis," he says, no limit can be drawn on what we could treat as "is this" or "is not this"; all *shi–fei* patterns are possible, none actual.

From that axis, however, we make no judgment. It is not a relevant alternative to the disputing perspectives. The absolute viewpoint neither advocates nor forbids any *dao*. Any practical guide is a possible path from the axis to a particular way of making distinctions.

Zhuangzi emphasizes the possibility of innumerable competing standpoints. Occasionally, however, he emphasizes the almost tragic inevitability involved once we take one possible path. Once we have started down a *dao*, we seem doomed to elaborate and develop it in a kind of "rush to death." Youth is the state of being comparatively open to many possible systems of *shi–fei*. As we grow and gain "knowledge," we close off possibilities and flexibility. Zhuangzi exploits the analogy of youth and flexibility. Nothing can free us from the headlong rush to complete our initial commitments to *shi* and *fei* as if they were oaths or treaties. We rush through life clinging to the alternative we judge as winning. "Is life really as stupid as this? Or is it that I am the only stupid one and there are others not so stupid?"

Those who call themselves "sages" project their point of view and prejudices on *tian* (nature:heaven) and then treat it as an authority. "Those who have arrived" allegedly know to treat everything as one – they reject the multiplicity of viewpoints as biased. Zhuangzi does not recommend that attitude. Instead of trying to transcend and abandon our usual or conventional ways of speaking, we should treat them as useful. They enable us to communicate and get things done. That is *all* one can sensibly ask of them.

Beyond what is implied in the fact that our language is useful, we do not know the way things are in themselves. We signal that lack of ultimate metaphysical knowledge when we call reality "*dao*." Treating it as an irreducible "one" (mysticism) differs only in attitude from saying nothing about it (skepticism). In the end, neither can say anything. Skeptics and mystics merely use a different emotional tone when saying their "nothing."

In a notoriously obscure passage, one of his characters is even skeptical about skepticism. However, he does not base this on the familiar Western concept of belief, i.e. he does not ask how he knows *that* he does not know. Zhuangzi's skepticism centers on the distinctions underlying words. He wonders if we know if we have distinguished correctly between "knowing" and "ignorance."

Zhuangzi's treatment of dreams also highlights his particular form of skepticism. He does not use dreaming to motivate sense skepticism. His doubts arise mainly from semantics. (Is there any real relation between our words and things?) Dreaming further illustrates a skeptical view that is rooted in worries about whether there is a right way to use a word to distinguish or "pick out" parts of reality. The "dreaming–waking" distinction is one we use to organize "what happens" (in the broadest sense). We have learned a way of using that distinction to bring unity or coherence to our experience.

In a dream, however, we can still make the distinction between dreaming and waking. Ultimately we can wonder if other ways of making the

distinction might work as well. For instance, Zhuangzi dreams in a particularly rich way of being a butterfly. On suddenly being Zhuangzi
again, he wonders how to distinguish his having dreamed a butterfly and
awakening, from his having just been a butterfly who is now dreaming
of being Zhuangzi.

Practical implications

What follows from Zhuangzi's skepticism and relativism? We should take
Zhuangzi to be reflectively aware that any advice he offers comes from
one perspective – his *ming* approach to discourse. Any advice will be
tenuous and hedged. First, Zhuangzi "mildly" recommends the kind of
perspective flexibility we noted above. He "recommends" it in the sense
one can "recommend" that one be young. To be young-at-heart-mind is
to be open to new ways of thinking and conceptualizing. The more committed you get to a scheme, as we saw, the "older" you become intellectually, until you are "dead" from learning.

   This practical line is paradoxical. Any reason we may have for being
flexible in adopting or tolerant to other points of view has to be a reason
that motivates us from our present point of view. We must be able to
envision how the alternative way of thinking will help us more with goals
we now have than our present scheme does. Since we judge from our
present scheme, we need not be open or tolerant of *any* other point of
view. Zhuangzi cannot argue for absolute tolerance. The limit on this
openness depends on our existing moral stance. From a *ming* standpoint, judgment is not only still possible, it is inescapable.

   Further, the motivation for being open to other schemes of knowledge presupposes the potential value of acquiring them. The openness
of youth is valuable only because it offers a greater range of possibilities of knowledge. If we were to treat openness as a principled
anti-knowledge stance, then perspectivalism would give us no reason to
value it.

   The second bit of advice is negative. We need not reject conventions.
To do so is wasteful and conventions can be useful since they allow coordination and communication. Again we must judge their usefulness
from our present standpoint.

   The third bit of advice is most famous. In the parable of "Butcher
Ding," Zhuangzi draws a favorable portrait of developing a *dao* to the
point of its being second nature. Highly honed skills invite paradoxical,
almost mystical, description. In performance we seem to experience a
unity of actor and action. Such practice is a way of losing oneself as much

as one might in contemplation or a trance. We can mystify ourselves by the fluid accuracy of our own actions. We do not understand how we do it – we certainly cannot explain it to others.

It is natural to express this ideal of skill mastery in language that suggests mystical awareness. Such skill normally conflicts with excessive self-consciousness and ratiocination. Internally it feels like we "flow with" some external force. Such language should not confuse us, however. The experience is compatible with Zhuangzi's perspective on perspectives. Examining the details of Butcher Ding's explanation of his skill illustrates why.

Note, first, that Butcher Ding's activity is cutting – dividing something into parts. While he is mastering his guiding *dao*, he perceives the ox already cut up. He comes to see the places he should cut as already existing spaces and fissures in the ox. The ox thus seems a perfect metaphor for our coming to see the world as divided into the "natural kinds." We internalize a language that serves some purpose. When we master a guiding *dao*, we seek to execute it in a real situation. Doing so requires finding distinctions in nature to match the concepts in the instructions. While acting, we do not have time to read the map; we see ourselves as reading *the world*.

Mastering any *dao* yields this sense of harmony with things. It is *as if* the world, not the instructions, guided us. At the highest levels of skill, we reach a point where we seem to transcend our own self-consciousness. Our normal ability to respond to complex feedback bypasses conscious processing. In our skilled actions, we have internalized a heightened sensitivity to the context.

The choice of a butcher for this parable also illustrates something about Zhuangzi's perspective. Asian cultures seldom hold butchering up as a noble profession. (Even the name "Ding" may be significant – it may not be his name but a sign of relatively low rank – something like fourth-place.) Zhuangzi's other examples of the theme of skill include the cicada catcher and wheelwright. Zhuangzi thus signals that this level of expertise is available within all activities.

Popular, romantic interpretations suggest this transcendent focus is available only for arts and physical activities. They read the point as an anti-intellectual one and insist that Zhuangzi's criticism of Hui Shi stems from the latter's rationalism. However, Zhuangzi follows his critical comments about Hui Shi with parallel observations about a zither player. What he criticizes is the aspiration to "total know-how," not any specific activity. Zhuangzi's "criticism" is that an exemplar of skill X is typically miserably inept at Y. These "criticisms" simply illustrate his view that defect always accompanies *cheng* (completion).

Zhuangzi's ambivalence about *cheng* poses a problem with the pre-scription to "achieve *dao* mastery." Any attainment leaves something out. To acquire and exercise any skill is to ignore others. We trade accomplishment at one skill for ineptitude at some other. If the renowned practitioners have reached completion, he says, then so has everyone. If they have not, no one can.

Thus, the three parts in Zhuangzi's *dao* pull in separate directions. We must treat each as tentative and conditional. The flexibility advice seems hard to follow if we also accept convention and work for single-minded mastery. That, in the end, may be the message of Zhuangzi's perspectivalism. We have limits . . . but we might as well get on with life.

Bibliography

Writings

Zhuangzi: Basic Writings, ed. Burton Watson (New York: Columbia University Press, 1964).
Chuang Tzu: The Inner Chapters, ed. Angus Graham (London: Allen & Unwin, 1981).
Zhuangzi: Mystic, Moralist and Social Reformer, ed. Herbert A. Giles (London: Allen & Unwin, 1981).

Further reading

Graham, Angus: "Chuang-tzu's Essay on Seeing Things as Equal," *History of Religions*, 9 (1969), 137–59.
Hansen, Chad: *A Daoist Theory of Chinese Thought* (New York: Oxford University Press, 1992).
Mair, Victor (ed.): *Experimental Essays on Chuang-tzu* (Honolulu: University of Hawaii Press, 1983).

40

Zhu Xi

Jonathan R. Herman

Apart from CONFUCIUS, LAOZI, and other seminal figures from the "Hundred Schools Period," Zhu Xi [Chu Hsi] (1130–1200 CE) is arguably China's most influential and studied philosopher, and his reach extends to areas of Chinese culture well beyond the academy. He was active at a time when intellectual and political structures in China were under considerable assault, as state Confucianism had been eclipsed by Daoist [Taoist] and Buddhist institutional gains, and the Song [Sung] Dynasty (960–1269) had suffered repeated setbacks at the hands of northern invaders. His activism on both scores led to an intermittent public life, with a stormy succession of government appointments, demotions, resignations, and dismissals. At the time of his death, he had actually been out of imperial favor for a few years, but his policies would eventually form the basis of a state-sponsored Confucian orthodoxy that remained intact until the demise of the dynastic system in the early twentieth century. His legacy endured through a series of curricular innovations in the public education system, the establishment of new types of civil service examinations, and the canonization of the "Four Books" (the *Analects* of Confucius, *Mencius*, the *Great Learning*, and the *Doctrine of the Mean*) to augment and eventually supercede the previously dominant "Five Classics" (the *Book of History*, the *Book of Odes*, the *Book of Changes*, the *Book of Rites*, and the *Spring and Autumn Annals*).

Despite Zhu Xi's considerable contributions to various elements of Chinese public life, he is best known as the architect (or at least the synthesizer) of the "School of Principle," the supposedly "rational" wing of the broad Confucian reform movement that had begun a century or so earlier and is known in the West as "neo-Confucianism." Not all of Zhu Xi's contributions were completely original, and he was admittedly indebted to a number of kindred philosophical spirits, notably Zhou Dunyi [Chou Tun-i], Cheng Yi [Ch'eng I], and Zhang Zai [Chang Tsai]. Nevertheless, Zhu Xi has in subsequent years so dominated the Chinese philosophical landscape that it is sometimes difficult for modern intellectual historians to separate the earlier Confucian legacy from the neo-Confucian ideological interpretation of it.

Zhu Xi's brand of neo-Confucianism begins with a set of metaphysical assumptions or observations that are in one sense purely monistic, in another sense somewhat dualistic. The starting point is the idea that the mechanisms of the universe are undergirded by a single principle (*li*) of coherence, and it is from this axiomatic foundation that Zhu Xi justifies conflating a number of different loaded terms from the Confucian lexicon. That is to say, while principle is indeed singular, it is manifest cosmologically as the "great ultimate" (*taiji*) [*t'ai-chi*], theologically as "heaven" (*tian*) [*t'ien*], existentially as "destiny" (*ming*), and ethically as "the way" (*dao*) [*tao*]. Moreover, it is impressed upon each human being as human nature (*xiao*) [*hsing*], which, in accord with the now "orthodox" interpretations of the fourth century BCE philosopher MENCIUS, is comprised of four incipient virtuous qualities – humanheartedness (*ren*) [*jen*], rightness (*yi*) [*i*], propriety (*li*), and wisdom (*zhi*) [*chih*] – virtues that can be cultivated through the efforts of the heart-mind (*xin*) [*hsin*] in the context of human culture (*wen*), the entire Chinese repository of refined moral, aesthetic, social, and historical resources. Perhaps the most significant innovation of this synthesis of established Confucian terminology is that the natural is not seen as distinct from the ethical; the principle by which the planets revolve in their orbits and the seasons follow in a cyclical manner is ultimately the same principle by which a ruler should care for the well-being of his or her subjects and a child should obey his or her parents. As Zhu Xi states aphoristically, echoing his eleventh-century forerunner Cheng Yi, in a passage that is quoted repeatedly in almost any work on Confucian metaphysics, "Principle is one; its manifestations are diverse." In short, human cultivation, however it is articulated, is nothing other than the task of learning the unitary, simultaneously natural and moral principle.

This philosophy takes a dualistic turn when Zhu Xi considers that a theory of principle alone describes only the patterns and norms of existence, and does not account for the actual constituents of existence, the ingredients that make up the phenomenal world. That is to say, positing an overarching principle of coherence is not sufficient to explain exactly what it is that coheres and how it does so. Principle, Zhu Xi contends, is "above form," but it is the world "below form" in which principle inheres. To address this, Zhu Xi echoes somewhat the dichotomy established a few centuries earlier in the Huayan [Hua-yen] Buddhist school, which differentiated between the realm of principle and that of phenomena (*shi* [*shih*]). In accord once again with Cheng Yi, Zhu Xi identifies the second piece of the metaphysical puzzle not as phenomena, but as *qi* (*ch'i*), a difficult concept that dates back to the "Hundred Schools Period" and is often translated tenuously by such phrases as "vital forces," "material force," or "psycho-physiological stuff." The idea of *qi*, which has since more or less found its way into English via popular interests in acupuncture, Chinese herbalism, and martial arts practices, essentially refers to the flux and flow of substance, material or otherwise, that constitutes the cosmos. In short, anything that has existential status – matter, energy, thought, etc. – is comprised of varying configurations of *qi*, and all such configurations are in some broad sense organically (or, as is sometimes suggested, *organismically*) related to one another. It should be noted that this is not akin to an atomic theory, an attempt to isolate the most minute components or building blocks of reality. Instead, it represents a holistic theory, concerned with understanding more how things interact than what their individual properties are.

The most immediate implication of this is that it recasts or at least makes explicit the purpose, if not the methods, of Confucian learning, which had sometimes been denigrated (or championed) as a secular philosophy of social ethics, a kind of "virtue" tradition emphasizing literary and cultural study, family and civic responsibility, and formalized ritual expression. With the neo-Confucian metaphysics in place, Zhu Xi raises the stakes of traditional education and self-cultivation considerably. While the early stages of classical learning may indeed entail the concrete lessons of "such-and-such a phenomenon" (particular ritual patterns, the virtue of filial piety, aesthetic disciplines of calligraphy and archery, etc.), the eventual goal is to generalize and internalize such lessons in order to "apprehend the many manifestations of moral principle." To underscore this redirection of Confucian thought, Zhu Xi introduces or reintroduces into the lexicon several ideas that become pregnant with new meanings in light of the *li–qi* dualism. For example, he draws from the newly canonized and rearranged *Great Learning* the concept of "the investigation of things" (*gewu*) [*ko-wu*], which had previously been a shorthand for the studious, incremental learning that had been the hallmark of Confucianism, but now refers also to the systematic scrutiny of the diverse configurations of *qi* for the purpose of discerning the principle that orders them. Similarly, the "extension of knowledge," also from the *Great Learning*, connotes not only the accumulated comprehension of things in their particularity, but the apprehension of how the particulars cohere in a greater unity. And the cultivation of "sincerity," discussed in both the *Great Learning* and the *Doctrine of the Mean*, relates initially to the earnest pursuit of personal virtues and ultimately to the full development of one's own nature, which allows one to "assist the transforming and nourishing powers of Heaven and earth." Even a deceptively simple idea like "inner mental attentiveness" or "quiet sitting" (*jingzuo*) [*ching-tso*], the closest Confucian analogue to Buddhist or Daoist meditative practice, becomes highly charged in the neo-Confucian context.

If there is some modicum of scholarly consensus that the quasi-monistic, quasi-dualistic metaphysics make up the core of Zhu Xi's philosophy, scholars have often focused their subsequent attentions in somewhat idiosyncratic ways, perhaps testifying above all else to the comprehensive, synthetic bent of his agenda. Nevertheless, there are a handful of avenues that are especially worthy of exploration, particularly those of human nature and religious experience. At first glance, one would anticipate from Zhu Xi a relatively straightforward attitude toward human nature, in that he directly identifies one's nature with principle and admittedly endorses the Mencian position on the innate goodness of the human heart-mind. However, Zhu Xi posits that human beings, by virtue of their concrete existence in time and space, have something of a "double endowment," including both an inherent nature that, in a manner of speaking, ontologically mirrors principle and an "existential nature" – literally, "the nature of one's *qi* constitution" – that describes the specific exigencies of one's own physical and mental attributes. Thus, humans are inherently and ontologically good, but one's existential endowments provide occasion for either the full realization of that goodness or the failure to fulfill one's potential. Phrased somewhat differently, just as the cosmos is a fundamentally sound and healthy organism, so too human beings are fundamentally in accord with its underlying principle. Yet, as one negotiates the particularities of one's own existence, one's own embodiment of *qi* evil may emerge, not as something possessed of independent ontological status, but as an existential problem to be addressed and overcome through learning and practice. Here, Zhu Xi is attempting (perhaps strategically) to thread a delicate metaphysical needle, as he is simultaneously affirming an optimistic, monistic base founded on the notion of principle and acknowledging the realistic possibilities and pitfalls of a world constituted by diverse configurations of *qi*.

Certainly, the bulk of Zhu Xi's work, as is often the case with much of Chinese philosophy, is concerned less with describing the world than with establishing foundations that enable human beings to live responsibility in the world, and even discussions of such matters as human nature are ultimately intended as justifications for very specific forms of sanctioned Confucian behavior. But again, the neo-Confucian metaphysics attaches a new significance to actions that might otherwise be interpreted as strictly mundane or secular, and it is here where there are very real suggestions of what might best be termed religious experience. Zhu Xi sometimes identifies the understanding of principle in ways that come closer to direct intuition or attunement than cognitive knowing. For example, he devotes considerable attention to a perplexing term, the "heart-mind of heaven and earth" (*tiandi zhi xin*) [*t'ien-ti chih hsin*], the "spiritually efficacious" (*ling*) impetus that brings principle into manifestation, that drives the generation and perpetuation of the cosmos. Moreover, Zhu Xi contends that the processes of Confucian learning, epitomized in classical study and the investigation of things, allow one to identify one's own heart-mind with the cosmic heart-mind and participate in its spiritual efficacy. This is not merely a claim that appropriate human practices amount to following principle; it is a contention, unusual in its resonance with forms of mystical philosophy thought to be at odds with "rational" neo-Confucianism, that knowledge of principle entails a direct apprehension of something tantamount to a kind of cosmic will, and that the ensuing moral and social actions are somehow the spontaneous expressions of that will.

Needless to say, Zhu Xi continues to provide the sinological community with tremendous challenges, as the extent of his philosophical contributions and their ramifications in various cultural areas are still being examined. He has, in recent years, been the subject of international conferences, specialized monographs, and comprehensive studies, which have explored Zhu Xi's relevance to the fields of ethics, theology, hermeneutics, literary theory, pedagogy, and several others. Ironically, his virtual obscurity in Western philosophical circles offers a sharp contrast with his historical significance within the Chinese philosophical landscape.

Bibliography

Writings

Learning to Be a Sage: Selections from the Conversations of Master Chu, Arranged Topically, trans. Daniel K. Gardner (Berkeley: University of California Press, 1990).
Reflections on Things at Hand: The Neo-Confucian Anthology, comp. Chu Hsi and Lü Ch'ien, trans. Wing-tsit Chan (New York: Columbia University Press 1967).

Further reading

Chan, Wing-tsit (ed.), *Chu Hsi and Neo-Confucianism* (Honolulu: University of Hawaii Press, 1986).

Chan, Wing-tsit, *Chu Hsi: New Studies* (Honolulu: University of Hawaii, 1989).

Tillman, Hoyt Cleveland, *Confucian Discourse and Chu Hsi's Ascendancy* (Honolulu: University of Hawaii, 1992).

Index